DESIGN METHODS AND APPLICATIONS FOR DISTRIBUTED EMBEDDED SYSTEMS

IFIP – The International Federation for Information Processing

IFIP was founded in 1960 under the auspices of UNESCO, following the First World Computer Congress held in Paris the previous year. An umbrella organization for societies working in information processing, IFIP's aim is two-fold: to support information processing within its member countries and to encourage technology transfer to developing nations. As its mission statement clearly states,

> *IFIP's mission is to be the leading, truly international, apolitical organization which encourages and assists in the development, exploitation and application of information technology for the benefit of all people.*

IFIP is a non-profit making organization, run almost solely by 2500 volunteers. It operates through a number of technical committees, which organize events and publications. IFIP's events range from an international congress to local seminars, but the most important are:

- The IFIP World Computer Congress, held every second year;
- Open conferences;
- Working conferences.

The flagship event is the IFIP World Computer Congress, at which both invited and contributed papers are presented. Contributed papers are rigorously refereed and the rejection rate is high.

As with the Congress, participation in the open conferences is open to all and papers may be invited or submitted. Again, submitted papers are stringently refereed.

The working conferences are structured differently. They are usually run by a working group and attendance is small and by invitation only. Their purpose is to create an atmosphere conducive to innovation and development. Refereeing is less rigorous and papers are subjected to extensive group discussion.

Publications arising from IFIP events vary. The papers presented at the IFIP World Computer Congress and at open conferences are published as conference proceedings, while the results of the working conferences are often published as collections of selected and edited papers.

Any national society whose primary activity is in information may apply to become a full member of IFIP, although full membership is restricted to one society per country. Full members are entitled to vote at the annual General Assembly, National societies preferring a less committed involvement may apply for associate or corresponding membership. Associate members enjoy the same benefits as full members, but without voting rights. Corresponding members are not represented in IFIP bodies. Affiliated membership is open to non-national societies, and individual and honorary membership schemes are also offered.

DESIGN METHODS AND APPLICATIONS FOR DISTRIBUTED EMBEDDED SYSTEMS

IFIP 18th World Computer Congress
TC10 Working Conference on Distributed and Parallel
Embedded Systems (DIPES 2004)
22–27 August 2004
Toulouse, France

Edited by

Bernd Kleinjohann
University of Paderborn, Germany

Guang R. Gao
University of Delaware, USA

Hermann Kopetz
Technische Universität Wien, Austria

Lisa Kleinjohann
University of Paderborn / C-LAB
Germany

Achim Rettberg
University of Paderborn / C-LAB, Germany

Springer-Science+Business Media, B.V.

Electronic Services <http://www.wkap.nl>

Library of Congress Cataloging-in-Publication Data

A C.I.P. Catalogue record for this book is available from the Library of Congress.

Design Methods and Applications for Distributed Embedded Systems
Edited by Bernd Kleinjohann, Guang R. Gao, Hermann Kopetz, Lisa Kleinjohann
and Achim Rettberg

ISBN 978-1-4757-8012-3   ISBN 978-1-4020-8149-1 (eBook)
DOI 10.1007/978-1-4020-8149-1

Contents

Preface

The IFIP TC-10 Working Conference on Distributed and Parallel Embedded Systems (DIPES 2004) brings together experts from industry and academia to discuss recent developments in this important and growing field in the splendid city of Toulouse, France.

The ever decreasing price/performance ratio of microcontrollers makes it economically attractive to replace more and more conventional mechanical or electronic control systems within many products by embedded real-time computer systems. An embedded real-time computer system is always part of a well-specified larger system, which we call an *intelligent product*. Although most intelligent products start out as stand-alone units, many of them are required to interact with other systems at a later stage. At present, many industries are in the middle of this transition from stand-alone products to networked embedded systems. This transition requires reflection and architecting: The complexity of the evolving distributed artifact can only be controlled, if careful planning and principled design methods replace the ad-hoc engineering of the first version of many standalone embedded products.

The topics which have been chosen for this working conference are thus very timely: model-based design methods, design space exploration, design methodologies and user interfaces, networks and communication, scheduling and resource management, fault detection and fault tolerance, and verification and analysis. These topics are supplemented by hardware and application oriented presentations and by an invited talk on "new directions in embedded processing - field programmable gate arrays and micro-processors" given by Patrick Lysaght, (Senior Director, Xilinx Research Labs, Xilinx Inc., USA). We hope that the presentations will spark stimulating discussions and lead to new insights. Since this working conference is organized within the 18th IFIP World Computer Congress, there are many possibilities to interact with experts from other scientific areas and to place the field of embedded systems into a wider context. We all hope that this working conference in this beautiful part of the world will be a memorable event to all involved.

Hermann Kopetz, Bernd Kleinjohann, Guang R. Gao,

Lisa Kleinjohann and Achim Rettberg

The original version of this book was revised.
An erratum to this book can be found at DOI 10.1007/978-1-4020-8149-1_33

IFIP TC10 Working Conference on Distributed and Parallel Embedded Systems (DIPES 2004)
World Computer Congress, August 22-27, 2004, Toulouse, France

General Chair
Bernd Kleinjohann

Co-Chairs
Guang R. Gao & Hermann Kopetz

Program Committee
Bernd Kleinjohann (Chair, Germany)
Guang R. Gao (Co-Chair, USA)
Hermann Kopetz (Co-Chair, Austria)
Arndt Bode (Germany)
Nikil Dutt (USA)
Bernhard Eschermann (Switzerland)
Uwe Glässer (Canada)
Uwe Honekamp (Germany)
Joachim Stroop (Germany)
Ahmed Jerraya (France)
Kane Kim (USA)
Moon Hae Kim (Korea)
Lisa Kleinjohann (Germany)
Rainer Leupers (Germany)
Erik Maehle (Germany)
Carlos E. Pereira (Brazil)
Peter Puschner (Austria)
Franz J. Rammig (Germany)
Achim Rettberg (Germany)
Bernd-Heinrich Schmitfranz   (Germany)
Flavio R. Wagner (Brazil)
Heinz-Dietrich Wuttke (Germany)
Ying C. (Bob) Yeh (USA)

Organizing Committee
Lisa Kleinjohann and Achim Rettberg

Sponsoring and Co-Organizing Institution
IFIP TC 10, WG 10.5, SIG-ES in co-operation with WG 10.1, 10.3, 10.4

Acknowledgement
We thank the entire organizing committee of the IFIP World Computer Congress 2004, the Congress Chair Jean-Claude Laprie and the Programme Chair Reino Kurki-Suoni for their support and for the local arrangements in Toulouse.

MDA PLATFORM FOR COMPLEX EMBEDDED SYSTEMS DEVELOPMENT

Chokri Mraidha, Sylvain Robert, Sébastien Gérard, David Servat
CEA LIST – CEA SACLAY
F-91191 Gif-sur-Yvette Cedex France
Phone : +33 169 085 039
{chokri.mraidha; sylvain.robert; sebastien.gerard ; david.servat}@cea.fr

Abstract: Moving from code-centric to model-centric development seems to be a promising way to cope with the increasing complexity of embedded real-time systems. The Object Management Group (OMG) has been recently promoting this approach, known as Model Driven Architecture (MDA). It relies on UML model refinement and transformation as the basic step of an iterative design process. This model-centric posture has raised many questions, among which the need for an integrated MDA-based developing environment is probably the most severe one. It directly affects the reality of the adoption of this good practice by software engineers. For several years, the CEA-LIST has been involved in the field of real-time systems research and development. This work resulted in the completion of the Accord/UML toolkit, which aims at providing users with a model-driven method and supporting tools. This paper outlines the Accord/UML approach focusing on the solving of complex real-time/embedded systems development issues in this MDA process.

Keywords: Model driven development, UML, Real-time embedded systems

1.   INTRODUCTION

Over the last few years, engineers have been faced with the problem of developing more and more complex embedded real-time systems in a world where time-to-market constraints are constantly increasing. Moving from code-centric to model-centric development brings significant answers to software complexity management. With its standardization the Unified Modeling Language (UML) [1] has become the lingua franca of object-oriented modeling. Existing UML-based approaches for real-time systems development [2, 3] still result in models that are hard to maintain and reuse. This drawback is principally due to the lack of model development methodologies.

The Model Driven Architecture (MDA) [4] initiative introduces architectural separation of concerns in order to provide portability, interoperability, maintainability and reusability of models. To achieve these goals, MDA recommends different kinds of models and describes ways to obtain these models from one another through model transformation processes. MDA relies on three kinds of models, which are the Computation Independent Model (CIM), the Platform Independent Model (PIM) and the Platform Specific Model (PSM).

The CIM is a view of a system from a computation independent viewpoint. This model focuses on the requirements of the system and its interactions with the environment while hiding the details of the structure of the system. In other words, the system is seen as a black box. The PIM focuses on the structure and operations of the system from a platform independent viewpoint while hiding details specific to a particular platform. In the PIM, the system is seen as a white box. The PSM combines the PIM with details specific to a particular platform to obtain a model dependent of that platform.

The idea is then to apply MDA tenets in order to facilitate development of real-time applications. Accord/UML [5, 6] is an MDA-oriented methodology entirely based on UML which aims at facilitating real-time software development by engineers who are not real-time experts. The first section of this paper gives an overview of the Accord/UML methodology, enhancing its compliance with the MDA approach. The second section accounts for several directions of research to deal with platform specificities issues for complex embedded real-time systems development, while putting emphasis on code generation process, before giving a short conclusion.

2.   OUTLINES OF THE ACCORD/UML PLATFORM

Accord/UML aims at providing users with an MDA-compliant methodology and connected tools dedicated to real-time systems design. This section briefly introduces of the Accord/UML methodology before giving an overview of its associated workbench.

2.1 The Accord/UML methodology

A prototype development with the Accord/UML methodology basically consists of three successive phases, each producing one of the three MDA model kinds. For each phase, Accord/UML provides guidelines and UML extensions (gathered in a UML profile), which enable users to model system real-time features. Moving from one phase to another is facilitated by partially automating model transformations.

The preliminary analysis phase deals with requirements capture. System requirements are identified and reformatted in a set of UML diagrams (use case diagrams and high-level scenario diagrams). The resulting model gives a better-formalized view of system functionalities regardless of its internal structure. This model, called Preliminary Analysis Model (PAM) in our methodology stands for the CIM MDA model.

In the detailed analysis phase, the objective is to move from the PAM to the Detailed Analysis Model (DAM), which is the Accord/UML vision of PIM. The system is decomposed in complementary and consistent sub models: structural models (mainly class diagrams), detailed interaction models (detailed scenarios diagrams), and behavioral model (statecharts and activity diagrams). Structural models are built following a generic pattern, which consists in separating system core features from its relationships with its environment. This approach notably favors reusability and permits to define a generic mapping from PAM to DAM. Modeling real-time structural features is eased by introducing the Real-Time Object concept [7, 8], an extension of UML active objects. As far as behavioral modeling is concerned, two aspects are separated [9]: the control view through statecharts, and the algorithmic view through activity diagrams completed by an UML Action Semantics [1] compliant Action Language [10]. To ensure determinism in modeling behavioral aspects, Accord/UML also provides through its profile a set of rules to specify UML semantics variation points in the one hand and clarify some ambiguous points on the other hand. The resulting model gives an *implementation language independent* executable specification of the system.

Finally, the aim of the prototyping phase is to obtain a complete running mock-up of the application from its DAM [11]. This model is the Prototyping Model (PrM), an Accord/UML equivalent of PSM. This model is then used as an input to a specialized C++ generator, handling notably system real-time features implementation. Eventually, a runtime framework is provided to support the execution of the synthesized code on top of a Real-Time Operating System: the Accord real-time kernel, and the Accord virtual machine. The so-obtained prototype can thus be validated by test.

2.2   The Accord/UML workbench

As depicted in Figure 1, the Accord/UML methodology support consists mainly of three parts: automatic synthesis of specific design patterns relating to real-time and distribution issues; full code generation (structure + behavior) toward the Accord runtime platform; the Accord platform itself implementing high level concepts of the methodology and running on Unix, Linux or VxWorks.

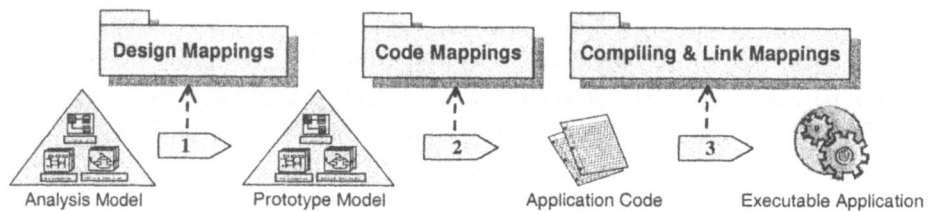

Figure 1: From analysis model to executable application.

The Accord/UML workbench relies on a generic UML-based CASE tool, Objecteering [12], which we customize for distributed real-time embedded systems design. This offers possibilities through its profile builder tool to implement UML profiles. Our toolset is then made of the Objecteering tool completed with additional modules implementing the Accord/UML profiles.

More precisely, in modeling phases, building models is done thanks to the Objecteering UML modeler, which provides a complete set of UML elements (e.g. use cases diagrams, class diagrams, state-machine diagrams, sequence diagrams...), but also using additional model elements defined in the context of the Accord/UML profiles and ensuring real-time features modeling. Stepping from one model to another is done as much as possible via Accord/UML specific model transformation rules. For instance, Accord/UML sets mapping rules to ensure automatic model transformation from Use Cases diagrams to Classes diagrams. The tenets of the approach being to define and implement as often as possible modeling rules to assist the engineer in building the application model. One could speak of MAC ("Modeling Assisted by Computer").

In addition, the Accord/UML tools provide the developer with means of validation in the earlier phases of the development. Firstly, structural and functional validation is carried out on the behavioral models. To this end, a connection has been made between Accord/UML and the Agatha tool [13-15], enabling automatic test case generation from the behavioral diagrams obtained during the detailed analysis phase. Secondly, a validation of quality of service (QoS) in terms of timing requirements is performed by a schedulability analysis of UML models [16]. This point will be discussed in more details in the following sections.

Once application models are completed, one may perform code generation from this model. To this purpose, Accord/UML provides a specialized code generator targeting C++ code (a C code generator being under development). This generator has been upgraded to integrate real-time features support conformant to the Accord/UML specification. This means that the generated code can be executed with support from the Accord kernel and Accord virtual machine [17] running on top of various operating systems, namely VxWorks, UNIX, or Linux.

3. PLATFORM DEPENDANCE ISSUES IN AN MDA PROCESS

In this section, we present the strategy adopted in Accord/UML to deal with real-time/embedded issues, before providing several examples assessing the relevance of our choices.

3.1 Rationale

Targeting real-time embedded applications instead of mainstream ones imposes a superset of constraints on the software developed, among which platform-related considerations and real-time features validation are prevailing. Actually, traditional real-time software design processes provide strategies and support tools to validate temporal (either application-specific or non-functional) properties of the system during the earlier phases of the design cycle. Moreover, in the context of embedded applications, the characteristics of the HW platform have a major influence on the final system temporal behavior and have to be taken into account to make relevant design choices. Integrating these issues in our MDA-compliant approach is thus one of the major challenges we had to face.

As a consequence, two principal objectives were aimed to in the design of our development methodology and tools: to provide a sufficient level of real-time features integration and providing ways to validate the application with respect to the HW platform, in a UML-based model-centric approach. This comes actually to an attempt to merge conflicting aspects, since the ultimate goal of the MDA approach is precisely to shield concerns linked to the platform (in terms of implementation language as well as targeted HW). Furthermore, the UML is a language, which natively provides only "raw" materials (model elements, extension mechanisms), which are voluntarily platform-independent and generalist. As a consequence, UML tools are usually designed to support mainstream software development and provide therefore very poor means of validating real-time properties. All these considerations have led us to differentiate three kinds of actions to perform:

- Adapt the UML to real-time issues, by adding or extending (with UML profiles) native model elements to provide proper ways to represent temporal features at the model level.
- Adapt existing validation strategies to our approach: this implies notably to bridge the gap between the UML and other more formal languages, and between UML modeling tools and validation tools.
- Ensure the suitability of the application with respect to its embeddability, by trying to express the HW platform characteristics at the model level and thus enabling to make design choices in accordance.

These directions have been applied and refined all along the design of our platform. In the next sections, we account for this process, by describing works addressing several specific aspects of MDA adaptation to real-time/embedded issues.

3.2   A generic architecture for smart-sensor networked application

This thread of work is focused on architectural aspects when dealing with embedded applications. Smart-sensor networked applications stand as the prototypical example of such complex, but fairly common type of architectures, featuring both a central computing resource, such as an embedded PC, and several electronic devices, such as sensors and actuators.

To cope with the integration of such heterogeneous type of both hardware and software pieces, the component paradigm is of great help. It helps give a likewise abstract view of the various parts of the system. Then the question remains as how to integrate those parts, given that, most of the time, each of them is devised in an independent fashion, which prevents from easy coping of, among many, communication matters.

This work [18, 19] is an attempt to provide a generic integration scheme in the form of a component-partition of such networked applications. In his proposition, a sensor is represented both at the application (embedded PC) and at hardware level by various components:

- At the hardware device level, the sensor is seen as two components. The first one provides interface to the hardware logic. It is specified according to the existing standards (IEEE and OMG [20, 21]). The second one embeds the user logic and functional features. Apart from some predefined interfaces it is left to the engineer to develop

– At the embedded PC level, each sensor is represented by a device-driver component, which realizes one among predefined communication patterns and provides specific service interfaces to talk to the sensor through the network. Both CAN and Ethernet protocols have been taken into account so far and special care has been given to the design of synchronization algorithms among all the device driver components, so that the whole communication delay is handled. All this logic is embedded in the device-driver model construct, from which code can then be generated.

This is a typical example of what MDA is promoting. The definition of generic integration patterns, giving a sound basis for modeling, which in turn, via code generation, is finely-tuned to specific targeted electronic device platforms.

3.3   Schedulability and performance analysis

This thread of work can be seen as a general concern for assessing system properties – functional as well as extra-functional – at the level of the model. Among those, schedulability and performance stand as the most severe ones that embedded systems are expected to provide.

Three subsequent PhD thesis have been led on this topic within our team. The pursued goal was, on the one hand to broaden the coverage of those aspects within the UML, and on the other hand to bridge the gap between such UML modeling constructs and the use of external validation tools.

As concerns the first aspect, a dedicated UML profile was designed to define a generic Action Language [10] suitable for expressing control and functional algorithms in an implementation-language-independent fashion. Besides, another profile was developed to enable the expression of worst-case execution time (WCET) properties at the model level. Based on these, both a static and a dynamic WCET analysis of the overall models are possible.

The second part consisted in an effort to derive from Accord/UML standard models a specific, scheduling-oriented model [16], suitable for interpretation within a symbolic execution based validation tool, Agatha [13, 14], developed at CEA-LIST. Once established, this link between both tool-chains enables a complete assessment of the scheduling properties of an application model, provided that WCET information is fed to the models. This approach was mainly intended for critical real-time systems, for which precise knowledge of WCET are more likely to be known.

Finally, an ongoing work is focused on performance assessment, based on the use of the enhancement of the Scheduling, Performance and Time UML profile [22] and on the generation of Layered Queuing Networks

(LQN) [23] from standard Accord/UML application models. In the same way as was done for the scheduling issue, we foresee here the opportunity to bridge the gap with tools that were devised to extract LQN properties.

3.4   From models to code

Real-time embedded systems have to meet various design constraints including consumption of energy or memory and a sufficient level of performance to satisfy real-time requirements. There are actually several kinds of real-time embedded systems. They cover a wide range of domains going from cell phones applications to nuclear power plants control systems or also spacecrafts embedded calculators. Each domain has its own constraints to meet. This concern takes place at every stage of the design process but the fact that code of the application is the last link in the chain, makes code generation an essential and critical phase of model-centric development. Code provided by generators has to meet constraints of the RT/E application itself but also has to take into account the limitation of the resources provided by the hardware supports of the application. Hence, code generation needs to be optimized for each targeted platform depending of the features it offers. Besides, there are often several solutions to generate code from a given model. For example, a state-transition model may be generated under the form of a set of nested switches [24], or using the state pattern [25], but also by generating tables. These three patterns of code generation will not have the same impact on energy, memory and performance features of the generated code.

These different patterns of code generation are proposed in the Accord/UML workbench. Hence, code for different optimization purposes can be generated from the same model. Currently, the user has to manually make the choice of the code generation pattern, but our goal is to have a "smart" code generator capable of making this choice as automatically as possible. More than constraints specifications, this requires an elaborated platform description model to gather sufficient amount of information and we also need to elaborate some heuristics, keeping in mind combinatorial explosion issues, to be able to make the most appropriate choice.

Another axis of our ongoing work on optimized code generation concerns the ability to quantify the efficiency of the generated code in terms of energy, memory or performance in order to validate the fulfilment of requirements. From our point of view, this is a very important challenge in order for model-driven development to be a success in real-time embedded system development domain.

4. CONCLUSIONS

We strongly believe that the MDA approach, or more generally design processes centered on models design, constitutes a powerful mean to facilitate real-time embedded systems development. However, this statement will be completely true only if support tools and design processes guidelines are defined and refined, taking into account the very specific aspects of this application domain.

This paper expands this core rationale by describing the Accord/UML platform, a combination of an MDA-compliant methodology and a supporting workbench for developing real-time systems. In Accord/UML, going through development process is eased by models transformation automation and code generation, and support is provided until code execution. In order to mitigate concerns linked to implementation, a seamless integration of embedded and real-time features is performed all along the development process, for instance by providing methods and tools for temporal validation, or by extending the UML to a "real-time UML". The relevance of our approach has been assessed in various applications from the automotive and telecom industry in the context of European project such as AIT-WOODDES, EAST, or ARTIST.

REFERENCES

1. OMG, *Unified Modeling Language: Superstructure Version 2.0*. 2003.
2. B.P. Douglass, *Real-Time UML : Developing Efficient Objects for Embedded Systems*. Object technology Series, ed. Addison Wesley. 98.
3. Bran Selic, Garth Gullekson, and Paul T. Ward, *Real time Object-oriented Modeling*. Wiley Professional Computing. 94: John Wiley & Sons, Inc.
4. OMG, *MDA Guide Version 1.0.1*. 2003, OMG.
5. Sébastien Gérard, et al. *Efficient System Modeling of Complex Real-time Industrial Networks Using The ACCORD/UML Methodology*. in *Architecture and Design of Distributed Embedded Systems (DIPES 2000)*. 2000. Paderborn University, Germany: Kluwer Academic Publishers.
6. S. Gérard, F. Terrier, and Y. Tanguy. *Using the Model Paradigm for Real-Time Systems Develoment: ACCORD/UML*. in *OOIS'02-MDSD*. 2002. Montpellier: Springer.
7. François Terrier, et al. *A Real Time Object Model*. in *TOOLS Europe'96*. 1996. Paris, France: Prentice Hall.
8. Sébastien Gérard, et al. *A UML-based concept for high concurrency: the Real-Time Object*. in *The 7th IEEE International Symposium on Object-oriented Real-time distributed Computing (ISORC 2004)*. 2004. Vienna, Austria.

9. Chokri Mraidha, et al. *A Two-Aspect Approach for a Clearer Behavior Model.* in *The 6th IEEE International Symposium on Object-oriented Real-time distributed Computing (ISORC'2003).* 2003. Hakodate, Hokkaido, Japan: IEEE.

10. Chokri Mraidha, et al., *Action Language Notation for ACCORD/UML.* 2003, CEA.

11. Patrick Tessier, et al. *A Component-Based Methodology for Embedded System Prototyping.* in *14th IEEE International Workshop on Rapid System Prototyping (RSP'03).* 2003. San Diego, USA: IEEE.

12. Softeam,*Objecteering,*http://www.obecteering.com.

13. C. Bigot, et al. *Automatic test generation with AGATHA.* in *TACAS.* 2003. Warsaw, Poland.

14. D. Lugato, et al., *Validation and automatic test generation on UML models : the AGATHA approach.* special issue of the STTT (Software Tools for Technology Transfer), 2004.

15. C. Bigot, et al. *A Semantics for UML specification to be validated with AGATHA.* in *ERTS'04.* 2004. Toulouse, France.

16. Trung Hieu Phan, et al. *Scheduling Validation for UML-modeled Real-Time Systems.* in *ECRTS 2003.* 2003. Porto, Portugal.

17. David Servat, et al. *Doing Real-Time with a Simple Linux Kernel.* in *RTLWS'2003.* 2003. Valencia, Spain.

18. C. Jouvray, et al. *Smart Sensor Modeling with the UML for Real-Time Embedded Applications.* in *IV2004.* 2004. Parma, Italy.

19. C. Jouvray, et al. *Networked UML modeling sensors.* in *ICTTA'04.* 2004. Damascus, Syria.

20. *IEEE Standard for a Smart Transducer Interface for Sensors and Actuators,* in *Network Capable Application Processor (NCAP) Information Model, IEEE Std 1451.1.* 26 june 99.

21. OMG, *Smart Transducers Interface - OMG.* 07 dec. 01.

22. OMG, *UML Profile for Schedulability, Performance and Time (ptc/02-03-02).* 2003, OMG. p. 154.

23. D.C. Petriu and C.M. Woodside, *Performance Analysis with UML: Layered Queuing Models from the Performance Profile,* in *UML for Real: Design of Embedded Real-Time Systems.* 2003, Kluwer Academic Publishers.

24. Miro Samek, *Practical Statecharts in C/C++: Quantum Programming for Embedded Systems.* 2002.

25. Erich Gamma, et al., *Design Patterns. Elements of Reusable Object-Oriented Software.* 1994: Addison-Wesley.

ON DETECTING DEADLOCKS IN LARGE UML MODELS

Based on an Expressive Subset

Michael Kersten and Wolfgang Nebel
University of Oldenburg
Department of Computing Science
michael.kersten@informatik.uni-oldenburg.de, nebel@informatik.uni-oldenburg.de

Abstract: The paper describes a method for the detection of deadlocks in large UML models of reactive systems. Therefore a multi-phase-approach will be presented which consists of the four phases: property extraction, potential deadlock analysis, deadlock reachability analysis and result visualisation.

Keywords: Deadlock detection, cycle detection, graph theory, reachability analysis, UML.

1. INTRODUCTION

In the last few years the Unified Modeling Language (UML) emerged to the standard modelling language in the field of object-oriented design. Even in technical domains like automotive and aircraft industry the application of UML has grown appreciable. Due to the fact of high safety requirements in these areas the combination of UML and formal methods is a popular object of research.

A very specific but practically relevant part of this field of investigation is the detection of deadlocks in UML models. Since they are very easy to model but hard to find by manual inspection, automatic methods for deadlock detection are convenient to reduce development costs and to enhance quality. Recent contributions (e.g. [3],[8]) allow the detection of deadlocks in UML models using model checking techniques. They are very general and allow the proof of absence of deadlocks as well as many other properties. Currently the systems to be checked are limited in size (see [1],[2],[6]) depending on the state representation used. A further restriction of the regarded contributions is the small supported subset of UML.

Hence, the model checking approach cannot be used for any given project without additional effort. In particular the rich set of expressive modelling concepts provided is the payoff of UML.

The presented contribution aims at the automatic detection of deadlocks in large reactive system designs modelled by a rich UML subset.

Therefore in section 1 an expressive UML subset for reactive systems, containing class, statechart, sequence and collaboration diagrams is introduced.

Based on this, in section 2, a multi-phase analysis method is provided, which allows the automatic detection of deadlocks. Subsequently we conclude the presented work.

2.   AN EXPRESSIVE UML SUBSET FOR REACTIVE SYSTEMS

In order to provide an expressive UML subset for reactive systems with the full usability it is necessary to include the most commonly used concepts. A minimal but complete subset of necessary concepts is hard to define by academic means. In the present case the concepts included are the achievement of an academia/industry co-project described in [5]. These are essentially concepts for the structural and logical decomposition, modelling of concurrency/parallelism aspects, and the definition of the behaviour of the system under development.

For the definition of the static structure the class diagram concepts of UML are used. Within class diagrams the package concept is used to provide a high-level logical decomposition of the system under development. In order to define the system border the package level stereotype ≪ *system* ≫ is used. The further decomposition of the system under development is done using classes and associations.

One important aspect of reactive systems is the concurrency. The first design decision in the reactive system design is the distinction between active and passive components. Therefore the UML provides the feature *isActive* which is anchored as an attribute of *class* in the UML metamodel. Following the definition of the UML specification (see [7]) a class is an active class, if its meta-attribute *isActive* is set to 'true'. The class thus has an own thread of control. Whether active classes on the same hierarchy level of a UML model are executed concurrently or in parallel is left open on this level of abstraction. In the later design phases this aspect may be refined using the stereotypes ≪ *task* ≫ and ≪ *hw* ≫. The former is used to denote software components which are running concurrently and the latter identifies hardware components which are running in parallel by default.

For the hardware/software-codesign more elaborate concepts are necessary which are beyond the scope of the present contribution.

Besides the structural modelling of the system under development the behavioural aspects are important. In our profile the internal behaviour of objects (instances of classes) is modelled using statemachines. For each active class a statemachine must be defined. Since passive classes have no own thread of control they have no own internal behaviour and therefore they have no associated statemachine. This does not apply for their operations. The behavioural modelling of class operations may be done using statemachines. For simplicity we state the following assumtions for the UML models under analysis:

1 Nested statecharts are not used,

2 Concurrent states are not used,

3 All active objects are created in the initial phase, later on, only passive objects are created using constructor methods,

4 Guards are boolean expressions over attribute and event-parameter values,

5 Time events are regarded as equal to completion events,

6 No usage of history states.

The assumptions 1-4 are only stated for simplicity reasons and do not limit the generality. Assumption 5 has no influence on the generality, too, but it is needed for the analysis. If time events are not regarded[1] as completion events the underlying deadlock model must be changed into a timed deadlock model. This would introduce a lot of effort without advancing the analysis.

Assumption 6 deliberately increases the generality of the modelling because from the authors standpoint the usage of the history state concept of the UML decreases the comprehensibility of the respective model in an irresponsible manner. Another important aspect of the reactive system modelling is the time modelling. In particular for real-time systems this is essential. For the purpose of deadlock detection we abstract from the timing aspects and therefore do not present our UML time modelling concepts (see [4]) within this paper.

---

[1]Since in the deadlock analysis time events are only regarded as completion events, the developer may use them as accustomed.

3.   A MULTI-PHASE AUTOMATIC DEADLOCK DETECTION METHOD

Our contribution is based on a multi-phase analysis process as shown in Fig. 1. In the first phase the deadlock relevant properties of the UML

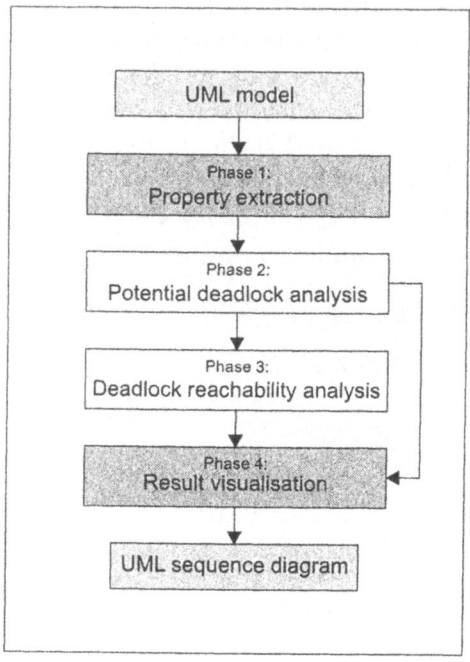

UML model

Phase 1:
Property extraction

Phase 2:
Potential deadlock analysis

Phase 3:
Deadlock reachability analysis

Phase 4:
Result visualisation

UML sequence diagram

Figure 1.   The multi-phase-method

model are extracted and stored in mathematical structures (e.g. lists, sets, tuples) which allow effective algorithms in the second phase.

There the UML statechart diagrams are analysed statically in order to find out which "wait-for"-relations between active objects exist. For this purpose the State-Wait-Graph is introduced which allows white box deadlock detection. In contrast to classical wait graphs, the State-Wait-Graph representation considers the internal state of the active objects expressed as statechart diagrams. The detection of cycles in the State-Wait-Graph indicates the existence and location of potential deadlocks.

Whether these potential deadlocks are reachable at run-time, depends on the binding of attributes and parameters of operation calls between active objects to actual values. These aspects are analysed in the third phase of the method, which performs a deadlock reachability analysis. For this purpose relevant execution paths are derived from the model and the associated transitions are analysed.

When a potential deadlock situation is reachable, this is detected by the method and the complete history of this deadlock can be stated. The included result visualisation mechanism generates a sequence diagram containing an illustration of the deadlock trace.

3.1   Property Extraction

In the property extraction phase all active classes of the UML model are analysed concerning their communication aspects. In concrete terms this means that for each active class the set of produced events and consumed events is calculated and stored in producer and consumer lists. For this purpose call events are regarded as consumer and call actions are regarded as producer of events. Thereby events are only considered if their consumer and producer are suitably associated.

3.2   Potential Deadlock Analysis

A potential deadlock is a cyclic wait situation between concurrent or parallel components of a system each within a specific state. Our respective deadlock model is the State-Wait-Graph (see Fig. 2). This is a directed graph in which each vertex represents an active object in a specific state (of the associated statechart diagram) and each edge represents a 'wait-for-relation'. The number of vertices of the State-

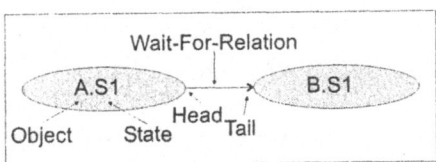

Figure 2.   Principle of a State-Wait-Graph

Wait-Graph is the same as the number of states of all statechart diagrams of the model which are associated to active classes. The number of edges depends on the transitions defined in these statecharts. The head of each edge is connected with the vertex waiting for some specific event. The vertex connected with the tail of the edge is a potential producer of this particular event.

The potential deadlock analysis starts with the creation of a State-Wait-Graph. This is done by operating on the structures (e.g. consumer and producer lists) created in the property extraction phase.

Having created the full State-Wait-Graph of the system, potential deadlock situations can be detected. A potential deadlock situation is

a situation in which two or more objects (each in a specific state) are waiting mutually for the production of a particular event.

In our approach the next phase is to detect all cycles in the State-Wait-Graph and then sort out the relevant ones. In contrast to classical wait-graphs (e.g. [9]), where each detected cycle is a potential deadlock the procedure is more complicated for State-Wait-Graphs due to their white-box-nature. Cycles with all vertices being of the same object (as shown in Fig 3) are not potential deadlocks but logical errors in the corresponding statechart diagram. Cycles with two or more vertices of different objects

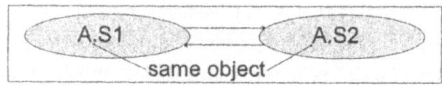

Figure 3.   Cycle within one object

are potential deadlock situations, if no object is involved with more than one state. Otherwise we denote them as 'cycles with over-involved objects' (see Fig. 4). The detection of all cycles in the State-Wait-Graph

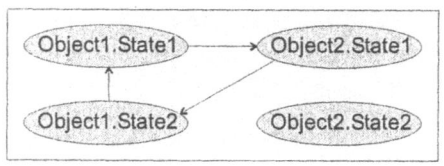

Figure 4.   Over-involved object

is done using an advanced depth-first-search algorithm which calculates all cycles of the graph and the partitioning within a single run. The pruning of logical errors and cycles with over-involved objects is done using set-operations.

After the pruning the remaining potential deadlock situations need to be examined concerning outgoing edges. This is done by traversing the graph and calculating the out-degree of each vertex. If all vertices have the $out-degree = 1$ the potential deadlock situation is called a potential deadlock in our approach. If there are vertices with an $out-degree > 1$ (as shown in Fig. 5) it depends on the target object of the edge leading out of the cycle, whether the cycle under examination is a potential deadlock. When the target object is not involved in the cycle the examined cycle is not a potential deadlock. Otherwise it must be checked, if the edge connects two states of the same object. If the check evaluates to true the potential deadlock is combined with a logical error and the logical error should be corrected before going on in the

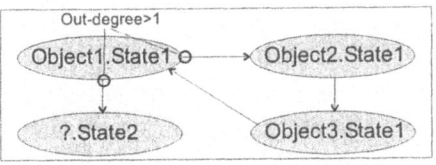

Figure 5.   Out transition of a cycle

deadlock detection. If it evaluates to false we have a further cycle in the State-Wait-Graph. In this case the next phase can be initiated because our cycle detection ensures that all cycles are found and all cycles are handled seperately in the further analysis.

Potential deadlock means, that it is statically possible that the deadlock occurs but whether this really may happen at run-time depends on some dynamic aspects of the model which are analysed in the next phase, the deadlock analysis phase.

If no potential deadlock is found in this phase, the system is deadlock free and the next phase may be omitted.

3.3   Deadlock Reachability Analysis

The purpose of the deadlock reachability analysis phase is to provide evidence for each detected potential deadlock found in the previous phase. This means to calculate the possible paths into the potential deadlocks detected using a search algorithm and to analyse whether these paths are executable by an heuristic simulation approach. As illustrated

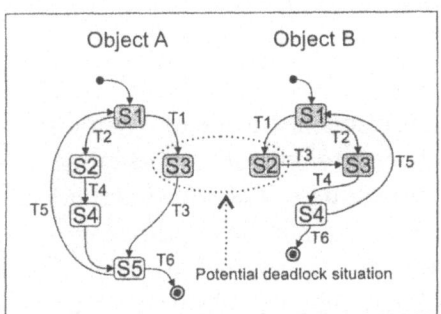

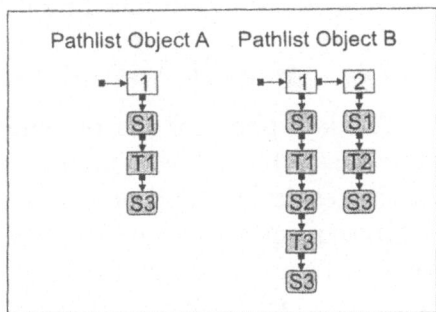

Figure 6.   An example of statecharts containing a potential deadlock

Figure 7.   An example of path lists

in Fig. 6, the search algorithm performs a specialised depth-first search for each relevant statechart diagram and stores all paths to potential deadlock states in a path list (see Fig. 7). Each path list contains all states and transitions of the respective path.

The path lists are used as input for the subsequent heuristic simulation. In the simulation the state machines are executed on a simulator which implements the exact UML semantics as defined in [7]. Besides very special features like the queue length and the evaluation order of expressions as defined in the semantics the following dynamic aspects of the model need to be considered: guard conditions, event parameter values and attribute values.

In the case that one or more paths into a potential deadlock situation exist it is sufficient to find one executable path during the simulation. The other case is the more expensive one. When all paths of the path list are executed once and no executable path is found, it cannot be stated whether there is an executable path or not. Even after theoretically infinitely many executions one cannot be sure that the next execution does not lead to a potential deadlock situation. In this case the simulation will break after an adjustable number of n executions and a corresponding warning is issued to the user.

The disadvantage of this heuristic simulation approach is that the non-existance of deadlocks cannot be proved if there are potential deadlocks found in phase 2 into which no executable path could be found after n executions.

In this infrequent case only an exhaustive search over a completely unfolded state space as model checking does could help. Since our approach basically adresses models which are to large for model checking there is no other solution than the usage of manual abstraction techniques in conjunction with advanced model checking techniques.

3.4   Result Visualisation

The last phase of the presented contribution is the result visualisation phase. Its task is to provide an easily comprehensible representation of the results of the deadlock detection procedure. Therefore extended UML sequence diagrams are applied. In Fig. 8 a simple deadlock situation is shown, in which, for simplicity, only the deadlocked states 'A.S1' and 'B.S2' are displayed. The corresponding result visualisation chart is

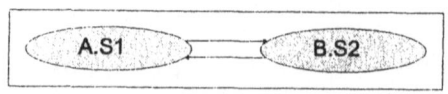

Figure 8.   Cycle in the State-Wait-Graph

given in Fig. 9. There it is apparent that the active objects A and B are running directly into a deadlock situation after being created from the system. Next to the sequence of communications ahead of the deadlock

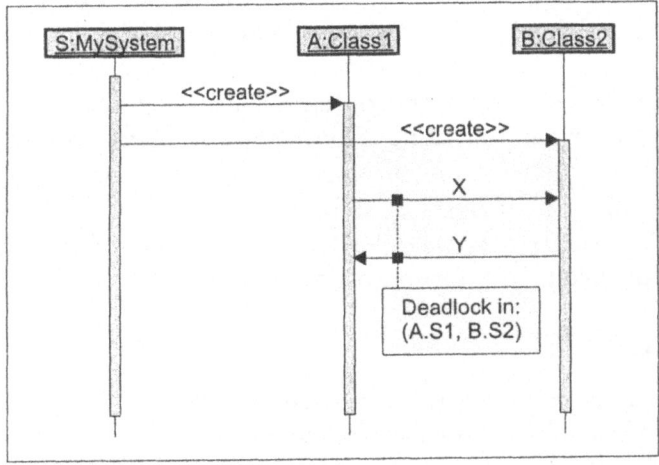

Figure 9. Example of a deadlock trace

situation the participating objects and states are relevant and presented to the user. Other visualisations are possible but not in the focus of this contribution.

4. CONCLUSION

We have presented a method for the detection of deadlocks in UML models of reactive systems. The present approach has two main advantages. First, the method supports an expressive set of UML concepts and thus real-world UML models of reactive systems can be checked without modification. Second, the size of models to be checked, may be significantly larger than a model checker can handle. Since the evaluation of the presented method is in progress, we will not give a full complexity analysis within the scope of the presented contribution but a rough estimate causes the assumption that the overall algorithm will be linear in the number of states and transitions multiplied by a factor depending on the number of potential deadlocks found, the number of reachable execution paths and a set of further internal parameters.

The main drawback is that in seldom cases (as discussed in section 3.3) the freedom of deadlocks cannot be stated and thus the method is not complete. Since in this case a corresponding message is issued to the user the creditability is not affected.

Another disadvantage is the loss of generality in contrast to model checking, which allows the proof of almost any property expressible in the particular logic dialect used.

For a class of applications the criteria model size and expressiveness of the supported UML subset are more important than the generality of properties.

The property extraction and potential deadlock detection phases are experimentally evaluated using a prototype implementation. The first results of this evaluation are promising, but it turned out that the creation of adequate UML models as input for the method is an extensive and difficult task. Hence, we defer the continuation of the experimental evaluation in favour of a formal proof.

REFERENCES

[1] J. R. Burch, E. M. Clarke, K. L. McMillan, D. Dill, and L. J. Hwang. Symbolic model checking: 10^{20} states and beyond. In *Information and Computation*, volume (98)2, pages 142–170. IEEE, 1992. also in 5th IEEE LICS 90.

[2] E. M. Clarke and H. Schlingloff. Model checking. In Alan Robinson and Andrei Voronkov, editors, *Handbook of Automated Reasoning*, chapter 21, pages 1367 – 1522. Elsevier Science Publishers B.V., 2000.

[3] Alexandre David, M. Oliver Möller, and Wang Yi. Verification of UML State-charts with Real-time Extensions. Technical report, Department of Information Technology, Uppsala University, http://www.it.uu.se/research, February 2003.

[4] Michael Kersten, Ramon Biniasch, Wolfgang Nebel, and Frank Oppenheimer. Die Erweiterung der UML um Zeitannotationen zur Analyse des Zeitverhaltens reaktiver Systeme. In R. Drechsler et al., editors, *GI/ITG/GMM Workshop 2003*, pages 11–20, Bremen, February 2003. Shaker Verlag.

[5] Michael Kersten, Jörg Matthes, Christian Fouda, Stephan Zipser, and Hubert B. Keller. Customizing UML for the Development of Distributed Reative Systems and Ada 95 Code Generation. *Ada User Journal*, 23(3), 2002.

[6] K. L. McMillan. *Symbolic model Checking*. Kluwer Academic Publishers, 1993.

[7] OMG. OMG Unified Modeling Language Specification (version 1.4). Technical report, OMG, http://www.omg.org, September 2001.

[8] Timm Schäfer, Alexander Knapp, and Stephan Merz. Model Checking UML State Machines and Collaborations. *Electronic Notes in Theoretical Computer Science*, 47, 2001.

[9] Mathias Weske. *Deadlocks in Computersystemen*. International Thomson Publishing GmbH, Bonn, Albany [u.a.], first edition, 1995. ISBN 3-929821-11-7.

VERIFICATION FRAMEWORK FOR UML - BASED DESIGN OF EMBEDDED SYSTEMS[*]

Martin Kardos and Yuhong Zhao
Heinz Nixdorf Institute, University of Paderborn, Germany

Abstract: System level design incorporating system modeling and formal specification in combination with formal verification can substantially contribute to the correctness and quality of the embedded systems and consequently help reduce the development costs. Ensuring the correctness of the designed system is, of course, a crucial design criterion especially when complex distributed (real-time) embedded systems are considered. Therefore, this paper aims at presenting a verification framework designated for formal verification and validation of UML-based design of embedded systems. It first introduces an approach of using the AsmL language for acquiring formal models of the UML semantics and consequently presents an on-the-fly model checking technique designed to run the formal verification directly over those semantic models.

Key words: embedded system design, UML, formal semantics, ASMs, AsmL, formal verification, model-checking

1. INTRODUCTION

The increasing complexity of today's embedded systems imposes new demands on the overall design process and on the used design languages and verification techniques. The *system level design* has become a hot topic in the research area of embedded systems and is gradually gaining popularity in the designer community. Typical for system level design are specification and modeling techniques offering facilities for coping with the system complexity such as structural decomposition, abstraction, refinement, etc. However, employment of these techniques into the design process of embedded systems can not succeed without appropriate support for

*This work has been supported by the German National Science Foundation (DFG)

embedded systems can not succeed without appropriate support for verification. Therefore, verification techniques are needed that are able to identify the design errors hidden in the abstract and often incomplete models at the earlier stages of the system level design.

The work presented in this paper deals with formal verification of UML-based design for embedded systems. The main objective resides in providing a unified verification framework based on a solid formal background that integrates formal verification techniques together with model-based validation techniques. In this way we believe that system designs of high complexity could be verified at early design phase of the system development lifecycle.

The remainder of the paper is organized as follows. Section 2 gives an overview of the proposed verification framework. Section 3 outlines the work on formalizing the UML semantics by means of the ASM-theory based specification language AsmL. Section 4 presents a model checking approach towards formal verification of the AsmL specifications. In this section, the focus is put on the description of an on-the-fly algorithm and its functional parts consequently followed by the introduction of possible enhancement towards the efficient model checking of distributed systems. In Section 5 the related work is discussed. Finally, the paper concludes with a brief outlook on the future work in Section 6.

2.   FRAMEWORK OVERVIEW

The proposed verification framework is depicted by means of a process flow diagram shown in the Figure 1. The input to the verification process (dashed box) is represented by an UML model describing the specified system. The verification process is further divided into two parallel branches, namely the formal verification and the validation. The main goal of the formal verification consists in proving the correctness of the required properties that a given UML model has to fulfill. This is achieved by incorporating model checking techniques into the verification framework. The validation branch, on the other hand, comprises of the methods for conventional model simulation amended by the model-based testing. Both branches are built upon a common formal background based on the theory of Abstract State Machines (ASMs) and are implemented in the AsmL language.

In the rest of the paper we focus only on the formal verification, i.e. the model checking of AsmL specifications. The simulation and model-based testing approaches are based on the tool support coming together with AsmL and are out of the scope of this paper.

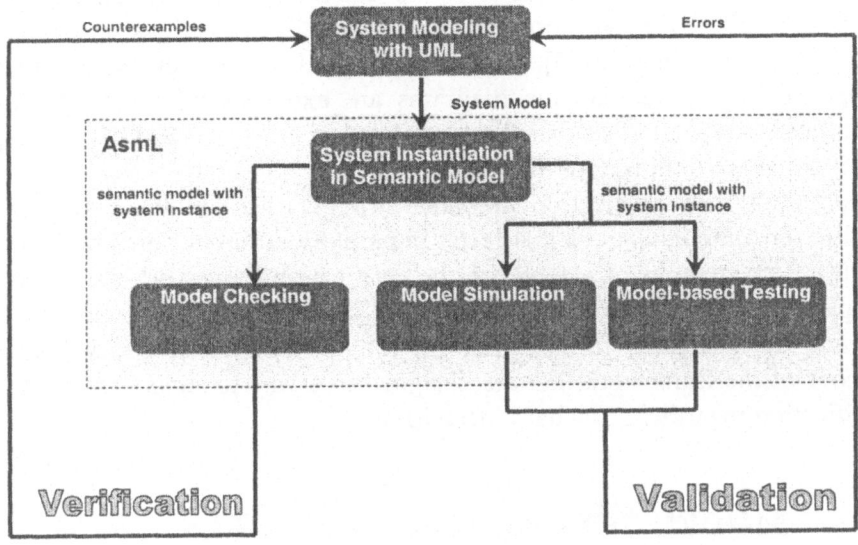

Figure 1. Verification framework for UML-based design

3.   FORMALIZING UML SEMANTICS

The main prerequisite for integration of the proposed verification methods into the verification framework is the presence of a rigorous formal semantics of the modeling paradigm, in our case represented by the Unified Modeling Language (UML 2.0) [1]. Therefore, choosing the right formal method is one of the crucial decisions to be taken. In our approach the *Abstract State Machines* (ASMs) [2] has been chosen as a suitable formalism to define the formal semantics of UML. The ASMs have approved their strong modeling and specification abilities in various application domains [3] also including work on formalization of selected parts of the older version of UML [4,5]. In particular, we adopted the AsmL language [6], an executable specification language built upon the theory of Abstract State Machines, to formally describe the UML semantics.

Formalizing the UML semantics is a tedious task, especially when the complexity and vastness of the whole UML 2.0 is considered. Therefore, our aim is not to formalize the complete semantics of UML. Instead, we consider only those UML diagrams that have been adopted into our design methodologies focusing on the two main application domains we are active in: the design of distributed production control systems and the design of self-optimizing multi-agent systems with mechatronic components. In the former, UML is applied to model distributed software for controlling production lines. We use UML structure diagrams, collaboration diagrams and state machine diagrams combined with modeling of actions by means of so-called Story Diagrams [7]. In the latter, similar diagrams are employed except that the state machine diagrams are extended with discrete time semantics. Due to the fact that the formalization process is out of the scope of this paper we omit further details.

Although both application domains strongly overlap, there still exist specific semantic deviations that result in partially different semantic models of UML written in AsmL. However, the verification framework presented in this paper does not depend on any semantic deviations. The solution resides in using the AsmL as formal platform for all verification and validation methods of the framework that are designed in a way to support any AsmL specification regardless of what it describes.

4.   MODEL CHECKING ASML MODELS

One of the qualities of AsmL is the high expressivity and richness of the language that allows us to keep the semantic models of UML in a readable and comprehensible form. This gives us flexibility in further maintenance of the semantic models and eases their modification and updating. However, in order to keep this advantage of AsmL we need to provide such a model checking approach that imposes least restrictions on the AsmL specification. Concretely, an AsmL specification should be allowed to fully exploit the robust data type system build in the AsmL, should allow dynamic object creation as well as usage of whole operational functionality provided by AsmL. The only constraint imposed on a specification is related to the size of its state space that has to be finite. The model checking approach presented in the next sections obeys all these requirements. It can be classified as an on-the-fly approach working over the explicit ASM state.

4.1   On-the-fly model checking

The intended model checking approach is depicted in the Figure 2. First of all, a particular AsmL specification and the property to be verified are provided as inputs. The property is specified in form of a temporal logic formula. In the first step, the temporal formula is transformed into a property automaton. As next, the AsmL specification is compiled and prepared for on-the-fly exploration. When both steps are successfully finished, the verification algorithm is started. During this process the state space exploration of a given AsmL specification is driven by the verification algorithm in an on-demand manner. The verification process may terminate in one of the following states: 1) in the OK state, after the whole state space has been explored and no contradiction of the property has been detected, 2) in the contradiction state, if a state of the system is found that does not satisfy the property and a counter example is produced 3) in the exception state, when an exception inside the specification is thrown during the state space exploration, and 4) in the user termination state, if the verification process was forced by the user to terminate.

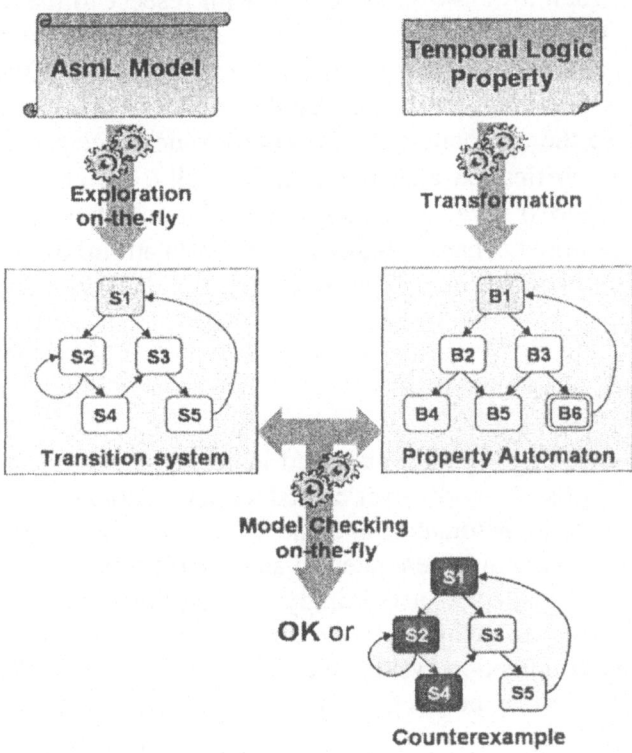

Figure 2. On-the-fly model checking of AsmL

4.1.1 Property specification and transformation

During model checking a system is verified against a property describing the desired system behavior. The property is expressed in form of a temporal logic formula. There exist several kinds of temporal logics, e.g. CTL, LTL, CTL* which usually differ in the set of expressible behaviors. In our approach we consider the CTL* logic that subsumes both CTL and LTL. The transformation of a CTL* formula into an automaton is done following the method introduced in [8]. This method uses a set of predefined goal-directed rules to derive the states of specialized tree automata called alternating Büchi tableau automata (ABTAs). An ABTA represents the property automaton showed in Figure 2.

4.1.2   Transition system construction

A transition system (a state transition graph) derived from an AsmL specification represents all possible runs of the specification. Obviously, the construction of such a transition system is, with respect to the needed time and resources, the most costly part of the overall model checking process. Therefore, we propose an on-the-fly construction approach that uses the exploration function built-in in the AsmL Toolkit. This function should allow us to drive the exploration of the system state space according to the demands of the verification algorithm. Additionally, the configurability of the exploration process gives us the apparatus to control how the state space is going to be explored. Thanks to this feature, even an infinite specification can be model checked within a fixed state space boundary (bounded model checking).

4.1.3   Verification algorithm

The model checking algorithm adopted in our approach originates in the work presented in [8]. It works over a product automaton, constructed from the produced property automaton and the transition system. Since, in our case, the transition system is generated in an on-the-fly manner, the original algorithm had to be adapted accordingly. In addition, the algorithm was redesigned in order to achieve a certain generics with respect to the implementations of transition system and property automaton. This gives us more freedom for experiments towards achievement of optimal implementations.

4.2   Incremental Model Checking

The presented model checking approach, similar to any other existing approaches, can show its weakness when it comes to verification of AsmL specifications that have a large state space. This is typical for example for distributed systems that consist of several interacting components running in parallel. In order to cope also with such distributed systems we propose a solution embedded into our verification framework. The main idea resides in defining an algorithm that is capable of executing the model checking in an incremental manner. The algorithm proposed here, depicted in Figure 3, can be seen as an enhancement of the on-the-fly algorithm presented above. It considers an AsmL specification consisting of several components (ASM agents) running in parallel and affecting each other only through their precisely defined communication. In addition, the properties to be verified are constrained to only ACTL formulas (the CTL formulas with only universal quantifiers).

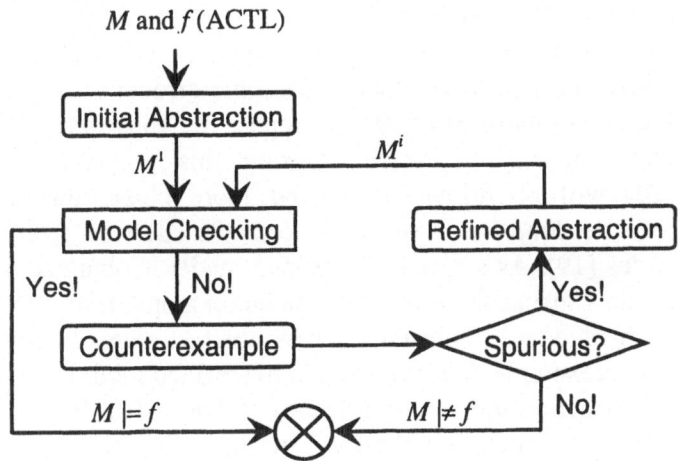

Figure 3. Control flow of incremental model checking

For an embedded system M with a finite set of variables $V = \{v_1, v_2, ..., v_n\}$ where each variable v_i has an associated finite domain D_i $(1 \le i \le n)$, the set of all possible states is $D = D_1 \times D_2 \times ... \times D_n$. Let P be the set of atomic propositions derived from the system. Then the system can be represented as a *Kripke* structure $M = (S, I, R, L)$ where $S = D$ is the set of states, $I \subseteq S$ is the set of initial states, $R \subseteq S \times S$ is the transition relation between states and $L: S \to 2^P$ is the labeling function. Given an ACTL property f, to avoid checking the satisfiability of f directly on M due to the state space explosion problem, we can obtain an abstract model (initial abstraction) from the original system by applying an appropriate abstraction function h to M. Intuitively, the abstraction function h induces an equivalence relation $\equiv_h$ on the domain D. That is, let d, e be states in D, then $d \equiv_h e$ iff $h(d) = h(e)$. It means that the equivalence relation $\equiv_h$ partitions D into a set of equivalence class denoted as $[D]_h = \{[d] \mid d \in D\}$ where $[d] = \{e \in D \mid h(e) = h(d)\}$. If we regard each equivalence class $[d]$ as a state from an abstract view, an abstract *Kripke* structure $M_h = (S_h, I_h, R_h, L_h)$ derived from M with respect to h can be defined as follows:

1. S_h is the abstract domain $[D]_h$;
2. $I_h = \{[d] \mid \exists e(e \in [d] \land e \in I)\}$;
3. $R_h = \{([d_1], [d_2]) \mid \exists e_1 \exists e_2(e_1 \in [d_1] \land e_2 \in [d_2] \land (e_1, e_2) \in R\}$;
4. $L_h([d]) = \cup_{e \in [d]} L(e)$.

Usually, the abstraction function h can be obtained by analyzing the dependency relationship between the variables in the system as well as the effect of these variables on the property to be verified. It is obvious that M_h

covers all possible behaviors of M but contains fewer states and fewer transitions than M. In this sense, M_h is an upper approximation to M, which means that an ACTL formula f *true* in M_h implies it's also *true* in M. However, in case that M_h falsifies f, the counterexample may be the result of some behavior in M_h which is not present in the original model M. Therefore, by refining M_h to a more precise model, i.e. far closer to M, it is possible to make the behavior which caused the erroneous counterexample disappear. For the refinement of M_h, we repeat the above procedure until a definite conclusion can be drawn. During this procedure, the initial abstraction M_h will be refined more and more close towards M. The refinement can be done based on the information derived from erroneous counterexamples [19]. As a result, the refined model is obtained by splitting the abstract state causing the erroneous counterexample into two subsets of the states, each of which represents a new abstract state. In this way, the erroneous counterexample does not exist in the refined model any more.

Given an abstraction function h, it is easy to know that the initial abstract model M_h can be constructed on-the-fly. Consequently, we can apply the on-the-fly model checking mentioned in section 4.1 to the abstract model of the original system M. If the abstract model satisfies f, then we can conclude the original system satisfies f. In case that a counterexample is found, we can locate the first abstract state which can cause the counterexample and then split the abstract state into two abstract states. Afterwards, we continue the on-the-fly model checking on this modified abstract model until a definite answer is obtained.

5.   RELATED WORK

Many methods on model checking UML model [9,10,11,12,13] have been presented in recent years. The basic idea of all these methods is to transform the UML model to the input language of an existing model checking tool, say SMV, SPIN or UPPAAL for example. In other words, the semantics of the UML model is reflected through the input language of some model checker. The expressiveness of the model checker's input language usually limits the expressiveness of the checked UML model. Unlike these methods, our method presented in this paper uses the ASM-based executable specification language AsmL to define the semantics of the UML model. The expressive power of AsmL allows us to formalize the semantics of any complex UML model that implies no constraints on used UML diagrams at the user's side. In addition, the resulting AsmL specification can be executed or tested by the tools coming with AsmL.

Of course, AsmL can also be used to do model checking. Since AsmL is quite a new language, there are no published approaches aimed at model checking AsmL yet. However, a few papers can be found concerning model checking of Abstract State Machines [14,15,16]. Basically, we can identify two main approaches both based on translation of the selected subsets of ASMs into the input language of an existing model checking tool. In the [14,15] an ASM model is first simplified by flattening the data structure and the corresponding ASM rules, and then translated (by direct mapping) to the SMV [17] input language. The approach introduced in [16] follows similar strategy, but uses the SPIN [18] model checker and its PROMELA language. The main drawbacks of both approaches consist in the constraints imposed on the supported ASM models. On the other hand, imposing such constraints seemed to be an inevitable decision in order to bridge the gap between the different expressive power of ASMs and the model checker languages. Our method can avoid this problem by model checking AsmL specifications directly.

6. CONCLUSION AND FUTURE WORK

In this paper we have presented a verification framework designated for formal verification and validation of UML-based design of embedded systems. The main ideas consist in using the AsmL specification language to define the formal semantic model of the supported part of UML and consequently applying model checking technique directly on the resulting AsmL semantic model. In addition, we have introduced two model checking methods, on-the-fly model checking and incremental model checking that we hope, are suitable for verifying large complex system models.

The work presented here is still an ongoing research work that needs to be evaluated in order to approve its practical utilization. Therefore, after finishing the implementation of the discussed methods we plan to focus on their evaluation by taking real system examples from the already mentioned application domains. Consequently, we plan to integrate the formal verification into our verification framework together with the simulation and model based-testing functions provided by the AsmL tools.

REFERENCES

[1] Object Management Group. UML Superstructure Submission V2.0. OMG Document ptc/02-03-02, January 2003. URL: http://www.omg.org/cgi-bin/doc?ad/2003-01-06.

[2] Y. Gurevich: Evolving Algebras 1993: Lipari Guide; E. Börger (Eds.): Specification and Validation Methods, Oxford University Press, 1995.

[3] Abstract State Machines web page: http://www.eecs.umich.edu/gasm/

[4] E. Börger, A. Cavarra, and E. Riccobene: An ASM Semantics for UML Activity Diagrams, in Teodor Rus, ed., Algebraic Methodology and Software Technology, 8th International Conference, AMAST 2000, Iowa City, Iowa, USA, May 20-27, 2000, Proceedings, Springer LNCS 1816, 2000, 293--308.

[5] K. Compton, J. K. Huggins, and W. Shen: A Semantic Model for the State Machine in the Unified Modeling Language. In Gianna Reggio, Alexander Knapp, Bernhard Rumpe, Bran Selic, and Roel Wieringa, eds., "Dynamic Behaviour in UML Models: Semantic Questions", Workshop Proceedings, UML 2000 Workshop, Ludwig-Maximilians-Universität München, Institut für Informatik, Bericht 0006, October 2000, 25-31.

[6] Y. Gurevich,W. Schulte,C. Campbell,W. Grieskamp. AsmL: The Abstract State Machine Language Version 2.0. http://research.microsoft.com/foundations/AsmL/default.html

[7] T. Fischer, J. Niere, L. Torunski, A. Zündorf: Story Diagrams: A new Graph Rewrite Language based on the Unified Modelling Language and Java; in Proc. of the 6th International Workshop on Theory and Application of Graph Transformation (TAGT), Paderborn, November 1998, LNCS, Springer Verlag.

[8] G. Bhat, R. Cleaveland, and A. Groce: Efficient model checking via Buchi tableau automata. Technical report, Department of Computer Science, SUNY, Stony Brook, 2000

[9] T. Schäfer, A. Knapp, and S. Merz. Model Checking UML State Machines and Collaborations. In *Proc. Wsh. Software Model Checking*, Volume 55(3) of *Elect. Notes Theo. Comp. Sci.*, Paries, 2001.

[10] A. Knapp, S. Merz, and C. Rauh. Model Checking Timed UML State Machines and Collaborations. *Proc. 7th Int. Symp. Formal Techniques in Real-Time and Fault Tolerant Systems*, LNCS 2469, pages 395-416. ©Springer, Berlin, 2002

[11] K. Diethers, U. Goltz and M. Huhn. Model Checking UML Statecharts with Time. In Proc. of the Workshop on Critical Systems Development with UML, 2002.

[12] A. David, M.Möller, and W. Yi. Formal Verification of UML Statecharts with Real-Time Extensions. In Proc. of FASE 2002 (ETAPS 2002). LNCS 2306, p218-232, 2002.

[13] S. Gnesi and D. Latella. Model Checking UML Statechart Diagrams using JACK. In *Proc. Fourth IEEE International Symposium on High Assuarance Systems Enginering*, IEEE Press, 1999.

[14] G. del Castillo and K. Winter: Model checking support for the ASM high-level language. In S. Graf and M. Schwartzbach, editors, Proc. on 6th Int. Conf. TACAS 2000, volume 1785 of LNCS, pages 331-346, 2000.

[15] Kirsten Winter: Model Checking Abstract State Machines, Ph.D. thesis, Technical University of Berlin, Germany, 2001.

[16] A. Gargantini, E. Riccobene, S. Rinzivillo: Using Spin to Generate Tests from ASM Specifications, In E. Börger, A. Gargantini, E. Riccobene, editors, Proc. of 10th International Workshop on Abstract State Machines 2003, Taormina, Italy, March 3-7, 2003

[17] K. McMillan: Symbolic Model Checking, Kluwer Academic Publishers, Boston (1993).

[18] G. J. Holzmann: The model checker SPIN. IEEE Transactions on Software Engineering, May 1997.

[19] E. Clarke, O. Grumberg, S. Jha, Y. Lu and H. Veith. Counterexample-guided abstraction refinement. In Computer Aided Verification, volume 1855 of LNCS, pp. 154-169, 2000.

LTL'S INTUITIVE REPRESENTATIONS AND ITS AUTOMATON TRANSLATION

Yuhong Zhao
Heinz Nixdorf Institute, University of Paderborn, Germany

Abstract: Compared with other verification methods, to some sense, model checking can be thought of as more attractive method to test hardware and software systems due to its automatic features. However, a stumbling problem is how to supply correct formal properties in logic to do model checking by system designers without specific mathematical background. This paper first presents two intuitive representations for the LTL formulas: one is graphical automaton-like; the other is textual regular-expression-like and then shows how these representations can be used to construct Büchi automata for LTL model checking.

1. INTRODUCTION

Software components have become an important part of the complex distributed (real-time) embedded systems, which usually run in a much more constrained environment than "traditional" computer systems and require consequently safety-critical and high-reliability to these systems. Therefore, one challenge today's system designers are facing is how to guarantee the correctness of such systems, especially when large concurrent and reactive systems are concerned. Moreover, in safety crucial applications, real-time requirements need to be considered, which further increase the difficulty of system development and validation. The non-determinism inherent in such applications usually makes them hard to test. However, formal methods for specifying and verifying systems can offer a greater assurance of correctness than traditional simulation and testing [CGP00].

Formal verification methods can ensure that a high-level system design really meets rigorously specified correctness requirements, thereby increaseing the possibility that faulty designs can be discovered at the earlier phases of system development. Temporal logics [CD88] are well-suited for specifying temporal properties of systems. Nevertheless, experiences show that specifications of even moderate-sized systems are too complex to be readily understood if without some expertise in idioms of the specification language [DAC99]. Consequently, system developers seldom make signifycant use of formal specification and verification techniques in practice.

In order to be widely adopted in the development of real world systems, formal specification and analysis methods should be made accessible to system designers and software engineers in the sense that users can express the properties of the systems about which they wish to reason as intuitively as possible and to confirm automatically that the design models of the systems satisfy the required properties. As a result, system developers can use formal specifications throughout the system lifecycle to guide development, maintenance and enhancement.

To do this, the author has presented intuitive representations for a widely used temporal logic called CTL* as well as its extensions with respect to time in [Zha03]. These representations include automaton-like graphical notations and regular-expression-like textual notations so as to fit into different needs. To some extent, these representations can offer a natural way to express system properties without sacrificing the benefits of the formal notation. Moreover, the intuitive representations of the LTL formulas can help to construct Büchi automata with features different from other methods [DGV99, Fri03, GL02, GO01, GPV⁺95, SB00, Tri02]. This method makes fairness constraints caused by the "U" operators disappeared and the resulting automata are the Büchi automata with only one acceptance conditions, instead of the generalized ones with multiple acceptance conditions.

Considering the limit of space, the main aim of the paper is to introduce the intuitive representations for LTL formulas and then present the automata translation method based on these intuitive representations. The remainder of this paper is structured as follows: Section 2 gives the preliminaries on linear temporal logic and on Büchi automata; Section 3 presents the intuitive representations for the LTL formulas; Section 4 addresses applying these representations to automata translation; Section 5 discusses related work and finally we draw conclusions in Section 6.

2.   PRELIMINARIES

Linear Temporal Logic(LTL)[Pnu81] is composed of *temporal operators* (**X**, **F**, **G**, **U** and **R**) which specify properties of a system execution path. LTL formulas are defined inductively starting from a finite set P of *atomic* *propositions*, the standard *Boolean* operators, and the temporal operators. Without loss of generality, given a system M, let π be an execution path; $p \in P$ be a proposition; f and g be LTL formulas. The interpretation of LTL can then be described as below:

1. $M, \pi \models p \quad \Leftrightarrow \quad p$ holds at the first state of π.
2. $M, \pi \models \neg f \quad \Leftrightarrow \quad f$ does not hold along π.
3. $M, \pi \models f \vee g \quad \Leftrightarrow$ either f or g holds along π.
4. $M, \pi \models f \wedge g \quad \Leftrightarrow$ both f and g hold along π.
5. $M, \pi \models \mathbf{X}f \quad \Leftrightarrow \quad f$ holds at the second state of π.
6. $M, \pi \models \mathbf{F}f \quad \Leftrightarrow \quad f$ holds at some state on π.
7. $M, \pi \models \mathbf{G}f \quad \Leftrightarrow \quad f$ holds at every state on π.
8. $M, \pi \models f \mathbf{U} g \quad \Leftrightarrow \quad f$ holds along π up to some state where g holds.
9. $M, \pi \models f \mathbf{R} g \quad \Leftrightarrow \quad g$ holds along π up to and including the first state where f holds.

Büchi automata are widely used in model checking to verify LTL formulas due to the characteristic that both the system model and the properties can be represented in an automaton form. There are several variants of Büchi automata. The variant typically used in model checking is Büchi automata with labels on transitions and simple accepting conditions defined in terms of states. Simply, a Büchi automata is a 6-tuple $<S, P, R, L, S_0, F>$, where S is a finite set of states, P is a finite set of propositions, $R \subseteq S \times S$ is a transition relation, $L: R \rightarrow 2^P$ is a transition labeling function, $S_0 \subseteq S$ is a set of initial states, and $F \subseteq 2^P$ is a set of accepting states.

3. LTL'S INTUITIVE REPRESENTATIONS

3.1 Graphical Representation

Without loss of generality, Figure 1 - Figure 5 illustrate the graphical representations for LTL formulas $\mathbf{X}f$, $\mathbf{F}f$, $\mathbf{G}f$, $f \mathbf{U} g$ and $f \mathbf{R} g$ respectively, each of which is composed of a dot "•" and a *path pattern*. Simply speaking, a dot "•" connects to the first position of a path pattern and a path pattern consists of *node*s and *edge*s: a node denotes a position on the path pattern, on which the formula "f" means only those states satisfying f can occur in this position (matching the node); an edge denotes the sequential order between states, on which a symbol "*" represents repeating zero or finitely many times and a symbol "∞" represents repeating infinitely many times. In addition, "T" refers to *true* representing "all states" in the system M; similarly, "F" refers to *false* representing "no state" if needed. Thus, path patterns can intuitively illustrate what states may occur in which positions on a matching path. In this sense, a path pattern can be seen as a type of those paths matching this path pattern and such a path can be seen as an instance of this path pattern.

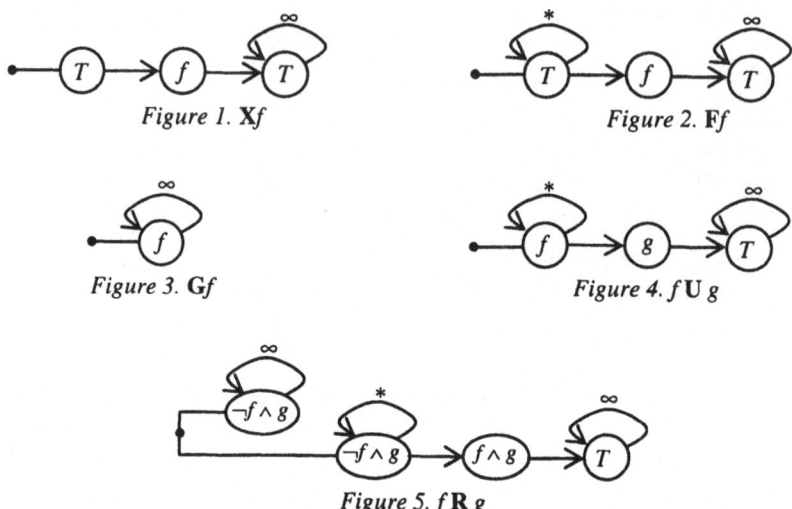

Figure 1. X*f*   Figure 2. F*f*

Figure 3. G*f*   Figure 4. *f* U *g*

Figure 5. *f* R *g*

The meanings of Figure 1 - Figure 5 are obvious, i.e., each path matching the above path patterns in *M* are the path satisfying the corresponding formula. But how about the more complicated LTL formulas with the nested sub-formulas? Let's take the formula **G**(*h* → **F**(*f* U *g*)) as an example. As a result, Figure 6 is the graphical representation in which the nodes with a dot "•" characterize the nested cases. That is, a path pattern connected to the dot "•" in a node of another path pattern represents a subformula. Therefore, a path starting from a state matching such a node should, on the one hand, conform to the path pattern starting from the node and, on the other hand, conform to the path pattern of the formula in the node at the same time. For example, a path from a state matching the node N_3 should follow both the path pattern starting from N_3 and the path pattern connected to the dot "•" in N_3. Note that this is different from Figure 5 which means a path should follow one of the two given path patterns. In addition, the negation form can be represented as "¬(•)". In this way, we can intuitively represent any

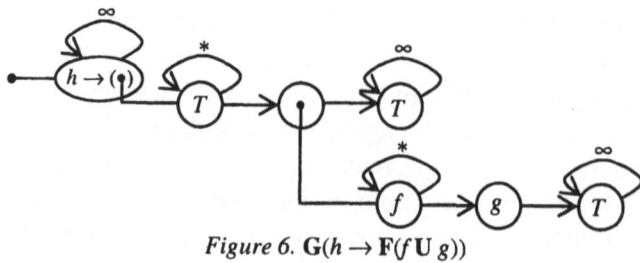

Figure 6. **G**(*h* → **F**(*f* U *g*))

complex LTL formulas. The *proof* is simple by structure induction and therefore omitted here.

3.2 Textual Representation

The idea of textual representation for LTL formulas is inspired by the form of regular expressions. However, in order to describe LTL formula intuitively in a textual way, we just borrow some notations of the traditional regular expressions and add some new notations to fit our needs.

The new notations related to logic operators are "~" denoting *Negation*, "|" denoting *Or*, "&" denoting *And*, "=>" denoting *Implication* and "<=>" denoting *Equivalence*. In particular, "!" is employed to force the formula immediately preceding it to repeat infinitely many times. The notations borrowed from the regular expressions are the operators related to concatenation and closure [HMU01] which also have a similar meaning here. In addition, "T" and "F" have the same meaning as in the graphical representation.

As a result, the basic LTL formula Xf can be written as "$TfT!$", Ff can be written as "$T*fT!$", Gf written as "$f!$", $f \cup g$ written as "$f*gT!$", and "$f \mathbf{R} g$" written as "$((\sim f\&g)! \mid (\sim f\&g)*(f\&g)T!)$". As for the complex LTL formulas, say $G(h \to F(f \cup g))$, its regular form is also easy to be obtained in this way, i.e., "$(h => T*(f*gT!)T!)!$". It's not difficult to reason that this textual repreesenttation has a direct one to one mapping with the corresponding graphical representation. Therefore, its semantics is the same as the graphical one. In fact, the regular form is another way to represent path patterns. Note that, to avoid ambiguity, this regular representation has to be parenthesized whenever need. Otherwise, the meaning of the expression "$(h => T*(f*gT!)T!)!$" would be not clear if the brackets surrounding the sub-expression "$f*gT!$" were missing.

4. LTL'S AUTOMATON TRANSLATION

Because the graphical and the regular representations for LTL formulas are essentially the same thing, here we only use the regular form to illustrate the translation procedure in this section. On the other hand, we suppose the LTL formula is of the restricted negation normal form, in which the negation is applied only to propositional variables.

4.1 Example

To ease the understanding of the translation procedure, let's first take an LTL formula $G(f \to Fg)$ as an example. According to Section 3, the textual form of $G(f \to Fg)$ is $(\sim f \mid T^*gT!)!$ representing an infinite sequence of nodes labeled with $(\sim f \mid T^*gT!)$. If we separate the first node from the sequence, the rest of the sequence still forms an infinite sequence. That is, $(\sim f \mid T^*gT!)!$ can be derived into two parts: $(\sim f \mid T^*gT!)! = (\sim f \mid T^*gT!)::(\sim f \mid T^*gT!)!$. Note that the double colon "::" here is employed to separate the two parts: the part before "::" is called *head*; the part after "::" is called *tail*. Intuitively, a path pattern can be seen as a sequence of nodes, in which the first node is *head* and the rest of the sequence *tail*. As for $(\sim f \mid T^*gT!)!$, its *head* is $(\sim f \mid T^*gT!)$ and its *tail* is $(\sim f \mid T^*gT!)!$. However, its *head* is still a path pattern not a state formula. Our goal is to transform a path pattern into its "normal" form, i.e., its *head* is state formula. Similarly, $T^*gT! = g::T! \mid T::T^*gT!$. According to the interpretation of LTL formulas, it's not difficult to reason that

$$
\begin{aligned}
(\sim f \mid T^*gT!)! \quad &= (\sim f \mid T^*gT!)::(\sim f \mid T^*gT!)! \\
&= (\sim f)::(\sim f \mid T^*gT!)! \mid (T^*gT!)::(\sim f \mid T^*gT!)!
\end{aligned}
$$

Moreover, since $(T^*gT!)$ is still a path pattern, $(T^*gT!)::(\sim f \mid T^*gT!)!$ can be further transformed as follows until all the *head* parts are state formulas:

$$
\begin{aligned}
(T^*gT!)::(\sim f \mid T^*gT!)! \quad &= (T::T^*gT! \mid g::T!)::(\sim f \mid T^*gT!)! \\
&= T::(\sim f \mid T^*gT!)! \ \& \ (T^*gT!) \mid g::(\sim f \mid T^*gT!)! \ \& \ T! \\
&= T::(\sim f \mid T^*gT!)! \ \& \ (T^*gT!) \mid g::(\sim f \mid T^*gT!)!
\end{aligned}
$$

Notice that $T!$ matches any infinite path, so $(\sim f \mid T^*gT!)! \ \& \ T! = (\sim f \mid T^*gT!)!$. $(\sim f \mid T^*gT!)!$ can be represented as the following normal form:

$$
(\sim f \mid T^*gT!)! \quad = (\sim f)::(\sim f \mid T^*gT!)! \mid T::(\sim f \mid T^*gT!)! \ \& \ (T^*gT!) \mid g::(\sim f \mid T^*gT!)!
$$

Similarly, the normal form of $(\sim f \mid T^*gT!)! \ \& \ (T^*gT!)$ is shown as below:

$$
\begin{aligned}
(\sim f \mid T^*gT!)! \ \& \ (T^*gT!) \quad &= (\sim f)::(\sim f \mid T^*gT!)! \ \& \ (T^*gT!) \mid \\
&\quad (\sim f \& g)::(\sim f \mid T^*gT!)! \mid \\
&\quad T::(\sim f \mid T^*gT!)! \ \& \ (T^*gT!) \mid \\
&\quad g::(\sim f \mid T^*gT!)! \ \& \ (T^*gT!) \mid \\
&\quad g::(\sim f \mid T^*gT!)!
\end{aligned}
$$

Let $A = (\sim f \mid T^*gT!)!$ and $B = (\sim f \mid T^*gT!)! \ \& \ (T^*gT!)$, then we have

$$
\begin{aligned}
A &= (\sim f)::A \mid g::A \mid T::B = (\sim f \mid g)::A \mid T::B \\
B &= (\sim f \& g)::A \mid g::A \mid (\sim f)::B \mid g::B \mid T::B = g::A \mid T::B
\end{aligned}
$$

which can be seen as a variant of context-free grammar productions. We can construct the Büchi automaton of $G(f \to Fg)$ as shown in Figure 7 from this production form.

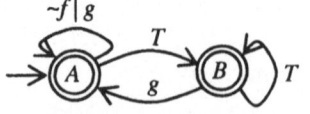

Figure 7. Büchi automaton of $G(f \to Fg)$

One problem that needs to make further explain is accepting condition. The Büchi automaton of $G(f \to Fg)$ contains two states A and B which are labeled with $(\sim f \mid T^*gT!)!$ and $(\sim f \mid T^*gT!)! \ \& \ (T^*gT!)$ respectively. According to the automaton construction, the state A labeled with $(\sim f \mid T*gT!)!$ means any infinite path starting from A matches $(\sim f \mid T*gT!)!$; the state B labeled with $(\sim f \mid T*gT!)!$ & $(T*gT!)$ means any infinite path starting from B matches $(\sim f \mid T*gT!)!$ and $(T*gT!)$ at the same time. It is easy to reason that the loop from B directly to B is not acceptable because the infinite part (i.e., $T!$) of $(T*gT!)$ is never matched. But the loop from B via A to B is acceptable because $(\sim f \mid T*gT!)!$ & $T! = (\sim f \mid T*gT!)!$. Consequently, both A and B are accepting states with such a constraint on B that the loop from B must go through A. In general, all the states on an accepting loop can not contain a common subformula of the form "$x*yT!$". Otherwise, the loop will always matche $x*yT!$ and thus can not match the infinite part of $x*yT!$ at all.

Note that in this automata translation procedure we do not need fairness constraints with respect to the (implicit) "U" operators in the given formula. The reason is $f \, U \, g = f*gT! = f::f*gT! \mid g::T!$. Let $A = f*gT!$ and $B = T!$, thus in the resulting automaton (Figure 8) only the state B labeled with $T!$ is the accepting state, which guarantees that g has already been held before arriving at B. In this aspect, this automata translation method differs from many other methods by explicitly denoting the path pattern following g.

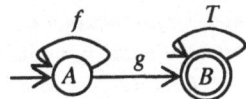

Figure 8. Büchi automaton of $f \, U \, g$

4.2   Translation Algorithm

The above example illustrates that the procedure of translating an LTL formula into Büchi automaton from its path pattern representation, which is similar to the tableau-constructing method. But the approach presented here is more simple and intuitive. Especially, the "U" operators are no longer a problem. In what follows, we'll present our algorithm by imitating the algorithm in [GPVW95]. Therefore, our algorithm has the same complexity as the algorithm in [GPVW95].

The basic data structure used in our algorithm is called *node*. The states of the automaton can be derived from *nodes*. A *node* is defined as below:

record *node* = [*formula*:	*Path-Pattern*,
head:	*Path-Pattern*,
tail:	*Path-Pattern*]

where the field *formula* keeps the textual path pattern of an LTL formula; the fields *head* and *tail* keep the *head* and the *tail* of the path pattern *formula* respectively. As a result, *formula* = *head::tail*. Our goal is to transform *formula* into its normal form, i.e., its *head* is a state formula. Obviously, the three fields together can uniquely identify a *node*. Intuitively, the successors of a *node* are the *node*s with *formula*s the same as *tail* of the *node* and the predecessors of a *node* are the *node*s with *tail*s the same as *formula* of the *node*. The edge between a *node* and its successor is labeled with *head* of the *node*. To some sense, the resulting automaton is a flattened path pattern.

Given an LTL formula *r* in a textual path pattern form, the function *create_graph* initiates the automaton construction procedure by applying *split* to the starting node with *formula* and *head* set to *r* and *tail* set to *T!*. As a result, *create_graph* returns a set of nodes, from which we can derive a Büchi automaton of *r*.

```
function create_graph(r: Path-Pattern): Node-Set
    return (split([formula ⇐ r, head ⇐ r, tail ⇐ T!], ∅));
end function
```

The recursive function *split* builds a tableau. It has two parameters: *node* denoting the current *node* to be processed and *node_set* a set of *node*s have been generated by now and returns an updated set of *node*s if possible.

```
function split(node: Node, node_set: Node-Set): Node-Set
    if ∃node'∈ node_set: head(node) = formula(node') then
        for each node'∈ node_set: head(node) = formula(node')
            node_set := node_set ∪ [formula    ⇐ formula(node),
                                    head        ⇐ head(node'),
                                    tail        ⇐ tail(node) & tail(node')];
        end for
        return (node_set);
    else if head(node) is a state formula then
        if head(node) ≠ F then
            return(split([formula ⇐ tail(node), head ⇐ tail(node), tail ⇐ T!],
                         node_Set ∪ {node}));
        else return (node_set);
        end if
    else if head(node) is of form f | g then
        node_set := split([formula ⇐ formula(node), head ⇐ f, tail ⇐ tail(node)],
                          node_set);
        return (split([formula ⇐ formula(node), head ⇐ g, tail ⇐ tail(node)], node_set));
    else if head(node) is of form f & g then
        node_set := split([formula ⇐ f, head ⇐ f, tail ⇐ T!], node_set);
        node_set := split([formula ⇐ g, head ⇐ g, tail ⇐ T!], node_set);
        for each node₁ in node_set with formula(node₁) = f and
            each node₂ in node_set with formula(node₂) = g do
            node_set := split([formula ⇐ formula(node),
                               head    ⇐ head(node₁) & head(node₂),
                               tail ⇐ tail(node) & tail(node₁) & tail(node₂)], node_set);
        end for
```

```
        return(node_set);
    else if head(node) is of form TfT! then
        return(split([formula ⇐ formula(node),
                      head  ⇐ T,
                      tail  ⇐ tail(node) & fT!], node_set));
    else if head(node) is of form f*gT! then
        node_set := split([formula ⇐ formula(node),
                           head  ⇐ g,
                           tail  ⇐ tail(Node) & T!], node_set);
        return(split([formula ⇐ formula(node),
                      head  ⇐ f,
                      tail  ⇐ tail(Node) & f*gT!], node_set));
    else if head(node) is of form f! then
        return(split([formula ⇐ formula(node), head ⇐ f, tail⇐ tail(node) & f!],
               node_set));
    end if
end function
```

4.3 Acceptance Condition

We can deduce the accepting states of the resulting automaton as follows. According to our automaton construction, a state labeled with a path pattern means any infinite path (loop) starting from the state matches the path pattern. Consequently, the infinite part of the path matches the infinite part of the path pattern. In addition, the *tails* of the *nodes* obtained from *create_graph* always have the conjunction form "x_1 & x_2 & ... & x_n" ($n \geq 1$) where x_i has a form of either "$x*yT!$" or "$x!$". Notice that a path pattern of the form "$TxT!$" or "$xT!$" is a special case of the form "$x*yT!$". This conjunction form requires any loop from the corresponding state in the automaton match the n path patterns $x_1, x_2, ..., x_n$ at the same time.

For convenience, we denote "x_1 & x_2 & ... & x_n" as a path pattern set $\{x_1, x_2, ..., x_n\}$. If all the states $s_1, s_2, ..., s_k$ on a loop share common path patterns of the form "$x*yT!$", say, $f*gT! \in path\_pattern\_set(s_1) \cap path\_pattern\_set(s_2) \cap ... \cap path\_pattern\_set(s_k)$), obviously, the loop will match $f*gT!$ forever but never get to the infinite part of $f*gT!$. Consequently, such a loop is not acceptable. However, if the above condition is not *true*, then we can say the loop is acceptable. In general, if a state in a resulting automaton has a loop starting from it and the states on the loop do not share common path patterns of the form "$x*yT!$", then the state is a (constrained) accepting state.

It's easy to reason that a state labeled with a path pattern of the form "$y_1!$ & $y_2!$ & ... & $y_n!$" is definitely an accepting state and a state labeled with a path pattern of the form "$x_1*y_1T!$ & $x_2*y_2T!$ & ... & $x_n*y_nT!$" is definitely not an accepting state. Therefore, a state contains path patterns of the two forms "*x*!" and "*x*yT*!" is an accepting state if there is a loop to it and the states on the loop do not share common path patterns of the form "*x*yT*!".

As mentioned in section 4.1, this automata translation procedure does not need fairness constraints with respect to the (implicit) "**U**" operators in the given formula and thereby differs from many other methods. According to the existing methods, for each subformula of the form "*f* **U** *g*", a set of accepting states $F_{f\mathbf{U}g} = \{s \in S : f \mathbf{U} g \notin s \text{ or } g \in s\}$ is produced. In case a formula contains multiple subformulas of the form "*f* **U** *g*", then the resulting automaton contains accordingly multiple sets of accepting states, so called generalized Büchi automaton. The path of a generalized Büchi automaton is accepted if for each set F_i of accepting states, there are infinitely many *s*'s on the path such that $s \in F_i$. Therefore, a generalized Büchi automaton is usually transformed into a normal Büchi automaton with only one set of accepting states by using a counter *i*: each state becomes a pair <*s*, *i*>. The counter is initialized to 0 and counts modulo *m* ($m = |F|$) where $F = \{F_0, F_1, ..., F_{m-1}\}$. It is increased whenever a state of the *i*th set $F_i \subseteq F$ is reached. As a result, only one set of accepting states, say $F_0 \times \{0\}$, is needed.

5.   RELATED WORK

Graphical representation, due to its visual effect, is popular in the process of system development. Some intuitive representations for temporal logic properties have been presented in recent years. Timing Diagrams [SD93] are a graphical notation for expressing precedence and causality relationships between events in a computation, the semantics of which is defined by a subset of temporal logics. Graphical Interval Logic (GIL) [DKM+94] is a visual temporal logic in which formulas resemble timing diagrams and can thus express a subset of temporal logic, too. Timeline notation captures the event-based LTL requirements [SHE01]. Constrained expression representation in [ABC⁺91] is essentially a regular expression which can not address infinite executions of the system. Regular CTL (RCTL) [BBL98] covers a rich and useful set of CTL formulas and regular expressions. Bandera Specification Language (BSL) [CDH⁺00] is a source-level model checking independent language for expressing properties of Java program actions and data.

For the automaton translation, many existing approaches [DGV99, Fri03, GL02, GO01, GPV⁺95, SB00, Tri02] are mainly based on the LTL formulas or alternating Büchi automata of the LTL formulas together with some simplification and optimization techniques to reduce the size of the resulting automata. In contrast, the method presented in this paper built the automata based on the path patterns of the LTL formulas. Path pattern is similar but different from alternating Büchi automaton in concept and use. We just use path pattern (formula) "x_1 & x_2 & ... & x_n," to label a state, but never think of such a state as a conjunction of n basic states labeled respectively with x_1, x_2, ..., x_n. A path pattern can characterize the whole path instead of the prefix of the path, say $\mathbf{F}g$, because path pattern ends with the infinite form "$x!$". Thus, path pattern does not need accepting states. Using path pattern does not need to transform $\mathbf{G(F)}$ into $\mathbf{R(U)}$ operator. Checking a (constrained) accepting state is simple and the resulting automaton can directly be used to do LTL model checking. That is to say, we can avoid the problem caused by the formula of form "$f\,\mathbf{U}\,g$" and obtain a "normal" Büchi automaton directly.

6. CONCLUSION AND OUTLOOK

Expressing complex requirements in logic is without doubt a challenging task. Therefore, this paper attempts to visualize the cryptic specifications to ease the question. By using path pattern, one can intuitively reason what type of states can occur in which positions on a path and both state- and event-based properties can be specified in a unified way. Moreover, path pattern can help to construct the normal Büchi automata, instead of the generalized ones, which different from many other translation methods in the aspect that this method avoids the problem caused by the "U" operator naturally. We plan to study on the simplification and optimization methods related to this automata translation way in the future.

REFERENCES

[ABC+91] G. S. Avrunin, U. A. Buy, J. C. Corbett, L. K. Dillon, and J. C. Wileden. Automated Analysis of Concurrent Systems with the Constrained Expression Tool-set. IEEE Transactions on Software Engineering, 17(11): 1024-1222, Nov. 1991.

[BBL98] I. Beer, S. Ben-David, A. Landver. On-the-fly Model Checking of RCTL Formulas. CAV'98, LNCS 1427, pp. 184-194.

[CD88] E. M. Clark, I. A. Draghicescu. Expressibility results for linear time and branching time logics. In Linear time, Branching time, and Partial order in Logics and Models for Concurrency, LNCS 354, pp. 428-437. Springer, 1988.

[CDH+00] J. C. Corbett, M. B. Dwyer, J. Hatcliff, and Robby. A Language Framework for Expressing Checkable Properties of Dynamic Software. In SPIN Software Model Checking Workshop, pp. 205-223. Stanford, CA. 2000.

[CGP00] E. M. Clark, Jr., O. Grumberg, and D. A. Peled. Model Checking. MIT Press. 1999.

[DAC99] M. B. Dwyer, G. S. Avrunin and J. C. Corbett. Pat-terns in Property Specifications for Finite-State Verification. In Proc. of the 21st International Conf. on Software Engineering, pp. 411-420. May, 1999.

[DGV99]   M. Daniele, F. Giunchiglia, and M. Vardi. Improved Automata Generation for Linear Temporal Logic. In Proc. of the 11th International Conference on Computer Aided Verification (CAV'99), Trento, Italy. Springer, LNCS1631.

[DKM+94] L. K. Dillon, G. Kutty, L. E. Moser, P. M. Melliar-Smith, and Y. S. Ramakrishna. A Graphical Interval Logic for Specifying Concurrent Systems. ACM Transactions on Software Engineering and Methodology, 3(2): 131-165, Apr. 1994.

[Fri03]   C. Fritz. Constructing Büchi Automata from Linear Temporal Logic Using Simulation Relations for Alternating Büchi Automata. In CIAA 2003, LNCS 2759, pp. 35-48, 2003.

[GL02]   D. Giannakopoulou and F. Lerda. From States to Transitions: Improving Translation of LTL formulae to Büchi Automata. In Formal Techniques for Networked and Distributed Systems - FORTE 2002, LNCS 2529, pp. 308-326, Texas, USA, November, 2002.

[GO01]   P. Gastin and D. Oddoux. Fast LTL to Büchi Automata Translation. In Proc. of the 13th International Conference on Computer Aided Verification (CAV'01). July, 2001, Paris, France. Springer, LNCS 2102.

[GPV+95] R.Gerth, D. Peled, M. Vardi and P. Wolper. Simple On-the-fly Automatic Verification of Linear Temporal Logic. In Proc. of the 15th IFIP/WG6.1 Symposium on Protocol Specification, Testing and Verification (PSTV'95). June, 1995, Warsaw, Poland.

[GPVW95] R.Gerth, D. Peled, M. Vardi and P. Wolper. Simple On-the-fly Automatic Verification of Linear Temporal Logic. In Proc. of the 15th IFIP/WG6.1 Symposium on Protocol Specification, Testing and Verification (PSTV'95). June, 1995, Warsaw, Poland.

[HMU01]   J. E. Hopcroft, R. Motwani, and J. D. Ullman. Introduction to Automata Theory, Language, and Computation (second edition). Addison-Wesley, 2001.

[Pnu81]   A. Pnueli. A temporal logic of concurrent programs. Theoretical Computer Science 13: 45-60.

[SB00]   F. Somenzi and R. Bloem. Efficient Büchi Automata from LTL Formulae. In Computer Aided Verification, 12th International Conference (CAV2000), LNCS 1855, pp. 249-263, 2000.

[SD93]   R. Schlör and W. Damm. Specification of system-level hardware designs using timing diagrams. In Proc. Europe Conf. Design Automation and Europe Event in ASIC Design, pages 518-524, Paris, Feb. 1993. IEEE Computer Society Press.

[SHE01]   M.H. Smith, G. J. Holzmann and K. Etessami. Events and Constraints: A Graphical Editor for Capturing Logic Requirements of Programs. In the 5th IEEE International Symposium on Requirements Engineering, pp. 14-23. Canada, August, 2001.

[Tri02]   X. Thirioux. Simple and Efficient Translation from LTL Formulas to Büchi Automata. In Electronic Notes in Theoretical Computer Science 66 No. 2(2002).

[Zha03]   Y. Zhao. Intuitive Representations for Temporal Logic Formulas. In Proc. of Forum on Specification and Design Language (FDL'03), pp. 405-413, Frankfurt, Germany, September, 2003.

MODELING AND VERIFICATION OF HYBRID SYSTEMS BASED ON EQUATIONS

Kazuhiro Ogata[1], Daigo Yamagishi[2], Takahiro Seino[2], Kokichi Futatsugi[2]

[1] *NEC Software Hokuriku, Ltd. / JAIST*

ogatak@acm.org

[2] *Graduate School of Information Science, JAIST*

{d-yamagi, t-seino, kokichi}@jaist.ac.jp

Abstract: We describe hybrid observational transition systems, or HOTSs. HOTSs are written in terms of equations and verified by means of equational reasoning. More concretely, CafeOBJ, an algebraic specification language, is used to specify HOTSs and verify that HOTSs have properties by writing proofs, or proof scores. One case study is used to demonstrate how to model hybrid systems as HOTSs, specify HOTSs in CafeOBJ and verify that HOTSs have properties with the CafeOBJ system.

Keywords: CafeOBJ, HOTS, hybrid systems, modeling, verification.

1.   INTRODUCTION

Embedded systems are inherently hybrid. Hybrid systems are sensitive to physical continuity such as real-time and real-temperature. Real-time systems are one sub-class of hybrid systems. Hybrid systems can be complex and subject to subtle errors. Therefore, several formal methods of modeling and verification of hybrid systems have been recently proposed(Kesten et al., 2000; Lamport, 1993; Lynch et al., 2003). Our method proposed in this paper is one of such formal methods. Our method is based on equations and equational reasoning. Equations are the most basic logical formulas and equational reasoning is the most fundamental way of reasoning(Gries and Schneider, 1993), which can moderate the difficulties of proofs that might otherwise become too hard to understand. Consequently, we expect that our method is easier to learn and use than existing formal methods for hybrid systems.

We have been successfully applying equations and equational reasoning to modeling and verification of distributed systems such as security protocols(Ogata and Futatsugi, 2003a; Ogata and Futatsugi, 2003b). The method used is called the OTS/CafeOBJ method(Ogata and Futatsugi, 2003c), in which systems are modeled as observational transition systems, or OTSs, which are written in CafeOBJ(Diaconescu and Futatsugi, 1998), an algebraic specification language. It is verified that systems have properties by writing proofs, or proof scores in CafeOBJ and executing the proof scores with the CafeOBJ system.

The OTS/CafeOBJ method is evolved in order to deal with hybrid systems. OTSs are a definition of transition systems for writing transition systems in terms of equations. An OTS consists of a set of observers, which correspond to variables in the usual transition system definition, a set of initial states and a set of transitions. Observers are functions that return observable values in an OTS. By introducing observers that return real numbers, called physical observers, OTSs can deal with hybrid systems. Such OTSs are called hybrid observational transition systems, or HOTSs. In this paper, we describe HOTSs and demonstrate that equations can be used to specify hybrid systems and equational reasoning can be used to verify that hybrid systems have properties using a case study in which a temperature stabilizer is modeled and verified.

The rest of the paper is organized as follows. Section 2 mentions CafeOBJ. HOTSs are described in Section 3. A temperature stabilizer is modeled and verified in Section 4. We finally mention related work in Section 5.

2.   CAFEOBJ IN A NUTSHELL

CafeOBJ(Diaconescu and Futatsugi, 1998) can be used to specify abstract machines as well as abstract data types. A visible sort denotes an abstract data type, while a hidden sort denotes the state space of an abstract machine. There are two kinds of operators to hidden sorts: action and observation operators. An action operator can change states of an abstract machine. Only observation operators can be used to observe the inside of an abstract machine. An action operator is basically specified with equations by describing how the value returned by each observation operator changes. Declarations of observation and action operators start with bop or bops, and those of other operators start with op or ops. Declarations of equations start with eq, and those of conditional ones start with ceq. The CafeOBJ system rewrites a given term by regarding equations as left-to-right rewrite rules.

3. HYBRID OBSERVATIONAL TRANSITION SYSTEMS

HOTSs are OTSs that are evolved by introducing physical observers in order to deal with physical continuity. We assume that there exists a universal state space called Υ. We also suppose that each data type used has been defined beforehand, including the equivalence between two values v_1, v_2 of the data type denoted by $v_1 = v_2$. Let R and R^+ be a set of real numbers and a set of non-negative real numbers, respectively. An HOTS $\mathcal{S}$ is defined as $\langle \mathcal{O}, \mathcal{I}, \mathcal{T} \cup \{\text{tick}_r \mid r \in R^+\}\rangle$ where

- $\mathcal{O}$: A set of observers. The set $\mathcal{O} = \mathcal{D} \cup \mathcal{P}$ is classified into the set $\mathcal{D}$ of discrete observers and the set $\mathcal{P}$ of physical observers. Each $o \in \mathcal{O}$ is a function $o : \Upsilon \to D$, where D is a data type. For each $p \in \mathcal{P}$, $D \subseteq R \cup \{\infty\}$.

  For each $p \in \mathcal{P}$, there are $l\,(\geq 1)$ aspects, each of which is denoted by a predicate $a_p^i : \Upsilon \to \{\text{true}, \text{false}\}$ where $i \in \{1, \ldots, l\}$. We suppose that the predicates are exhaustive and exclusive. For each aspect denoted by a_p^i, we have a value $\iota_{a_p^i}$ and function $f_{a_p^i} : R^+ \to R$ such that $f_{a_p^i}(0) = 0$. $\iota_{a_p^i}$ is the initial value returned by p as the aspect denoted by a_p^i starts and $f_{a_p^i}$ denotes how values returned by p change in the aspect as time goes by. There is a special physical observer $now : \Upsilon \to R^+$. There is one aspect called *cosmos* for now, ι_{cosmos} is 0 and $f_{cosmos}(t) = t$. now serves as the master clock that returns the time amount that has passed after starting the execution of $\mathcal{S}$.

  Given two states $v_1, v_2 \in \Upsilon$, the equivalence between two states, denoted by $v_1 =_{\mathcal{S}} v_2$, with respect to $\mathcal{S}$ is defined as $v_1 =_{\mathcal{S}} v_2 \stackrel{\text{def}}{=} \forall o \in \mathcal{O}.o(v_1) = o(v_2)$.

- $\mathcal{I}$: A set of initial states such that $\mathcal{I} \subseteq \Upsilon$. Master clock now initially returns 0.

- $\mathcal{T} \cup \{\text{tick}_r \mid r \in R^+\}$: A set of conditional transitions. Each $\tau \in \mathcal{T} \cup \{\text{tick}_r \mid r \in R^+\}$ is a function $\tau : \Upsilon/=_{\mathcal{S}} \to \Upsilon/=_{\mathcal{S}}$ on equivalence classes of Υ with respect to $=_{\mathcal{S}}$. Let $\tau(v)$ be the representative element of $\tau([v])$ for each $v \in \Upsilon \cup \{\text{tick}_r \mid r \in R^+\}$ and it is called *the successor state* of v with respect to τ.

  The condition of a transition $\tau \in \mathcal{T} \cup \{\text{tick}_r \mid r \in R^+\}$ is called the effective condition. The effective condition is supposed to satisfy the following requirement: given a state $v \in \Upsilon$, if the effective condition of τ is false in v, then $v =_{\mathcal{S}} \tau(v)$.

For each $\tau \in \mathcal{T}$, the effective condition of τ consists of the physical part c_τ^p and the non-physical part c_τ. There is also the time advancing condition c_τ^t corresponding to c_τ^p. Any $\tau \in \mathcal{T}$ does not change values returned by *now*.

Each *tick$_r$* is a time advancing transition, where $r \in R^+$. Given a state $\upsilon \in \Upsilon$, $now(tick_r(\upsilon))$ is $now(\upsilon) + r$ if for each $\tau \in \mathcal{T}$, c_τ^t keeps holding while r time units are passing, and is $now(\upsilon)$ otherwise. *tick$_r$* does not change values returned by any discrete observers.

Observers and transitions may be indexed such as $o_{i_1,\ldots,i_m}$ and $\tau_{j_1,\ldots,j_n}$, where $m, n \geq 0$ and we assume that there exist data types D_k such that $k \in D_k$ $(k = i_1, \ldots, i_m, j_1, \ldots, j_n)$.

An execution of $\mathcal{S}$ is an infinite sequence $\upsilon_0, \upsilon_1, \ldots$ of states satisfying

- *Initiation*: $\upsilon_0 \in \mathcal{I}$,

- *Consecution*: For each $i \in \{0, 1, \ldots\}$, $\upsilon_{i+1} =_{\mathcal{S}} \tau(\upsilon_i)$ for some $\tau \in \mathcal{T}$.

- *Time Divergence*: As i increases, $now(\upsilon_i)$ increases without bound.

A state υ is reachable with respect to $\mathcal{S}$ if and only if there exists an execution of $\mathcal{S}$ in which υ appears. Let $\mathcal{R}_\mathcal{S}$ be the set of all reachable states with respect to $\mathcal{S}$.

All properties considered in this paper are invariants, which are defined as follows:

$$\text{invariant } p \stackrel{\text{def}}{=} \forall \upsilon \in \mathcal{R}_\mathcal{S}.p(\upsilon).$$

Let x be all free variables in invariant p. We suppose that invariant p is interpreted as $\forall x.(\text{invariant } p)$ in this paper. When proof scores are written to prove $\forall x.(\text{invariant } p)$, x are replaced with constants that denote arbitrary values corresponding to x and the universally quantifier is eliminated. If a variable is existentially quantified in invariant p, the variable is replaced with a Skolem constant or function and the existential quantifier is eliminated.

HOTSs are written in CafeOBJ as OTSs. Observers and transitions are denoted by CafeOBJ observation and action operators, respectively. We prove a predicate invariant to an HOTS by reduction, case analysis and/or induction as we prove a predicate invariant to an OTS. In any case, proofs, or proof scores are written in CafeOBJ. A method of writing proof scores of invariants for OTSs is described in (Ogata and Futatsugi, 2003c), which can be used for HOTSs.

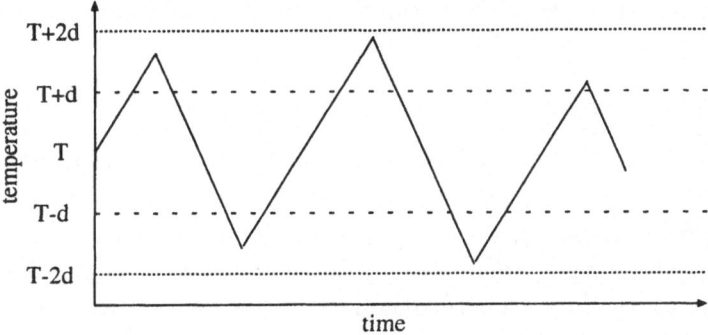

Figure 1. Behavior of the temperature stabilizer.

4. TEMPERATURE STABILIZER

Let us consider a temperature stabilizer that keeps the temperature between $T - 2 \times d$ and $T + 2 \times d$, where $d > 0$. The temperature stabilizer consists of two processors called Cooler and Heater. Cooler lowers the temperature $b\,(> 0)$ per unit time if it is active, while Heater raises the temperature $a\,(> 0)$ per unit time if it is active. Cooler or Heater is active, and only one of them is active. Cooler can become active if the temperature is greater than or equal to $T + d$ and must become active by the time when the temperature is greater then $T + 2 \times d$. Heater can become active if the temperature is less than or equal to $T - d$ and must become active by the time when the temperature is less than $T - 2 \times d$. Initially the temperature is T and Heater is active. The behavior of the temperature stabilizer is depicted in Figure 1.

Modeling

The temperature stabilizer is modeled as an HOTS.

Observers.

Discrete observers.

- *phase* : $\Upsilon \rightarrow \{\text{true}, \text{false}\}$. It means that the temperature is heated if it returns true and the temperature is cooled otherwise. It initially returns true.

- *point* : $\Upsilon \rightarrow R^+$. It returns the latest time when the temperature has become heated (or cooled) if the temperature is heated (or cooled). It initially returns 0.

- value : $\Upsilon \to R$. It returns the temperature at the time returned by *point*. It initially returns T.

Physical observers.

- *temp* : $\Upsilon \to R$. It returns the temperature, initially T. There are two aspects heating and cooling that are denoted by *phase* and $\neg phase$, respectively. ι_{heating} is the value returned by *temp* as the aspect changes to heating from cooling and $f_{\text{heating}}(t) = a \times t$. ι_{cooling} is the value returned by *temp* as the aspect changes to cooling from heating and $f_{\text{cooling}}(t) = -b \times t$.

- *now* : $\Upsilon \to R^+$.

Transitions.

- *cool* : $\Upsilon \to \Upsilon$. Given a state $v \in \Upsilon$, $c_{cool}(v)$ is *phase*(v) and $c^{\text{p}}_{cool}(v)$ is *temp*(v) $\geq T + d$. $c^{\text{t}}_{cool}(v, r)$ is *value*(v) + $f_{\text{heating}}(now(v) + r - point(v)) \leq T + 2 \times d$ if $c_{cool}(v)$ holds, and is true otherwise. If both $c_{cool}(v)$ and $c^{\text{p}}_{cool}(v)$ hold, then *phase*(cool(v)) is false, *point*(cool(v)) is *now*(v) and *value*(cool(v)) is *temp*(v). In any case, *temp*(cool(v)) is *temp*(v).

- *heat* : $\Upsilon \to \Upsilon$. Given a state $v \in \Upsilon$, $c_{heat}(v)$ is $\neg phase(v)$ and $c^{\text{p}}_{heat}(v)$ is *temp*(v) $\leq T - d$. $c^{\text{t}}_{heat}(v, r)$ is $T - 2 \times d \leq$ *value*(v)+$f_{\text{cooling}}(now(v)+r-point(v))$ if $c_{heat}(v)$ holds, and is true otherwise. If both $c_{heat}(v)$ and $c^{\text{p}}_{heat}(v)$ hold, then *phase*(heat(v)) is true, *point*(heat(v)) is *now*(v) and *value*(heat(v)) is *temp*(v). In any case, *temp*(heat(v)) is *temp*(v).

- $tick_r$: $\Upsilon \to \Upsilon$ ($r \in R^+$). Given a state $v \in \Upsilon$, if both $c^{\text{t}}_{cool}(v, r_1)$ and $c^{\text{t}}_{heat}(v, r_1)$ holds for any r_1 such that $0 \leq r_1 \leq r$, $now(tick_r(v))$ is *now*(v) + r, and *temp*($tick_r(v)$) is *value*(v) + $f_{\text{heating}}(now(v) + r - point(v))$ if *phase*(v) is true, and is *value*(v)+$f_{\text{cooling}}(now(v) + r - point(v))$ otherwise.

The HOTS is written in CafeOBJ. The signature is as follows:

```
*[Sys]*
-- any initial state
op init : -> Sys
-- observation operators
op phase : Sys -> Bool        op point : Sys -> Real+
op value : Sys -> Real        op temp  : Sys -> Real
op now   : Sys -> Real+
--  action operators
op cool : Sys -> Sys          op heat : Sys -> Sys
```

```
op tick : Sys Real+ -> Sys
```

Sys is the hidden sort denoting the state space. A comment starts with -- and terminates at the end of the line. Constant init denotes any initial state. Bool, Real+ and Real are the visible sorts denoting the truth values, R^+ and R, respectively. You can imagine what the observation and action operators denote.

In the following, let S and R be CafeOBJ variables whose sorts are Sys and Real+, respectively. The equations defining cool are as follows:

```
op c-cool : Sys -> Bool
eq c-cool(S) = phase(S) and ((T + d) <= temp(S)) .
--
ceq phase(cool(S)) = false if c-cool(S) .
ceq point(cool(S)) = now(S) if c-cool(S) .
ceq value(cool(S)) = temp(S) if c-cool(S) .
eq  temp(cool(S))  = temp(S) .
eq  now(cool(S))   = now(S) .
ceq cool(S)        = S if not c-cool(S) .
```

Operator c-cool denotes $c_{cool} \wedge c_{cool}^{\mathrm{p}}$. Term cool(S) denotes the successor state of state S after applying transition *cool* denoted by action operator cool. The six equations from the bottom describe how to change the values returned by observers when *cool* is applied. For example, the sixth equation from the bottom says that the value returned by observer *phase* changes to false when *cool* is applied in a state where $c_{cool} \wedge c_{cool}^{\mathrm{p}}$ holds, and the last equation says that nothing changes when *cool* is applied in a state where $c_{cool} \wedge c_{cool}^{\mathrm{p}}$ does not hold.

heat is defined likewise.

The equations defining tick are as follows:

```
op c-tick : Sys Real+ -> Bool
eq c-tick(S,R)
   = (phase(S) implies
     ((value(S) + f-heat((now(S) + R) - point(S)))
      <= (T + (2 * d)))) and
     (not phase(S) implies
     ((T - (2 * d))
      <= (value(S) + f-cool((now(S) + R) - point(S))))) .
--
eq  phase(tick(S,R)) = phase(S) .
eq  point(tick(S,R)) = point(S) .
eq  value(tick(S,R)) = value(S) .
ceq temp(tick(S,R))
    = (if phase(S) then value(S) + f-heat((now(S) + R) - point(S))
                   else value(S) + f-cool((now(S) + R) - point(S)) fi)
      if c-tick(S,R) .
ceq now(tick(S,R))   = now(S) + R if c-tick(S,R) .
```

```
ceq tick(S,R)        = S if not c-tick(S,R) .
```

Operator `c-tick` denotes $c_{cool}^t \wedge c_{heat}^t$. Operators `f-cool` and `f-heat` denote $f_{cooling}$ and $f_{heating}$, respectively. The six equations from the bottom describe how to change the values returned by observers when transition $tick_r$ denoted by action operator `tick` is applied.

Verification

We verify that the temperature is surely kept between $T - 2 \times d$ and $T + 2 \times d$. To this end, all we have to do is to prove the following predicate invariant to the HOTS:

$$T - 2 \times d \leq temp(v) \wedge temp(v) \leq T + 2 \times d. \tag{1}$$

To prove (1) invariant to the HOTS, we need to prove the following predicates invariant to the HOTS:

$$point(v) \leq now(v), \tag{2}$$
$$T - 2 \times d \leq value(v), \tag{3}$$
$$value(v) \leq T + 2 \times d. \tag{4}$$

The four predicates are proved invariant to the HOTS by induction on the number of transitions applied by writing proof scores in CafeOBJ.

Before writing proof scores, we first write a module, say INV, in which the four predicates are expressed as CafeOBJ terms as follows:

```
eq inv1(S) = (T - (2 * d)) <= temp(S) and temp(S) <= (T + (2 * d)) .
eq inv2(S) = point(S) <= now(S) .
eq inv3(S) = (T - (2 * d)) <= value(S) .
eq inv4(S) = value(S) <= (T + (2 * d)) .
```

We next write a module, say ISTEP, in which basic formulas to prove in each inductive case are expressed as CafeOBJ terms as follows:

```
eq istep1 = inv1(s) implies inv1(s') .
eq istep2 = inv2(s) implies inv2(s') .
eq istep3 = inv3(s) implies inv3(s') .
eq istep4 = inv4(s) implies inv4(s') .
```

Constants s and s' denote an arbitrary state and a successor state of s.

We then write four proof scores of (1), (2), (3) and (4). In this paper, we describe the inductive case in which $tick_r$ denoted by `tick` preserves (1). The state space, or the case is first split into two subcases: one where the condition denoted by `c-tick(s,r)` holds and the other where it does not. Since $tick_r$ does not change anything in a state in which the condition does not hold, $tick_r$ surely preserves (1).

The case in which the condition holds is divided into two: one where both `phase(s)` and `(value(s) + f-heat((now(s) + r) - point(s)))` `<= (T + (2 * d))` hold and the other where `phase(s)` does not hold and `(T - (2 * d)) <= (value(s) + f-cool((now(s) + r) - point (s)))` holds. The former is also split into three: (i) `point(s) <= now(s)` does not hold, (ii) `(T - (2 * d)) <= value(s)` does not hold and (iii) both `point(s) <= now(s)` and `(T - (2 * d)) <= value(s)` hold, and the latter is also split into three: (iv) `point(s) <= now(s)` does not hold, (v) `value(s) <= (T + (2 * d))` does not hold and (vi) both `point(s) <= now(s)` and `value(s) <= (T + (2 * d))` hold. Cases (i) and (iv) use (2) to strengthen the inductive hypothesis denoted by `inv1(s)`, case (ii) uses (3) to strengthen the inductive hypothesis and case (v) uses (4) to strengthen the inductive hypothesis.

In this paper, the proof passage of case (i) is shown, which is as follows:

```
open ISTEP
-- arbitrary objects
  op r : -> Real+ .
-- assumptions
  -- eq t-tick(s,r) = true .
  eq phase(s) = true .
  -- eq (value(s) + f-heat((now(s) + r) - point(s)))   <= (T + (2 * d))
  --     = true .
  eq (value(s) + (a * ((now(s) + r) - point(s)))) <= (T + (2 * d))
     = true .
  --
  eq point(s) <= now(s) = false .
-- successor state
  eq s' = tick(s,r) .
-- check
  red inv2(s) implies istep1 .
close
```

Constant `r` denotes an arbitrary non-negative real number. `(value(s) + (a*((now(s) + r) - point(s))))) <= (T + (2 * d))` is the normal form of `(value(s) + f-heat((now(s)+r) - point(s))) <= (T + (2 * d))` in the sense of term rewriting. In order to make effective use of the declared equation, the left-hand side should be in normal form. The proof passage is executed by the CafeOBJ system, which returns `true`. This means that $tick_r$ preserves (1) for any $r \in R^+$ in this subcase.

The proof passages of the remaining subcases are written likewise.

5. RELATED WORK

Lamport(Lamport, 1993) proposes a method of specifying and reasoning about hybrid systems in TLA+. TLA+ is a formal specification language based on TLA, the Temporal Logic of Actions. Systems are specified in terms of temporal logic formulas. Kesten, et al.(Kesten et al., 2000) propose phase transition systems for modeling hybrid systems and a rule for proving invariants of hybrid systems. Phase transition systems are described graphically, which seems suited for small examples. Lynch, et al.(Lynch et al., 2003) propose hybrid I/O automata that are I/O automata that are evolved for modeling and analyzing hybrid systems. They verify that a hybrid system meets its specification by proving that there exists a simulation relation from a hybrid I/O automata modeling the hybrid system to a hybrid I/O automata describing the specification.

Lamport points out that any formal method that can be used to model and verify concurrent systems can be applied to distributed, real-time and/or hybrid systems. Phase transition systems and hybrid I/O automata are basically such examples, and so is our proposed method. One important difference between our method and the existing ones is that our method intensively uses equations and equational reasoning, which makes our method relatively easy to learn and use.

Maude, a sibling language of CafeOBJ, can be used to specify and analyze hybrid systems(Ölveczky and Meseguer, 2000) and is equipped with an LTL model checker. Maude can be used to complement our method. Design and implementation of a tool that translates CafeOBJ specifications into Maude ones is part of our future work.

REFERENCES

Diaconescu, R. and Futatsugi, K. (1998). *CafeOBJ Report*, volume 6 of *AMAST Series in Computing*. World Scientific, Singapore.

Gries, D. and Schneider, F. B. (1993). *A Logical Approach to Discrete Math*. Texts and Monographs in Computer Science. Springer, NY.

Kesten, Y., Manna, Z., and Pnueli, A. (2000). Verification of clocked and hybrid systems. *Acta Informatica*, 36:837–912.

Lamport, L. (1993). Hybrid systems in TLA+. In *Hybrid Systems*, volume 736 of *LNCS*, pages 77–102. Springer.

Lynch, N., Segala, R., and Vaandraager, F. (2003). Hybrid I/O automata. *Information and Computation*, 185:105–157.

Ogata, K. and Futatsugi, K. (2003a). Formal analysis of the *i*KP electronic payment protocols. In *ISSS 2002*, volume 2609 of *LNCS*, pages 441–460. Springer.

Ogata, K. and Futatsugi, K. (2003b). Formal verification of the Horn-Preneel micropayment protocol. In *VMCAI 2003*, volume 2575 of *LNCS*, pages 238–252. Springer.

Ogata, K. and Futatsugi, K. (2003c). Proof scores in the OTS/CafeOBJ method. In *FMOODS 2003*, volume 2884 of *LNCS*, pages 170–184. Springer.

Ölveczky, P. C. and Meseguer, J. (2000). Real-Time Maude: A tool for simulating and analyzing real-time and hybrid systems. In *WRLA 2000*, volume 36 of *ENTCS*. Elsevier.

DISTRIBUTION OF TIME INTERVAL BETWEEN SUCCESSIVE INTERRUPT REQUESTS

Wojciech Noworyta

Institute of Engineering Cybernetics - Wroclaw University of Technology

Abstract: In majority of computer systems, the most time-critical tasks are performed by interrupt service routines. In some cases pooling methods are utilized, especially when I/O hardware is not capable of stand-alone operation. When these two approaches are mixed together conflicts are likely. Pooling procedure may not tolerate delays caused by interrupts and interrupt-driven procedures may not be able to wait until pooling driver finishes its job. In various systems some of the time-critical operations can be repeated or skipped, if CPU fails to service them in time. Statistical methods can be used to verify if system performance satisfies requirements. To apply them the distribution function of time interval between two consecutive interrupt requests is calculated on the basis of a simple theoretical model. The model is then verified by empirical measurements.

Key words: interrupt, distribution function, streams merging, performance modeling.

1. INTRODUCTION

Observations of program execution performance have been taken using the most widespread hardware and operating systems (Windows 98/me/XP, Linux) and embedded processor MB91F362. In all cases a significant influence of operating system jobs and interrupt-driven activity has been detected. Asynchronous tasks particularly affect "smoothness" of execution making application response time random and unpredictable. These effects can be easily observed in low-end systems during multimedia playback. Methods of compensating IRQ introduced slowdowns may be applied to restore acceptable quality of real-time performance [1]. Since interrupts have the highest priority a vast majority of internal kernel functions must be able to tolerate unexpected delays during execution [2].

Execution of application while interrupts are enabled can be compared to queuing model where streams of requests are merged into one queue. When the queue is empty an application code is executed [3]. Queuing models with mixed type streams are not popular. Coexistence of periodical and random events results in very complex equations or problematic assumptions [4].

Many publications focus on scheduling algorithms that should give best overall quality of service of a real-time system [5]. The statistic nature of interrupts and other factors causing execution time uncertainty is rarely taken into account. Sometimes the simplest algorithms like Earliest Deadline First are suggested to be the most efficient solution [6].

In contrast to hard real–time systems where well-timed response must be assured soft real–time approach relays on statistical assurance of required performance [7]. Since average number of missed deadlines is not a good metrics n-out-of-m is proposed [8].

2.   MODEL OF INTERRUPT REQUESTS

To investigate a nature of interrupt request process a spectral density of the empirically measured time between interrupts was plotted. Two components were observed: single periodical and the white noise. Such spectrum proves that interrupts can be categorized as:
- system timer interrupt
- random interrupts from other sources

It is known, that interrupts from peripheral devices are not 100% random. The observation of spectral plot shows that collection of all interrupts makes good approximation of the white noise in the majority of the cases.

Let's assume computer system where two types of interrupts are present. There is only one periodical timer interrupt and unlimited number of random interrupts. The nature of interrupts is as follows:
- Timer interrupt with frequency $f_x = 1/t_{xI}$ is requested periodically in fully deterministic manner.
- Peripheral interrupts are requested randomly according to Poisson process with parameter λ. If many sources of random interrupts are present, with intensities $\lambda_1, \lambda_2, \ldots \lambda_n$ that they can be described as one process with intensity $\lambda = \lambda_1 + \lambda_2 + \ldots + \lambda_n$.

All interrupts are treated identically. The cumulative distribution function of time between two consecutive interrupt requests is to be calculated.

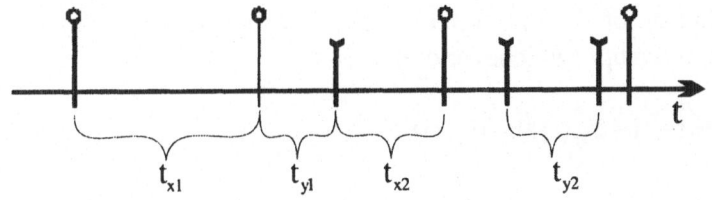

Figure 1. Interrupt requests and time intervals between them

Example interrupt requests and time intervals are presented on figure 1. Timer interrupts are marked with circle while random ones are marked with arrow-tail. The time interval can be measured between:
- two timer interrupts t_{x1}
- timer interrupt and random interrupt t_{y1}
- random interrupt and timer interrupt t_{x2}
- two random interrupts t_{y2}

Non-zero correlation between t_{y1} and t_{x2} is not taken into account since only distribution of time interval between (any) two interrupts is calculated.

2.1   Weighted sum of alternative distributions

To calculate the CDF of time between two consecutive requests two alternative cases should be considered:
- time interval begins after timer interrupt (t_{x1} or t_{y1}) with probability p_1
- time interval begins after random interrupt (t_{x2} or t_{y2}) with probability p_2

Cumulative distribution function is then calculated as a weighted sum of distribution functions of two alternative cases.

In sufficiently long time period T→∞ it is expected to appear $T*f_x$ timer interrupts and $T*\lambda$ random interrupts so the probabilities are:

$$p_1 = \frac{f_x}{f_x + \lambda} \quad \text{and} \quad p_2 = \frac{\lambda}{f_x + \lambda} \tag{1}$$

If the last interrupt was timer interrupt:

CDF of the interval t_{x1} from a timer interrupt to the next timer interrupt:

$$F_{x1}(t) = \mathbf{1}(t - t_{x1}) \tag{2}$$

CDF of the time interval t_{y1} from a timer interrupt to the nearest random:

$$F_{y1}(t) = \mathbf{1}(t)(1 - e^{-\lambda t}) \tag{3}$$

Distribution of the time interval from a timer interrupt to the next timer or random interrupt (whichever comes first):

$$F_1(t) = 1 - (1 - F_{x1}(t))(1 - F_{y1}(t)) \tag{4}$$

$$F_1(t) = \begin{cases} 0 & \text{for } t \le 0 \\ 1 - e^{-\lambda t} & \text{for } 0 < t \le t_{x1} \\ 1 & \text{for } t > t_{x1} \end{cases} \tag{5}$$

If the last interrupt was a random interrupt then the cumulative distribution functions of time interval to next interrupt are given as follows:

CDF of the interval t_{x2} from a random interrupt to the next timer interrupt

$$F_{x2}(t) = \begin{cases} 0 & \text{for } t \le 0 \\ t\, f_x & \text{for } 0 < t \le t_{x1} \\ 1 & \text{for } t > t_{x1} \end{cases} \tag{6}$$

There is no synchronization between timer and random interrupts so it's not known when the last timer interrupt was generated and when to expect the next. Due to periodic nature of timer interrupts, the next timer interrupt must appear within $1/f_x$ time. The probability is equally spread in $(0, 1/f_x)$.

CDF of the time t_{y2} from a random interrupt to the next random interrupt:

$$F_{y2}(t) = \mathbf{1}(t)(1 - e^{-\lambda t}) \tag{7}$$

Distribution function of time interval from a random interrupt to any interrupt (whichever comes first) is given the equation:

$$F_2(t) = 1 - (1 - F_{x2}(t))(1 - F_{y2}(t)) \tag{8}$$

$$F_2(t) = \begin{cases} 0 & \text{for } t \le 0 \\ 1 - e^{-\lambda t} + t f_x e^{-\lambda t} & \text{for } 0 < t \le t_{x1} \\ 1 & \text{for } t > t_{x1} \end{cases} \tag{9}$$

2.2   Cumulative distribution function

The Bayes equation for total probability is used to get the cumulative distribution function as a weighted sum of distribution functions of previously shown alternative cases.

$$F(t) = p_1 F_1(t) + p_2 F_2(t) = \frac{f_x}{f_x + \lambda} F_1(t) + \frac{\lambda}{f_x + \lambda} F_2(t) \qquad (10)$$

After simplification and grouping of variables:

$$F(t) = \begin{cases} 0 & \text{for } t \le 0 \\ 1 - e^{-\lambda t} + \dfrac{f_x \lambda}{f_x + \lambda} t e^{-\lambda t} & \text{for } 0 < t \le t_{x1} \\ 1 & \text{for } t > t_{x1} \end{cases} \qquad (11)$$

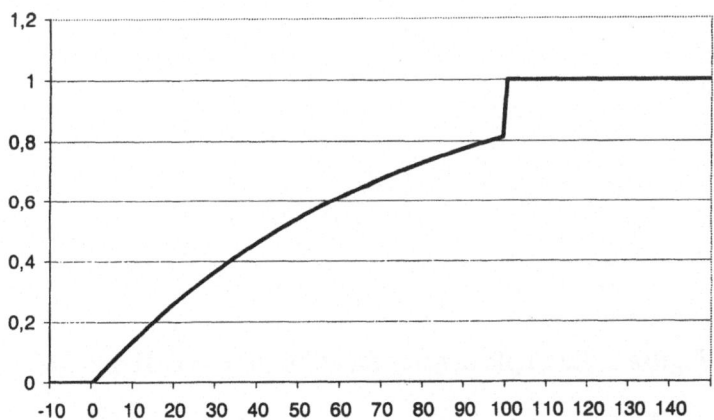

Figure 2. Example distribution function for $f_x = 0.01$ and $\lambda = 0.01$

The cumulative distribution function has following properties:
- Equals zero for negative time values
- Equals one for $t > 1/f_x$
- Is continuous excluding $t = 1/f_x$
- Difference of left and right side limits at $t = 1/f_x$ equals $f_x/(f_x+\lambda)\exp(-\lambda/f_x)$
- Is differentiable in all range excluding $t = 0$ and $t = 1/f_x$
- Is integrable in all its range - it consist of sum $const + e^t + t e^t$

2.3   Density and intensity

The first derivative of the distribution function (density function)

$$f(t) = \begin{cases} 0 & \text{for } t \leq 0 \\ \left(\dfrac{2f_x\lambda + \lambda^2}{f_x + \lambda}\right)e^{-\lambda t} + \dfrac{f_x\lambda^2}{f_x + \lambda}\left(te^{-\lambda t}\right) & \text{for } 0 < t < t_{x1} \\ \dfrac{f_x}{f_x + \lambda}\exp(\dfrac{\lambda}{f_x})\ \delta(t - t_{x1}) & \text{for } t = t_{x1} \\ 0 & \text{for } t > t_{x1} \end{cases} \qquad (12)$$

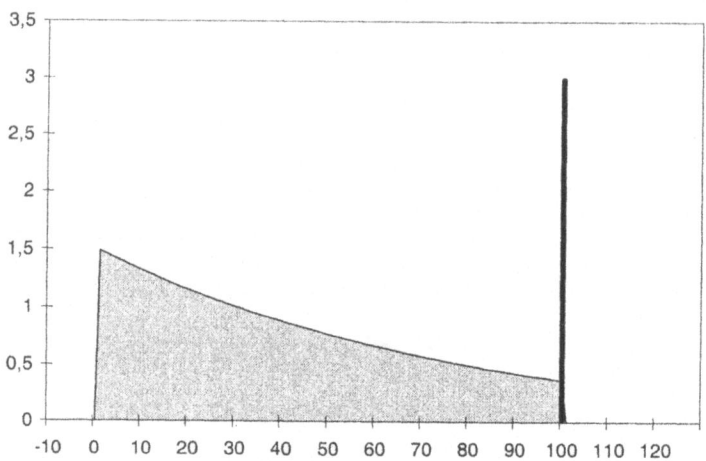

Figure 3. Example density function for $f_x = 0.01$ and $\lambda = 0.01$

Density function of distribution of time interval between interrupts:
- Produces positive values in range $(0, 1/f_x)$
- Has Dirac's delta at $t = 1/f_x$
- Is descending in range $(0, 1/f_x)$, slower than exponential distribution

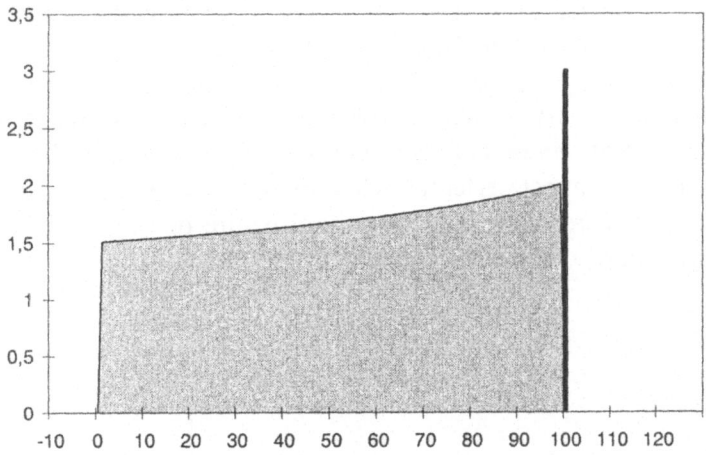

Figure 4. Example intensity function for $f_x = 0.01$ and $\lambda = 0.01$

The intensity function of interrupt requests has following properties:
- Produces positive values in range $(0, 1/f_x)$
- Has Dirac's delta at $t=1/f_x$
- Is ascending in range $(0, 1/f_x)$
- If $\lambda \gg f_x$ is similar to intensity of exponential distribution
- If $\lambda \ll f_x$ produces small values for $t=(0, 1/f_x)$, Dirac's delta is dominating

3.   EMPIRICAL RESULTS

Observations of moments when interrupts are requested have been taken to construct empirical distribution of time between two consecutive requests. Fast spin-lock procedure was used as a measuring routine and good approximation of CPU utilization by pooling driver or user multimedia application. To get reliable results 10^{10} measurements have been taken during each experiment. In most experiments $10^5 - 10^6$ request were detected. Density function of time interval between two consecutive interrupts has been plotted because it graphically shows better the nature of distribution than the cumulative distribution function. Having so big collection of empirical data, very high level of confidence was expected during statistical tests. Unfortunately majority of statistical analysis applications are not capable of proper handling of such large sets of data.

The histogram (density function) for Pentium III – 450MHz system working under Windows 98 is presented on figure 5. Nearly 700 thousands intervals has been measured and shown giving good approximation of distribution shape. Horizontal axis represents length of time interval expressed in processor clock periods (450MHz). Vertical axis represents the number of samples that fit in range $(t, t+dt)$. Density function has not been scaled to have integral equal one. Empirical results are plotted as black line. Additionally light-gray line of theoretical histogram has been plotted. In the left part of the figure they fit almost perfectly, while the Dirac's delta is left hand diffused. Due to $f_x > \lambda$ relation, the descending nature of density function is weak, although can be observed.

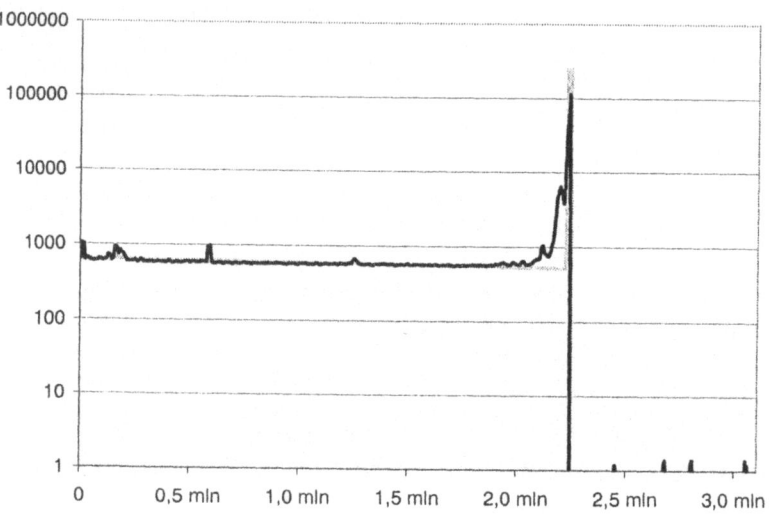

Figure 5. Empirical density function for $f_x = 200$Hz and $\lambda = 81$

Time interval between two consecutive interrupts seen by user-level application may significantly differ from the real one. The histogram (density function) of time interval between interrupts for Pentium 4 system 2,5GHz working under Win-XP system is presented on figure 6. Three interrupt requests of periodic nature can be observed in this system. Additionally a small peak at 78 million cycles occurs. The reason for odd shape of histogram is that a measuring procedure runs as a normal user-level process in highly over-loaded single-processor system. When CPU is switched to another process the spin-lock loop used for measurement can not detect interrupts since it is not running. In fact there is only one periodic interrupt in presented system - the first peak in histogram at $\tau=1.33$ms. The second peak occurring at 4τ the third at 12τ and the fourth at 24τ are caused by scheduler that stopped measuring procedure giving other programs 4, 12, or 24 "chunks" of CPU time. Since processor's clock count register (used for measurement) was incremented while spin-lock procedure was sleeping the application after wake-up observed it as a single, very long interrupt.

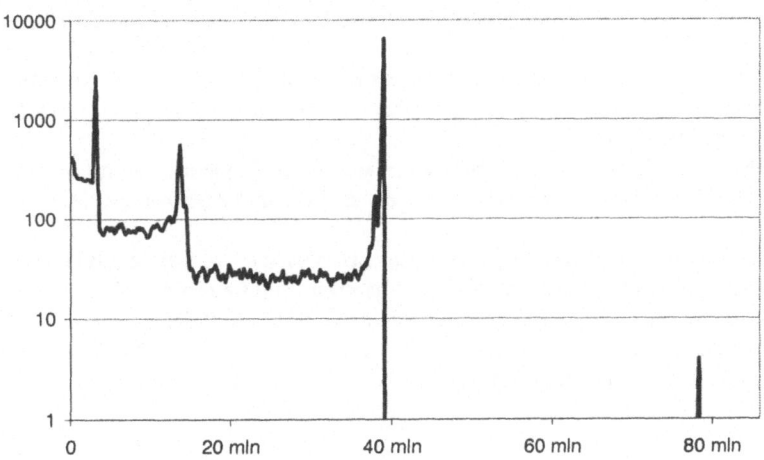

Figure 6. Empirical density function from application point of view

4.   CONCLUSION

Statistical analysis of interrupt request behavior can be a helpful tool in design and validation of systems with coexisting interrupt driven and pooling I/O service routines. Additionally the influence of interrupt requests on application execution is significant in soft time critical programs such as audio or video recording and playback. Presented simple model of delays caused by operation system can be effective means of describing execution platform from the applications point of view without going into details of hardware and system software. Statistical description of machine and system influence on application is far less exact than behavioral model of operating system, but also far more simple and easy to apply. Model of interrupts slowing down application execution can be regarded as formal method of defining "smoothness" of application execution. Presented model is especially suited to low-end audio and video systems rapidly growing in popularity.

5.   REFERENCES

[1] L. Abeni, G. Lipari, "Compensating for interrupt process times in real-time multimedia systems", *Third Real-Time Linux Workshop*, Milano 2001.

[2] L. Abeni, "Coping with interrupt execution time in real-time kernels: a non intrusive approach", *Proceedings of the IEEE Real-Time Systems Symposium WIP*, London 2001.

[3] R. Nelson, *Probability, Stochastic Processes and Queuing Theory – The Mathematics of Computer Performance Modeling*, Springer Verlag, New York 1995

[4] W. Noworyta – "Universal Model of Interval between Interrupt Requests" – to be published

[5] M. Gardner, J. Liu, "Performance of Algorithms for Scheduling Real-Time Systems with Overrun and Overload", *IEEE Proceedings 11th Euromicro Conference Real-Time Systems*, June 1999.

[6] Wolfgang A. Halang, "Contemporary research on real-time scheduling considered obsolete", *27th IFAC/IFIP/IEEE Workshop on Real-Time Programming*, May 14-17 2003 Lagow, Poland.

[7] B. Srinivasan, S. Pather, R. Hill, F. Ansari, D. Niehaus, "A firm real-time system implementation using commercial off-the-shelf hardware and free software", *Proceedings of the IEEE Real-Time Technology and Applications Symposium*, 1998.

[8] G. Bernat, A. Burns, A. Llamosi, "Weakly Hard Real-Time Systems", *IEEE Transactions on Computers* Vol. 50 No. 4 April 2001

A MEMBERSHIP AGREEMENT ALGORITHM DETECTING AND TOLERATING ASYMMETRIC TIMING FAULTS

Håkan Sivencrona[1], Mattias Persson[2] and Jan Torin[2]
[1]SP Swedish National Testing and Research Institute, Software Electronics, Brinellgatan 4, SE-501 15 Borås, Sweden; [2]Chalmers University of Technology, Department of Computer Engineering, Rannvagan 6, SE 412 96 Göteborg, Sweden

Abstract: Our paper presents a new membership agreement algorithm that address asymmetric timing faults and includes a new tool simulating TTP/C clusters. The proposed algorithm flags deviating or slightly untimely messages to assure that single marginal transmitting faults are detected and that only the faulty node will be expelled. The tool can demonstrate the behavior of membership agreement algorithms such as the original TTP-C1 algorithm or our modified flagging algorithm. The performed simulations use experimental results from heavy-ion fault injection logged timing faults. The gathered results show the rare faults, which made a network using the original algorithm either collapse or become degraded, are detected and handled with the new algorithm without loss of more than the faulty node.

Key words: Membership agreement; Asymmetric timing faults; Fault detection.

1.   INTRODUCTION

A severe type of communication faults is the infamous Byzantine fault class, which includes so-called slightly-out-of-specification faults[1], SOS, which may cause inconsistencies at the communication level in distributed systems when a number of nodes receive a message while other nodes fail to correctly receive the same message. This may affect the application with problems such as reaching application consensus.

In the FIT project (IST-1999-10748)[2], a time-triggered architecture[3] was evaluated by use of several fault injection techniques. One major finding was that the fault detection and error processing with respect to SOS faults was insufficient[1], which had major effects on the application due to communication black out and the degraded operation of the cluster.

There are basically two approaches to design a system for a specific fault tolerance: a) to have sufficient redundancy to mask the Byzantine fault[4], b) to implement methods to identify (diagnose) and reconfigure the system before additional faults arrive[5-7]. We present a diagnosis algorithm where the basic idea is that messages are "quality stamped" with respect to the timelines they demonstrate at each receiving node. The designed algorithm differs significantly compared to the original implementation of TTP/C where no effort has been put to detect a specific node, rather the caused inconsistency, solved through minority partition reintegration.

The paper is organized as follows. First we briefly present TTP/C, especially mechanisms[8-11] vital for the development and understanding of our algorithm such as membership agreement and clique avoidance. Secondly Byzantine faults and slightly-out-of-specification faults are described. Then the membership agreement is presented with respect to asymmetric faults while the simulation tool is presented in section five. Section six contains the simulation results while section seven concludes the paper.

2.   TIME-TRIGGERED PROTOCOL CLASS C

TTP/C[3] basically provides three services; clock synchronization[9], deterministic message sending, and a membership service[8]. The clock synchronization information uses the FTA clock synchronization algorithm where the time data is extracted from the arrival of the latest four messages. The two most extreme clock values are removed and the sum of the remaining clocks' values is averaged, a correction term. The nodes will adjust their clocks with the correction term and thus remain synchronized with the cluster.

The membership agreement[8,10] in TTP/C is represented by a unique identification vector, which is stored in all nodes as a local membership vector. All nodes update the membership information continuously. The membership service is closely coupled to features such as clique avoidance[10], which further improve the error handling capabilities in a distributed system.

If the membership vectors differ between sending and receiving nodes, the CRC calculation should not produce a readable message. When a CRC error is found, the receiving node raises a membership error for the sending node locally (after some internal checks such as implicit acknowledgement algorithm, see below) and the corresponding membership vector value is set to false. If the frame is not semantically correct it is considered as an invalid frame, which could be due to a transmission error, and the membership bit is in this case set to false. If a node discovers that it is not in agreement with the majority of the active nodes in the cluster, it is not allowed to send and has to reintegrate this is guaranteed by the clique avoidance algorithm.

Starting with its own sending slot all nodes in a cluster counts all incorrect nodes in a fail counter, FC and correct nodes in an accept counter, AC during one TDMA round. $AC + FC = n$, where n is the number of nodes in the system before failure (or operating). Null frames are not counted by either FC or AC and it is assumed that all nodes detect Null frames thus n is decreased by detected Null frames. If $FC > 1$ the cluster is considered a partitioned cluster otherwise the acknowledgement algorithm is enough to retain a consistent cluster.

A node may transmit if $FC < n/2$ if n is even and $(n+1)/2$ if n is odd which results in that FC must be $< n/2$. An in depth explanation can be found in[10].

When a node, lets say A, has sent a message it usually (can be a sending error) increases the AC counter. If it detects a CRC error during the two succeeding TDMA slots it does not passively await the resolution of the upcoming situation. TTP/C has an algorithm to address this situation, the implicit acknowledgement algorithm.

The algorithm introduces the denotation of first and second successor. If the first succeeding node B does not have the same membership list, A decides to preliminary remove B from its local membership list and increases its FC. If it was B that was receive-faulty the situation will be solved by a second successor node, C. If C sends a syntactically correct message, e.g. with B removed from the membership, node A is acknowledged. If not, B is probably acknowledged and A has been removed from Cs membership, A is thus not acknowledged. A was as a result faulty. A removes itself from the membership list but adds both B and C to the membership list and updates AC and FC correspondingly and then reintegrates. The implicit acknowledgment algorithm is completed.

3. BYZANTINE FAULTS

Since its initial presentation the Byzantine Generals problem[12] has been the subject of intense academic scrutiny, leading to the development of numerous Byzantine-tolerant algorithms and architectures[6,7,13]. A sub-class of Byzantine faults are slightly-out-of-specification faults[1] which occur in the transition between the analog and discrete world. In the time domains these faults occur when entities get different views of the time, a marginal transmission. A message that is timely at a certain node may be considered as untimely at another node due to different drifts of the local clocks or internal errors.

In TTP/C all nodes have a start of frame window where an expected message must be received (with respect to start of frame transmission) to be processed further by the node and application. This window is usually so small that a feasibly low jitter can be achieved. When the receive window has opened up for message reception a counter is incremented every microtic, from for example -40 microtics before expected arrival time and up to 40 microtics after expected arrival time, a span of 81 microtics. Within this span the design specific window is specified, for example -20 < acceptable reception time < 20 microtics. Settings for this window depend on the size of the TDMA slots and the time for a TDMA round.

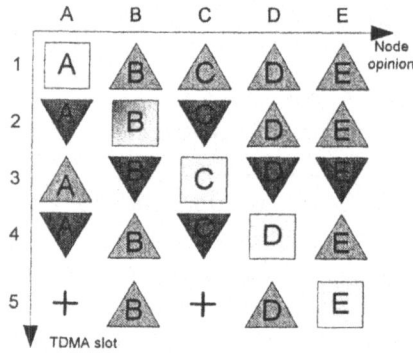

Figure 1. TTP/C membership agreement and clique avoidance handling an Asymmetric fault (node B sending in slot two) + = nodes resetting

In Figure 1, an asymmetric fault scenario is shown. Triangles pointing upward mean agreement with the sent message while triangles that point down is in disagreement while squares mean sending node. When *B* transmits, second row, node *A* and *C* raise an error. *D* and *E* on the other hand accept the message.

In the third TDMA slot (when *C* sends its opposing opinion to the system) the inconsistency is known to parts of the system (node *B*, *D* and *E*) while *A* still regards the upcoming situation as a normal fault (non-asymmetric).

D is the next node to transmit and must now decide which opinion it should have (Assume for a while that the message sent by *C* can be viewed by *D*, in TTP/C this would have caused a CRC error). In TTP/C it does not accept the message from *C*. We now have a situation where two nodes out of five have expressed their opposing view. *D* uses, in this case, the clique avoidance algorithm to decide. The upcoming situation is solved as described in Figure 1. Node *A* and *C* will cease their transmission because their fail counters will be larger than their accept counters. The faulty node is on the other hand still synchronized and remains undetected.

4. FLAGGING ALGORITHM

The proposed algorithm uses some assumptions. Only one node is faulty during one TDMA round. The algorithm is assumed to be a transparent layer on top of the ordinary TTP/C mechanisms, not voiding any of the original properties.

Following assumptions have been used with respect to the receive window, see Figure 2:

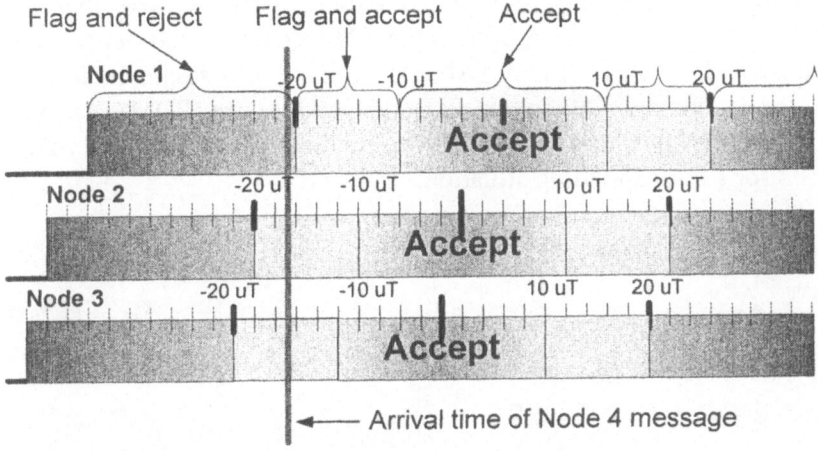

Figure 2. The modified receive window where node 4 is received early, too early by node 1

- A message (node) is declared invalid and removed from membership list (if it arrives later than 20 microtics or earlier than 20 microtics from expected arrival time. −20 < expected arrival < 20, a window of 40 microtics. A message received outside this window of 40 microtics is also flagged.
- A node is not allowed to transmit if the own clock synchronization calculation results in a clock correction term that is larger than 10 microtics
- A message that arrives within 10 to 20 microtics from expected time is declared as a message possible SOS-message. The message is flagged in an internal register by the communication controller.
- A node that has a non-empty flag register will not immediately remove disagreeing nodes without an extra check with respect to flag position

If a received message, *M*, is declared invalid due to a faulty CRC calculation (non-readable message) the receiving node *R* will check its flag register for flags, since voting message *M* as invalid at this state could result in that the majority regards *R* as a faulty node. *R* will thus assume that the flag corresponds to a node *F* that the sending node *S* has removed from its membership, thus causing the CRC error. *R* changes the corresponding bit in the membership vector and recalculates the CRC. Following this assumption node *R* tries once more to access message *M* and if this succeeds it will accept the message as valid assuming that it was because of a timing fault *S* had removed *F* which *R* did only flag. All other nodes that have the same view about this node and flagged the same will update their membership vectors correspondingly. All nodes will thus have removed node F that was flagged by everyone but the faulty and removed from membership by at least one. In cases when not all nodes, except the faulty, have flagged the node the original algorithm will solve the situation. All nodes will then recount their accepted messages and update their fail counters and accept counters accordingly. This way all nodes should, in case of a single fault, have the same consistent view of operating nodes within one TDMA round. Any shortage of the algorithm will be solved within a second TDMA round, see Figure 3 for a corresponding situation.

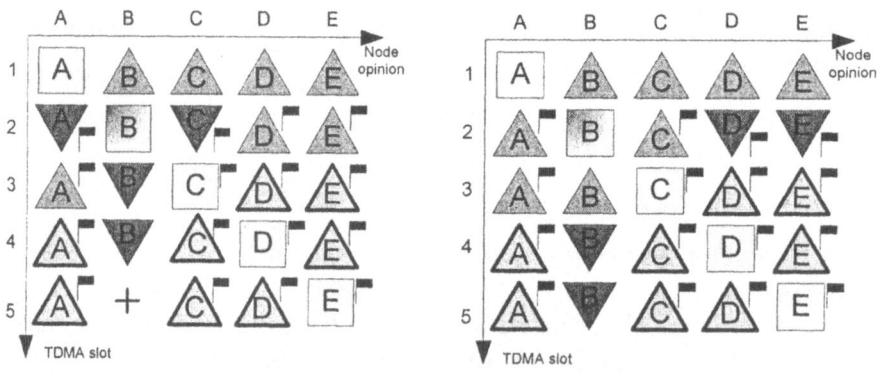

Figure 3. Membership behavior under two fault scenarios

One variation of an SOS faults shows up if the third node, *C*, flags message *B* and transmits this knowledge. *C* has thus not removed *B* from membership while the successor *D* has already done so, see Figure 3 (right). This means that node *D* will receive a message that could differ on two places with respect to the own membership list (*D* has already removed *B* from membership and has a pending membership change on *C*, meaning it would have removed *C* from the membership list using the original algorithm). But *C* and *D* do only disagree about their opinion concerning *B*.

Node *D* will still keep the opinion about *B* and raise a CRC error on *B*, but accept node *C*. *D* will be notified about this agreement about *B* upon inverting the membership bit in question (flagged position). This will cause a transient inconsistency in the system, which is a complex state, meaning we disagree over one message but accepts each other, which is against the prerequisite of the original membership agreement protocol utilization but a prerequisite for the accurate operation of the flagging algorithm.

Figure 3 furthermore shows that node *D* and *E* did not accept the message in TDMA slot 2 and that node *C* must change its already public membership view. *D* and *E* will *win* while *A* and *C* will adapt to this view.

The algorithm is interpreted in Figure 4 which shows the flowchart of the algorithm which is then implemented and tested using our tool.

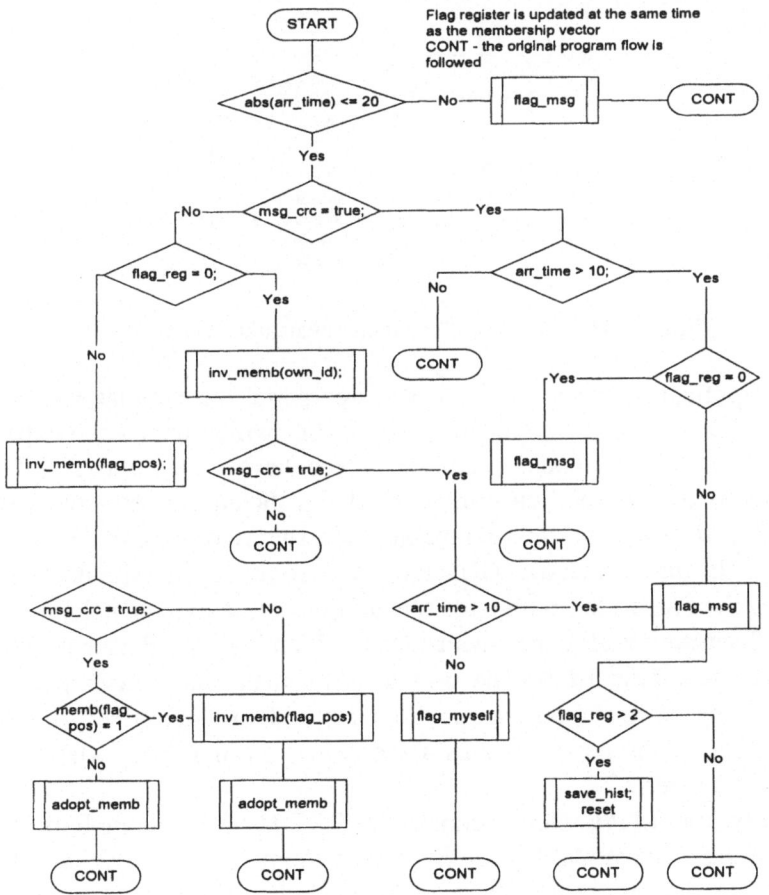

Figure 4. A flowchart of the algorithm

5. SIMULATION SETUP

The purpose of the TTP/C algorithm simulator is to provide a simple simulation environment for a TTP/C network. It simulates a network of $n+1$ nodes, where n is the number of nodes for which experimental log files exists, where one node is assumed to be the fault-injected without any logged data available, see Figure 5.

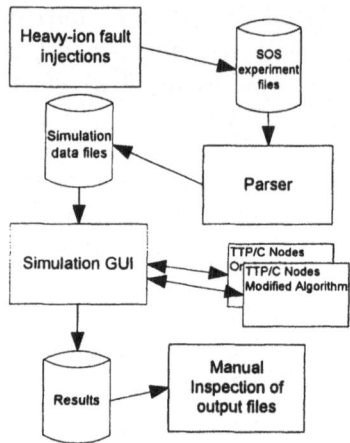

Figure 5. The basic work flow of the simulation tool environment

The application mainly consists of three parts; the Simulator GUI which controls the flow of the application, the Parser which parses the experiment files and the TTP/C Node, simulating the behavior of a real TTP/C node. Using the object orientation principle, all significant data structures such as the TTP/C Message and the Membership Vector are represented by objects.

Through the Simulator GUI the user controls the simulation. After invoking the Parser, the Simulator sets up the simulation and calls the TTP/C nodes. Because not all experiment logs are identical, the Parser is actually a Java interface. This allows the user to tailor-make one Parser per log file type, as long as it contains a specified method to parse a set of log files. When running, the parser creates a scenario from n-1 files, where n is the size of the cluster.

Finally, the TTP/C Nodes consists of TTP/C protocol implementations. Utilizing the same versatility as the Parser, the protocol is also an interface. Simplifying the program flow, each simulated node actually processes all messages received from one TDMA round at the same time. The TTP/C message is distributed to all "nodes" in the network, using the Membership vector calculated by the protocol implementation and the time drift obtained from the same slot in the logged scenario.

6.   SIMULATION RESULTS

The SOS scenarios were first executed with the original algorithm. Figure 6 shows the last part of the printout of one experiment. When the same object file was executed using the flagging algorithm the cluster remained synchronized but the faulty node was detected and expelled from the membership at all nodes.

One type of scenario was not solved perfectly. The flagging algorithm did not resolve situations when more than one node was badly synchronized, meaning this node did not flag the SOS-node. But the cluster remained synchronized in throughout al test cases but in some cases with two nodes expelled.

```
Node 3: Message from node 0;
Sender 0, NULLFRAME
Node 3 thinks node 0 is NOK
Node 3: Message from node 1;
Sender 1, NULLFRAME
Node 3 thinks node 1 is NOK
Node 3: Message from node 2;
Sender 2, NULLFRAME
Node 3 thinks node 2 is NOK
Node 3 Membership: 0x0
Performing acknowledgement algorithm,
my memb is 0x0 and the 1st succ's
message is Sender 0, NULLFRAME
Performing check 2A because 1st Succ
sent a null frame
Node 3 NOT acknowledged
Round 4, Slot 19, Got message Sender 3,
NULLFRAME
ALL NODES KICKED OUT
Simulation Aborted
   ***Simulation complete!***
Node 0gets drift 5
Node 1gets drift 9
Node 2gets drift 2
Exiting...
```

```
Node 3: Message from node 0;
Sender 0, Drift = 0, Membership = 0x7
Node 3 thinks node 0 is OK!
Node 3: Message from node 1;
Sender 1, Drift = 0, Membership = 0x7
Node 3 thinks node 1 is OK!
Node 3: Message from node 2;
Sender 2, Drift = 0, Membership = 0x7
Node 3 thinks node 2 is OK!
Node 3 Membership: 0x7
Performing acknowledgement algorithm,
my memb is 0x7 and the 1st succ's
message is Sender 0, Drift = 0, Membership = 0x7
Performing check 2A because 1st Succ thinks I'm out
Node 3: Check 2B passed!
Node 3 NOT acknowledged
Round 9, Slot 39, Got message Sender 3,
NULLFRAME
Node 0gets drift 5
Node 1gets drift 9
Node 2gets drift 2
   ***Simulation complete!***
```

Figure 6. Scenarios using old algorithm (left) and the flagging algorithm (right) where node 3 is the faulty node

7.   CONCLUSION

We have presented an algorithm for increasing the tolerance against asymmetric timing faults in a time-triggered protocol (TTP-C1). The major conclusion is that any single untimely node will be disclosed and that a global agreement can be reached about the system state, including time within two TDMA rounds.

The algorithm does not guarantee that all SOS faults are detected, at least not with respect to the chosen parameters. The success depends on the ratio between the different windows, e.g. the width of the flag window compared to accept window.

We have furthermore provided and presented an uncomplicated simulator GUI for a TTP/C network. The TTP/C Simulator can mimic a TTP/C network of $n+1$ nodes, where n is the number of nodes for which log files exists, where one node is assumed to be a fault-injected node without any logged data available, as was the case when a single TTP/C communication controller was injected with heavy-ions.

REFERENCES

1. H. Sivencrona, P. Johannessen, M. Persson and J. Torin, Heavy-ion Fault Injection in the Time-triggered Communication Protocol. Proc. First Latin American Symposium on Dependable Computing (LADC03), São Paulo, Brazil, October (2003).
2. FIT-project at http://www.cordis.lu/ist/projects/99-10748.htm, (2002).
3. H. Kopetz, TTP/C Protocol, Available at http://www.ttpforum.org. (1999).
4. K. Driscoll, B. Hall, H. Sivencrona and P. Zumsteg, Byzantine Fault Tolerance, from Theory to Reality. Proc. 22nd International Conference on Computer Safety, Reliability and Security (SAFECOMP03), pp. 235-248, Edinburgh, Scotland, UK, October 2003.
5. J. Rushby, Systematic Formal Verification for Fault-Tolerant Time-Triggered Algorithms, IEEE Transactions on Software Engineering, Volume 25, Number 5, September, pp: 651-660, (1999).
6. A. Ademaj, H. Sivencrona, G. Bauer and J. Torin, Evaluation of Fault Handling of the Time-Triggered Architecture with Bus and Star Topology. Proc. International Conference on Dependable Systems and Networks (DSN 2003), pp. 123-132, San Francisco, USA, (2003).
7. K. Hoyme and K. Driscoll, SAFEbus. Proc. Digital Avionics Systems Conference (AIAA-11), pp. 68 -73, Seattle, WA, USA, (1992).
8. H. Kopetz, G. Grünsteidl and J. Reisinger, Fault-Tolerant Membership Service in a Synchronous Distributed Real-Time System, in Dependable Computing for Critical Applications, pp. 411- 429, Springer-Verlag, Vienna, Austria, (1991).
9. H. Kopetz and W. Ochsenreiter, Clock Synchronization in Distributed Real-Time Systems, IEEE Transactions on Computers. Vol. 36, Nr. 8, pp. 933-940, (1987).
10. G. Bauer and M. Paulitsch, An Investigation of Membership and Clique Avoidance in TTP/C, Proc. of the 19th IEEE Symposium on Reliable Distributed Systems, pp. 118-124, Nuremberg, Germany, (2000).
11. A. Merceron, Proving "no Cliques" in a Protocol, Computer Science Conference, (ACSC 2001), Proc. 24th Australasian, pp: 134 –139, (2001).
12. L. Lamport, R. Shostak and M. Pease, The Byzantine generals problem, ACM Transactions on Programming Languages and Systems, vol. 4 issue 3, pp. 382-401, (1982).
13. L. Gong, P. Lincoln and J. Rushby, Byzantine Agreement with Authentication: Observations and Applications in Tolerating Hybrid and Link Faults. Proc. Dependable Computing for Critical Applications (DCCA-5), volume 10 of Dependable Computing and Fault Tolerant Systems, pp. 139-157. IEEE Computer Society, (1995).

TEMPORAL BOUNDS FOR TTA : VALIDATION

K. Godary, I. Augé-Blum, A. Mignotte
CITI Lab. / INSA Lyon - 21 av. J. Capelle 69621 Villeurbanne, France
karen.godary@insa-lyon.fr, isabelle.auge-blum@insa-lyon.fr, anne.mignotte@insa-lyon.fr

Abstract: In the context of real-time fault-tolerant architecture, as TTA (Time-Triggered Architecture), the temporal validation of the system behavior is very important. Indeed, the fault-tolerant mechanism execution must respects several temporal constraints. To validate the mechanism behaviors, and to give their maximum execution time (temporal bound), we propose here a temporal validation methodology for TTA. This methodology uses the UPPAAL tool, based on the timed automata and the model-checking analysis. This methodology allows us to extract the temporal bounds of the TTA services.

Keywords: Time-Triggered Architecture, Embedded real-time networks, Fault tolerance, Temporal validation, UPPAAL modeling.

1.   INTRODUCTION

Motivation.   TTA (Time-Triggered Architecture) (Kopetz, 1998, TTP, 2002) is a real-time network architecture for embedded systems. It is mainly used for automotive embedded applications. This architecture is based on two primary concepts : time triggered protocol and fault tolerance. These concepts are performed by a number of services defined in TTA specifications. Furthermore, the services are defined by using basic algorithms such as : synchronization, membership fault detection, or reintegration.

An application using TTA will require temporal guarantees on the temporal behavior of the architecture. The execution time of the algorithms and services has an influence on the behavior of the application level. Therefore, they have to be validated within a specific fault environment. For a specific service, its maximum execution time (its temporal bound), must never be superior to a fixed deadline. In this article we are going to define these bounds and describe the validation process to obtain them.

State of the art.   TTA specifications definition (TTP, 2002) allows extraction of basic temporal bounds. Obviously, these bounds are not validated by the specifications definition. While it is quite easy for elementary services to extract their bounds on simplified hypothesis, it is more difficult for regular TTA services. For instance, the clock precision is never taken into account, nor complex fault hypotheses.

On one hand, formal proofs (Pfeifer, 2003, Rushby, 2002, Bouajjani and Merceron, 2002) validate basic algorithms. For example in (Pfeifer, 2000), the membership algorithm is formally verified with the PVS theorem prover. This article proves the convergence of the algorithm. Yet, it does not define its temporal bound.

On the other hand, another approach is developed in (Bouajjani and Merceron, 2002), which gives a parametric proof of clique avoidance and membership correctness. These algorithms can be modeled by graphs, used to prove their temporal bounds. In the study, a bound is given for the detection of one fault, with simplified hypotheses. However this study is based on graph theory, a method too specific to be applied to all TTA algorithms.

All these formal methods are applicable on basic algorithms. Nevertheless they are difficult to be used on combination of services, or for the whole architecture. However the proven properties can be used as hypotheses in several other validation methodologies including the one presented in this article.

Other approaches produce deadline verification at a higher level. In (Caspi et al., 2003) for instance, the design of the whole system is based on a LUSTRE model, including temporal information and constraints, mapping on the hardware architecture, and the related scheduling. Temporal constraints are validated during scheduling. In this context, the TTA bus is modeled by a TDMA (Time-Division Multiple Access) round. Nevertheless, the deadline of a message transmission on the bus do not take into account the presence of faults nor fault tolerance. Such an approach would take fault tolerance into account if the temporal information are bounded durations (message transmission for instance) including faults. This is the aim of our approach.

Our approach is based on UPPAAL (Larsen et al., 1997). This tool has already been used for verification of other protocols (Jensen et al., 1996, Lönn and Pettersson, 1997, Lindahl et al., 1998). For instance, the study in Lönn and Pettersson, 1997 is similar to our method : the TDMA protocol is modeled in Uppaal, some properties are verified, and a parameterized deadline bound is extracted. But this study did not verify the protocol in the fault tolerance context, nor the whole architecture (it did not consider the applicative levels).

In this article, we propose an approach to find parameterized temporal bounds of TTA behavior, based on specific fault hypotheses. TTA is described in the next section. Our approach uses bounds already defined in TTA specifications or other publications. We extract new bounds by analysis of timed automata models. This approach is defined in the third section. Section 4 gives an illustrating example (the reintegration mechanism). Then section 5 presents experiments and results on our methodology.

2.   TTA BASIC DEFINITION

Architecture

TTA (Kopetz, 1998) is composed of a cluster, i.e. a set of nodes connected through a communication network based on TTP/C (Time Triggered Protocol class C) (TTP, 2002). A node is composed of four independent levels : the application level; the real-time operating system (RTOS), compatible with the OSEKTime specifications (OST, 2001); the FTLayer (Bauer and Kopetz, 2000), compatible with the FTCom (Fault Tolerant Communication) specifications (FTC, 2001) (this level is in charge of redundancy, which is the base of fault-tolerance); and the TTP/C controller (TTP, 2002).

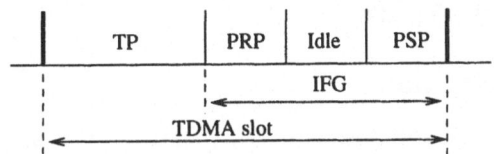

Figure 1.   Temporal slot decomposition

Time Triggered Protocol

TTP/C is based on a static and predefined scheduling. It implements a broadcast communication using the TDMA strategy. Moreover, the bus access is guaranteed by autonomous subsystems, bus guardians, which prevent the nodes to emit at the wrong time.

Information about transmitted data and emission dates are stored in a static table : the MEDL (MEssage Descriptor List), included in each node. Then, clock synchronization is necessary. It is based on the comparison between the time of the real arrival of each message and the expected time given by the MEDL.

A slot is the smallest unit of the communication phase. The slots are grouped together in a TDMA round. Each slot is dedicated to the transmission of a node. The usual system phase is a cyclic execution of all TDMA rounds : the cluster cycle. A slot is composed of 4 phases (figure 1) :

- *Transmission Phase (TP)* : a TDMA slot begins with the transmission of a message on the bus.

- *Post Receive Phase (PRP)* : allows the evaluation of received data and the execution of protocol services.

- *Pre-Send Phase (PSP)* : necessary to load the schedule information from the MEDL and to prepare the data transmission of the next slot.

- *Idle phase* : the duration of the PRP and PSP depends on the actions performed. So the Idle phase is used to stretch the slot to the duration fixed by the schedule designer.

The set of phases without transmission on the bus is called Inter-Frame Gap (IFG). It is the set of the three phases PRP, Idle and PSP.

3.   METHODOLOGY

Our methodology is based on model validation. The chosen formalism is a specific timed automata implemented in the UPPAAL tool (Larsen et al., 1997). Its associated model-checker enables to check reachability properties by an exhaustive analysis of all the possible behaviors of the system. More discussions on different possible modeling formalisms are in Godary et al., 2004b. For more information on the UPPAAL tool see for instance Pettersson, 1999 or Bengtsson and Yi, 2004).

Methodology definition

Our methodology is composed of two phases. The aim of the first step (illustrated figure 2) is to obtain an abstracted and verified UPPAAL model of TTA. Then, the aim of the second one is to extract parameterized formulae for temporal bounds of mechanisms and services of TTP/C, such as mode change, reintegration (of a TTA node after a fault) or initialization.

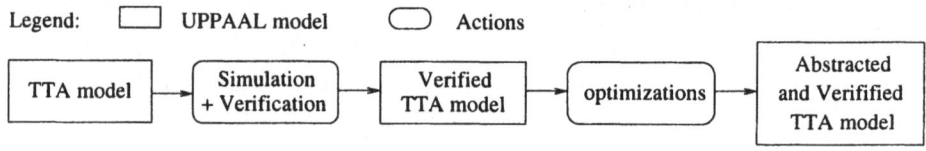

Figure 2.   Methodology - step 1

Step 1 : Abstracted and verified model (figure 2).

From the referring document TTP, 2002 a first model of TTA is built in UPPAAL. To guarantee the expected behavior, we check our model with formal verification of behavioral properties (for instance, one can check that two states are never reached at the same instant). More information on the initial model, and some results on this formal verification are given in the section 4

After those simulation and verification, we obtain a verified TTA model.

The problem of this model is combinatorial explosion. Therefore, some abstraction rules have been applied to simplify the analysis method implemented in UPPAAL. This abstracted TTA model keeps the same behavior, but it is easier to analyze. Basically, we have applied the following abstraction rules: reduction of the number of variables, automata, clocks, and interleaving. More details on these rules can be found in Godary et al., 2004a.

Finally, we have obtained an abstracted and verified TTA model.

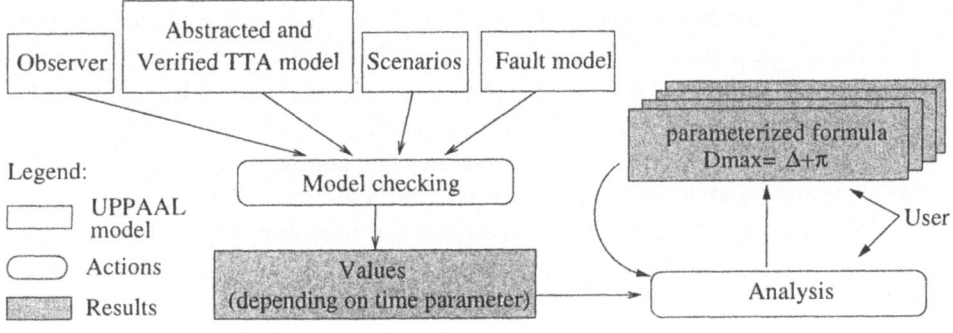

Figure 3. Methodology - step 2

Step 2 : Parameterized formula (figure 3).

Each basic mechanism is expressed in the UPPAAL model : either with an explicit modeling of its behavior, or with a representation of its characteristics. For instance, the synchronization algorithm is represented by the fact that all the local clocks of the nodes are synchronized within a fixed interval π. This abstraction is possible because this algorithm has already been validated (Pfeifer, 2003).

The basic mechanism model is completed with a Test automaton to verify with the model-checker that a deadline value D is never reached. This deadline value is a parameter of the system model. Then different values of D are verified by dichotomy, until the worst-case scenario is found. This worst-case behavior is the temporal bound of the studied mechanism.

Then, the same model is used with different values of parameters (such as clock drift or slot duration). We obtain a set of values depending on system parameters. We analyze them to deduce parameterized formulae for each bound.

Now, our methodology is going to be illustrated in more details with a complete analysis of the reintegration mechanism of TTA. This is a simple example which can help to understand its interest.

4.   ILLUSTRATION ON A BOUND : REINTEGRATION

The reintegration service

The reintegration of a node can occur when one of the TTA basic algorithms detects a fault. Then the faulty node transits in passive state, and waits for reintegration. All the nodes however continue to perform TDMA principle, and the non-faulty nodes continue a normal execution.

The faulty node has a slightly different behavior. In the PSP, if the next slot is the one of the faulty node, the faulty node checks if it can transit to active state. The condition for that is that the controller has received at least MIC (Minimum Integration Count) correct frames since it has failed. Then the node reintegrate the cluster (transits to active state) and can send its frame.

The exact bound is validated between the beginning of the reintegration (i.e. the detection of the fault which causes the transition of the faulty node to passive state), and the end of the reintegration (i.e. its transition to active state).

Hypotheses

- **Time-triggered concept** : Some TTA mechanisms are supposed to be correct, as there have already been formally validated in the literature (Pfeifer, 2003, Rushby, 2002, Bouajjani and Merceron, 2002) : membership, clique avoidance and clock synchronization algorithms. These algorithms provide the basis of the time-triggered strategy : a global view of the system for all the non faulty nodes. All the nodes are synchronized with a maximal clock drift π.

- **Architecture** : The model includes a cluster of 4 nodes with bus guardians in a one bus topology. No redundancy is considered.

- **Fault hypotheses** : In faulty models, we consider that only one fault at a time can occur during one TTA cluster cycle, which corresponds in our model to two TDMA rounds. This is realistic considering the usual fault hypotheses in automotive applications; but it rejects repetitive faults or combination of faults. In non faulty models, the only fault modeled is the one which initiates the reintegration process. It does not interfere with the reintegration itself, and thus not with the bound value.

Model

The model is composed of several automata : one MEDL, one central bus-guardian, one test automaton, one overall behavior manager and a set of automata for each node (the scheduler, the host_ftlayer level and the controller). They are not presented here because of the limited place.

A fault detection cause the starting of the deadline verification : the test automaton (see figure 4) transits to the *Reintegration* state on the *reintegration_begin* signal from the controller. Similarly, the end of the reintegration is indicated to the test automaton with the *reintegration_end* signal. If this signal is not received before the end of the deadline (*clock==deadline*), the test automaton transits to the *Error* state. The deadline verification is then the verification of the Fault state reachability.

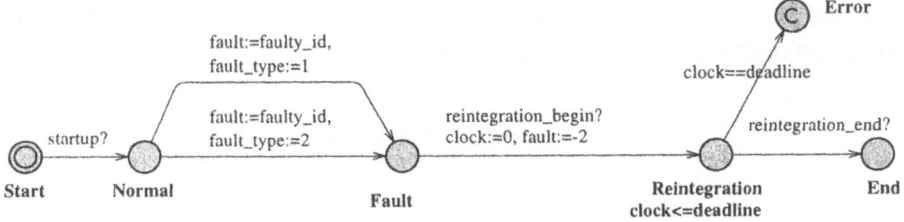

Figure 4. Test automaton

Validation

Verification results. Few results of the reintegration deadline verification are given as example in table 1. These results are the same for all faulty nodes. The CPU times and memory sizes have been measured for the verification of the property of the deadline, in the case the *Error* state is reached.

Table 1. Reintegration deadline verification

π	Δ_{slot}	Δ_{TP}	Δ_{PRP}	D_r	CPU time	Memory size
2	300	220	40	1542	2.74	19752KB
4	300	220	40	1544	2.74	19716KB
2	350	220	40	1842	2.85	26948KB
2	400	200	40	2162	2.41	16620KB

Analysis - worst scenario. The figure 5 illustrates the first line of table 1, for the faulty node 2. This worst scenario exists for a fault detected in the PRP of the slot which is two slots before the faulty node one. In this case, at the next node PSP, the reintegration condition ($integration > MIC$ with $integration$ the number of received correct frames) is not fulfilled, and then the node must waits for its next PSP, i.e. one round later.

Analysis - parameterized formulae. In the model, the node transits to passive state only at the end of the PRP. Thus, for the maximal bound, we add Δ_{PRP} at the bound verified on the model: $D_{Reint} = D_r + \Delta_{PRP}$.

The IFG phase duration is calculated by adding the other durations of the slot phases: $\Delta_{IFG} = \Delta_{PRP} + \Delta_{idle} + \Delta_{PSP}$

The parameterized formula is extracted by the worst case analysis of different scenarios, as shown in figure 5. Then we have: $D_r = \Delta_{round} + \Delta_{slot} + \Delta_{idle} + \Delta_{PSP} + \pi$ and $D_{Reint} = \Delta_{round} + \Delta_{slot} + \Delta_{IFG} + \pi$.

This formula is confirmed with all the results of table 1. For example, with the first line of this table : $D_r = 1542 = 5 * 300 + (300 - 220 - 40) + 2$.

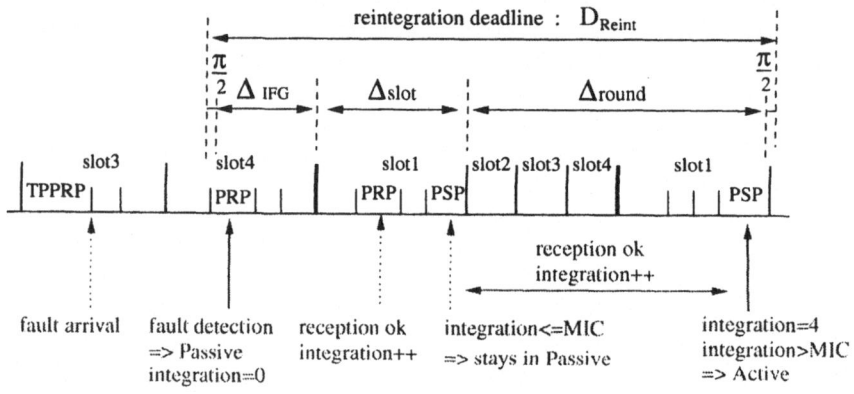

Figure 5.   Worst reintegration scenario for node 2

5.   EXPERIMENTS AND RESUTLS

Each of the UPPAAL models has been verified proving a number of properties on the UPPAAL model-checker. For instance, the cyclic infinite behavior is guarantee verifying the deadlock property. Another example is the verification of the reachability of the reintegration *Error* state.

This section gives bounds for the TTA services. On one hand, some elementary bounds for TTA algorithms are given by the TTA specification TTP, 2002 : Δ_{cycle} for the clock synchronization algorithm and Δ_{round} for the membership loss detection. Another one is given with formal verification in Bouajjani and Merceron, 2002 : $2 * \Delta_{round}$ for the clique avoidance algorithm.

In the other hand, our methodology was first performed on bounds validation for basic services. These bounds can be seen table 2. The fault hypotheses are the ones fixed in section 4. The communication blackout detection service is the only service which necessarily works under a longer time fault (more than one frame failed).

Table 2. TTA services bounds

Services	Maximal bounds
Without Faults	
Initialization	$MIC + (N + 1) * \tau_{round}$
Reintegration	$\Delta_{round} + \Delta_{slot} + \Delta_{IFG} + \pi$
Reinitialization	$3 * \Delta_{round} + (MIC - 1) * \Delta_{slot} + \Delta_{IFG} + \pi$
Mode change	$\Delta_{cycle} + \Delta_{round} + \Delta_{PSP} + \pi$
With Faults	
Communication blackout check	$\Delta_{round} + \Delta_{slot}$
Reintegration	$\Delta_{round} + 2 * \Delta_{slot} + \Delta_{IFG} + \pi$
Reinitialization	$3 * \Delta_{round} + \Gamma_{int} * \Delta_{slot} + \Delta_{IFG} + \pi$

Another interesting study to do is the bound validation of the composition of several mechanisms. All TTA mechanisms are not independent and the temporal bound of the composition is not the sum of the different mechanism bounds. Specific analyses have to be done to extract these bounds.

This section shows as an example, the composition of both the detection mechanism of membership loss fault, and the reintegration service. The bound is not detailed here, and is done with simple fault hypotheses : the fault causing the membership loss is a symmetric one (it has the same effect in all the nodes), and there is no other faults during the rest of the service execution.

The temporal bound of the membership loss detection can be extract from the specification : Δ_{round}. The one of the reintegration service is given in table 2 : $\Delta_{round} + \Delta_{slot} + \Delta_{IFG} + \pi$. The sum of this two services bounds is then superior two rounds and one slot. But the real temporal bounds is equal to $2 * \Delta_{round}$. This difference is because the sum do not take into account that this is the same node which is concerned with the two mechanisms. And the worst case do not happened for both mechanisms for the same node. Moreover, this bound is still an overvaluation of the real combined bound. Indeed, the membership loss detection bound used is the one given in the specification, and we do not modeled and analyze the worst case in details.

6. CONCLUSION

We defined a methodology to determine temporal bounds for basic TTA services and algorithms. These bounds are parameterized values. They should be used at higher levels for temporal validation of application.

In the future we expect to complete our UPPAAL models. Indeed, some combination of services have to be bounded. Moreover, other fault hypotheses can be modeled. As bounds are calculated in reasonable CPU time, our methodology could be applied to more complex models.

REFERENCES

(2001). *OSEK/VDX Fault Tolerant Communication - Version 1.0*. http://www.osek-vdx.org/.

(2001). *OSEK/VDX Time-Triggered Operating System - Version 1.0*.

(2002). *Time-Triggered Protocol TTP/C, High-Level Specification Document - 1.0.0*. TTTech Computertechnik AG, Time-Triggered Technology, Vienna, Austria. http://www.ttech.com.

Bauer, G. and Kopetz, H. (2000). Transparent redundancy in the time-triggered architecture. In *Int. Conf. on Dependable Systems and Networks (DSN 2000)*, New York, New York.

Bengtsson, J. and Yi, W. (2004). Timed automata : Semantics, algorithms and tools. Uppsala University.

Bouajjani, A. and Merceron, A. (2002). Parametric verification of a group membership algorithm. In *7th Int. Symp. on Formal Techniques in Real-Time and Fault Tolerant Systems (FTRTFT'02)*, volume LNCS 2469, pages 311–330, Oldenburg (Germany).

Caspi, P., Curic, A., Maignan, A., Sofronis, C., Tripakis, S., and Niebert, P. (2003). From simulink to scade/lustre to tta: a layered approach for distributed embedded applications. In *Proc. of the 2003 ACM SIGPLAN conference on Language, compiler, and tool for embedded systems*, pages 153–162. ACM Press.

Godary, K., Augé-Blum, I., and Mignotte, A. (2004a). Evaluation of model abstractions for the temporal validation of tta with uppaal. Technical Report RR2004-2, Lab. CITI, INSA Lyon.

Godary, K., Augé-Blum, I., and Mignotte, A. (2004b). Sdl and timed petri nets versus uppaal for the validation of embedded architecture in automotive. Technical Report RR2004-1, Lab. CITI, INSA Lyon.

Jensen, H. E., Larsen, K. G., and Skou, A. (1996). Modelling and analysis of a collision avoidance protocol using spin and uppaal. In *In Proc. of the 2nd SPIN Workshop*, New Jersey, USA. Rutgers University.

Kopetz, H. (1998). The time-triggered architecture. In *IEEE Int. Symp. on Object-Oriented Real- Time Distributed Computing (ISORC'98)*, volume LNCS 2469, Kyoto, Japan.

Larsen, K., Pettersson, P., and Yi, W. (1997). UPPAAL in a nutshell. *International Journal on Software Tools for Technology Transfer*, 1(1):134–152.

Lindahl, M., Pettersson, P., and Yi, W. (1998). Formal Design and Analysis of a Gear-Box Controller. In *Proc. of the 4th Workshop on Tools and Algorithms for the Construction and Analysis of Systems*, LNCS. Springer–Verlag.

Lönn, H. and Pettersson, P. (1997). Formal Verification of a TDMA Protocol Startup Mechanism. In *Proc. of the Pacific Rim Int. Symp. on Fault-Tolerant Systems*, pages 235–242.

Pettersson, P. (1999). *Modelling and Verification of Real-Time Systems Using Timed Automata: Theory and Practice*. Phdthesis - technical report docs 99/101, Department of Computer Systems, Uppsala University.

Pfeifer, H. (2000). Formal verification of the ttp group membership algorithm. In *IFIP, Int. Conf. on Formal Description Techniques for Distributed Systems and Communication protocols and Protocol Specification, Testing and Verification, FORTE/PSTV 2000*, Pisa, Italy.

Pfeifer, H. (2003). *Formal Analysis of Fault-Tolerant Algorithms in the Time-Triggered Architecture*. PhD thesis, Universitat Ulm, Germany.

Rushby, J. (2002). An overview of formal verification for the time-triggered architecture. In Damm, W. and Olderog, E.-R., editors, *Formal Techniques in Real-Time and Fault-Tolerant Systems*, LNCS, Oldenburg, Germany. Springer-Verlag.

AN ACTIVE REPLICATION SCHEME THAT TOLERATES FAILURES IN DISTRIBUTED EMBEDDED REAL-TIME SYSTEMS

Processors and communication links failures

Alain Girault[1], Hamoudi Kalla[1], and Yves Sorel[2]

[1]*INRIA Rhône-Alpes, 655 avenue de l'Europe, 38334 Saint-Ismier cedex, FRANCE*
{ alain.girault,hamoudi.kalla } @inrialpes.fr

[2]*INRIA Rocquencourt, B.P.105 - 78153 Le Chesnay Cedex, FRANCE*
yves.sorel@inria.fr

Abstract: Embedded real-time systems are being increasingly used in a major part of critical applications. In these systems, critical real-time constraints must be satisfied even in the presence of failures. In this paper, we present a new method-based on graph transformation that introduces fault-tolerance in building embedded real-time systems. The proposed method targets distributed architecture and can tolerate a fixed number of arbitrary processors and communication links failures. Because of the resource limitation in embedded systems, our method uses a software-based replication technique to provide fault-tolerance. Finally, since we use graph transformation to perform replication, our method may be used by any off-line distribution-scheduling algorithm to generate a fault-tolerant distributed schedule.

Keywords: Distributed and embedded systems, real-time systems, fault-tolerance, active replication, graph transformation.

1. INTRODUCTION

Distributed and embedded real-time systems, such as transportation (e.g., aircrafts and automobiles), nuclear, robotics, and telecommunication, requires high dependability (Avizienis et al., 2000), where system failures during execution can causes catastrophic damages. These systems must function with high availability even under hardware and software faults. Fault-tolerance (Jalote, 1994) then becomes an important key to establish dependability in these systems. Hardware and software redundancy are well-known effective methods for hardware fault-tolerance (Guerraoui and Schiper, 1996), where extra hardware (e.g., processors, communication links) and software (e.g., tasks, messages) are added into the system to deal with hardware faults. However, hardware techniques based on *hardware* solutions are not preferred in most embedded systems due to the limited resources available, for reasons of weight, encumbrance, energy consumption, or price constraints.

In this paper, we present our most recent work for integrating fault-tolerance in SYNDEX (http://www-rocq.inria.fr/syndex), a system level CAD software tool for optimizing the implementation of real-time embedded applications on multicomponent architectures. The method we present extends (Girault et al., 2001; Girault et al., 2003) by tolerating also communication links failures, and is more general than (Dima et al., 2001) since it can tolerate an arbitrary number of processors failures and an arbitrary number of communication links failures.

The paper is organized as follows. Section 2 describes the related work. Section 3 presents the various models used by our method and states our fault-tolerance problem. Section 4 presents the proposed approach for providing fault-tolerance. Section 5 explains how to use our solution with some existing distribution-scheduling heuristics to generate fault-tolerant schedules. Finally, section 6 concludes and proposes directions for future research.

2.   RELATED WORK

Related work in software fault tolerance approaches for distributed and embedded real-time systems falls in several categories. Relatively to fault hypothesis, we are interested in three fault-tolerant approaches: processors fault-tolerance, communication links fault-tolerance, and processors/communication links fault-tolerance.

In the first category of approaches that tolerates processors failures, several algorithms-based on scheduling heuristics have been proposed. They are based on *active software redundancy* (Breland et al., 1994; Hashimoto et al., 2002) or *passive software redundancy* (Ahn et al., 1997; Oh and Son, 1997). In the active redundancy technique, multiple redundant copies of a task are scheduled on different processors, which are run in parallel to tolerate a fixed number of processor failures. For instance, an off-line scheduling algorithm that tolerates a single processor failure in multiprocessor systems is presented in (Hashimoto et al., 2002). In the passive redundancy technique, also called primary/backup approach, a task is replicated on primary and backups replicas, but only the primary replica is executed. If it fails, one of the backups is selected to become the new primary. For instance, a fault-tolerant real-time scheduling algorithm that tolerate one processor failure in a heterogeneous distributed system is presented in (Qin et al., 2002), where failures are assumed to be permanent.

In the second category of approaches that tolerates communication links failures, several techniques have been proposed, which are based on *proactive* and *reactive* schemes. In the proactive scheme (Fragopoulou and Akl, 1995), multiple redundant copies of a message are sent along disjoint paths. However, in the reactive scheme (Sriram et al., 1999), one copy of the message, called primary, is sent, and if it fails, another copy of the message, called backup, will be transmitted.

Finally, the last category of approaches tolerates both processors and communication links failures (Gummadi et al., 2003; Zheng and Shin, 1998; Dima et al., 2001). For instance, in (Gummadi et al., 2003), failures are tolerated using the fault recovery scheme and a primary/backups strategy. Our solution is more general since it can tolerate *arbitrary* processors and communication links failures, and it may be used by *any* off-line distribution-scheduling heuristic to generate a fault-tolerant distributed code.

3. MODELS

3.1 Algorithm model

The algorithm is modeled by a *data-flow graph* ($\mathcal{A}lg$). Each vertex is an *operation* and each edge is a *data-dependence*. A data-dependence corresponds to a data transfer from a producer operation to a consumer operation, defining a partial order on the execution of operations. This partial order relation is denoted by $\triangleright$. Operations of $\mathcal{A}lg$ can be either an external input/output operation or a computation operation. Operations with no predecessor (resp. no successor) are the input interfaces (resp. output), handling the events produced by the sensors (resp. actuators). The inputs of a computation operation must precede its outputs. Moreover, computation operations are side-effect free, i.e. the output values depend only of the input values. The algorithm graph is executed repeatedly at each input event from the sensors in order to compute the output events for the actuators.

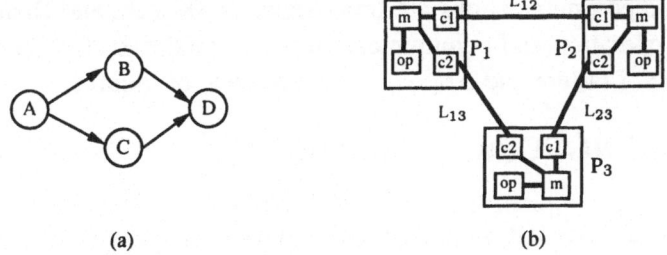

(a)	(b)

Figure 1. (a) Algorithm graph; (b) Architecture graph.

Figure 1(a) gives an example of $\mathcal{A}lg$, with four operations: A (sensor), B and C (computations), and D (actuator), and four data-dependences: $A \triangleright B$, $A \triangleright C$, $B \triangleright D$, and $C \triangleright D$.

3.2   Architecture model

The architecture is modeled by a graph (Arc), where vertices are processors, and edges are bidirectional point-to-point communication links. In the sequel, we write "links" instead of "point-to-point communication links".

A processor P is a graph made of one operator op, one local memory m, and at least one communicator c. An operator op executes sequentially operations of Alg, reads from and writes data into its local memory m. A communicator c_i cooperates with another communicator c_j in order to execute sequentially transfers of data stored in the memory (send or receive) between processors through a link.

Figure 1(b) gives an example of Arc, with three processors P_1, P_2, and P_3, and three links L_{12}, L_{13}, and L_{23}, where each processor is made of one operator (op), one local memory (m), and two communicators ($c1$ and $c2$).

To each operator op we associate a list of pairs ($o,d/op$), where d is the worst case execution time (WCET) of the operation o on operator op. Also, to each communicator c, we associate a list of pairs ($dpd,d/c$), where d is the worst case transmission time (WCTT) of the data-dependence dpd on communicator c. Since the target architecture is heterogeneous, the WCET (resp. WCTT) for a given operation (resp. data-dependence) can be distinct on each operator (resp. communication link).

3.3   Failure model

We consider only processors and communication links failures, where failures are assumed to be a fail-silent (also known as fail-stop), i.e. a component works correctly or stops functioning (becomes silent). Recent studies on modern processors have shown that a fail-silent behavior can be achieved at a reasonable cost (Baleani et al., 2003). We assume that at most $\mathcal{N}_{PF}$ processors and $\mathcal{N}_{LF}$ links may fails.

As we consider off-line distribution-scheduling heuristics, the execution of operations and communications are time-triggered (Kopetz and Bauer, 2002), that is, each operation and communication is assigned two start-dates: St_{best} in the absence of failure and St_{worst} in the presence of failures.

4.   THE PROPOSED APPROACH

In this section, we present our approach based on software redundancy to tolerate processor and link failures. We propose to use *graph transformation* to perform software redundancy, where a given input algorithm graph (Alg) is transformed into a new algorithm graph (Alg^*) augmented with redundancies. Then, operations and data-dependences of Alg^* can be distributed and scheduled on a specified target distributed architecture (Arc) to generate a fault tolerant distributed schedule. The global picture of our methodology is shown in Figure 2.

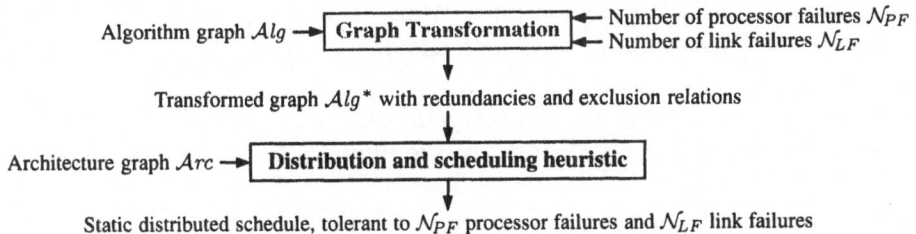

Figure 2. Global picture of our methodology.

In this section, we concentrate on the first step, the transformation of Alg into Alg^*. We first present a method that tolerates only processors failures, next we present a method that tolerates only links failures, and finally we present a combined method that tolerates both processors and links failures.

4.1 Tolerating processor failures

In order to tolerate at most $\mathcal{N}_{PF}$ processor failures, we propose to use the same principle as in (Girault et al., 2003): each operation has $\mathcal{N}_{PF}+1$ replicas scheduled on $\mathcal{N}_{PF}+1$ distinct processors. The system's communication links are assumed to be fault-free.

The transformation of Alg into Alg^* is performed in two steps. Initially, each operation o_i of Alg is replicated in Alg^* on $\mathcal{N}_{PF}+1$ *exclusive replicas* o_i^1, ..., $o_i^{\mathcal{N}_{PF}+1}$ (the set of o_i's replicas is noted $\mathcal{R}ep(o_i)$); two operations o_i^1 et o_i^2 are exclusive if and only if they are two identical replicas of the same operation o_i and they must be scheduled on distinct processors. In the second step, each replicated operation of Alg^* must receive its inputs data $\mathcal{N}_{PF}+1$ times from each of its predecessors. Therefore, each data-dependence $data_i$ of Alg is replicated in Alg^* on $\mathcal{N}_{PF}+1$ exclusive replicas $data_i^1, \ldots, data_i^{\mathcal{N}_{PF}+1}$; two data-dependences $data_i^1$ et $data_i^2$ are exclusive if and only if they are two identical replicas of the same data-dependence $data_i$ and they must be scheduled on disjoint paths (see Figure 3(a) for $\mathcal{N}_{PF}=1$).

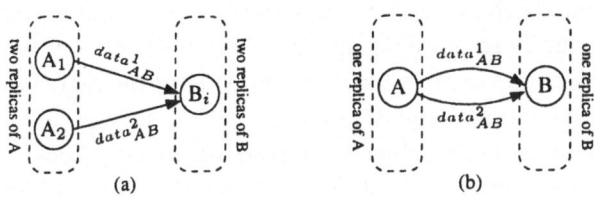

Figure 3. (a) Processor failures; (b) Link failures.

4.2 Tolerating link failures

To tolerate at most $\mathcal{N}_{LF}$ link failures, we propose to use the same principle as in tolerating processors failures, which is based on the following graph transformation. We don't need to replicate operations because the processors are assumed to be fault-free. Therefore, each data-dependence $data_i$ of $\mathcal{A}lg$ is replicated in $\mathcal{A}lg^*$ on $\mathcal{N}_{LF}+1$ exclusive replicas $data_i^1, data_i^2, \ldots, data_i^{\mathcal{N}_{LF}+1}$ between any two dependent operations (see Figure 3(b) for $\mathcal{N}_{LF}=1$).

4.3 Tolerating processor and link failures

To tolerate at most $\mathcal{N}_{PF}$ processor and $\mathcal{N}_{LF}$ link failures, we first replicate each operation o_i of $\mathcal{A}lg$ in $\mathcal{A}lg^*$ on $\mathcal{N}_{PF}+1$ exclusive replicas (set $\mathcal{R}ep(o_i)$), as shown in Figure 4(a), wherein operations A and B of Figure 1(a) are replicated on $\mathcal{N}_{PF}+1$ exclusive replicas. Then, each replicated operation of $\mathcal{A}lg^*$ must receive its input data $\mathcal{N}_{PF}+\mathcal{N}_{LF}+1$ times from each of its predecessors. Therefore, each data-dependence $data_i$ of $\mathcal{A}lg$ is replicated in $\mathcal{A}lg^*$ on $\mathcal{N}_{PF}+\mathcal{N}_{LF}+1$ exclusive replicas, as shown in Figure 4(a), wherein the data-dependence A ▷ B is replicated $\mathcal{N}_{PF}+\mathcal{N}_{LF}+1$ times between the replicas $\mathcal{R}ep(A)$ of A and each replica of B.

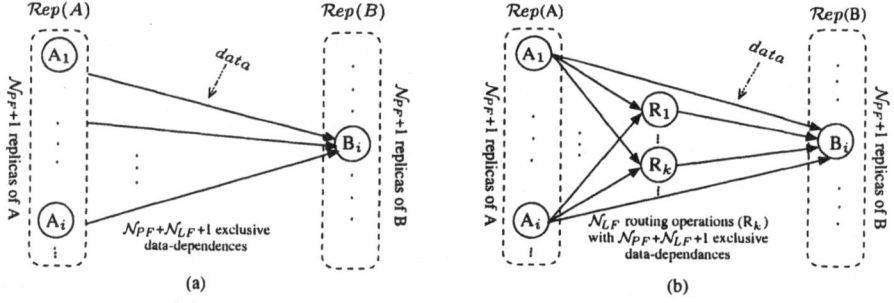

Figure 4.   (a) Initial transformations for $\mathcal{N}_{PF} \geq 0$ and $\mathcal{N}_{LF} \geq 0$; (b) Final transformations.

The problem of this scheme is to find a distribution of these exclusive dependences of $\mathcal{A}lg^*$ between the replicas $\mathcal{R}ep(A)$ of A. The requirement is to tolerate only $\mathcal{N}_{PF}$ processor failures and $\mathcal{N}_{LF}$ link failures. Therefore, we propose a distribution which is *less expensive* in terms of communications.

To present as clearly as possible our distribution technique, we present initially its principles in the case $\mathcal{N}_{PF}=1$ and $\mathcal{N}_{LF}=1$ for the algorithm sub-graph of Figure 5(a). Figures 5(b) and 5(c) are the two first steps of our approach, before the distribution itself, which is performed in two steps, illustrated in Figures 5(d) and 5(e). Since $\mathcal{N}_{PF}=1$ and $\mathcal{N}_{LF}=1$, $\mathcal{R}ep(A)$ and $\mathcal{R}ep(B)$ contain each two replicas. Furthermore, the data-dependence A ▷ B is replicated three times.

First, we connect each replica of A with one of these three data-dependences, as shown in Figure 5(d). Next, we first replace the third data-dependence by a new operation R_1. We call this new operation a *routing operation*, its duration is *null* (the set of all routing operations from A to B is noted $\mathcal{R}ep(A \triangleright B)$). Finally, we connect all the replicas $\mathcal{R}ep(A)$ of A to R_1 which is also connected to each replica of B, as shown in Figure 5(e). The purpose is to make sure that each replica of B has *three* distinct sources from which it will receive the data-dependence $A \triangleright B$, so that if any two sources fail (two because here $\mathcal{N}_{PF}+\mathcal{N}_{LF}=2$), then these failures will be masked by the third source. Thus, for any i, operations A_1, A_2 and R_i are exclusive and must be implemented on distinct processors. Also, the data-dependences $A_1 \triangleright B_i$, $A_2 \triangleright B_i$, and $R_i \triangleright B_i$ are exclusive and must be implemented on disjoint paths. Such exclusive relations are given with the final transformed graph $\mathcal{A}lg^*$ to the distribution/scheduling heuristic (see Figure 2).

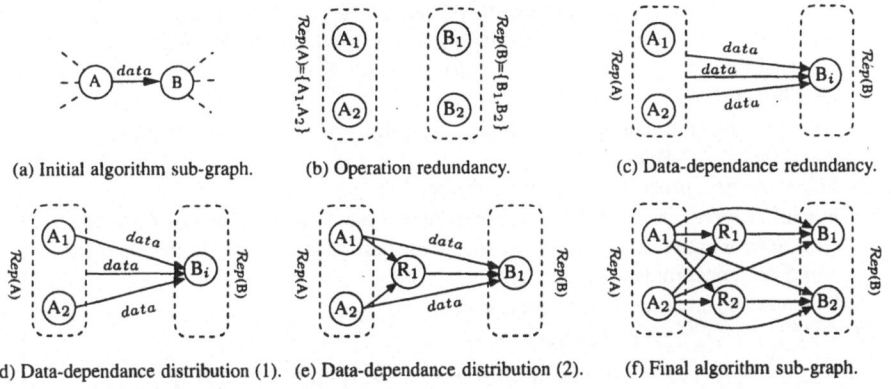

(a) Initial algorithm sub-graph.   (b) Operation redundancy.   (c) Data-dependance redundancy.

(d) Data-dependance distribution (1).   (e) Data-dependance distribution (2).   (f) Final algorithm sub-graph.

Figure 5.   Distribution scheme for $\mathcal{N}_{PF}=1$ and $\mathcal{N}_{LF}=1$.

In the general case, $\mathcal{N}_{PF} \geq 0$ and $\mathcal{N}_{LF} \geq 0$, the transformation scheme of $\mathcal{A}lg$ on $\mathcal{A}lg^*$ is illustrated in Figure 4(b), where each operation is replicated in $\mathcal{A}lg^*$ on $\mathcal{N}_{PF}+1$ exclusive replicas, and each data-dependence is replaced by $\mathcal{N}_{LF}$ routing operations R_k, $\mathcal{N}_{PF}+1$ data-dependences between $\mathcal{R}ep(A)$ and each R_k, and one data-dependence between each R_k and each B_i. The operations in $\mathcal{R}ep(A)$ and in $\mathcal{R}ep(A \triangleright B)$ are exclusive and must be implemented on distinct processors. Also, all replicated data-dependences $A \triangleright B$ and $R \triangleright B$ are exclusive and must be implemented on disjoint paths.

5.   DISTRIBUTION/SCHEDULING HEURISTIC

Our method may use the distribution-scheduling heuristic DSH proposed in (Grandpierre et al., 1999). As required by our graph transformation method, we modify the DSH heuristic to take into account the exclusive relations between operations and data-dependences. The modified heuristic is formally described in Figure 6. We use the two functions $succ(o)$ and $pred(o)$ to denote the sets of successor and predecessor operations of o in Alg^*.

Inputs = a transformed algorithm graph Alg^*, a list of exclusions $\mathcal{E}xcl$, an architecture
       graph $\mathcal{A}rc$, some real-time and distribution constraints;
Output = a fault-tolerant distributed static schedule of Alg^* onto $\mathcal{A}rc$;
Begin
   $O_{cand}^{(0)} :=$ {operations of Alg^* without any predecessor}; $O_{sched}^{(0)} := \emptyset$;
Repeat
  1. **For each $B_i \in O_{cand}^{(n)}$ do**
     1.1. **If B_i is a routing operation then** Compute the set $\mathcal{P}(B_i)$ of processors,
       such that for each $p \in \mathcal{P}$:
        a. There exist $\mathcal{N}_{PF}+1$ disjoint paths from processors implementing
          operations of $\mathcal{R}ep(A_j)$ to p, for any A_j predecessor of B_i;
        b. p must comply to all exclusions in $\mathcal{E}xcl$ concerning B_i;
     1.2. **Else** Compute the set $\mathcal{P}(B_i)$ of processors, such that for each $p \in \mathcal{P}$:
        a. There exist $\mathcal{N}_{PF}+\mathcal{N}_{LF}+1$ disjoint paths from processors
          implementing operations in $\mathcal{R}ep(A_j) \cup \mathcal{R}ep(A_j \triangleright B_i)$ to p;
        b. p must comply to all exclusions in $\mathcal{E}xcl$ concerning B_i; **End if**
     1.3. **If** the set $\mathcal{P}(B_i)$ is empty **then** return "Fail"; **End if**
  End for each
  3. Select the most urgent operation B_{urgent} of Alg^* using the schedule pressure
     and the sets $\mathcal{P}(B_i)$;
  4. Select the best processor p_{best} from the set $\mathcal{P}(B_{urgent})$;
  5. **For all** A_j predecessor of B_{urgent}, schedule all the data-dependences $A_j \triangleright B_{urgent}$
     on several paths leading to p_{best}, such that these paths comply to the exclusions
     in $\mathcal{E}xcl$ concerning $A_j \triangleright B_{urgent}$;
  6. Schedule B_{urgent} onto the processor p_{best};
  7. $O_{sched}^{(n+1)} := O_{sched}^{(n)} \cup \{B_{urgent}\}$;
  8. $O_{cand}^{(n+1)} := O_{cand}^{(n)} - \{B_{urgent}\} \cup \{o \in succ(B_{urgent}) \mid pred(o) \subseteq O_{sched}^{(n+1)}\}$;
Until $O_{cand}^{(n+1)} = \emptyset$;
End

Figure 6.   The DSH distribution-scheduling heuristic.

At each step (n) of the heuristic, for each candidate operation B_i in $O_{cand}^{(n)}$, we compute the set $\mathcal{P}(B_i)$ of processors that can execute B_i and comply to the concerned exclusions of $\mathcal{E}xcl$. Then, the most urgent candidate operation B_{urgent} is selected to be scheduled thanks to the *schedule pressure* function defined in (Grandpierre et al., 1999). Then, among the set $\mathcal{P}(B_{urgent})$, the processor p_{best}, where B_{urgent} will finish at the earliest date, is selected to execute B_{urgent}. But before B_{urgent} is actually scheduled onto p_{best}, all the required data-dependences are scheduled on paths, possibly disjoint depending again on the concerned exclusions of $\mathcal{E}xcl$. Finally, the lists $O_{sched}^{(n)}$ of scheduled operations and $O_{cand}^{(n)}$ of candidate operations are updated.

Finally, the proposed general transformation scheme enables us to generate a fault-tolerant distributed schedule of the new algorithm graph Alg^* onto the architecture graph $\mathcal{A}rc$. The following theorem proves that it is, by construction, tolerant to any combination of at most $\mathcal{N}_{PF}$ processors failures and at most $\mathcal{N}_{LF}$ communication links failures.

THEOREM 1 *Let Alg be an algorithm graph and $\mathcal{A}rc$ an architecture graph. Let Alg^* be the new algorithm graph obtained by applying the transformation of Figure 4(b) to Alg. Let Sys be the system obtained by distributing and scheduling Alg^* onto $\mathcal{A}rc$ w.r.t. the exclusion relations required by the graph transformation having led to Alg^*. If at most $\mathcal{N}_{PF}$ processor failures and $\mathcal{N}_{LF}$ communication links failures occur in Sys, then at least one replica of each operation will remain active.*

Proof. Since each operation is replicated $\mathcal{N}_{PF}+1$ times, since all these $\mathcal{N}_{PF}+1$ replicas are scheduled onto distinct processors, and since at most $\mathcal{N}_{PF}$ processors can fail simultaneously, then at least one replica of each operation is scheduled onto a processor that will remain valid. We therefore need to prove that any operation scheduled onto an active processor is active, i.e., that it receives correctly all its required inputs from all its predecessor operations.

Let o_j^m be such an operation, namely the mth replica of operation o_j. For each of its predecessor operations o_i, thanks to the same argument as above, there exists at least one replica o_i^k scheduled onto a valid processor. By construction, there exist $\mathcal{N}_{LF}+1$ data-dependences between o_i^k and o_j^m. Thanks to the exclusion lists given to the distribution/scheduling heuristic, these $\mathcal{N}_{LF}+1$ data-dependences are scheduled onto $\mathcal{N}_{LF}+1$ disjoint paths. Since at most $\mathcal{N}_{LF}$ communication links can fail simultaneously, then at least one of these data-dependences will remain valid. Hence o_j^m will receive correctly its input from o_i^k. We have thus proved that any operation scheduled onto an active processor will receive correctly all its input data from all its predecessors in Alg, and will therefore be executed correctly. $\qquad\square$

6. CONCLUSION

We have investigated methods to mask hardware failures in heterogeneous distributed systems with point-to-point communication links. We have proposed a new method that tolerates at most $\mathcal{N}_{PF}$ arbitrary processors and at most $\mathcal{N}_{LF}$ arbitrary communication links failures. It is a software solution, based on active redundancy to mask the hardware failures. It proceed in two steps: first a graph transformation, and then an off-line distribution-scheduling heuristic. The graph transformation adds software redundancy to the original algorithm graph Alg: we obtain a new algorithm graph Alg^* with redundancy, along with exclusion relations. Then, the distribution-scheduling heuristic is applied to map Alg^* onto a given architecture graph $\mathcal{A}rc$. As a result, it generates a static schedule of Alg^* onto $\mathcal{A}rc$, which is tolerant to the required processors and communication links failures.

Currently, we are working on a new solution to take into account distributed architectures with bus communication links. We also plan new solution to take sensors/actuators failures into account.

REFERENCES

Ahn, K., Kim, J., and Hong, S. (1997). Fault-tolerant real-time scheduling using passive replicas. In *PRFTS'97*, Taipei, Taiwan.

Avizienis, A., Laprie, J.-C., and Randell, B. (2000). Fundamental concepts in dependability. In *ISW-2000*, pages 7–12, Boston, Massachusetts, USA.

Baleani, M., Ferrari, A., Mangeruca, L., Peri, M., Pezzini, S., and Sangiovanni-Vincentelli, A. (2003). Fault-tolerant platforms for automotive safety-critical applications. In *CASES'03*, San Jose, USA. ACM.

Breland, M.A., Rogers, S.A., Brat, G., and Nelson, K.L. (1994). Transparent fault-tolerance for distributed Ada applications. In *Proceedings of the Conference on TRI-Ada '94*, pages 446–457. ACM Press.

Dima, C., Girault, A., Lavarenne, C., and Sorel, Y. (2001). Off-line real-time fault-tolerant scheduling. In *Euromicro PDP'01*, pages 410–417, Mantova, Italy.

Fragopoulou, P. and Akl, S.G. (1995). Fault tolerant communication algorithms on the star network using disjoint paths. In *Proceedings of the HICSS'95*, Kingston, Canada.

Girault, A., Kalla, H., Sighireanu, M., and Sorel, Y. (2003). An algorithm for automatically obtaining distributed and fault-tolerant static schedule. In *DSN'03*, San Francisco, USA.

Girault, A., Lavarenne, C., Sighireanu, M., and Sorel, Y. (2001). Fault-tolerant static scheduling for real-time distributed embedded systems. In *ICDCS'01*, pages 695–698, Phoenix, USA. IEEE. Extended abstract.

Grandpierre, T., Lavarenne, C., and Sorel, Y. (1999). Optimized rapid prototyping for real-time embedded heterogeneous multiprocessors. In *7th International Workshop on Hardware/Software Co-Design, CODES'99*, Rome, Italy.

Guerraoui, R. and Schiper, A. (1996). Fault-tolerance by replication in distributed systems. In *Proceeding Conference on Reliable Software Technologies*, pages 38–57. Springer-Verlag.

Gummadi, K.P., Pradeep, M.J., and Murthy, C.S. Ram (2003). An efficient primary-segmented backup scheme for dependable real-time communication in multihop networks. *IEEE/ACM Trans. on Networking*, 11(1).

Hashimoto, K., Tsuchiya, T., and Kikuno, T. (2002). Effective scheduling of duplicated tasks for fault-tolerance in multiprocessor systems. *IEICE Transactions on Information and Systems*.

Jalote, P. (1994). *Fault-Tolerance in Distributed Systems*. Prentice Hall, Englewood Cliffs, New Jersey.

Kopetz, H. and Bauer, G. (2002). The time-triggered architecture. *Proceedings of the IEEE, Special Issue on Modeling and Design of Embedded Software*.

Oh, Y. and Son, S.H. (1997). Scheduling real-time tasks for dependability. *Journal of Operational Research Society*, 48(6):629–639.

Qin, X., Jiang, H., and Swanson, D.R. (2002). An efficient fault-tolerant scheduling algorithm for real-time tasks with precedence constraints in heterogeneous systems. In *ICPP'02*, pages 360–386, Vancouver, Canada.

Sriram, R., Manimaran, G., and Murthy, C. Siva Ram (1999). An integrated scheme for establishing dependable real-time channels in multihop networks. In *ICCC'90*, pages 528–533.

Zheng, Q. and Shin, K. G. (1998). Fault-tolerant real-time communication in distributed computing systems. In *IEEE Trans. on Parallel and Distributed Systems*, pages 470–480.

DEVELOPMENT OF DISTRIBUTED AUTOMOTIVE SOFTWARE
The DaVinci Methodology

Dr. Uwe Honekamp, Matthias Wernicke
Vector Informatik GmbH, Dep. PND - Tools for Networks and distributed Systems

Abstract: The software complexity in modern vehicle electronic systems is increasingly growing. Vehicle projects have to take into account a growing number of interconnected functions, which are jointly developed by many persons in many different companies. For facing these challenges, new design methodologies for a formalized and partially automated software development are required.

The DaVinci design methodology has been developed to match the specific requirements of distributed automotive systems. This includes the function-oriented design of the system structure as well as the deployment on a network and software integration on ECUs (electronic control units). Such a design serves as basis for an automatic code generation process, which integrates the applications into an efficient ECU target architecture with real-time operating system (RTOS) and communication stack.

Typical scenarios during the development processes like the reuse, exchange and integration of design data are supported and combined with a flexible configuration management. PC-based test environments may be used for functional integration tests or verification of the network communication.

This article is supposed to give a brief overview of the methodology as well as some selected aspects of its implementation in the DaVinci tool suite.

Key words: Design methodology, distributed embedded systems, automotive.

1.   INTRODUCTION

The software architecture of typical automotive systems in general is required to fulfil important requirements, the most prominent being:

– *Independence of software component from each others*: it must be feasible to independently develop and test self-contained functions of the automotive software. Only by this means it is possible to **reuse** particular software components among model families.

– *Independence from particular network topology*: it must be possible to **map** a particular collection of communicating software components to a variety of network topologies.

– *Efficiency*: the **overhead** imposed by the conformance to a standard software architecture is required to be as **small as possible**. Of course, the optimal solution would be not to generate any overhead at all.

As a response to these requirements the DaVinci methodology has been developed. DaVinci supports the independence of "pieces of software" from each others by defining the so-called *software component.*

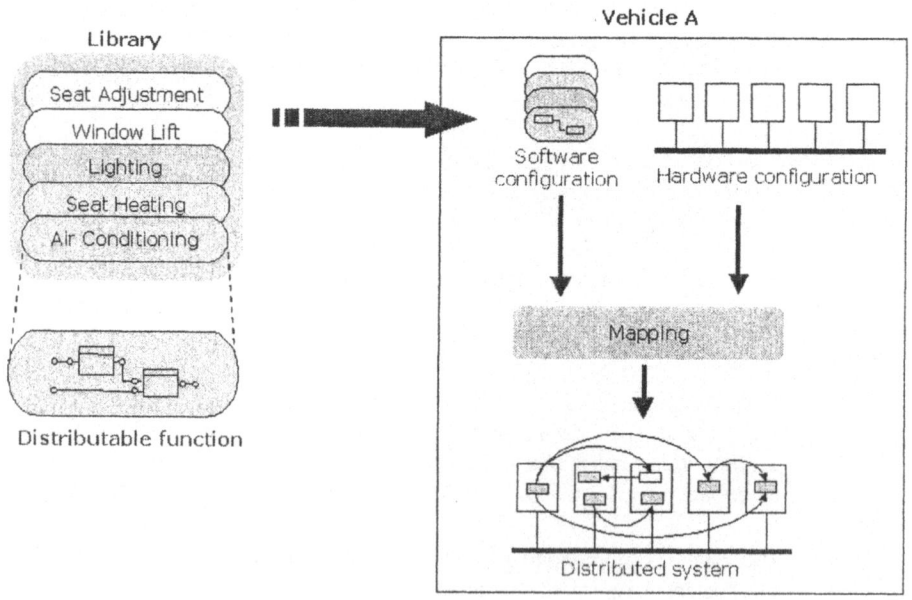

Figure 1. Distributed System

The combination of particular *software components* to form a logically consistent higher functionality is called a software configuration. In other words: the software configuration represents a graph of *software components.*

Furthermore, it is possible to model relevant hardware components (i.e. ECUs, communication buses, sensors, actuators). By this means a graph of hardware elements is formed.

In order to define a concrete network of *electronic control units* (ECU) for a particular car model the software graph has to be mapped on the hardware graph. The result is called a *mapping system*. The latter is the basis for sophisticated code generation activities that mainly resolve the abstract interfaces defined in the *software component*. By this means the strict interfaces leave virtually no overhead.

The persistent storage of DaVinci model elements is based on XML. Model elements that belong together are arranged in a so-called workspace. The latter, on the other hand, can be associated to a *configuration management* repository to support team-based development of DaVinci models.

The main field of application for DaVinci is the specification of so-called body electronics (e.g. power windows, climate control, seat adjustment, lighting, etc.). It is planned to extend the applicability of the DaVinci methodology to other automotive domains such as power train, chassis, etc. in the future.

2. DAVINCI DESIGN ELEMENTS

2.1 Software Component

Obviously, the main point for achieving independence of *software components* is the definition of strict interfaces among *software components* as well as to the underlying hardware and standard services (RTOS, communication drivers, network management, etc.).

A further point to take into account is the granularity of software gathered in a *software component*. The latter is defined as the minimum self-contained reusable software unit.

Software components can be arranged hierarchically such that *software components* (without behavioural description) contain other *software components*.

The behaviour of a *software component* can be modelled either directly by means of the C language or by means of some behaviour modelling tool such as The Mathwork's Simulink™ or I-Logix' Statemate™.

Furthermore, dSPACE's TargetLink™ can be used for behavioural modelling to support the creation of series production code from Simulink™ models.

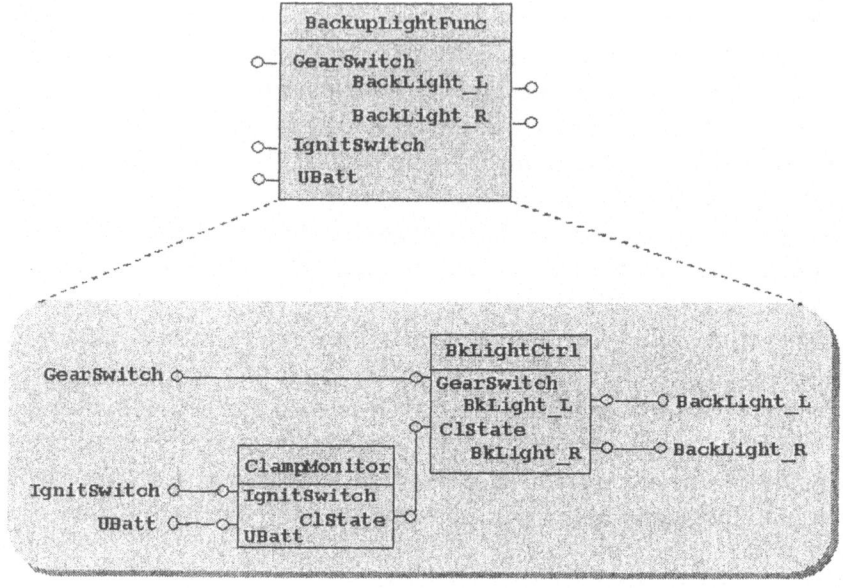

Figure 2. Example of a hierarchical software component

The architecture of Vector's DaVinci Tool Suite provides a generic adapter concept that allows to easily integrate additional behaviour modelling tools on customer's demand.

2.2   Signal

A signal is used for interconnecting *software components* with each others. Furthermore, a signal can be used to connect a *software system* (see ch. 2.4) to hardware devices such as *sensors* and *actuators*.

Signals maintain several properties such as the data type, the conversion formula from the physical domain to the data type as well as several automotive-specific properties like a timeout value.

2.3   ECU State Machine

The so-called *ECU state machine* is part of the abstraction mechanisms specially introduced to yield a maximum hardware independence of *software components. ECU state machines* define special states in which an ECU can operate as well as the possible transitions between states.

Software components, on the other hand, may define so-called *procedures* that implement special behaviour of the *software component* according to the current state of the *ECU state machine*.

Of course, the full power of *ECU state machines* as a means of abstraction is provided only if all ECUs (to which a particular *software component* can be mapped) implement an instance of the same *ECU state machine*.

2.4 Software System

A *software system* is a collection of *software components* connected by *signals*. The purpose of a *software system* is to gather *software components* to form a higher functionality based on the interaction of the particular *software components*.

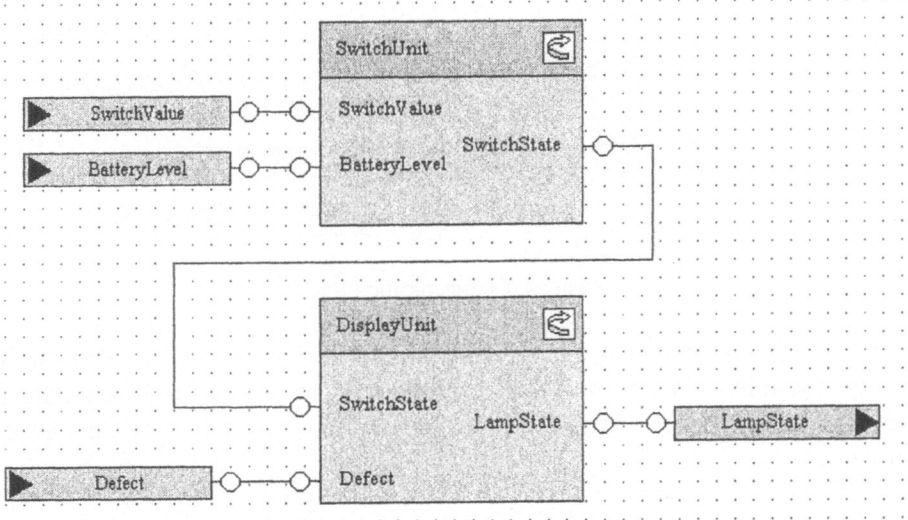

Figure 3. Example of a simple software system.

Another perspective of a *software system* is the representation of the entire (as far as DaVinci in concerned) software functionality of the network of ECUs in a car.

3.   DAVINCI IMPLEMENTATION ELEMENTS

3.1   BUS

A *bus* is used to express a communication device among the collection of ECUs in a network. In general, several types of buses (e.g. CAN, LIN, MOST, FlexRay, etc.) could be used in a network of automotive ECUs. Furthermore, several disjoint buses of the same type (e.g. CAN) could be used to form subnets connected to each others by gateway ECUs.

DaVinci currently supports the definition of CAN networks. Gateways are supported but the gateway functionality must be explicitly specified by a *software component*.

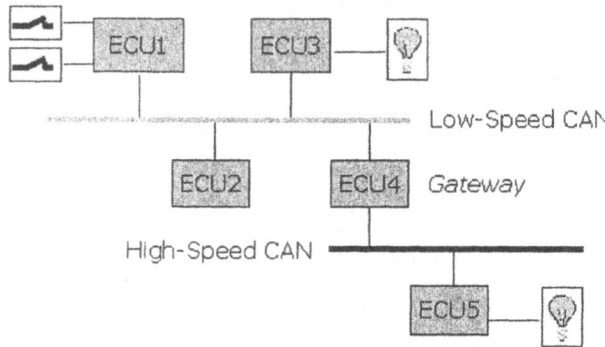

Figure 4. Communication Bus

For the future, DaVinci will not only support a wide range of buses but it will be possible to automatically determine the communication behaviour of gateway ECUs based on the formal description of the communication network.

3.2   ECU

An *ECU* obviously is used to carry out computations, i.e. host a collection of *software components* as described by the mapping description. An *ECU* can have *sensors* and *actuators* that resolve particular signals.

In other words: *software components* interact (via *signals*) with the real world by means of *sensors* and *actuators* provided by the *ECU* onto which the *software component* is mapped.

Furthermore, the description of an *ECU* consists of a reference to a particular *ECU state machine*.

For supporting the generation of target code, it is possible to specify the type and (if applicable) variant of the underlying microcontroller.

3.3 Hardware System

A *hardware system* is the direct counterpart of the concept of the *software system*, i.e. it describes a collection of *ECUs* as well as the communication *buses* used to interconnect particular *ECUs*.

3.4 Mapping System

A *mapping system* defines a particular combination of a *hardware system* and a *software system*. Furthermore, the mapping of *software components* to *ECUs* as well as the mapping of *signals* to bus messages are essential parts of the description of a *mapping system*.

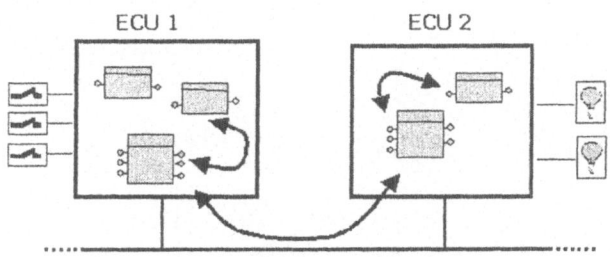

Figure 5. A simple mapping system

4. DAVINCI TARGET ARCHITECTURE

As mentioned before, the abstract interfaces defined by the DaVinci methodology at some point in time must be resolved such that *software components* can be embedded into a defined target architecture with maximum efficiency.

DaVinci's code integration capabilities allow the seamless integration of heterogeneous *software components*, e.g. legacy C Code and model-based developed components.

The standardized target architecture used for DaVinci models is depicted in *Figure 6*. As sketched by the picture, the target architecture itself consists of self-contained modules some of which must be specially generated according to the DaVinci model configuration.

Other modules exist as predefined source code but must be configured (i.e. header files containing configuration information must be created). Both generation and configuration of software modules is carried out by specially tailored code generation tools.

One of the most prominent code generation issues is the generation of a communication stack that provides signal access in the context of a so-called *interaction layer* to *software components*.

The underlying RTOS must be configured as well. The configuration depends on the mapping of *software components* as well as the assignment of priorities to tasks.

Furthermore, timing constraints concerning bus communication must also be taken into account, i.e. it must be made sure that messages with a high priority are send by tasks that as well are executed under a high priority.

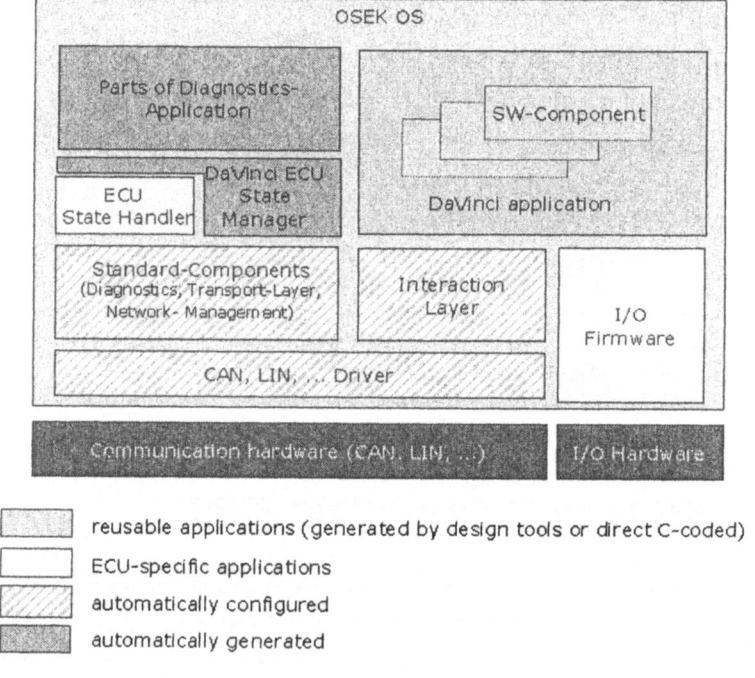

Figure 6. DaVinci target architecture

The currently supported range of microcontroller targets consists of the Motorola PowerPC series for embedded applications as well as on the Star12 microcontroller. Further targets are supported on demand.

For diagnostics purposes Vector's CANdesc software module can be integrated to DaVinci applications. Supported interaction layers are

GMLAN, DBKom, and derivatives of the Vector IL. For calibration and measurement purposes it is possible to add a CCP driver as well.

5. TEST OF SOFTWARE COMPONENTS

A very typical constraint of the development of ECU software is the fact that in early phases of the development project the target hardware does not yet exist.

This fact should not have an impact on the activities on the software side. For this purpose it is essential to have a test platform that emulates especially the communication hardware.

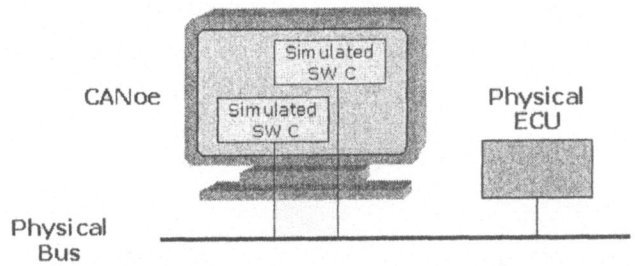

Figure 7. CANoe test environment

This requirement is fulfilled by the software tool CANoe that has as well been developed by Vector Informatik GmbH. The functionality of CANoe, however, is not limited to mere simulation.

It is possible to simulate particular nodes of a communication bus that otherwise already exists in hardware, i.e. physically existing ECUs can be conveniently combined with simulated ones and perform realistic real-time communication among each others. This concept is depicted by *Figure 7.*

DaVinci supports CANoe as an experimentation platform for early phases of a network project. It is possible (by means of a predefined target configuration) to generate the target architecture code such that the entire ECU including applications, communication stack and RTOS can be simulated by CANoe.

6. DISTRIBUTED DEVELOPMENT

Large software projects in the automotive domain are usually distributed among several supplier companies under the control of the car manufacturer.

A tool suite for carrying out large software project must therefore support the distributed development of software.

For this purpose DaVinci provides several features:

- It is possible to attach a DaVinci workspace to a configuration management repository thus enabling DaVinci to be used by the development team of at least an entire company.
- DaVinci provides sophisticated import and export mechanisms that are capable of dealing with the formal model without uncovering subjects to intellectual property (e.g. the structure of a control algorithm implemented to realize a specific *software component*). This technique can be used to share DaVinci model elements among developers of different companies. Please consult *Figure 8* for more details.

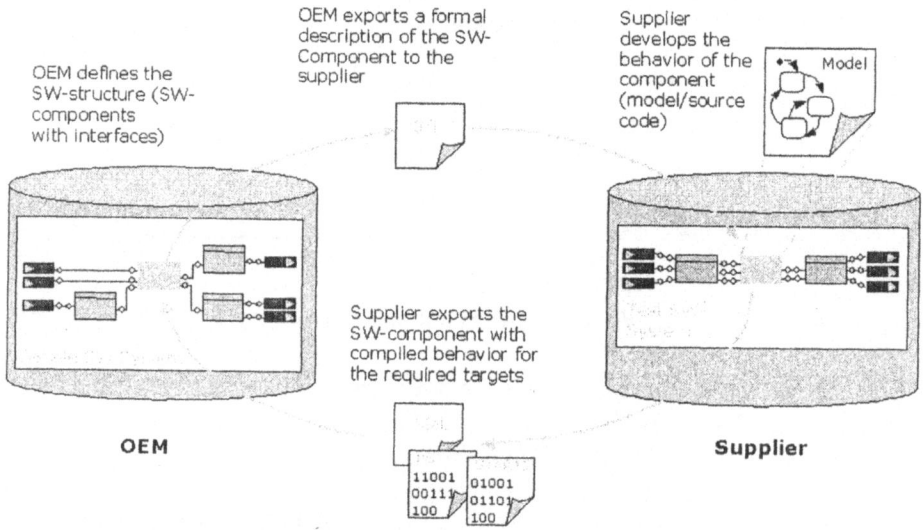

Figure 8. Distributed development using DaVinci

7. FUTURE PROSPECTS

The DaVinci methodology as well as the corresponding tool suite is subject to continuous improvement. Among other things this applies in particular to the introduction of further behaviour modelling tools as well as the support for additional microcontroller targets.

EXPERIENCES FROM MODEL BASED DEVELOPMENT OF DRIVE-BY-WIRE CONTROL SYSTEMS

Per Johannessen[1], Fredrik Törner[1] and Jan Torin[2]
[1]Volvo Car Corporation, Department 94221, ELIN, SE-405 31 Göteborg, SWEDEN;
[2]Chalmers University of Technology, Computer Engineering, SE-412 96 Göteborg, SWEDEN

Abstract: Research in distributed dependable control systems within the automotive industry is of high importance today. One reason is the introduction of more mechatronical systems. Volvo Car Corporation and the Royal Institute of Technology initiated a joint project in October 2002 to target this technology change. The project was named FAR, which stands for Function and ARchitecture integration. FAR focused on the development of drive-by-wire systems using model based development. The deliveries from the project were a tool chain for automatic code generation from Matlab Simulink and Matlab Stateflow models and also a prototype vehicle in scale 1:5. It was a very successful project and the result was delivered to Volvo Cars in June 2003. The project deliveries have been further developed at Volvo Cars since then. Primarily, a new hazard analysis method has been developed and new fault tolerance mechanisms have been implemented.

Key words: dependable systems; drive-by-wire; model based development; hazard analysis; redundancy; fault tolerance; electrical architecture; time-triggered CAN; case study.

1. INTRODUCTION

The automotive industry faces new challenges as more functionality is implemented using mechatronical solutions. At the same time, challenges as increased complexity and high dependability requirements must be handled. The dependability requirements will be in the same order as for fly-by-wire systems. It is also crucial to meet low development costs, short development time, high degree of reusability, and quality targets.

Therefore, the automotive industry needs new approaches in product development and engineers skilled to develop mechatronical system. These were the main reasons for initiating this project. In the FAR project, Volvo Cars and the Royal Institute of Technology reached these objectives in a successful cooperation.

There were many lessons learned and valuable outcomes from the FAR project. The model based development used, allowed the project to handle the complexity of the given task. The prototype car that was developed has been used to implement and evaluate several design concepts like a fault tolerant electrical architecture and redundancy strategies. Further, the car implemented the time triggered CAN protocol, TTCAN. TTCAN gave the required support to synchronize the nodes in the cluster.

When the first phase of the FAR project was finished, the prototype moved to Volvo Cars in Gothenburg. At Volvo Cars, the main research was in the area of electrical architectures. It is mainly this work that is presented in this paper. Particularly the focus has been on an actuator based hazard analysis and fault tolerance mechanisms that uses inherent redundancy. This hazard analysis was used to guide the design of the implementation.

The paper starts with a short introduction to the dependability approach including hazard analysis and fault tolerance mechanisms in Section 2. Section 3 describes different architecture views that were developed and implemented in the prototype. The prototype is described in Section 4 and Section 5 summarizes the conclusions from the project.

2.   DEPENDABILITY APPROACH

The development of safety critical mechatronical products require structured design methods to assure system dependability. In this work, the focus was on an actuator based hazard analysis and specific redundancy strategies for fault tolerance.

2.1   Actuator Based Hazard Analysis

In the early stages in the design process, an actuator based hazard analysis was performed. The method used has been developed from the work by Johannessen (2001) and Papadopoulos (1999). Since it is the actuators that affect the system's environment, this actuator based approach is the logical approach for an early hazard analysis.

The failure classes used in this analysis are; *omission, commission,* and *stuck.* These classes are the worst case failures for any mechanical actuator. The class *omission* is interpreted as no energy is available at the actuator, *commission* is interpreted as maximum energy is applied to the actuator, and *stuck* is interpreted as a mechanical locking.

The chosen failure classes represent the three main failures of an actuator. Therefore, the analysis can indicate which state is the preferred fail state. For instance, if a brake failing in an *omission* state is less severe than both the *commission* and *stuck* states, then *omission* is the preferred fail state for the brake actuator. All failure classes are applied to each actuator and the system effect is analyzed.

The used severity levels are described in IEC-61508 (IEC 1998). They are *Catastrophic, Critical, Marginal,* and *Negligible.* These failure classes are used in a unique criticality ranking where the distribution between the severity levels for each failure class is considered. The sum of the distribution terms is 100%. This can be seen in the example in Table 1.

To be able to do a quantitative analysis, each severity level is assigned a weight, as shown in parenthesis in Table 1. The weights are application dependent, e.g. *Negligible* is of higher importance in a consumer product than for an industry product. The product of the severity level and the distribution numbers are added to a criticality number for each failure class.

Table 1. Example of actuator based hazard analysis for one brake actuator.

Failure Class	System severity	Distribution	Criticality	...
Omission	Catastrophic (10)	70%		
	Critical (6)	20%	8.4	
	Marginal (2)	10%		
	Negligible (1)	0%		
Commission	Catastrophic (10)	90%		
...			...	
Stuck	Catastrophic (10)	80%		
...			...	

The hazards that have a criticality that exceeds a predetermined threshold need to be handled. This method also supports a solvability analysis, where different design solutions are compared with each other. The analysis gives an indication of the best soultion.

In the FAR project, this hazard analysis gave valuable input to the design and implementation, particularly for fault handling concepts at the actuator level.

2.2   Redundancy Strategies for Fault Tolerance

The redundancy strategies used are described by Johannessen (2003) and Forsberg (2003) and include inherent redundancy, scalable software redundancy and local redundancy. These redundancy strategies are implemented in a top down approach starting with the most cost efficient strategy, which is the inherent redundancy. The most expensive approach, local redundancy, is used to fulfill fault tolerance requirements of permanent faults when inherent redundancy is impossible.

The inherent redundancy requires fail-silent actuators to be efficient. In FAR this is achieved by using wheel nodes that monitor each other by a fault handler module. The front and rear wheel nodes are grouped together to achieve a more dynamically stable system. The disable signals are directly connected to the actuators and are activated by the monitoring node to avoid unintended behavior. It is vital that the signal is an active action by the monitoring node. This approach requires a sane node to shut down the controlled node. A schematic of this solution is shown in Figure 2. An alternative solution that was implemented was to reset the controlling node instead of disabling the actuator. However, this approach was analyzed to be less safe since a reseted node has to reintegrate in the system. Therefore, it was used as a secondary fault handling mechanism.

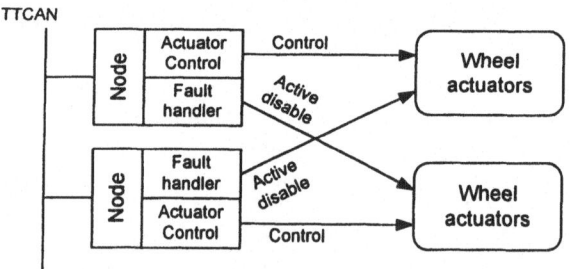

Figure 1. The monitoring node concept used to achieve fail-silent actuators.

3.   ARCHITECTURE VIEWS

The FAR architecture is a further development of the Sirius 2001 architecture (Johannessen 2003) and the conceptual study of a distributed JAS 39 Gripen architecture (Forsberg 2003). This updated FAR architecture contains several different views. In this section, the functional, logical, hardware, software, deployment, and TTCAN views are described.

To capture the requirements of the system, a functional view is first developed. The logical view is highly integrated with the vehicles dynamic functionality developed in Matlab Simulink and Matlab Stateflow. One further step towards the implementation is the software view that integrates all software components in the complete system. The hardware view describes the target system onto which the functions developed in the Matlab tools will execute. To integrate the functional, software and hardware systems, a deployment view is needed. This view is also important when implementing fault tolerance and redundancy. The TTCAN view describes the communication system used in the project.

3.1   Functional View

UML Use cases were used in the early design phases to capture the requirements of the project. Figure 1 shows the project's Use case diagram. This diagram includes three users; the *Project Stakeholder*, the *Driver* of the car, and the *System Developer*. The *Project Stakeholder* is interested in the project as a whole, for visualizing new technology, education and research activities and also for marketing purposes. Both the *Project Stakeholder* and the *System Developer* can be a *Driver,* who operates the prototype vehicle. The *System Developer* is the engineer that develops the system and uses it for experiments.

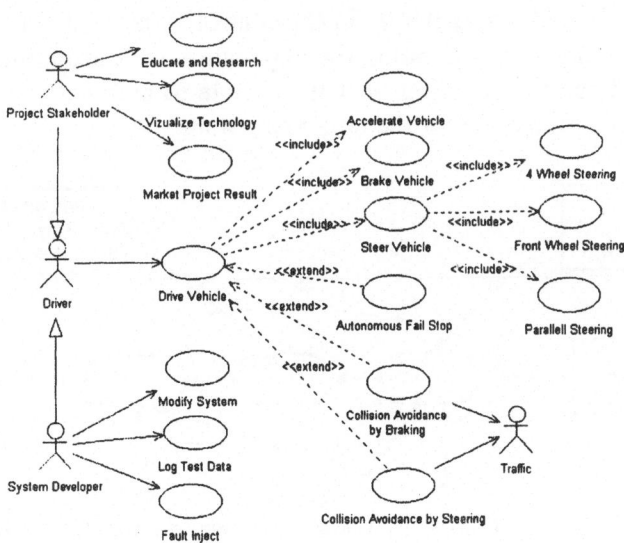

Figure 2. The FAR UML Use case diagram

3.2   Logical View

The logical view shown in Figure 3 is the basis in the scalable software redundancy strategy described by Johannessen (2003). Further, many control-by-wire systems can be modeled and designed according to the model in Figure 3. The global control functionality considers vehicle dynamics and the local control functionality handles loop closure for all actuators. All objects should be designed with as few dependencies as possible to support reusability and reduce complexity.

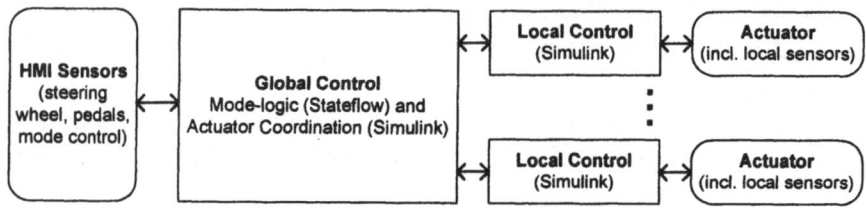

Figure 3. The logical view of the FAR architecture.

3.3   Software View

The software view in Figure 4 is the base for automatic code generation from Matlab Simulink and Matlab Stateflow using dSPACE TargetLink. Further, the clock tick from the TTCAN controller is used for distributed node synchronization. By separating the application code from the low level code such as I/O and scheduling, it was possible to automatically generate and modify application code for the target hardware.

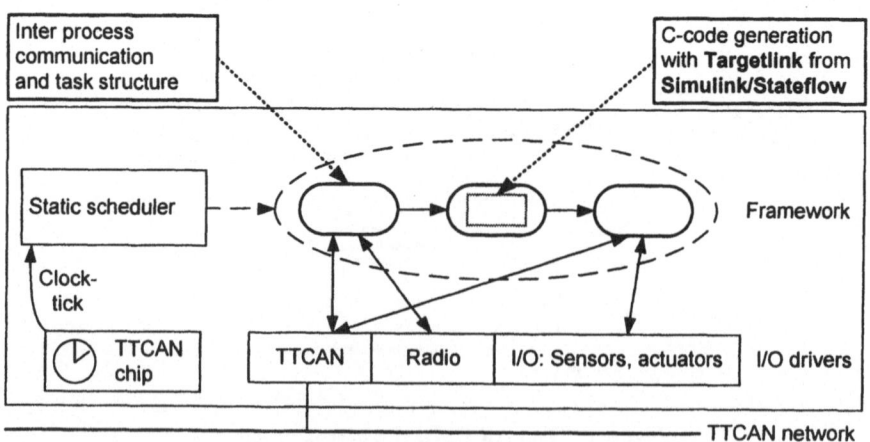

Figure 4. The software view of the FAR project.

3.4   Hardware View

The hardware view in Figure 5 shows the hardware components used in the system. There are six Motorola 68340 microcontrollers connected with a TTCAN network. The microcontrollers run at 25 MHz and are equipped with external A/D and D/A converters.

Each wheel has a dedicated node and there is one node for environment sensors. To coordinate the whole system there is one driver node that is connected through a radio link to a HMI node. The HMI node is further connected to a joystick or a steering wheel and pedals.

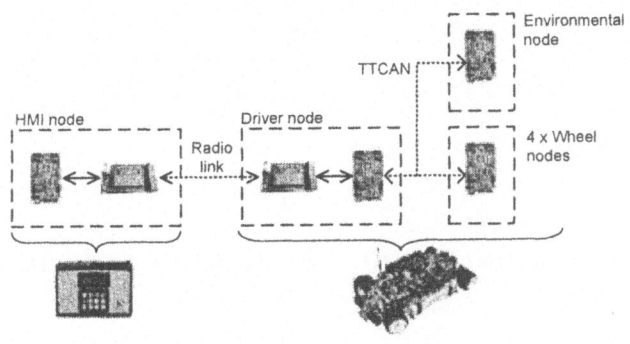

Figure 5. The Hardware view of the FAR car

3.5   Deployment View

The deployment view in Figure 6 is vital for implementing redundancy strategies and fault tolerance concepts described in section 2.2. In the scalable software redundancy concept, several instances of the global control calculations are executed in the distributed system and the results are shared in the cluster using a broadcast communication system.

Since all results from the global calculations are broadcasted, all nodes have a consistent view of the system. These broadcasted results are voted on in each wheel node, which gives a high degree of fault tolerance for transient faults.

Further, the par-wise monitoring and fault handler in Figure 2 was implemented. This applies to the brake, steer and drive actuators. Figure 6 shows these mechanisms for the front right node denoted FR. The other nodes are symmetrically identical.

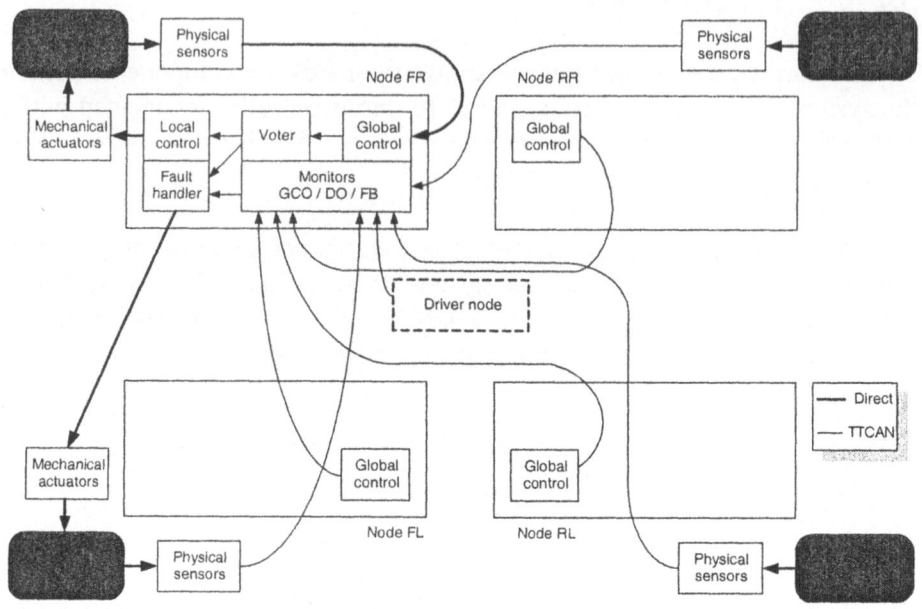

Figure 6. The deployment view of the FAR project with fault handling strategies for the front right wheel node.

3.6   TTCAN View

The communication protocol that was implemented in the FAR platform was TTCAN (ISO 2003). TTCAN was chosen since it is a potential protocol for the automotive industry that would fulfill the system's requirements. The protocol supports both time triggered and event triggered operation. Event triggered operation is implemented in the protocol using standard CAN arbitration mechanisms.

TTCAN is particularly useful in distributed control systems since the TTCAN controllers can provide a clock tick. These clock ticks can be used to synchronize the nodes in the cluster. All clocks in a TTCAN cluster are synchronized by CAN messages distributed by redundant time masters. Further, time triggered communication is predictable in the time domain.

The FAR car uses time triggered operation and approximately 20% of the available bandwidth. However, the communication could be further optimized. The cycle time of the communication system was 32 ms and consequently the global cycle frequency was 31 Hz.

4. PROTOTYPE

The developed car prototype has four-wheel steering, individual braking and four-wheel drive, with a total of three actuators per wheel. The car, shown in Figure 7 can be programmed into several modes of operation, including three different types of steering and three different types of wheel drive. This prototype will be valuable as a basis for future projects with drive-by-wire research.

Figure 7. The developed prototype vehicle in scale 1:5.

5. CONCLUSIONS

This project allowed us to verify some concept in the development of drive-by-wire systems. Primarily, many dependability increasing concepts were validated, both to provide fault tolerance and also to be implementable in an embedded system.

The developed hazard analysis method also proved useful in the development process. It efficiently identifies real and critical failures that need to be handled. This is a requirement in the development of safety critical systems. By combining criticality and distribution of criticality for each failure class, valuable information could be obtained.

The use of TTCAN gave valuable insights. It is a highly interesting protocol, not only as a replacement of traditional CAN, but also as a communication protocol for safety critical real-time systems.

The developed prototype vehicle has shown to be as useful as expected. It is always preferred to have a real system when demonstrating new functionality or implementing new concepts to increase understandability.

It is also important to consider the teams developing the drive-by-wire systems. These mechatronical systems have a very high degree of complexity and also many degrees of freedom that give a larger possible solution space. The designers need some form of tools to handle the complexity. In this project the complexity was handled using several architectural views. Since each view considered only one aspect the complexity was manageable by the designers.

ACKNOWLEDGEMENTS

We wish to thank Professor Törngren and his students at the Royal Institute of Technology who built the FAR car and developed the framework for the automatic code generation. Further, we wish to thank Roger Johansson at Chalmers University of Technology for his support on the hardware used.

The project was funded by The Program Board for the Swedish Automotive Research Program at VINNOVA, the Swedish Agency for Innovation Systems.

REFERENCES

Forsberg, K., *Design Principles of Fly-By-Wire Architectures*, PhD. Thesis, Dept. of Computer Engineering, Chalmers University of Technology, Goteborg, Sweden, 2003.

IEC, *IEC-61508: Functional safety of electrical/electronic/programmable electronic safety-related Systems*, International Electro-technical Commission, 1998.

ISO, *Working Draft ISO 11898-4 - Road Vehicles – Controller Area Network (CAN) – Part 4: Time Triggered Communication*, International Organization for Standardization, 2003.

Johannessen, P., System Safety Design of the SIRIUS 2001 Drive-by-Wire Car – In Retrospect, *Proceedings of the International System Safety Conference 2003*, Ottawa, Canada, 2003.

Johannessen, P., Grante, C., Alminger, A., Eklund, U., and J. Torin, Hazard Analysis in Object Oriented Design of Dependable Systems, *Proceedings of the 2001 International Conference on Dependable Systems and Networks*, Goteborg, 2001, pp. 507-512.

Papadopoulos, Y. and McDermid, J., Hierarchically Performed Hazard Origin and Propagation Studies, *Proceedings of SAFECOMP'99, 18th International Conference on Computer Safety, Reliability and Security*, Toulouse, 1999.

HARDWARE DESIGN AND PROTOCOL SPECIFICATION FOR THE CONTROL AND COMMUNICATION WITHIN A MECHATRONIC SYSTEM

André Luiz de Freitas Francisco[1], Achim Rettberg[2] and Andreas Hennig[2]

[1]*University of Paderborn – MLaP, Pohlweg 98, D-33098 Paderborn, Germany,*
Tel:. +49 5251 605576, Fax: + 49 5251 605579,
Email: Andre.Francisco@MLaP.de;
[2]*University of Paderborn – C-LAB, Fuerstenallee 11, D-33102 Paderborn, Germany,*
Tel:. +49 5251 606110, Fax: + 49 5251 606065,
Email: Achim.Rettberg@c-lab.de, Andreas.Hennig@c-lab.de

Abstract: This paper describes a communication system for the test track that will be used to develop the components of a new train concept, the RailCab. The demand for flexible hardware architecture and optimized communication channels motivated this project. The aim of the network is to control frequency converters for linear motor sections placed along the track. The vehicles that are moving along the track at a given time will issue the commands to each motor. In order to optimize the communication functions, new hardware components and a new protocol were designed, so that modules accessing network are able to do this in a more direct way.

Key words: Mechatronic systems, hardware design, protocol specification, control systems, communication systems.

1.   INTRODUCTION

Stand-alone systems are increasingly becoming obsolete. For some applications, they are considered useless in comparison to the distributed ones, the latter being able to use all the features that are present on each element of a network. Distributed systems are especially useful in constructing complex systems that comprise different function modules; they offer the possibility of sharing resources and can be used together nodes that can cooperate to accomplish a certain task.

Although the number of communication interfaces available on the market has largely increased in the past decades, there are still new applications which make specific demands that cannot be completely fulfilled by the available standards in terms of cost/benefit or even particular technical characteristics [9]. The special case to be described in this work requires a protocol that has to guarantee very short latency times (some microseconds at most) but can sometimes dispense extremely high bandwidths as the packets transmitted are relative small and the number of nodes is restricted.

The case study presented here is the RailCab [1] test track. The RailCab, developed at the University of Paderborn, is an innovative variation of conventional trains and based on individual, autonomous shuttles that can be ordered by a client to transport him/her directly from one city to another. The service being personalized, there is no need for the passenger to change trains or wait for fixed departures: the shuttle just sets off at the defined time and location and travels to its destination non-stop. This technology is based on linear motors which are used to move and brake the shuttles and can be installed on existing railroad tracks. The whole track is made up of a succession of linear-motor sections which can be controlled individually. For the shuttle to run smoothly and at a defined velocity, a linear motor has to be synchronized to its respective neighbors as the vehicle is passing over them. However, not only the motors have to be synchronized but their current must also be controlled by a local ECU. To provide these features, a networking system is required that can be optimized to this application. The aim of this paper is to propose a concept to be used with the first prototypes on the test track and to present the basic protocol and hardware platform required to accomplish this task.

2.   TEST TRACK

The RailCab test track was built up at the University of Paderborn on a scale of 1:2.5 and has a total length of about 530 meters. It is made up of the rail track itself and 83 linear-motor sections, each one controlled by a servo device; all of these are distributed to 4 stations along the track. Additionally, there is a control room where the track functions are coordinated and monitored. Figure 1 represents the track.

The servos, or frequency converters, are made up of a processing unit and power electronics. The processing unit is the component where the current controller for the servo runs. This unit also provides communication interfaces (CAN-bus and RS-485) to other equipments. At present, the entire network operates using the CAN-bus interface which allows an external system to set the reference values for the motor frequency, amplitude, and phase. However, the RS-485 (SSI) interface is faster and provides features that surpass those of the CAN-bus. Extra features include, e.g., the possibility to let the controllers run externally, using only the servo sensors for reading signals and writing values for high voltages to registers in the frequency converter that is then in charge to generate the power outputs. Due to its advantages, the RS-485 servo interface was chosen for the network described in this paper.

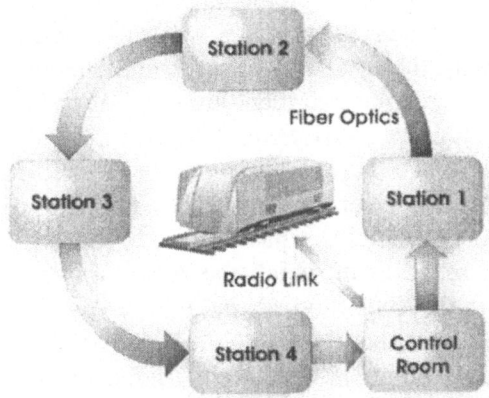

Figure 1. RailCab test track

Networking between the control room and the servo stations is done via a fiber optic (see [6], [7]) channel where all five nodes are interconnected by a point-to-point link that represents a ring topology (fig. 1).

So far two communication interfaces that are going to be used for the actual implementation were described: RS-485 for the servos and fiber optics between the stations. For these links to communicate with one another, additional interfaces and hardware are required and will be described in the following sections.

3. NETWORK FUNCTIONALITIES

The proposed network is intended to gradually provide new functionalities according to the following three steps:

1. Establishment of a networking system that, from a remote operation point, will be able to distribute reference values to all linear motors on the track. These reference values are set by a pre-defined unit located at the control room. At this stage the timing requirements are not as strict

as those for the following two steps once the current controllers run on the servos themselves.

2. Disabling of the internal current controllers of the servos and implement them using an external ECU. This will make possible the tests of new control strategies for the linear motors - one of the tasks of the RailCab development team. To implement this second stage the Motorola PowerPC MPC555 microcontroller will be used. A set of four boards, each containing one of these processors, is going to be connected to the network, initially in a remote position, to control the entire track. Some prior tests have shown that implementation of the current controllers at sampling rates of 8 kHz requires almost the entire microcontroller capacity; as a result, the four boards can simultaneously control up to 4 linear-motor sections. Although there are many more sections to control, four boards should be sufficient because initially there will be simultaneously no more than two shuttles on the track, and each one of them requires a maximum of only two sections operating at a given time (considering that the vehicle is passing from one section to the next). This illustrates a scenario in which the processing power is scheduled dynamically to the active motors, in an "on demand" manner. The immediate advantage is that the number of hardware elements needed to implement the controllers is drastically reduced; on the other hand, though, the communication requirements will increase significantly because the controllers are in a remote position and have to use the network to transfer the servo's input/output data.

3. The third step is meant to minimize the communication drawbacks by distributing the controllers evenly along the track, thus reducing demands on the network bandwidth and creating segments that can make safety or operability decisions autonomously if, for example, the connection to the respective neighbors is interrupted. Another possibility here is to build the ECUs using FPGAs as processing elements. Such devices are appropriate for fast and parallel computations and could therefore be used to implement the current controllers.

Now that the basic idea for the network has been expounded, we can go on to propose appropriate hardware devices.

4.   HARDWARE PLATFORM

The hardware described here is based on the Rabbit system [2], [8]. The Rabbit platform is intended for the rapid prototyping of distributed mechatronic systems and made up of three main boards: one with an MPC555 PowerPC, another with a Xilinx Virtex-E FPGA, and the last including a FireWire (IEEE 1394) communication interface. The new processing hardware developed is to be used as an ECU for the current controllers and makes use of the concept of microcontroller/FPGA integration. Although the FireWire module is no longer available on the new hardware, there are also some new communication interfaces, such as 4 LVDS (low-voltage differential signaling) [10] ports and a 10/100 Mbps Ethernet port. Additional features include the possibility for the microcontroller to program the FPGA or its Prom, as well as the FPGA to write the MPC555 memories. This is especially helpful if some reprogramming tasks must be performed remotely (some dozens of meters away), which is the case for the test track. The diagram of this board is shown in figure 2:

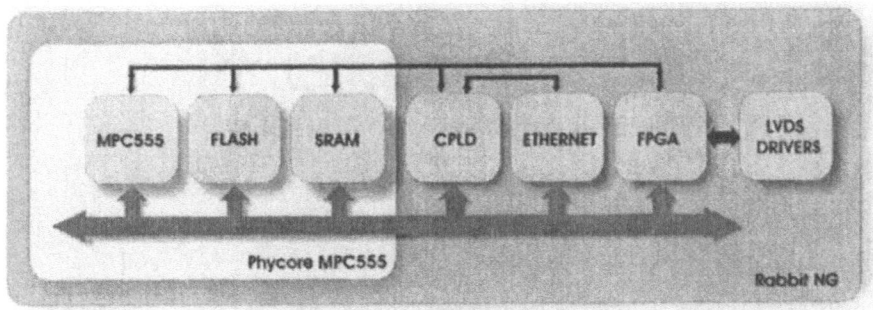

Figure 2. Rabbit NG platform

Communication among all the boards takes place mainly via the LVDS interface. This serial standard offers high signaling rates, but is restricted to just about 40 Mbps for each pair of wires on the boards for this system. Each one of the so-called LVDS ports available on the board contain actually four differential pairs; thus the total throughput for each of the four ports is about 160 Mbps. The reason for using this standard is that it is a merely physical one, i.e., the entire protocol that is being used over it can be implemented to met the requirements of specific applications. As the network proposed in this paper basically defines a new protocol, the choice of the LVDS standard is justified. All LVDS interfaces are connected to the FPGA, where the entire protocol is actually implemented. The programming language chosen for this purpose was VHDL.

As stated above, communication infrastructure between the stations on the track uses fiber optics only. In order to transmit the data of the LVDS interface transparently via optical fibers an adapter board was also built up. With this solution, it will not matter to the user if electrical or optical cables are used to connect two boards. Fiber optics is a good solution for the link between the stations because the involved distances are rather high for electrical cables and also due to the fact that the linear motors' electromagnetic fields may cause interferences on electrical cables.

At this point, there is still the need to connect the motor servos to the network. Because the servos have their own communication standard, a third board (called SSI) must also be developed. This board operates as a bridge between the LVDS (network) and RS-485 (servo) interfaces. Once again an FPGA is used as the processing element for this task.

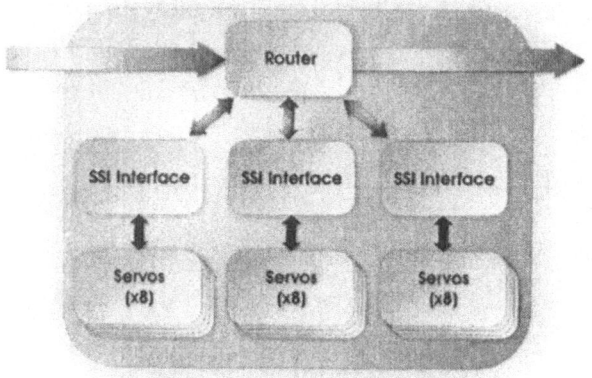

Figure 3. Architecture of a station

Now that we have described the boards, we need an architecture to combine them. The architecture of the four servo stations is shown in figure 3. For these stations, each SSI board has connections for up to 8 servos and a LVDS link to a router (fig. 3). The router is actually the MPC555 board with a LVDS-to-fiber optics, but is represented as a single block for simplification.

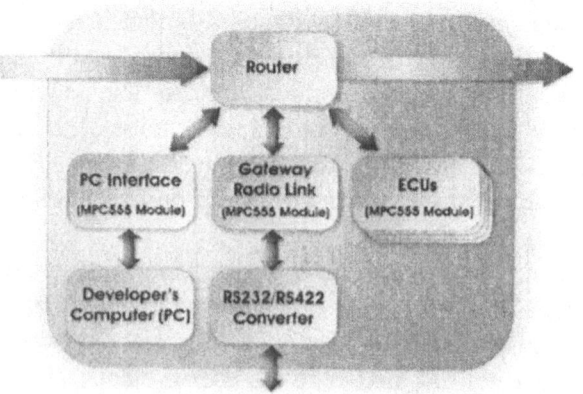

Figure 4. Architecture of a garage

The architecture for the control room is different (figure 4) because its functions differ from those of the servo stations. The basic difference is that the ECUs are for the first development phase centralized in the control room. Additionally, one processing board operates as a gateway for a radio link between the test track and the shuttles and another one is used as an interface to a developer's PC via Ethernet communication.

5.   PROTOCOL SPECIFICATION

All the messages in the proposed network fit into one packet. A message is sent only once and will not be repeated even if an error is detected. A node address serves as a unique identifier for each component on a network. Thus, as this project has many similarities with standard networks, it resembles sometimes the Internet Protocol Addressing [3] strategies. The messages that pass through the network can have different purposes. For this reason, four different types of messages were defined: emergency, synchronization, data, and maintenance. The priority scheme is very simple: it considers just the type of message and the order of arrival. As regards priority, the order of the messages from the highest to the lowest is: emergency, synchronization, data, and maintenance.

There are many techniques to detect garbled messages. Three of them are the most common ones used in data communications: Checksum, Error Detection, and Error Correction. Check Sum is a method that uses module summation to detect errors in a stream of data. The problem is that the probability of not identifying an error is equal to the sum of all bits in the message. Error correction can be implemented in two different ways: error correction by itself, in the form of Forward Error Correction (FEC), and strategies such as Automatic Repeat Request (ARQ) that function in combination with a retransmission of corrupted data. Although the first is a good technique, error detection is generally preferred. The main reason is that the number of overhead bits required to implement error detection is much smaller than the number of bits needed for correction [4]. The CRC is a very powerful error detection technique used to obtain data reliability and is easy to implement. In order to employ this technique, the transmitter appends an extra n-bit sequence to every frame. In the present project, it was chosen the 16 bit standard polynomial, the "CRC-16".

To receive data from the memory and send it to the network, it is necessary to modify the data into the correct data format. Another task that has to be implemented is retrieval of the line status, which is used by the memory controller. The main modules specified to fulfil those tasks are the following: *Receiver, Transceiver, Manager, Switching Matrix,* and *Registers* (see figure 5).

The *Receiver* receives the data stream and store 16 bits segments in a FIFO. Furthermore, it has a ready/acknowledge handshaking mechanism with the Switch Manager. When the *Receiver* sets "ready", the priority of the current block is available at the outputs. When a CRC error is detected, the packet is ignored, the FIFO is emptied and the *Receiver* waits for a new packet.

The *Transceiver* transmits the contents of the four message types according to the given priority, if messages are available. It is ensured that the message with the highest priority is transmitted first. It is not necessary to calculate the CRC because it is already calculated by the manager.

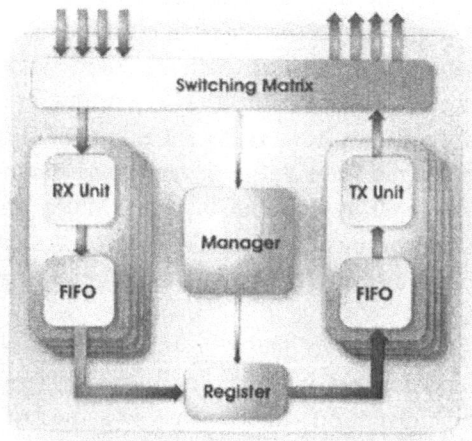

Figure 5. Modules of the protocol implementation

The *Switching Matrix* is necessary to speed communication up. Once the destination address of an incoming packet has been received, and the respective output channel is idle, the data stream is directly sent to the destination.

The *Manager* receives requests from the *Receiver* (RX) and the *Switching Matrix* and then directs the received packet to the transmit memory of the *Transceiver* via an internal bus. The *Registers* are necessary to store the packets internally.

5.1   Memory Management

The RAM memory available in FPGAs for data storage is limited (e.g., Spartan-IIE™ FPGAs range from 32 to 288 kbits) [5]. For this reason, it is necessary to manage the memory to get the most advantage of each free bit space. Many generic algorithms could be implemented to this purpose. Most of them are based in linked queues, binary trees, or even mapping tables that contain information about each space in the memory.

The memory management of this project should be simple. Besides choosing the best algorithm to fit the project needs, it was necessary to think about logical space constraints in FPGAs. Each *Receiver* has only one FIFO to store the incoming messages. A *Transceiver* needs four FIFOs, one for each message type. For the *Transceiver,* a method based on queues was created, considering all the constraints and features of the specific protocol and available hardware configuration. This method uses the memory and takes care of the performance of the concurrent running processes.

Figure 6 illustrates the way the memory management works within the *Transceiver.* For each type of message, one FIFO was created for each transmission channel. The horizontal lines in figure 6 represent the FIFOs, considering the whole illustration as a matrix. The memory manager uses the next available space on the FIFO to store the message. To specify the destination, the *Manager* reads the destination address from the incoming packets and directs it to the appropriated output FIFO. A transmission channel pools the FIFOs, starting from the highest to the lowest priority. After the message is send it is popped from the FIFO.

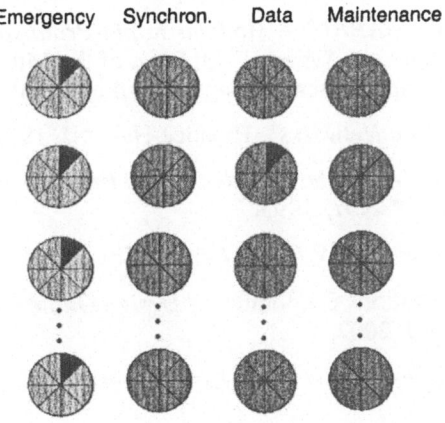

Emergency   Synchron.   Data   Maintenance

Figure 6. Memory management scheme

5.2   Implementation

All the VHDL code was developed using the Xilinx™ ISE 6.2 software. To simulate these designs Synopsys™ and ModelSim™ were employed. The MPC555 software was developed using Metrowerks™ Codewarrior 6.5 compiler.

6.   CONCLUSION AND FUTURE WORK

The present paper briefly described the RailCab project. It also presented the hardware, including the protocol to control the RailCab test track. In combination with the hardware boards, it was possible to specify a software protocol and a management of data passing through a network. All these features were implemented by means of VHDL, with access to the higher-level function enabled by a microcontroller programmed in C. The standards used in the physical layer were LVDS, Fiber Optics, and RS-485.

The approach presented has supplied all the bases for the specifications. After putting the communication system in operation, the experience gathered testing mechatronic functions can be used as a feedback in view of the design of a system for a 1:1 realization, which surely has many more requirements (e.g., safety and extensibility). In addition, the flexibility of the hardware allows scenarios including different topologies and protocols, which are naturally important when implementing new approaches and evaluating trade-offs.

REFERENCES

[1]   University of Paderborn. *"Neue Bahntechnik Paderborn"*. 2002.

[2]   Zanella, M., et. al. *"RABBIT: A Modular Rapid-Prototyping Platform for Distributed Mechatronic Systems"*. In: Proc. of the 14th Symposium on Integrated Circuits and Systems Design; Brasília, Brazil, 2001.

[3]   Black, Uyless. *"Data Networks"*. Prentice-Hall, NJ, 1989.

[4]   Williams, Ross N. *"A Painless Guide to CRC Error Detection Algorithms"*. *Rocksoft Technical Report*, 1993.

[5]   Xilinx Inc. *"Spartan-II 2.5V FPGA Family Manual"*. San José, CA, 2000.

[6]   Radiant Communications Corporation. *"Design Guide – Fiber Optic Basics"*. South Plainfield, NJ, 2002.

[7]   Agilent Technologies. *"Fiber Optic Components Cookbook"*. Palo Alto, CA, 2002.

[8]   De Freitas Francisco, André Luiz. *"Realization of controllers for mechatronic systems using FPGAs"*. Bachelor-Thesis, University Paderborn/MLaP, 2001.

[9]   Helmers, Scott A. *"Data Communications: A Beginner's Guide to Concepts and Technology"*. Prentice-Hall, NJ, 1989.

[10] National Semiconductor. *"LVDS Owner's Manual"*. Santa Clara, CA, 2000.

A DECENTRALIZED SELF-ORGANIZED APPROACH FOR WIRELESS SENSOR NETWORKS

Jean-Paul Jamont, Michel Occello, André Lagrèze
Laboratoire de Conception et d'Intégration des Systèmes
Institut National Polytechnique de Grenoble
F-26000 Valence, France
jean-paul.jamont@esisar.inpg.fr, michel.occello@iut-valence.fr, andre.lagreze@iut-valence.fr

Abstract: This paper deals with an application of multiagent systems to management in wireless sensor networks (WSN). This WSN will be applied to monitor an underground hydrographic network (the EnvSys project). We present the EnvSys project, the multiagent systems (MAS) and their application in WSN. After we propose an adaptive infrastructure of autonomous agents to route the information in the best way, in consideration to strong constraints on energy resources. Interesting simulation results are discussed.

Keywords: Multiagent system, wireless sensor network, self-organization.

1. INTRODUCTION

Considering complex embedded control systems as decentralized cooperative nodes networks is a recent but attractive way to design intelligent applications.

In some cases, especially for aggressive environment applications, nodes cannot be interconnected through classical field buses and wireless technology is required. The whole system becomes an open network of intelligent autonomous embedded entities controlling sensors and actuators.

We introduce in this paper a multiagent approach to design such applications. Further, we intend to show that using behavior modelling, cooperative aspects and organizational techniques of multiagent systems allows increasing the overall efficiency of embedded systems.

In a first section we describe the EnvSys project, an underground river instrumentation system, which motivates this study. We expose in a second section multiagent systems (MAS) and their application to wireless intelligent sensor networks (WSN). We then propose our multiagent approach based on self-organization to manage the functional integrity of the decentralized embedded nodes network. Finally, after a presentation of our simulation platform and of some quantitative results, we give an insight to the operational embedded architecture.

2.   THE ENVSYS PROJECT

2.1   Origin and issue

The purpose of the ENVironment SYStem project is to monitor an underground river system (Jamont, J.-P. et al, 2002). At the origine of this project are the difficulties to measure various parameters in an underground river system is a complex task : access to this type of underground galleries requires help from speleologists, installation of wire communications networks is difficult, especially because an hydrographic system has a chaotic structure and, in the case of radio communication, the underground aspect complicate wave propagation (these techniques are not totally mastered).

The general idea of the project is to study the feasibility of a WSN from an existing physical layer. This will allow wireless instrumentation of a subterranean river system. Such a network would present an important interest in many domains: the study of underground flows, the monitoring of deep collecting, flooding risk management, river system detection of pollution risks, etc.

In a subterranean river system, the interesting parameters to measure are numerous: temperature of air and water, air pressure and if possible water pressure for the flooded galleries, pollution rate by classical pollutants, water flow, draft speed, etc. All this information will be collected at the immediate hydrographic network exit by a work station like a PC. These data will be processed to activate alarms, study the progress of a certain pollution according to miscellaneous measuring parameters, determine a predictive model of the whole network by relating the subterranean parameters measures of our system with the overground parameters measures more classically on the catchment basin.

Every sensor has a limited transmission range due to rock blocks properties. This limitation results from three points: the technological solutions which are used to achieve the sensor transmission module (frequency, power, antenna), the implementation of these solutions and, finally, the environment. Indeed, according to the obstacles it will have to go through, the electromagnetic waves will not be usable at the same distance for each direction. The transmission zone will not be modeled by a sphere.

2.2 Difficulties of communication management in wireless sensor networks

WSN are a particular type of adhoc network. In adhoc network, communication between two hosts is generally not direct. To communicate, they require help from others host. It is a multihop communication. Thus, the sensors have two tasks : make their own measure and assure routing functionnality for others sensors. This multihop caracteristic create an important routing problem (routing consist to find the path between a sender to a receiver node) because all the adhoc routing protocol use flooding technics (in a flooding scheme a host give the message to all its neigboors etc.) and the location updating is difficult (location updating consist to maintening information about its neighboors).

A lot of problems are added in the case of WSN. An overview of these difficulties, collectively accepted today, is given in (Zhang, W. et al, 2002). Some of them concern the sensors (hardware limitation for financial cost reason) and its energy ressource. Sensor's battery are difficult to replace, one of the global system aim so to reduce as possible the energy cost. When it has nothing to do generally for conserving energy they enter in a sleep mode. When they communicate they must use good routing protocol and optimal way (generally the criteria will be the number of hop). An agressive environment like the underground river system can cause some internal fault for sensors. So WSN must be very adaptive, fault tolerant and self-stabilized : a sensor failure must not have an important impact on the system. This system must provide reliable communication and, sometimes, adapt to "real-time" constraints. Furthermore, in the case of mobile devices the infrastructure of sytems are not persistant.

Our work deals with the analysis of the problem using a MAS approach. The main contribution of the work presented in this paper is situated at a logical level : we don't discuss about the physical layer. We talk about the monitoring of this system, the complex environment, the kind of intelligence giving to the network.

3. MULTIAGENT AND WSN

3.1 Agents and multiagents systems

An agent is a software entity endowed with autonomous behaviors and embedded in an environment which it can perceive and in which it acts.

This entity has its own objective. Autonomy is the main concepts in the agent issue: it is the ability of agents to control their actions and their internal states. The autonomy of agents implies no centralized control. The power of an agent decomposition is the decentralization of the intelligence, i.e. the decision capabilities, and of entities' knowledge.

A MAS is a set of agents situated in a common environment, which interact and attempt to reach a set of goals. Through these interactions a global behavior can emerge. The emergence process is a way to obtain, from cooperation, dynamic results that cannot be predicted in a deterministic way.

The multiagent methods aim at decreasing the complexity of system design by a decentralized analysis. There are several MAS methods (Iglesias, C. et al, 1998) among which most are centered on the analysis of agents'tasks as the methods Gaia and MaSE, others on the roles or on the organization as the method AALAADIN.

We are thereafter going to be interested in the AEIO decomposition. We will follow the method of multiagent design discussed in (Occello and Koning, 2000), associated to this MAS decomposition. It proposes a decomposition according to four axes collectively accepted today. The *agent axis* (A) gathers all elements for defining and constructing these entities. The *environment* axis (E) deals with elements necessary for the MAS realization such as the perception of this environment and the actions one can do on it. The *interaction axis* (I) includes all elements which are in use for structuring the external interactions among the agents (agent communication language, interaction protocols) The *organization axis* (O) allows to order agent groups in organization determined according to their roles.

We chose to apply this multiagent method for our problem because it privileges an explicit description of the interactions and the environment.

3.2   Wireless sensor networks management

WSN management and MAS.   The distributed and open nature of WSN means that the MAS approach is an adapted answer. Another advantage of this approach is the external representation of the interactions and of the organization. External representations offer multiple possibilities such as the monitoring by an external observer.

A few works reaching the same objectives show that the approach is interesting. We can quote the ActComm (Gray, 2000) project which is a military project for which the routing of information is essential: it aims at studying the communication management between a soldier team and a military camp via a satellite. We can also mention the work of (Petriu,

E.M. et al, 2002) on wireless networks of mobile autonomous intelligent sensors where agents are used to achieve flexible and open cell assembly. Another example is the Unmanned Ground Vehicle Program ARPA's project (Cook,D.J. et al, 1996) which approaches the information management resulting from a group of autonomous observation military vehicles. The problem described in (Zhang, W. et al, 2002) is very similar to our problem but the approach is very different since the used technique is based on distributed stochastic algorithms.

MAS are used in very active way for service descriptions and service discovery in ad-hoc networks (Chen, H. et al, 2000).

WSN and routing protocol. The WSN associated routing protocols are centered on the flooding techniques. There are three differents type of routing protocols families. The *reactive* protocols using no routing table. The main idea of this family is to reduce the flows by creating clusters for example. The *proactive* protocols using routing tables, periodically updated, and for those it is necessary to exchange control packets (energy cost). The *hybrid* protocols adopting the reactive protocol behavior and, if necessary, using routing tables for increasing efficiency.

4. A MAS FOR WSN COMMUNICATION MANAGEMENT

4.1 AEIO analysis of this problem

As previously examined, this approach is articulated around four axes.

The environment axis. The environment will be made of the measurable information. It is deterministic, non episodic, dynamic and continuous. Agents are situated but don't know their position.

The organization axis. In this type of application no one can control the organization a priori. Relations between agents are going to emerge from the evolution of the agents'states and from their interactions. We are going to be content with fixing the organization parameters, i.e. agents'tasks, agents'roles.

The organizational basic structures (see fig 1) are composed of one *group representative agent* (managing the communication in his group), some *connection agents* (they know different representative agents and they can belong to several groups) and some *ordinary members* (active in the communication process only for their own tasks. They don't ensure information relay).

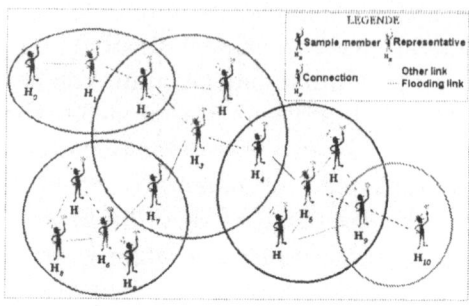

Figure 1.   Group organisation for communication management

Because a representative agent is the most sollicited agent in a group, the best one having the most important level of energy and the most important number of neighbors. We use a role allocation based self-organization mechanism involving the election of a representative agent based on a function which estimates the adequation between it desire to be the boss and its capacity to be. The organization is modified only when a problem occurs. We don't try to maintain it if we have no communication.

The interaction axis.   The agents will interact only with the agents in acquaintance (an agent is in acquaintance with another if it is aware of its existence). Agents interact by asynchronous exchange of messages (without rendez vous). Among the different protocols that we use, the choice of an introduction protocol is essential. Indeed, this protocol allows to the agents to be known, i.e. to bring their knowledge and their know-how to the agents' society. We defined thirteen different types of small messages.

The agent axis.   Sensors are modeled by agents. These agents have hybrid architectures, i.e. a composition of some pure types of architectures. Indeed, the agents will be of a cognitive type in case of a configuration alteration, it will be necessary for them to communicate and to manipulate their knowledge in order to have an efficient collaboration. On the other hand, in normal use it will be necessary for them to be reactive (stimuli/response paradigm) to be most efficient.
The agents have then to achieve a *measuring function* (the main work of a sensor, it consists in interacting with the environment to acquire information about one of the environment parameters) and a *communication task* for giving (if necessary) the information to other devices or relay-

ing neighbor's messages. All the agents have the same communication capabilities but the communicated data depend of their roles.

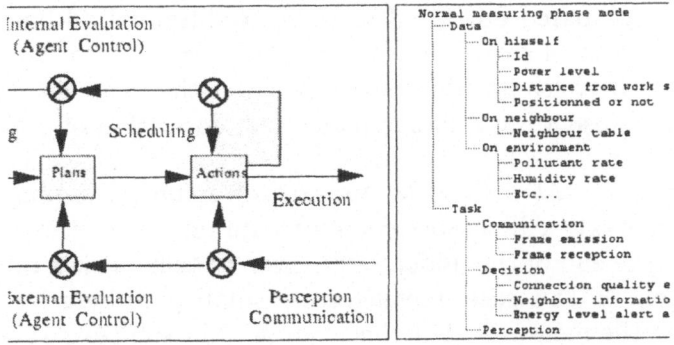

Figure 2.   Agent architecture and agent tasks tree

Using a hybrid architecture for the agents enables to combine the strong features of each of reactive and cognitive capabilities seen before. The ASTRO hybrid architecture (Occello, M. et al, 1998) is especially adapted to a real time context. The integration of deliberative and reactive capabilities is possible through the use of parallelism in the structure of the agent. Separating Reasoning/Adaptation and Perception/Communication tasks allows a continuous supervision of the evolution of the environment. The reasoning model of this agent is based on the Perception/Decision/Reasoning/Action paradigm. The cognitive reasoning is thus preserved, and predicted events contribute to the normal progress of the reasoning process.

5.   THE EXPERIMENTATION

In order to evaluate and improve such agents' software architectures and the cooperation techniques that they involve, we introduce a simulation stage in our development process.

5.1   Simulation Results

The simulation first allowed us to experiment our approach and the software solutions that we provide for the various problems. We can also quantify the emergence inferred by the MAS approach in this case.

The simulation software structure is very basic. In fact, we have two types of components: SimSensor and SimNetwork. A SimSensor component simulates the sensor behavior. It possesses its own model and architecture. All the sensors have the same communication capabilities.

They transmit their requests to the SimNetwork component sends this information to all sensors which can receive them, in the environment. SimNetwork can appear as the inference mechanism for the simulation.

We have compared our MAS to three traditionnal ad-hoc protocols. The DSDV protocol and the natural DSR protocol do not appear in this comparaison because its efficiency were lower than the ehanced version of DSR which use a route maintenance (memorization of main route).

Use case 1. At a first, let us present some performances in the ENVSYS context. All sensors communicate only with the workstation situated at the end of the undergound river system : it is a unidirectionnal protocol. In this case, messages are small (one byte for data type and four for the measure). For this example, three messages are send by five second. The same scenario is applied for the different protocols.

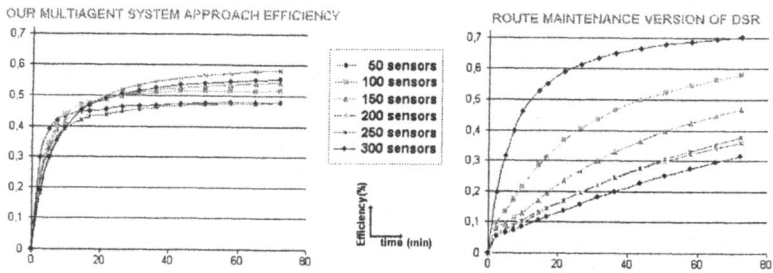

Figure 3. Approach comparison for unidirectionnal use case

We can see that the benefit (fig 3) of our approach is important. Quickly our routing method can deliver all messages with a good efficiency. Higher is the number of sensors better is the reactivity of our approach. We must note that if the system knows no pertubation or mobility variation of DSR will be better from an efficiency point of view. It is normal because in this case DSR learns all the routes (succession of sensors) allowing to communicate with the workstation. It is not really the case of our approach witch reason from the group and not from the sensors. One consequence is that the route used by the messages with our approach are not optimal.

Use case 2. In this case, we are in the ENVSYS context where the sensors communicate together for elaborating more complex measures. We choose to give to the message a size of thirty bytes. In this case the behavior of our approach is much better than DSR because is route management it more complicated. If we add some perturbations on these

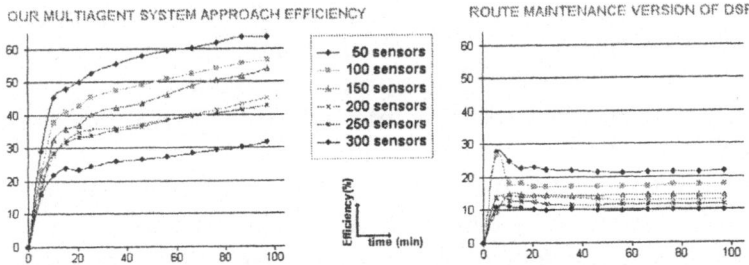

Figure 4. Approach comparison for the multidirectionnal use case

scenarios (one perturbation by three minutes) the efficiency is nearly the same (it is not the case for the DSDV protocol).

5.2 The operational embedded architecture

Therefore, we will demonstrate the feasibility of our approach. For the sensors we have chosen a classical three-layers architecture (physical layer/Link layer/Applicative layer).

We use the physical layer which is employed by NICOLA system, a voice transmission system used by the French speleological rescue teams (Graham, 1999). This layer is implemented in a digital signal processor rather than a full analogic system. Thereby we can keep good flexibility and we are able to apply further a signal processing algorithm to improve the data transmission.

The link layer used is a CAN (Controller Area Network) protocol stemming from the motorcar industry and chosen for its good reliability. The applicative layer is constituted by the agents' system. The agents are embedded on autonomous processor cards. These cards are equipped with communication modules and with measuring modules to carry out agent tasks relative to the instrumentation. These cards supply a real time kernel. The KR-51(the kernel's name) allows multi-task software engineering for C515C microcontroller. We can produce one task for one capability. We can then quite easily implement the parallelism inherent to agents and satisfy the real-time constraints.

6. CONCLUSION

This software agent architecture is embedded on autonomous processor cards. The MAS, which we are creating, is open: adding a sensor does not require a manual reconfiguration. Most of sensors'dysfunctions should not threaten the functional integrity of the whole system which should be fault tolerant. All the sensors have a hybrid decisionnal architecture based on the ASTRO model. Through the simulation step, we can already notice what the MAS approach provides:

1. The emergent feature , which is inferred by the MAS, makes the system fault tolerant to changes of the environment in which it evolves.

2. Agents present interesting features of software engineering such as genericity allowing an easy evolution of the applications.

3. Generic aspects of agents allows us to envisage differents applications for this network type such as diagnosis, risk management, data fusion...

In a near future, we want to analyse the effect of a recursive mechanism on this application to increase its efficiency in the case of a very pertubated context. We project to apply our approach to other applications such as health monitoring and movement tracking. For these applications, eavesdrop can introduce new problems on messages security.

REFERENCES

Chen, H. et al (2000). Service discovery in the future electronic market. In *Working notes of Seventeenth National Conference on Articial Intelligence, Eleventh Innovative Applications of AI Conference*, Austin.

Cook,D.J. et al (1996). Decision-theoric cooperative sensor planning. *IEEE Transactions on Pattern Analysis And Machine Intelligence*, 18.

Graham, N. (1999). The Nicola Mark II a New Rescue Radio for France. In *The CREG Journal*, volume 38, pages 3–6.

Gray, R. (2000). Soldiers, agents and wireless networks: A report on a military application. In *Proceedings of the Fifth International Conference and Exhibition on the Practical Application of Intelligent Agents and Multi-Agents*, Manchester, England.

Iglesias, C. et al (1998). A survey of agent oriented methodologies. In *Proceedings of ATAL 98 - Workshop on Agent Theories, Architectures, and Languages*, volume LNAI 1555, pages 163–176, Paris, France. Springer-Verlag.

Jamont, J.-P. et al (2002). A multiagent system for the instrumentation of an underground hydrographic system. In *Proceedings of IEEE International Symposium on Virtual and Intelligent Measurement Systems*, Mt Alyeska Resort, AK, USA.

Occello, M. and Koning, J. (2000). Multi-agent based software engineering: an approach based on model and software reuse. In *From Agent Theory to Agent Implementation II - EMCSR 2000 Symposium*, pages 645–657, Vienna.

Occello, M. et al (1998). Designing organized agents for cooperation in a real time context. In Drogoul, A., Tambe, M., and Singh, J., editors, *Collective Robotics*, volume LNCS/LNAI 1456, pages 25–73. Springer-Verlag.

Petriu, E.M. et al (2002). Intelligent robotic sensor agents for enviroment monitoring. In *Proceedings of IEEE International Symposium on Virtual and Intelligent Measurement Systems*, pages 19–20.

Zhang, W. et al (2002). Distributed problem solving in sensor networks. In *AAMAS'02*, pages 15–19.

A SOFTWARE ARCHITECTURE AND SUPPORTING KERNEL FOR LARGELY SYNCHRONOUSLY OPERATING SENSOR NETWORKS

K. H. (Kane) Kim, C.S. Im, M.C. Kim, Y.Q. Li, S.M. Yoo, and L.C. Zheng
DREAM Lab, Dept. of EECS, University of California, Irvine, CA, 92697 U.S.A.
http://dream.eng.uci.edu

Abstract: The *largely synchronous sensor network software architecture* (LaSSeNSA) was formulated with the goal of enabling efficient construction of sensor networks that are easily analyzable and can rarely run into a chaotic situation. There are largely three parts in LaSSeNSA; (1) Global time based coordination of uses of shared communication channels; (2) Global time based coordination of group configuration updates; and (3) Global time based coordination of sensing, communication, and relay activities. The essence of LaSSeNSA as well as various issues related to optimal implementation is presented. For efficient implementation of LaSSeNSA, a sensor node operating system supporting *time-triggered functions* (TTFs) is highly desirable. Our first prototype of TTF support facility was built as an RT subsystem on a small-footprint time-sliced multi-threading kernel. The prototype including both the kernel and the TTF support subsystem is called the *TTF Support OS* (TSOS). Major features of TSOS and a sensor network application development experiment are also presented.

Key words: Sensor, network, real time, time-triggered, TTF, service function, TDMA, TCoDA, wireless, kernel, synchronous, LaSSeNSA, analyzable.

1. INTRODUCTION

Tiny communicating sensors which consume low power and contain sensing, computation, and wireless communication components, are appearing with steadily growing capabilities and varieties [Agr00, Aky02, Hil02, Levo2, She01]. Such sensors are called *C-sensors* in this paper. New potential applications of networks of such C-sensors are recognized continuously in military and commercial areas such as command-control, surveillance, environment monitoring, targeting system, etc., although their practical deployments may be still several years away.

Due to their low costs, C-sensors may be densely deployed inside or close to the object of interest, dynamically forming a cooperative sensor network. We judge that one of the key technological issues in developing applications of C-sensor networks is to enable harmonious orderly cooperation among the C-sensors to meet real-time (RT) application goals. Cooperation among the C-sensors is needed mainly due to the reliability and functionality characteristics of C-sensors as well as due to the nature of the typical applications. To be more specific, the following causes exist.

(1)   The radio communication mechanisms of C-sensors typically have short communication ranges.   Multi-hop store-and-forward modes of communications are inevitable.

(2)   Applications often require fusion of data from multiple geographically dispersed C-sensors.

(3)   C-sensors are often deployed in rough environments and thus temporary or permanent failures of C-sensors are significantly more frequent than the failures of nodes in networks of office computers are.   Healthy neighbors of failed C-sensors must thus cooperate to bypass the failed C-sensors or take over their duties and work toward the application goals.

(4) Since C-sensors are often deployed in high density, not all of them need to be activated at any given time to meet the application requirements. This then offers opportunities for cooperative power saving, i.e., permitting some non-essential C-sensors in hibernating modes.

Simplistic designs of sensor nodes to exhibit poorly coordinated highly probabilistic self-centered behavior are bound to result in C-sensor networks which operate in chaotic manners and cannot accomplish RT applications successfully. For example, consider a spy-tracking application involving C-sensors spread out in a field to detect and track any intruding spy in the field. Sensor nodes might use magnetic, acoustic, or other types of sensing mechanisms for the detection and tracking purpose. As spies are tracked, their position reports are sent to a command station equipped with storage and long-distance communication capabilities which are not available in C-sensors. In this spy-tracking C-sensor network, poorly coordinated C-sensor nodes will frequently collide in accessing communication channels. Consequences will then be untimely arrivals of sensor reports at command stations and untimely arrivals of sensor adjustment commands at sensor nodes, which directly lead to application failures. Message forwarding functions will be highly unreliable, too. Poorly coordinated C-sensor nodes are also bound to produce sensor reports which collectively contain little more than what can be provided by a small subset. As multiple spies move around, the sensor-network will be plunged into a chaos.

Coordinated behavior of C-sensor nodes must be achieved by means involving little or modest amount of wireless communications. Coordination mechanisms requiring high-frequency message communications cannot be effective. They may actually add to the forces inducing a chaos. The recognition of this nature led us to explore the principle of *global-time-based coordination of distributed actions* (TCoDA) [Kop97]. Here coordination is realized by use of globally referenced time information, or for short, *global time*, rather than "last-minute" exchange of messages.

We started with applying the TCoDA principle to the wireless communication area, which quickly led us to adopting the TDMA (time-division multiplexed access) approach. Later we saw the needs for well coordinated behavior in other areas as well, e.g., coordination of sensing times of distributed sensors, dynamic formation and reconfiguration of closely interacting sensor-groups, etc. Subsequent efforts for exploring the TCoDA principle in a top-down manner in the context of C-sensor networks, led us to the formation of a new software architecture named the *largely synchronous sensor network software architecture* (LaSSeNSA). The main purpose of this paper is to discuss the essence of LaSSeNSA as well as various issues related to optimal implementation.

Our subsequent studies on implementation approaches for LaSSeNSA produced an idea that if the sensor node operating system (OS) supports *time-triggered functions* (TTFs), not only efforts for implementation of C-sensor network application systems but also their analysis and validation efforts are greatly simplified. The most general form of a TTF can be expressed as,

"*From GlobalTime* = T1 *to T2, Do an execution of the TTF body Every* P *time-units* (= *iteration-interval*) *By* GCT"

where GCT denotes the *guaranteed completion time* [Kim00]. TTFs make it very simple to implement periodic tasks which are often needed in sensor reading, communication, etc.

After some analysis and preliminary experimental investigations, we judged that in spite of the small memory foot-print requirements inherent in C-sensors, it was well worth equipping C-sensors with OS mechanisms supporting TTFs. In principle, TTFs can be facilitated on both *multi-threading OSs* and *single-threading non-preemptive task* (STNT) *OSs* (which are equipped with device drivers and use a single thread to execute both commanded and interrupt-triggered tasks in first-in-first-out (FIFO) manners). Although we first devised an approach for supporting TTFs on STNT OSs [Kim03], our first prototype of TTF support facility was built as an RT subsystem on a small-footprint time-sliced multi-threading kernel. The prototype including both the kernel and the TTF support subsystem is called the *TTF Support OS* (TSOS). TSOS adopted some device drivers included in TinyOS, an STNT OS developed at UC Berkeley [Hil02], with some modifications.

We have performed a spy-tracking experiment by using the Mica sensor nodes equipped with TSOS and magnetic sensing mechanisms and acoustic sensing mechanisms. The results clearly indicated the promising nature of LaSSeNSA and TSOS. Both TSOS and the experiment performed are also discussed in this paper.

This paper starts in Section 2 with a discussion on the essence of LaSSeNSA. Several issues related to efficient implementation are discussed. The main features of TSOS are discussed in Section 3. The spy-tracking experiment is discussed in Section 4 and the conclusion is provided in Section 5.

2.   THE ESSENCE OF LASSENSA

The C-sensors such as Mica sensor platforms have the following common characteristics.

(1) The amount of memory available, including both RAM and flash ROM, is fairly small although its continuous increase can be safely predicted. 32 KB RAM and 512 KB ROM may become available in 2005.

(2) The wireless communication mechanisms are limited in their communication ranges (up to 200 feet) and bandwidth. The number of channels is limited to one or a few. Controlling the communication ranges to stay below the maximum possible range is usually needed to enable reasonable chances for multiple simultaneous inter-node message communications.

(3) The batteries cannot be recharged easily in most application environments.

(4) An RS232 or similar serial communication port is an optional item. This can be used for loading a program onto the flash ROM and message communication between a command station and its slave C-sensor.

Given these characteristics and the possibility of deploying dense networks of C-sensors in application fields, effecting well-coordinated operations of C-sensors is a research issue of critical importance. LaSSeNSA was devised to enable avoiding chaotic situations arising from poorly coordinated behavior of C-sensors. Therefore, it should be relatively easy for developers of sensor network applications based on LaSSeNSA to avoid facing an explosion in the number of special cases to be dealt with.

There are largely three parts in LaSSeNSA and they are discussed in the following subsections.

2.1 Global time based coordination of uses of shared communication channels: TDMA

A well-established cost-effective way for letting distributed nodes share wireless communication channels is to enforce TDMA rules [Kop97]. It is our judgment that TDMA schemes are particularly attractive in C-sensor network environments. TDMA is effective in preventing collisions among C-sensors which can listen to each other. It is well known that in light-traffic conditions, TDMA has the drawback of relatively high overhead. However, this small drawback is more than compensated by the enormous advantages which become evident in typical C-sensor network application environments where wireless communication bandwidths are severely limited precious resources and collision costs are severe.

In the case of the prototype C-sensor developed at UC Berkeley and called the Mica platform, there is only one frequency radio channel of 40Kb/S bandwidth [Hil02]. In applications involving dense networks of this type of C-sensors, the time costs for collision detections and repeated competitions for accessing channels easily become prohibitively high unless sensor nodes are designed to access channels in well coordinated manners.

On the other hand, in large-scale networks, nodes separated beyond certain distance cannot talk and listen to each other. Therefore, grouping the nodes into closely cooperating groups and making groups provide *message-forwarding services* to other groups are essential requirements.

For the sake of simplicity in discussing the basic requirements and the promising approaches, we will consider C-sensors all of which share single fixed-frequency radio communication channel. In LaSSeNSA, a node-group has the following characteristics:

(1) Every node-group is a TDMA group.

(2) Each node-group has at least one member which can communicate with a non-member. Such a member is called a *gateway node.*

(3) Each node-group has one *group-master node* which should have the capability of talking to and listening from every member node.

(4) A member of a group, which is not the group-master, is called a *worker node.* A worker can send a message to another normally via the master of the group. Therefore, worker nodes do not communicate directly among themselves. Naturally, workers in a group *must always listen during the slots belonging to their master.*

An ideal situation is where each node-group has one and only one gateway node. In such a case, the only constraint on multiple simultaneous message broadcasts is:

(C1) No more than one message broadcast which can be heard by a gateway node during the time-slots paid attention by the gateway node should be generated within the sensor network.

Enforcing C1 requires global knowledge on the network status, especially knowledge on which node can listen to which other nodes. Moreover, the function of assigning group membership and TDMA slots to individual members can be a computationally intensive one. Therefore, in LaSSeNSA, that job is held by a relatively powerful node called the *region-command station*. A region-command station is usually a general-purpose server computer with relatively powerful hardware components (e.g., CPU, memory, and disk), abundant energy sources, and strong connections (e.g., wired connections) to the application customers. It collects data from all sensor groups via wireless communication channels and sends useful information to the application customers. It may use a C-sensor as a slave connected through a wire, e.g., serial communication wire, to itself. In a large-scale application, there may be multiple region-command stations which can interact through high-bandwidth high-reliability connections.

Figure 1 illustrates a sensor network instance of LaSSeNSA consisting of 7 active C-sensors and one region-command station. The 7 active C-sensors form 3 C-sensor groups. Each C-sensor group has a group-master node. The link between two C-sensors represents the reachability of radio transmission from one of the two to the other. We initially treated each link as a symmetric two-way link [Kim03] but recently we refined LaSSeNSA to recognize possibilities of asymmetric wireless reachabilities between a pair of C-sensors. For example, Node 4 can hear message broadcasts by the region-command station and Node 5 but the latter nodes cannot hear message broadcasts by the former node.

The TDMA slot assignment for all sensor groups is made by the region-command station. More details regarding the TDMA slot assignment for all

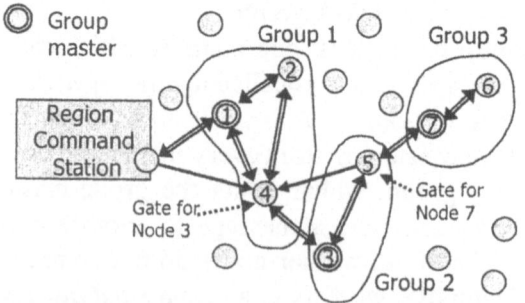

Figure 1. Sensor Groups in a C-sensor network

sensor groups can be found in [Kim03].

The global time base which is an essential ingredient in implementing the TDMA approach can be established in various ways nowadays. If GPS receivers are parts of the sensor nodes, then a global time base of microsecond-level precision can be established easily. Otherwise, a master-slave scheme which involves time announcements by the master as well as exploitation of the knowledge on the message delay between two nodes, can be used to establish a global time base of about 10 millisecond level precision with the C-sensors such as Mica platforms.

2.2   Global time based coordination of group configuration updates: Dynamic TDMA grouping

The scheme in LaSSeNSA for admitting a newly awakened node into an existing cooperating sensor group was formulated with the following challenging goals:

(1) As a newly awakened node joins an existing cooperating group, the members of the group should be able to continue their application tasks *without significant interruptions* due to the joining of the new node.

(2) Upon becoming awakened, a node should be able to join an existing group, receive an assignment of an application-specific task, and start performing its application task *within an acceptable time bound*.

(3) When a member node crashes and thus loses its membership of a group, remaining members of the group should not experience any unacceptable interruptions in their application tasks.

Therefore, the group configuration update is a dynamic process and the scheme adopted is called the *dynamic TDMA grouping scheme*.

We initially formulated the dynamic TDMA grouping scheme with the simplistic assumption about the symmetry in wireless reachability between every pair of C-sensors [Kim03] but recently we refined the scheme to handle the cases of asymmetry in wireless reachability between pairs of C-sensors. As a result, the complexity of the scheme grew considerably.

The asymmetry in wireless reachability between a member node and a newly joining node can be detected in various manners. One such case is depicted in Figure 2. A newly joining node N can hear from the group-master M and three workers, W1, W2, and W3. It thus announces its liveliness. M will not forward the liveliness report of N to the command station since it does not hear the liveliness report. After a while, W1, W2, and W3 detect the liveliness report of N and realize that M has not heard it. The three workers then alert M of N's liveliness report. M forwards it to the command station. Various possible cases have been considered and an admission protocol which accounts for all those cases has been established.

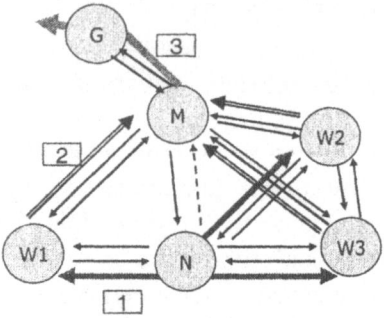

Figure 2. Admission of a node in a case of asymmetry in reachability

Due to the space limit, all those cases are not discussed here.

An additional aspect of the dynamic TDMA grouping scheme is related to the cases where C-sensors are too densely populated in certain parts of the application field. How the sensor nodes will be clustered or spread out geographically is not always predictable at design time. In the case of an excessively dense population, it is not desirable to keep all the C-sensors running all the time. An excessively dense sensor network will unnecessarily burden the communication channels while producing the amount of valuable information which is nearly the same as that which can be obtained with the operation of a subset of the sensors. Therefore, if a node in an area where active worker nodes are already densely populated, announces its liveliness, then it is assigned the role of an *auxiliary worker* under the dynamic TDMA grouping scheme. An auxiliary worker is allowed to occasionally share TDMA slots of a nearby worker to provide its sensor reports. Therefore, workers can cover the application field without the help of auxiliary workers but the overall sensing accuracy can be improved by receiving occasional helps from auxiliary workers.

Optimal assignment of sensor-groups and TDMA slots is the duty of the region-command station and a very complicated subject. So far, we have adopted a heuristic approach. Much further study is needed in this area.

The orderly joining scheme discussed in this section can be extended easily to fit the case where multiple frequency channels are used. The orderly joining enabled is another significant advantage of LaSSeNSA.

2.3   Global time based coordination of sensing, communication, and relay activities

Each member of a sensor group must operate one or more sensing mechanisms during the time-slots in which it does not have to pay attention to communication channels [Kim03].

LaSSeNSA allows fine-precision coordination of the timings of sensing activities in multiple C-sensors. Coordination of the timings of communication and relay activities in different C-sensors is also not difficult. TDMA slot assignment can also be done to reflect such coordination goals.

3.   TTF SUPPORT OS

As mentioned in Section 1, we believe that TTF is a sound fundamental building-block for constructing LaSSeNSA systems. We first devised an approach for supporting TTFs on STNT OSs [Kim03]. However, a prototype implementation of such a TTF support facility has not been completed yet. Instead, our first prototype of a TTF support facility was built as an RT subsystem on a small-footprint time-sliced multi-threading kernel running on the Mica platform. The prototype including both the kernel and the TTF support subsystem is called the *TTF Support OS* (TSOS). A substantial part of the structuring approaches and resource management techniques adopted in TSOS originated from our previous research on middleware support for high-level RT distributed computing objects [Kim97, Kim99, Kim00, Kim02]. Some major features of TSOS are briefly discussed in this section.

3.1   Threads and dynamic binding

In LaSSeNSA, applications are programmed as a set of TTFs. Each TTF is then assigned a thread within TSOS. This assignment or *TTF-thread binding* is a dynamic binding.

To be more specific, TTFs are dynamically registered to TSOS by applications. The registration parameters of TTFs, including the timing requirement specifications, a pointer to its code body, and the interrupt mask specification, are stored in a list called the TTF List within TSOS. The TTF List is periodically examined by the TTF scheduler within TSOS and when the next execution round of a TTF is found to be approaching within a pre-determined time-window, the TTF is bound to an available thread.

3.2   Two-level scheduling

TSOS enables applications to specify special grouping of TTFs. TTFs without such specification belong to the main group. Typically applications involve one or two groups of TTFs. TSOS then attempts to provide one virtual machine to each TTF group.

TSOS manages multiple *ready queues* and each ready queue corresponds

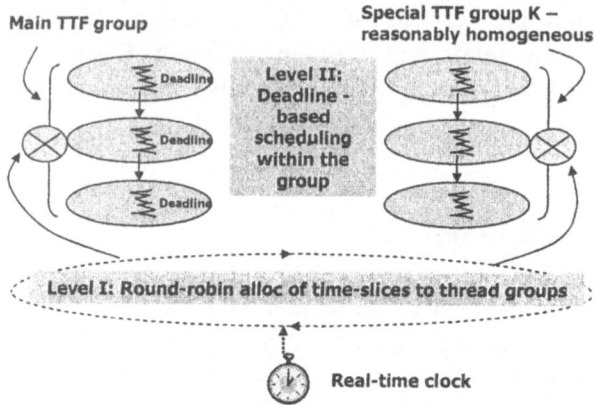

Figure 3. Two-level scheduling of TTF-threads in TSOS

to one TTF group. The two-level scheduler of TSOS selects one of multiple groups as the running group in the round-robin fashion. Therefore, if there are two TTF groups, time-slices are strictly alternatively given to the TTF groups. Within the running group, the time-slice is given to a TTF-thread following the policy of earliest-deadline-first or its variation. Figure 3 depicts this two-level scheduling structure.

The criteria for forming groups are a subject for much further study. We initially adopted this grouping approach for the cases where separating a group of compute-bound TTFs from the group of I/O-bound TTFs gave certain advantages in terms of performance prediction, search for effective in-group scheduling approaches, etc.

3.3   Critical sections

TSOS does not provide semaphores or mutexes for critical sections because these mechanisms may cause non-deterministic timing behavior of user applications in forms that make the timing analysis of user applications quite complicated. Instead, the protection of critical sections can be achieved via the *thread-to-thread atomic section* (TTAS) [Kim99].

4.   AN EXPERIMENTAL SPY-TRACKING SENSOR NETWORK

We have performed a spy-tracking experiment by using the Mica sensor nodes equipped with TSOS. The microcontroller in the Mica C-sensor platform used in our prototype implementation is Atmega 128 which has a 8-bit RISC CPU core running at the frequency of 7.3728MHz, 64K of program memory, 4K of data memory, and several peripherals including SPI, USART,

ADC, and digital I/O ports. The sensing mechanisms used in this experiment include a magnetic sensor and an acoustic sensor. Two core requirements of this application are timely sensing of moving objects and dynamically configuring an ad hoc network for delivering sensor data from all C-sensors to designated region-command stations. To fulfill these requirements, three TTFs were designed and implemented on TSOS:

(1) The TTF for periodic sensing of moving objects with the scheduling frequency of 20.83Hz;

(2) The TTF for radio transmission with the scheduling frequency of 1.736Hz; and

(3) The TTF for handling incoming radio messages with the scheduling frequency of 20.83Hz.

All these TTFs have an RT requirement in the sense that a small deviation of execution timing of any TTF may cause a loss of message or message collision during ratio communication and a wrong decision on sensing objects.

We ran this application with 24 C-sensors in a 4x6 grid network with the grid spacing of 4 ft. These 24 C-sensors build up an ad hoc network in an incremental fashion as each one of the C-sensors joins the current network. One of the 24 C-sensors plays a role of a slave / gateway to a command station where human operators can also monitor the operation of the sensor network. This slave is connected to a PC via serial communication.

We achieved the 410 usec jitter in global clock synchronization with the local real-time clocks set to operate at the resolution of 30.5 usec. In addition, our TDMA protocol showed an average 95.6% of successful radio message transmission between any two adjacent motes in the network. This result is an indirect demonstration of the strong RT scheduling ability of TSOS that has not been seen much in the C-sensor network field so far. The smooth spy-tracking performance demonstrated had not been shown much either in the past C-sensor network field.

5. CONCLUSIONS

LaSSeNSA is a C-sensor network architecture which exploits the TCoDA principle extensively. Its main advantages are in making the application systems easily analyzable. Its optimal implementation in various application environments is regarded as a fruitful area for future research.

The current TSOS was developed for platforms not containing GPS receivers. We plan to develop another version of TSOS for platforms equipped with GPS sensors. Further performance evaluations of TSOS are in plan.

ACKNOWLEDGMENT

The research work reported here was supported in part by the NSF under Grant Numbers 02-04050 (NGS) and 03-26606 (ITR), in part by the US DARPA under Contract F33615-01-C-1902 monitored by AFRL, and in part by a gift from Microsoft Corp. No part of this paper represents the views and opinions of any of the sponsors mentioned above.

REFERENCES

[Agr00] Agre, J. and Clare, L., "An integrated architecture for cooperative sensing networks", *IEEE Computer*, Vol. 33, Issue 5, May 2000, pp.106-108.

[Aky02] Akyildiz, I.F., Su, W., Sankarasubramaniam, Y., and Cayirci, E., "A survey on sensor networks", *IEEE Communications Magazine*, Vol. 40, Issue 8, Aug. 2002.

[Hil02] Hill, J.L. and Culler, D.E., "Mica: a wireless platform for deeply embedded networks", *IEEE Micro*, Vol. 22, Issue 6, Nov/Dec 2002, pp.12-24.

[Kim97] Kim, K.H., "Object Structures for Real-Time Systems and Simulators", *IEEE Computer*, Vol. 30, No.8, pp. 62-70, August 1997.

[Kim99] Kim, K.H., Ishida, M., and Liu, J., "An Efficient Middleware Architecture Supporting Time-Triggered Message-Triggered Objects and an NT-based Implementation", *Proc. ISORC '99 (IEEE CS 2nd Int'l Symp. on Object-oriented Real-time distributed Computing)*, May 1999, pp.54-63.

[Kim00] Kim, K.H., "APIs for Real-Time Distributed Object Programming", *IEEE Computer*, June 2000, pp.72-80.

[Kim02] Kim, K.H., "Commanding and Reactive Control of Peripherals in the TMO Programming Scheme", *Proc. ISORC '02 (IEEE CS 5th Int'l Symp. on Object-Oriented Real-Time distributed Computing)*, Crystal City, VA, April 2002, pp.448-456.

[Kim03] Kim, K.H., and Li, Y.Q., "Toward Easily Analyzable Sensor Networks via Structuring of Time-Triggered Task", *Proc. FTDCS 2003 (9th IEEE Workshop on Future Trends of Distributed Computing Systems)*, San Juan, Puerto Rico, May 2003.

[Kop97] Kopetz, H., '*Real-Time Systems: Design Principles for Distributed Embedded Applications*', Kluwer Academic Publishers, ISBN: 0-7923-9894-7, Boston, 1997.

[Lev02] Levis, P., and Culler, D., "Mate: A Tiny Virtual Machine for Sensor Networks", *ASPLOS*, Dec. 2002.

[She01] Shen, C.C., Srisathapornphat, C., and Jaikaeo, C., "Sensor information networking architecture and applications", *IEEE Personal Communications*, Vol. 8, Issue 4, Aug. 2001, pp.52-59.

ADAPTIVE BUS ENCODING SCHEMES FOR POWER-EFFICIENT DATA TRANSFER IN DSM ENVIRONMENTS*

Claudia Kretzschmar, Markus Scheithauer, and Dietmar Mueller
Dpt. of Systems and Circuit Design
Chemnitz University of Technology, Germany
clkre@infotech.tu-chemnitz.de

Abstract: Power dissipated on global DSM buses increasingly influences total chip power consumption. In order to reduce that portion, activity minimizing bus encoding schemes are applied. Thereby adaptive techniques have a higher potential in reducing transitions than static schemes. However, they are susceptible to rarely but occuring transmission errors since the encoding rule on decoder side is calculated from the received data. Once a different encoding rule is calculated there is no re-synchronization. In this paper we present a new approach which eliminates the dependency on the received data. The encoding rule of both, coder and decoder is updated by partial runtime reconfiguration. In combination with a static scheme we could achieve a reduction in activity of up to 26%. In comparism with an adaptive scheme the hardware requirements were reduced by up to 50%.

Keywords: Adaptive bus encoding, DSM, Partial run-time reconfiguration

1. INTRODUCTION

Technology scaling into the deep sub micron range (DSM) allows the realization of embedded systems on a single chip. Due to the extended functionality and the higher integration density both, power dissipation and power distribution over the whole chip are becoming limiting factors [Sylvester and Keutzer, 1998]. Since the reliability of a circuitry can be guaranteed only until a certain thermal threshold the reduction of power dissipation becomes increasingly important.

Embedded systems realized in DSM technologies are proposed to be implemented in a tile-like structure since DSM effects can be almost neglected in

*This work is funded by the Deutsche Forschungsgemeinschaft DFG within the VIVA research initiative under MU 1024/5-4

modules with 50 to 100 k gates [Sylvester and Keutzer, 2001]. They communicate with each other over high capacitive global system buses or extended
networks on chip (NoC) [Benini and DeMicheli, 2002] which are dominated
by parasitic DSM effects such as capacitive and inductive coupling. As a result the communication becomes error-prone and lossy. The signal integrity
on these communication channels can be improved by repeaters which additionally increase the power dissipated on global wires [Sylvester and Keutzer,
2001]. Therefore wires contribute a main and even increasing portion to the
overall power dissipation of embedded systems. The power consumed on sys-
tem buses can be calculated by the well-known formula: $P = \frac{1}{2}V_{dd}^2 f \sum_{i=1}^{n-1} C_{L_i}\alpha_i$
where V_{dd} is the supply voltage, f the frequency, C_i the capacitance and α_i the
switching activity of line i, respectively. Although modern technologies allow a high flexibility of the used supply voltage such as voltage islands, both
V_{dd} and frequency are determined by performance requirements. The wire capacitance, depends on the distance of the modules and the layout. Only the
switching activity can directly be influenced by the designer.

One approach is the application of transition-minimizing bus encoding
schemes which either work statically or adaptively. Due to their reactivity
to varied statistics adaptive schemes usually outperform static schemes with
respect to the reduction in activity. The required adaption of the encoding
rule is concurrently performed at coder and decoder based on the uncoded
data. Therefore adaptive techniques rely on error-free transmission. However,
errors occur on DSM transmission channels which can result in a different,
non re-synchronizable decoding rule. In this paper we present a new approach
which eliminates the susceptibility to errors. It exploits a new trend in complex
ASICs: embedded FPGA (eFPGA) which are tailored on specific functional
requirements in order to provide more flexibility [IBM, 2003]. Implemented
in eFPGAs, partial dynamic reconfiguration allows the replacement of coder
and decoder with a more suited one during operation.

The remainder of the paper is structured as follows. Section 2 gives an
overview of the related work. The fundamentals of the proposed scheme are
presented in sect. 3. In Sect. 4 the hardware platform and the realization are
described while in Sect. 5 experimental results are presented. The paper will
be summarized in Sect. 6.

2.   RELATED WORK

In the literature a huge number of bus encoding techniques were published.
Applying such methods transitions are displaced from high capacitive bus lines
into the less-capacitive encoder-decoder (codec) circuitry under exploitation of
different characteristics of the data stream.

Depending on the way the encoding rule is implemented into the codec system encoding techniques are either *static* or *adaptive*. The encoding rule of *static* schemes has to be optimized at design time for an application-specific data stream. Examples tailored on the high in-sequence portion of address buses are Gray encoding [X.L.Su et al., 1994] and combined schemes such as T0-BI, Dual-T0 and Dual-T0-BI [Benini et al., 1998]. Instruction- or data bus streams have a different characteristics and require therefore other techniques such as the 1bit redundant Businvert encoding (BI) [Stan and Burleson, 1995], which is the only static scheme that does not require a priori knowledge of statistical parameters of the data stream or the Partial Businvert encoding scheme (PBI) [Shin et al., 1998] encoding only a sub set of bus lines with high activity. A third class of static schemes focuses on the minimization of activity on adjacent lines. Coupling activity contributes due to the higher coupling capacitances in DSM technologies mainly to overall power dissipation. Example schemes are the coupling-driven Businvert [Kim et al., 2000] and the Odd/Even Businvert scheme [Zhang et al., 2002].

Most of the static schemes mentioned so far achieve a high encoding efficiency if the data transmitted corresponds to the streams they are optimized for. If the statistical parameters vary over time as this is usually the case for *real* applications, the encoding efficiency decreases dramatically as shown in [Kretzschmar et al., 2003]. In contrast to that adaptive schemes such as presented in [Benini et al., 1999], the Adaptive Code-book Method [Satoshi Komatsu et al., 2000] and the Adaptive Partial Businvert (APBI) [Kretzschmar et al., 2000] which adapts the set of bus lines to encode, outperform static schemes in terms of encoding efficiency due to the adaption of the encoding rule. In the last few years the number of adaptive schemes increased. Only a few can be mentioned here: the Frequent Value encoding (FV) [Yang and Gupta, 2001], the Adaptive Encoding Scheme ADES [Lv et al., 2002] and the Adaptive Probability Based Mapping (APBM) [Kretzschmar et al., 2003] for data buses and the Address Encoding using Self-Organizing Lists [Mamidipaka et al., 2001] and ETAM++ [Lekatsas and Henkel, 2002] for address buses.

Starting from the identical initial encoding rule, coder and decoder of adaptive schemes concurrently perform an update based on the uncoded or decoded data, respectively. As long as the transmission is error-free both compute the same encoding rule. However, wires in DSM technologies are susceptible to transmission errors which can result in a different encoding rules. Therefore the encoding rule has to be computed at a central place from which it is transferred to coder and decoder. If being transmitted over the bus error correction is compulsory. Furthermore activity is generated and additional bandwidth or wires are required which is infeasible in complex circuits. Therefore we propose the utilization of embedded FPGAs (eFPGA) as presented by XILINX Inc. and IBM Corp. [IBM, 2003]. eFPGAs will be included in complex circuits in order to introduce more flexibility in complex ASICs. The areas are tailored to the needs of the function to be realized. Implementing the codec system on eFPGAs provides the adaptability of the encoding scheme while simultaneously eliminating the dependence on transmission errors. Additionally our approach reduces the overall hardware overhead.

3.   FUNDAMENTALS OF THE SCHEME

The principle of the proposed encoding using eFPGAs is shown in Fig. 1. In the depicted example circuit the 3 modules X, Y and Z are connected via a transition minimizing codec system to the bus. The data sent by the source module X is transmitted in activity reduced fashion over the bus. Each of the receiving modules Y and Z is connected to a decoder which recovers the original data. Coder and decoder circuitry are implemented as partial runtime reconfigurable (pRTR) modules into the eFPGAs. At design time a static encoding scheme is selected based on the statistics of an application-specific data stream. The corresponding codec macros are loaded at setup time into the eFPGAs.

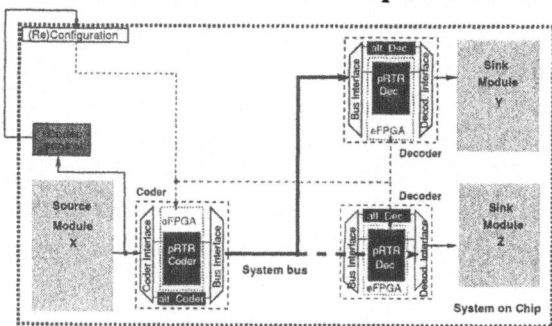

Figure 1.   Principle of runtime exchange of encoding techniques using eFPGA

Since the statistics of real-life data streams usually changes over time the encoding efficiency of the selected static technique decreases. Therefore the scheme has to be adapted to varied statistical parameters during operation. The implemented codec control block observes relevant parameters in a window of fixed size and periodically selects a suited scheme. The corresponding coder and decoder(s) are loaded into the eFPGAs by runtime reconfiguration. In contrast to traditional adaptive schemes which concurrently observe the statistics in coder and decoder, our proposed technique implements a single observation block within the circuit which is sufficient even if more than one receiver is connected to the source. Thereby the hardware overhead is significantly reduced in comparism with published adaptive schemes. However, the most important advantage is the decoupling of the decoding rule from the received data. Possible transmission errors will not impact the computation of the decoding rule anymore.

While being reconfigured data can not be processed by the codec system. The required alternative data path for the reconfiguration period can be realized either by wires bypassing the pRTR codec or a simple encoding scheme. Simply bypassing the pRTR codec requires very little hardware overhead. On the other hand the encoding efficiency deteriorates dependent on the reconfiguration duration. In contrast to that providing a different codec system introduces additional hardware overhead which results in a higher total area but improves the overall encoding efficiency. The total power dissipation can be kept low by switching off the alternative codec during periods of "normal" operation. The tradeoff between cost and gain of the two possibilities determines which alternative to use.

For the realization of the proposed adaptive scheme on eFPGAs two different possibilities of adaptation exist. The two variations which differ in their observation and reconfiguration complexity, will be discussed in the following.

3.1 Dynamic exchange of the encoding scheme

This variation is based on experimental results which show that the encoding efficiency of different encoding techniques distinguishes if applied to a number of data streams. In order to achieve the maximum encoding efficiency always the most suited encoding scheme has to be selected for the current data. The encoding scheme is exchanged by replacing it with the new, more efficient one during operation as depicted in Fig. 2. If for instance a data stream of an i.i.d. source is transmitted BI is optimal [Stan and Burleson, 1995] while for other streams PBI or PBM might achieve a more efficient reduction in activity. Since the schemes exploit different characteristics of the data streams

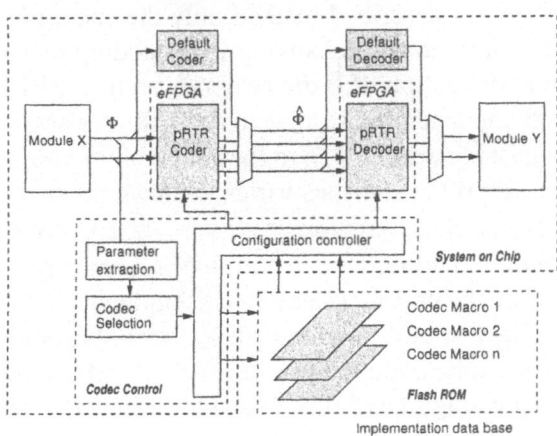

Figure 2. Dynamic replacement of encoding schemes using eFPGA

the codec control block has to observe the parameter set for each of the considered techniques such as line transition activity or data word probability. In a very complex process the codec control block has periodically to evaluate the results of each observed parameter set in order to determine which scheme would achieve the highest encoding efficiency for the current data stream characteristics. After initiating the reconfiguration and switching the data transmission to the alternative data path the configuration controller loads the selected codec macro from the flash ROM into the eFPGA. After the reconfiguration the transmission is switched back to the pRTR codec system by the codec control block.

While this approach allows the highest flexibility with respect to the encoding scheme to be selected and the best adaption to the current data statistics it requires a high effort. The number of schemes to consider is restricted by the size of the flash ROM and the number of parameter sets to be observed and evaluated in the codec control block since it directly influences the area and power requirements. The most decisive drawback of this variation is that a large eFPGA is required in order to provide enough area for each coder and decoder, respectively of the considered static schemes. The size of the eFPGA determines the cost of the circuit as well as the reconfiguration duration. Since during the reconfiguration data is sent either non- or less effective encoded the overall encoding efficiency is directly influenced.

Due to the previously mentioned drawbacks we propose a simplified version of the partial runtime reconfiguration which is described in the next section.

3.2   Dynamic adaption of the encoding rule

Figure 3 shows how dynamic reconfiguration is used in the simplified variation for the adaption of encoding schemes in integrated DSM circuits. In contrast to the previously described method only the encoding rule of a static scheme is optimized instead of exchanging the encoding technique. That approach allows the optimization of static schemes such as PBI or PBM for the current data stream characteristic similar to APBI or APBM without the susceptibility to transmission errors. Due to the adaptability a high encoding efficiency can be achieved if the statistics varies while simultaneously alleviating some of the drawbacks of the previous variation. In comparison with the dynamic exchange of the encoding scheme the eFPGA area is reduced drastically since only that part of the codec system which implements the encoding rule has to be updated. The rest of the codec system does not change and can therefore be fabricated in conventional ASIC technology which reduces the chip cost while providing enough flexibility to adapt the scheme. The smaller eFPGA area results in a reduced reconfiguration duration which requires less data words to be encoded by the default codec during the reconfiguration period. Therefore the influence of the default encoding method is decreased which increases the overall performance especially if data is not encoded alternatively.

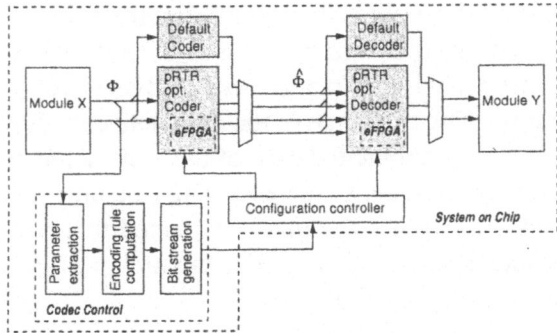

Figure 3.   Dynamic adaption of the encoding rule using eFPGA

Also the codec control block is significantly simplified since for the adaption of one scheme only a single parameter set has to be observed.

In order to eliminate the flash ROM which is used to store all possible codec macros we propose to expand the codec control block by a bit-stream generation block. The updated bit-stream containing the new encoding rule is computed and directed to the configuration pins of the eFPGA. This approach allows the self-reconfiguration of the circuit.

In order to keep the hardware overhead and the power dissipation of the codec control block as low as possible we decided to implement the second approach which realizes the adaption of the encoding rule instead of the exchange of the complete encoding technique. As a representative for all possible static schemes we chose PBI and periodically adapted the set of bus lines to include into encoding. We refer to it as PBI-Reconf.

4.   TEST PLATFORM

4.1   Hardware

We implemented the proposed partial run time reconfigurable encoding scheme on a XILINX VIRTEX FPGA XCV1000, since we did not have on our disposal integrated circuits containing eFPGAs. XILINX VIRTEX FPGAs consist of configurable logic blocks (CLB) which are arranged in columns and rows. Each CLB contains 2 Slices with 2 logic cells (LC) each. A LC is formed by a flip flop (FF) and a 4-input look up table (LUT) which are used to realize the logic function. In order to (re)configure the FPGA according to the required function a bit-stream is generated from a RTL description and loaded via the configuration pins into the FPGA. Thereby the smallest reconfigurable unit is a frame which spreads over all rows of a certain column.

Due to the bit-stream structure all rows of the concerned column are involved in a reconfiguration. Therefore the modules have to be placed carefully so that a partial run time reconfiguration does not affect logic of other modules.

In [Haase et al., 2002] the authors developed a method for circuit partitioning together with an automated design flow based on XILINX standard tools in order to produce the partial bit streams used to dynamically reconfigure the FPGA during runtime. The exchange of the complete encoding scheme would require synthesis, place and route for each of the considered codecs. Since we restrict ourselves to the adaption of the encoding rule only a single bit-stream has to be generated, from which the part is extracted that contains the encoding rule for the codec system. That partial bit-stream is taken as a basis to periodically generate the updated bit-stream.

4.2   Implementation

PBI can be adapted to the statistics of the current data stream if the sub bus to be encoded is periodically selected. Included lines are transmitted inverted if more than a half of the considered lines would switch. It means that transitions are only detected for selected bus lines and the value to which the number of switching lines is compared has to be updated for each configuration. Furthermore only lines which are included into encoding are inverted while non-included lines are transmitted uncoded independent of the number of transitions. Corresponding lines have to be masked. On decoder side the inversion is selectively applied according to a mask. For the PBI-Reconf coder we placed the 2 required LUTs per bus line in the reconfigurable area in order to influence the functionality as described. According to the configured function of the LUT the bits are correspondingly processed. The inversion threshold is formed by the outputs of $log(\frac{buswidth+1}{2})$ LUTs. The decoder implements one reconfigurable LUT per line which does the selective inversion. For a 32 bit bus it results in 69 reconfigurable LUTs for coder and 32 for decoder. A column in the XCV1000 contains 64 rows which corresponds to 128 LUTs per slice. The reconfiguration of the experimental environment can not be restricted to the utilized LUTs. Instead all LUTs of the corresponding slice of the column are covered. In contrast to that only used resources are reconfigured in the eFPGA. In order to converge the reconfiguration time of the two approaches all the reconfigurable LUTs of coder and decoder were placed in a single column of the VIRTEX FPGA.

The codec control block consists according to Fig. 3 of a parameter observation block, a mask computation logic and a bit-stream generation unit. The first two blocks correspond to the mask computation block of APBI but are required only once per PBI-Reconf circuit. The bit-stream generation unit alters the LUT bits of the partial bit-stream according to the new mask. Each of the 16 bits of a LUT is situated in a different frame. Therefore 16 Frames with 39 words have to be reconfigured. Since the LUT bits are placed very regularly in the bit-stream a few counters suffice to find their positions. According to the new subset of bus lines the bit-stream is altered and routed to the configuration pins of the FPGA. The codec control block switches data transmission to the alternative data path during the reconfiguration and back to the adapted PBI-Reconf codec system afterwards.

5.   EXPERIMENTAL RESULTS

We implemented the proposed PBI-Reconf encoding for a bus width of 32 lines in the FPGA test environment and conducted experiments with the following set of test data streams:

- **art**: A random, segmented data stream with a varying distribution of activity in each segment.
- **eps**: An ASCII file in encapsulated postscript format.
- **gzip**: Gzip binary (example for an executable file).
- **ppm**: A composed PPM image stream consisting of 4 different images with varying statistics.
- **gauss**: White Gaussian noise.

The statistical parameters were observed in a window of fixed size. Subsequently a new mask was computed. For the experiments we first read the partial configuration bit-stream using the reconfiguration pins of the FPGA before it was altered according to the new mask and reloaded. The reconfiguration was done in the SelectMap mode with a reconfiguration clock of 45 MHz. During the reconfiguration period continuously data was transmitted either with no encoding (PBI+NE) or BI encoding (PBI+BI).

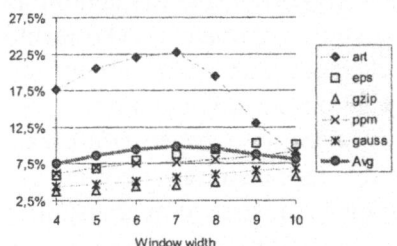
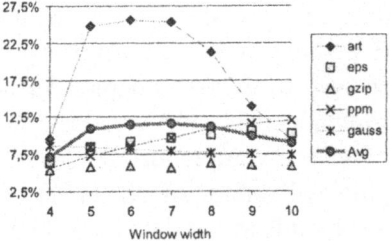

Figure 4. Relative activity reduction as function of window width: PBI-Reconf with no default encoding (PBI+NE)

Figure 5. Relative activity reduction as function of window width [bit]: PBI-Reconf with BI as default codec (PBI+BI)

In a first experiment we determined the influence of the window width which is used for parameter observation on the encoding efficiency. The relative savings for the test data streams are depicted as a function of *window width* given in *bit* for no alternative encoding in Fig. 4 and for BI encoding during the reconfiguration period in Fig 5. Although the encoding efficiency is as expected influenced by the alternative encoding both plots show a dependency on the window width. The most efficient reduction is achieved for *art* since adaptive schemes can exploit the strongly over time varying activity profile. The efficiency varies for the streams. In order to achieve the maximum reduction for each data stream different window widths would be required. Since we focus on a general-purpose scheme the average performance *Avg* is regarded. The highest average reduction is achieved for window widths between 2^5 (window width 5) and 2^7 (window width 7).

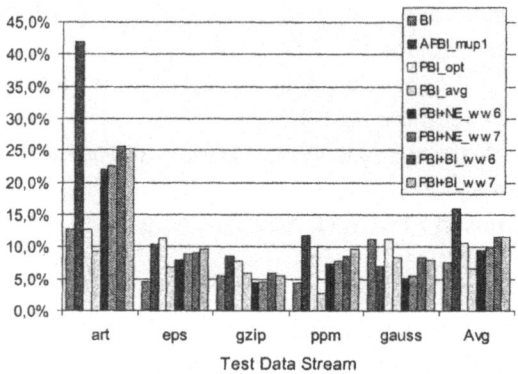

Figure 6. Comparism of the relative reduction in activity

In a second experiment the savings were compared to other encoding schemes: APBI, BI and PBI. PBI was optimized for each of the streams which is indicated by the subscript *opt*. Additionally we investigated in real-life conditions when PBI encodes streams with different statistical parameters. The results are marked by the subscript *avg*. The most efficient reduction in activity was achieved by APBI as depicted in Fig. 6 since the optimization can be applied instantaneously. Nevertheless, that opportunity does not exist in DSM technologies anymore since the scheme is susceptible to transmission errors. The optimized version of PBI is very efficient as long as the data to be transmitted corresponds to the data the scheme is optimized for. Otherwise the efficiency decreases as shown by PBI_{avg}. The proposed PBI-Reconf performs in both variations (BI and NE) comparable to PBI_{opt}. In both variations it outperforms BI by 25 to 50 percent.

In a next experiment we investigated in the hardware requirements. The codec control block which comprises of parameter extraction, encoding rule computation and bit-stream generation unit used for manipulating the partial bit-stream accordingly was described in synthesizable VHDL. We synthesized the block for our target FPGA. The hardware requirements were compared with that of APBI and BI. The results are presented in Tab. 1. As the figures indicate APBI requires compared to BI, a very high overhead in order to adapt the encoding rule periodically to the statistics of the data stream. The main

Table 1.   Hardware requirements on XILINX VIRTEX FPGA

Scheme		FG	CY	DFF
APBI$_{mup1}$	cod	725	9	344
	dec	569	9	314
BI	cod	115	0	98
	dec	32	0	65
CC$_{PBI,Reconf}$		732	26	308
1Source, 1Sink	APBI	1294	18	658
	PBI-Reconf	879	26	471
1Source, 2Sink	APBI	1863	27	972
	PBI-Reconf	911	26	536

portion of the increased hardware overhead is caused by the mask computation block (MC) which observes the statistics and computes a new encoding rule. In contrast to that our proposed PBI-Reconf scheme requires a single observation block per circuit and a PBI codec system with the complexity of BI which is periodically adapted by partial reconfiguration. The second part of Tab. 1 shows the requirements for an adaptive codec system with one or two sinks, respectively. In comparism with APBI our approach reduces the hardware requirements by about 30% if a single sink is connected to the bus. If more receivers are implemented the savings increase even more. For 2 sinks the hardware can be reduced to about 50% of a comparable APBI codec while the adaption is independent of any transmission errors on the bus.

6.   CONCLUSIONS

The experimental results confirm the efficiency of our proposed scheme. We achieved a higher encoding efficiency than BI and the average PBI with both variations of alternative encoding. Since the reconfiguration process lasts longer than the application of the new mask in APBI the reduction in activity was lower than for APBI. The most important advantage is the independence of transmission errors. Unlike APBI the encoding rule of the decoder is not derived from the received data but computed in the central codec control block and applied by partial reconfiguration. Therefore the scheme is suited for application in DSM environments where, due to coupling effects, transmission errors on system buses occur from time to time. In contrast to that the encoding rules of APBI diverge from each other as soon as a transmission error results in a different encoding rule on decoder side. The investigations in the hardware overhead showed that in comparism to APBI the overall hardware overhead including the bit-stream generation could be reduced by about 30 %. That benefit even increases if data is transmitted to more than one receiver. Furthermore the approach is very flexible regarding the scheme which is adapted. Instead of PBI which we chose as an example also one of the schemes which takes into account coupling activity such as coupling-driven BI or odd/even BI can be applied.

REFERENCES

Benini, L. and DeMicheli, G. (2002). Networks on chips: A new soc paradigm. *IEEE Jounal on Computer*, pages 70–78.

Benini, L., Macii, A., Macii, E., Poncino, M., and Scarsi, R. (1999). Synthesis of Low-Overhead Interfaces for Power-Efficient Communication over Wide Buses. In *36th DAC*.

Benini, L., Micheli, G. De, Macii, E., Sciuto, D., and Silvano, C. (1998). Address Bus Encoding Techniques for System-Level Power Optimization. In *DATE*.

Haase, A., Kretzschmar, C., Siegmund, R., Mueller, D., Schneider, J., Boden, M., and Langer, M. (2002). Design of a Reed Solomon Decoder using Partial Dynamic Reconfiguration of XILINX Virtex FPGAs - A Case Study. In *DATE*, Paris, France.

IBM (2003). Embedded fpga cores. http://www-3.ibm.com/chips/products/asics/products/cores/efpga.html.

Kim, Ki-Wook, Baek, Kwang-Hyun, Shanbhag, Naresh, Liu, C.L., and Kang, Sung-Mo (2000). Coupling-driven signal encoding scheme for low-power interface design. In *ICCAD*.

Kretzschmar, C., Siegmund, R., and Mueller, D. (2000). Adaptive Bus Encoding Technique for Switching Activity Reduced Data Transfer over Wide System Buses. In *PATMOS 2000*, pages 66–75, Goettingen, Germany. Springer.

Kretzschmar, C., Siegmund, R., and Mueller, D. (2003). Low Power Encoding Techniques for Dynamically Reconfigurable Hardware. *Special issue of the Kluwer Journal of Supercomputing*, 26(2):185–203.

Lekatsas, H. and Henkel, J. (2002). ETAM++: Extended Transition Activity Measure for Low Power Address Bus Designs. In *ASP-DAC*, pages 113–120.

Lv, T., Wolf, W., Henkel, J., and Lekatsas, H. (2002). An adaptive dictionary encoding scheme for soc data buses. In *Proceedings of DATE*, page 1059. IEEE Computer Society.

Mamidipaka, M., Hirschberg, D., and Dutt, N. (2001). Low power address encoding using self-organizing lists. In *ISLPED*, pages 188–193. ACM Press.

Satoshi Komatsu, Makoto Ikeda, and Kunihiro Asada (2000). Bus Data Encoding with Adaptive Code-book Method for Low Power IP Based Design. In *International Workshop on IP based design and Synthesis*, pages 77–81.

Shin, Youngsoo, Chae, Soo-Ik, and Choi, Kiyoung (1998). Partial Bus-Invert Coding for Power Optimization of System Level Bus. In *ISLPED*, pages 127–129.

Stan, Mircea R. and Burleson, Wayne P. (1995). Bus-Invert Coding for Low-Power I/O. In *Transactions on VLSI Systems*, volume 3, pages 49–58.

Sylvester, D. and Keutzer, K. (1998). Getting to the Bottom of Deep Submicron. In *ICCAD*.

Sylvester, D. and Keutzer, K. (2001). Impact of Small Process Geometries on Microarchitectures in Systems on a Chip. *Proceedings of the IEEE*, 89(4):467–489.

X.L.Su, X.Y.Tsui, and Despain, A.M. (1994). Saving Power in the Control Path of Embedded Processors. *IEEE Design and Test of Computers*, 11:24–30.

Yang, J. and Gupta, R. (2001). Fv encoding for low-power data i/o. In *International symposium on Low power electronics and designISLPED*, pages 84–87. ACM Press.

Zhang, Yan, Lach, John, Skadron, Kevin, and Stan, M. (2002). Odd/even bus invert with two-phase transfer for buses with coupling. In *ISLPED*, pages 80 – 83. ACM.

A NOVEL APPROACH FOR OFF-LINE MULTIPROCESSOR SCHEDULING IN EMBEDDED HARD REAL-TIME SYSTEMS

Raimundo Barreto[1], Paulo Maciel[1], Marília Neves[1], Eduardo Tavares[1], Ricardo Lima[2]

[1] *Centro de Informática (CIn) at Universidade Federal de Pernambuco (UFPE). PO Box 7851, 50732-970 Recife-PE-Brazil.*

{ rsb,prmm,mln2,eagt } @cin.ufpe.br.

[2] *Departamento de Engenharia da Computação - Universidade de Pernambuco Recife-PE-Brazil*

ricardo@upe.poli.br

Abstract: There are two general approaches for scheduling tasks in real-time systems: runtime and pre-runtime scheduling. However, there are several situations where the runtime approach does not find a feasible schedule even if such a schedule exists. The proposed approach uses state space exploration for finding a pre-runtime scheduling. The main problem with such methods is the space size, which can grow exponentially. This paper shows how to minimize this problem, and presents a depth-first search method on a timed labeled transition system derived from the time Petri net model.

Keywords: Embedded real-time systems, scheduling, formal methods, and time Petri nets.

1. INTRODUCTION

Embedded hard real-time systems are dedicated computer applications having to satisfy stringent timing constraints. For meeting this requirement, scheduling performs an important role. There are two general approaches for scheduling tasks: runtime and pre-runtime scheduling. In *runtime scheduling*, the schedule is computed on-line as tasks arrive, using a priority-driven approach. However, there are situations where this approach may constrain the possibility of finding a feasible schedule, even if such schedule exists [10–11]. The approach presented in this paper is *pre-runtime scheduling*, where schedules are computed entirely off-line. This solution reduces context switching, its execution is predictable, and excludes the need of complex operating systems. In safety-critical systems the predictability is an important matter, mainly due to the use of arbitrary precedence and exclusion relations. In accordance with [11], pre-runtime scheduling is often the only means of providing predictability in complex systems. This work uses *state space exploration* since it presents a complete automatic strategy for verifying finite-state systems [6]. In spite of the fact that a scheduling can be found using this strategy, this may be limited by the excessive size of its state space. The proposed approach tackles this problem by applying techniques for state space reduction, and a depth-first search algorithm. This paper is an extension of ours previous work [3], which presents how to reach feasible schedules by using a time Petri net model on uniprocessor architectures.

2.   RELATED WORK

Xu and Parnas [10]present a branch-and-bound algorithm that finds an optimal pre-runtime schedule on a single processor for real-time process segments with release, deadlines, and arbitrary exclusion and precedence relations. Despite the importance of their work, it does not present real-world experimental results. Abdelzaher and Shin [1]proposed an extension of [10]in order to deal with distributed real-time systems. This algorithm takes into account delays, precedence relations imposed by interprocess communications, and considers many possibilities for improving the scheduling lateness at the cost of complexity. The scheduler synthesis proposed by Altisen et.al. [2]synthesizes all *dynamic on-line scheduling* satisfying a given property. In spite of they have claimed that using *synchronization modes* the complexity is reduced, they do not directly address the state explosion problem, stressed by the authors as a limitation of their approach. Several authors also use Petri nets in scheduling theory. However, most of them are only concerned with schedulability analysis. For instance, Bruno et. al. [4]present a schedulability analysis, using high-level Petri nets. However, their work does not generate feasible schedules, but it relies on Xu and Parnas' algorithm [10]in order to find them.

Comparing our approach with other works (e.g., [1, 9]), it differs in the sense that: (i) their works model the *scheduling problem*, whilst our work models the tasks of a system. For this reason, they may have better performance in some situations. Nevertheless, time efficiency is not a critical concern when considering schedules computed off-line. However, our solution can also generate timely and predictable scheduled code, which is difficult in their works. (ii) using Petri net analysis techniques allows one to check several system properties. Although state space exploration is not new, at the best of our present knowledge, there is no similar work that uses formal methods for modeling real-time systems, and finds a feasible pre-runtime schedule considering multiprocessor architectures.

3. COMPUTATIONAL MODEL: SYNTAX AND SEMANTICS

The computational model syntax is given by a time Petri net [7], which is a Petri net extended with time, and its semantics is given by its time labeled transition system. A time Petri net (TPN) is a bipartite directed graph represented by a tuple $\mathcal{P}= (P, T, F, W, m_0, I)$. P (places), and T (transitions) are two types of nodes. The edges are represented by $F \subseteq (P \times T) \cup (T \times P)$. $W : F \rightarrow \mathbb{N}$ represents the weight of the edges. A TPN marking m_i is a vector $m_i \in \mathbb{N}^{|P|}$, and m_0 is the initial marking. $I : T \rightarrow \mathbb{N} \times \mathbb{N}$, represents the timing constraints, where $I(t) = (EFT(t), LFT(t)) \ \forall t \in T$. $ET(m_i)$ is a set of enabled transitions in marking m_i. Let M be the set of all reachable markings of $\mathcal{P}$. $C \in \mathbb{N}^{|ET(M)|}$ is a clock vector, which represents the time elapsed since the respective transition enabling. In order to facilitate the TPN's analysis, it is defined the dynamic firing interval $(I_D(t) = (DLB, DUB)$, where $DLB(t) = max(0, EFT(t) - c(t))$ and $DUB(t) = LFT(t) - c(t)$. $I_D(t)$ is dynamically modified whenever the respective clock variable is incremented, and t does not fire.

The set of states S of $\mathcal{P}$ is given by $S \subseteq (M \times \mathbb{N}^{|ET(M)|})$, that is, a single state is defined by a pair (m, c), where m is a marking, and c is its respective clock vector for $ET(m)$. The initial state is $s_0 = (m_0, c_0)$, where $c_0(t) = 0 \ \forall t \in ET(m_0)$. $FT(s)$ is the set of firable transitions at state s defined by: $FT(s) = \{t_i \in ET(m)|DLB(t_i) \leq min(DUB(t_k))\forall t_k \in ET(m)\}$, where $FT \subseteq ET \subseteq T$. The *firing domain* for t at a specific state s, is defined by: $FD_s(t) = [DLB(t), min\,(DUB(t_k))], \forall t_k \in ET(m)$.

The semantics of a TPN $\mathcal{P}$ is defined by associating a TLTS $\mathcal{L_P}= (S, \Sigma, \rightarrow, s_0)$ such that: (i) S is a finite set of discrete states of $\mathcal{P}$; (ii) $\Sigma \subseteq (T \times \mathbb{N})$ is an alphabet of labels representing activities. The labels are (t, θ) corresponding to the firing of a firable transition (t) at a specific time value (θ) in the firing interval $FD(s), \forall s \in S$; (iii) $\rightarrow \subseteq S \times \Sigma \times S$ is the transition relation; and (iv) s_0 is the initial state of $\mathcal{P}$.

Let $\mathcal{L_P}$ be a TLTS derived from a time Petri net $\mathcal{P}$, and $s_i = (m_i, c_i)$ a reachable state. $s_j =\mathtt{fire}(s_i, (t, \theta))$ denotes that firing a transition t at time θ from the state s_i, a new state $s_j = (m_j, c_j)$ is reached, such that:
(i) $\forall p \in P, \ m_j(p) = m_i(p) - W(p, t) + W(t, p)$;

$$(ii)\forall t_k \in ET(m_j), C_j(t_k) = \begin{cases} 0, & if(t_k = t) \\ 0, & if(t_k \in ET(m_j) - ET(m_i)) \\ C_i(t_k) + \theta, & else \end{cases}$$

The firing of a transition t_i, at a specific time θ_i in the state (s_{i-1}) defines the next state (s_i).

Let $\mathcal{L_P}$ be a TLTS of a TPN $\mathcal{P}$, where s_0 its initial state, $s_n = (m_n, c_n)$ a final state, and $m_n = M^F$, which is the desired final marking. $s_0 \xrightarrow{(t_1, \theta_1)}$

$s_1 \overset{(t_2,\theta_2)}{\longrightarrow} s_2 - - \to s_{n-1} \overset{(t_n,\theta_n)}{\longrightarrow} s_n$ is defined as a *feasible firing schedule*, where $s_i = \text{fire}(s_{i-1}, (t_i, \theta_i))$, $i > 0$, if $t_i \in FT(s_{i-1})$, and $\theta_i \in FD_{s_{i-1}}(t_i)$. As it is presented later, the modeling methodology guarantees the final marking M^F is well-known since it is explicitly modeled.

4. TEST MODEL

Let $\mathcal{T}$ be the set of tasks in a system. Let τ_i be a periodic task defined by $\tau_i = (ph_i, r_i, c_i, d_i, p_i)$, where ph_i is the initial phase (delay associated to the first time request of a task after the system starting); r_i is the release time (interval between the beginning of a period and the earliest time that a task execution can be started); c_i is the worst case computation time; d_i is the deadline (interval between the beginning of a period and the time when the task must be completed); and p_i is the period (time interval in which the task must be executed). Let $\tau_k = (c_k, d_k, min_k)$ be a sporadic task, where c_k is the worst case computation time; d_k is the deadline; and min_k is the minimum period between two activations of task τ_k. A task is classified as sporadic if it can be randomly activated, but the minimum period between two activations is known. As pre-runtime approaches may only schedule periodic tasks, the sporadic tasks have to be translated to an equivalent periodic task [8]. A task τ_i *precedes* task τ_j, if t_j can only start execution after t_i has finished. A task τ_i *excludes* task τ_j, if no execution of t_j cannot start while task t_i is executing. Exclusion relations may prevent simultaneous access to shared resources. Each task $\tau_i \in \mathcal{T}$ consists of a finite sequence of *task time units* $\tau_i^0, \tau_i^1, \cdots, \tau_i^{c_i-1}$, where τ_i^{j-1} always precedes τ_i^j, for $j > 0$. A task time unit is the smallest indivisible granule of a task, during which it cannot be preempted by any other task. A task can also be split into more than one *subtasks*, where each subtask is composed by one or more task time units.

5. MODELING REAL-TIME SYSTEMS

Hard real-time systems are those that besides its functional correctness, timeliness must be satisfied. The modeling phase is very important to attain such constraints.

5.1 Scheduling Period

The proposed method schedules the set of periodic tasks occurring in a period that is equal to the least common multiple (LCM) of the periods of the given set of tasks. The LCM is also called *schedule period* (P_S). Within this new period, there are several *tasks instances* of the same task, where $N(t_i) = P_S/p_i$ gives the instances of t_i. For example, consider the following task model consisting of two tasks: $t_1 = (0, 0, 2, 7, 8)$ and $t_2 = (0, 2, 3, 6, 6)$.

In this particular case, $P_S = 24$, implying that the two periodic tasks are replaced by seven new periodic tasks ($N(t_1) = 3$, and $N(t_2) = 4$), where the timing constraints of each task instance has to be transformed to consider that new period [10].

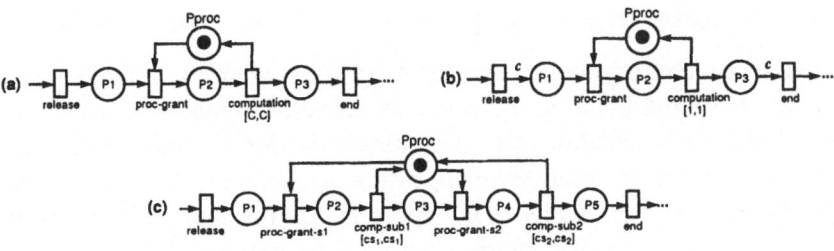

Figure 1.   Modeling Scheduling Methods

5.2 Scheduling Methods

Figure 1 presents three ways for modeling scheduling methods, where $c = cs_1 + cs_2$ is the task computation time (cs_1 and cs_2 are computation times for the first and last subtask, respectively):

a) *all-non-preemptive*: processor is just released after the entire computation be finished. Figure 1(a) shows that computation transition timing interval has bounds equal to the task computation time (i.e., $[c, c]$);

b) *all-preemptive*: tasks are implicitly split into all possible subtasks. This method allows running other *conflicting tasks*, meaning that one task could preempt another task. It is worth observing, the difference between the timing interval for the computation transition and the arc weight in Figures 1(a) and 1(b).

c) *defined subtasks*: tasks are split into more than one explicitly defined subtasks. Figure 1(c) shows two subtasks.

5.3 Tasks Modeling

Figure 2 is also used to show (in dashed boxes) the three main *building blocks* for modeling a real-time task. These blocks are: *(a) Task Arrival*, which models the periodic invocation for all task's instances. Transition t_{ph} models the initial phase, whilst transition t_a models the periodic arrival for the remaining instances; *(b) Deadline Checking*, where it is used elementary net structures to capture deadline missing. Some works (e.g. [2]) extended the Petri net model for dealing with deadline checking. *(c) Task Structure*, which models: release time, processor granting, computation, and processor releasing. Figure 2 presents a non-preemptive TPN model for the example presented in previous subsection. It does not model the seven task instances. Instead, it models only the two original tasks, and the time period of every task instances.

5.4   Modeling Interprocessor Communication

Processors are connected to one (or more) bus, which is modeled as a resource that is shared by all processors and accessed in mutual exclusion. The proposed approach schedules the communication for avoiding network contention. Otherwise, it could result in different execution times for different runs of the same system, which is not appropriated for hard real-time systems. It is supposed that: (i) the communication time between tasks in the same processor is negligible; and (ii) the communication is synchronous (blocking). Figure 3 presents a model for two interprocessor communicating tasks (ping and pong). The task ping computes and sends a data to pong. When the data arrives, the task pong computes and sends a new data to ping, and this

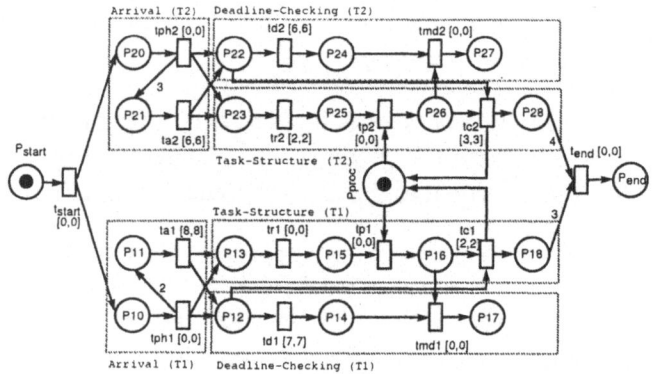

Figure 2.   Petri net model

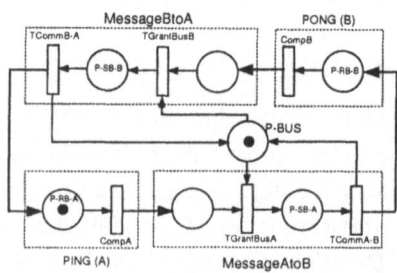

Figure 3.   A Simple Example of Interprocessor Communication

```
1  scheduling-synthesis(S,MF,TPN)
2  {
3     if (S.M = MF) return TRUE;
4     tag(S);
5     PT = remove-undesirable(partial-order(firable(S)));
6     if (|PT| = 0) return FALSE;
7     for each (⟨t,θ⟩ ∈ PT) {
8        S'= fire(S, t, θ);
9        if (untagged(S') ∧ scheduling-synthesis (S',MF,TPN)){
10          add-in-trans-system (S,S',t,θ);
11          return TRUE;
12       }
13    }
14    return FALSE;
15 }
```

Figure 4.   Scheduling Synthesis Algorithm

procedure repeats indefinitely. The bus is modeled by a place (P-BUS) shared by all tasks. The communication time is attached to transitions TCommA-B and TCommB-A. The places P-SB-A and P-SB-B model sending buffers, whilst places P-RB-A and P-RB-B model receiving buffers.

6.   PRE-RUNTIME SCHEDULING

This section shows a technique for state space minimization, the algorithm that implements the proposed method, and an application of the algorithm.

6.1   Minimizing State Space Size

Partial-Order Reduction.   If activities can be executed in any order, such that the system always reaches the same state, these activities are *independent*. Partial-order reduction methods exploit the independence of activities [6]. An independent activity is one that is not in conflict with other activity, that is, when it is executed it does not disable any other activity, such as: arrival, release, precedence, computation, processor releasing, and so on. This reduction method proposes to give for each class of activities a different *choice-priority*. Dependent activities, like processor granting and exclusion relations, have lowest priority. Therefore, when changing from one state to another, it is sufficient to analyze the class with highest choice-priority and pruning the other ones. This reduction is important due to two reasons: (i) it reduces the amount of storage; and (ii) when the system does not have a feasible schedule, it returns more rapidly.

Undesirable States.   Section 5 presents how to model undesirable states, for instance, states that represent missed deadlines. The proposed method is interested for schedules that do not reach any of these undesirable states.

6.2   Pre-Runtime Scheduling Algorithm

The algorithm proposed (Fig. 4) is a depth-first search method on a TLTS. The *stop criterion* is obtained whenever the desirable final marking M^F is reached. Considering that, (i) the Petri net model is guaranteed to be bounded, and (ii) the timing constraints are bounded and discrete, this implies that the TLTS is finite and thus the proposed algorithm always finishes. When the algorithm reaches the desired final marking (M^F), it implies that a feasible schedule was found (line 3). The state space generation is modified (line 5) to incorporate the state space pruning. PT is a set of ordered pairs $\langle t, \theta \rangle$ representing for each firable transition (post-pruning) all possible firing time in the firing domain. The *tagging scheme* (lines 4 and 9) ensures that no state is visited more than once. The function `fire` (line 8) returns a new generated state (S') due to the firing of transition t at time θ. The feasible schedule is represented by a TLTS generated by the function `add-in-trans-system` (line 10). The whole reduced state space is visited only when the system does not have a feasible schedule.

Table 1.   Illustrative example

st	PT	trans+time	st	PT	trans+time	st	PT	trans+time
0	{tstart}	{tstart,0}	12	{tr2}	{tr2,0}	19	{tp2}	{tp2,0}
1	{tph1,tph2}	{tph1,0}	13	**{tp1,tp2}**	**{tp1,0}**	20	{ta1}	{ta1,2}
2	{tph2}	{tph2,0}	14	{tc1}	{tc1,2}	21	{tr1}	{tr1,0}
3	{tr1}	{tr1,0}	15	{tp2}	{tp2,0}	22	{tc2}	{tc2,1}
4	{tp1}	{tp1,0}	16	{ta2}	{ta2,2}	23	{tp1}	{tp1,0}
5	{tr2}	{tr2,2}	17	**{td2}**	**{td2,0}**	24	{ta2}	{ta2,1}
6	{tc1}	{tc1,0}	13	**{tp2}**	**{tp2,0}**	25	{tc1}	{tc1,1}
7	{tp2}	{tp2,0}	14	{tc2}	{tc2,3}	26	{tr2}	{tr2,1}
8	{tc2}	{tc2,3}	15	{tp1}	{tp1,0}	27	{tp2}	{tp2,0}
9	{ta2}	{ta2,1}	16	{ta2}	{ta2,1}	28	{tc2}	{tc2,3}
10	{ta1}	{ta1,2}	17	{tc1}	{tc1,1}	29	**{tend}**	**{tend,0}**
11	{tr1,tr2}	{tr1,0}	18	{tr2}	{tr2,1}			

6.3   Application of the Algorithm

Table 1 depicts the execution of the algorithm applied to the time Petri net model of Figure 2. In this table, at state 13, two transitions (tp_1 and tp_2) are firable. The possible execution of task $T1$ (choosing tp_1 for firing) is a wrong choice since, after that, task $T2$ misses its deadline (state 17). The algorithm *backtracks* to state 13 and try the alternative, now granting the processor to the task $T2$ (firing tp_2). This new decision leads to a feasible schedule, since in the state 29 the firing of transition t_{end} reaches the desired final marking (M^F).

Table 2. Experimental results summary

Example	instances	state-min	found	time (s)
Simple Control Appl	**28**	**50**	**50**	**0.005**
Robotic Arm	37	150	150	0.03
Xu (example 3)	4	171	1566	0.82
Xu (figure 9)	5	281	2387	3.41
Mine Pump Control	782	3130	3255	11.6

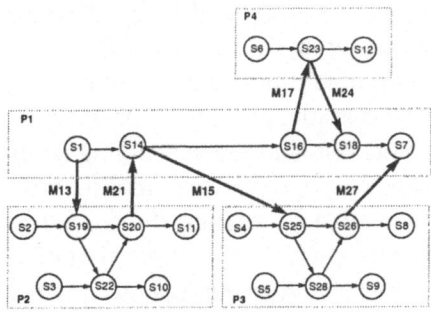

Figure 5. Case Study Graph

7. EXPERIMENTAL RESULTS

Table 2 shows a summary of the experimental results. All experiments were performed on a Pentium-III 600 Mhz dual processor. In order to depict the practical usability of the proposed method in more details, one of the examples is considered, *a simple control application*. This case study is described originally in [5]. The system consists of a sensory device mounted on a motorized platform that must detect and track specific objects in the environment. Four processors connected by a single bus control the system. The model consists of 6 tasks split into 22 subtasks, which exchanges 10 messages, 6 of them are sent across processor boundaries. Figure 5 shows the computational graph for this application, presenting the subtasks allocated to processors, and its communication pattern. In this graph each node is labeled with the corresponding subtask number, arcs representing local communication are treated as precedence relation, and each arc representing an interprocessor communication is labeled with a corresponding *message identification*. The proposed algorithm founds a feasible scheduling with no overhead, since it only examined the minimum number of states (in this case 50 states) in 5 milliseconds.

8.   CONCLUSIONS

This paper proposed a formal modeling methodology based on time Petri nets, and a framework for pre-runtime scheduling on multiprocessors using a reduced state space exploration algorithm. In spite of this analysis technique is not new, to the best of our knowledge, there is no work reported similar to ours that models hard real-time systems and finds (whether one exists) a respective pre-runtime scheduling. The real-time task specification can be very general, since it can have resource and timing constraints, and intertask relations, such as precedence and exclusion relations. The proposed algorithm is a depth-first search method on a finite TLTS derived from a TPN model. When searching for a feasible schedule, the algorithm suffers from the state space explosion problem. In order to maintain the state space growth under control, the proposed method uses minimization techniques. The algorithm presented here always finds a schedule, provided that one exists.

The proposed modeling and the scheduling synthesis are an important step toward embedded real-time software synthesis tools. So, it is planned to generate complete executable code from the formal model. This can be solved through TPN with tasks, which is an extension of TPN, which annotates transitions with program code. Another extension is to take into account different operational modes in the pre-runtime scheduling.

REFERENCES

[1] T. F. Abdelzaher and K. G. Shin. Optimal combined task and message scheduling in distributed real-time systems. In *Proc. IEEE RTSS*, pages 162–171, December 1995.

[2] K. Altisen, G. Göbler, A. Pnueli, J. Sifakis, S. Tripakis, and S. Yovine. A framework for scheduler synthesis. *IEEE Real-Time System Symposium*, pages 154–163, Dec 1999.

[3] R. Barreto, S. Cavalcante, and P. Maciel. A time petri net approach for finding pre-runtime schedules in embedded real-time systems. In *1st Int. Workshop on Embedded Computing Systems (ECS'04)*. IEEE CS Press, march 2004.

[4] G. Bruno, A. Castella, G. Macario, and M. Pescarmona. Scheduling hard real time systems using high-level petri nets. *13th ICATPN*, pages 93–112, Jun 1992.

[5] M. DiNatale and J. A. Stankovic. Dynamic end-to-end guarantees in distributed realtime systems. In *Proc. of the IEEE Real-Time Systems Symposium*, pages 216–227, 1994.

[6] P. Godefroid. *Partial Order Methods for the Verification of Concurrent Systems: An Approach to the State-Explosion Problem*. PhD Thesis, University of Liege, Nov. 1994.

[7] P. Merlin and D. J. Faber. Recoverability of communication protocols: Implicatons of a theoretical study. *IEEE Transactions on Communications*, 24(9):1036–1043, Sept. 1976.

[8] A. K. Mok. *Fundamental Design Problems of Distributed Systems for the Hard-Real-Time Environment*. PhD Thesis, MIT, May 1983.

[9] J. Xu. Multiprocessor scheduling of processes with release times, deadlines, precedence, and exclusion relations. *IEEE Trans. Soft. Engineering*, 19(2):139–154, February 1993.

[10] J. Xu and D. Parnas. Scheduling processes with release times, deadlines, precedence, and exclusion relations. *IEEE Trans. Soft. Engineering*, 16(3):360–369, March 1990.

[11] J. Xu and D. Parnas. On satisfying timing constraints in hard real-time systems. *IEEE Trans. Soft. Engineering*, 1(19):70–84, January 1993.

SCHEDULABILITY ANALYSIS AND DESIGN OF REAL-TIME EMBEDDED SYSTEMS WITH PARTITIONS

David Doose, Zoubir Mammeri
IRIT - Paul Sabatier University Toulouse, France
{doose, mammeri}@irit.fr

Abstract: Resource partitioning is used to run several independent applications on the same hardware while avoiding error propagation. However, classical methods of validation and design are not adapted to this technique, so new methods have to be elaborated. In this paper, we define four utilization bounds, which give sufficient conditions to guarantee an execution sequence without timing faults as long as the utilization rate of the system remains under the bound. They can of course be used to validate a system with partitions, but the fact that they are based on a partial knowledge of the system allows to use them during system design. This latter point is interesting since we can thus validate a system whose parameters are not yet completely defined, which can greatly reduce the cost by avoiding many backtracks in development cycle.

1. INTRODUCTION

The use of computers in industrial processes that involve critical application [1] induces changes in the design of systems. To run several applications simultaneously on the same systems, one can choose a distributed or centralized architecture. The first solution avoids propagation of errors between independent applications [2] but its cost increases with the number of applications (including the costs of space, a major issue in avionics for instance [3, 4]). Besides it is possible nowadays to centralize computations owing to computer performances, which have increased and are still increasing faster than embedded applications complexity.

However, costs reduction must not cut down on safety. That is why we need to develop new methods to design, validate and safely execute independent applications in a centralized environment. Many researches have been conduced in this area and many kinds of solutions were proposed [1, 5], among which partitioning [6–8].

Partitioning is an interesting solution, which allows to run several applications on the same hardware while keeping their independence and the safety requirements. The ARINC-653 [9] standard is a typical example of partitioning, that uses both strict resource partitioning and time partitioning. This time partitioning is based upon a multi-level or hierarchical scheduler [10–12] composed of a cyclic scheduler for the partitions, and a fixed-priority scheduler for the tasks inside a partition. The layer organization offers modularity and re-usability [13], which reduces the cost of the systems. Many recent real-time systems [14, 15] use it, and moreover classical methods of validation [16] can be used without any particular problem for this kind of systems, which makes the partitioning solution an almost perfect one.

However, the use of a fixed-priority scheduler is a problem regarding performance, since the utilization bounds are quite low [17, 18]. A dynamic priority scheduler (such as EDF) would be useful to increase the scheduling capacity of partitioned systems. And thus the cost of the system.

The cost of validation also has to be considered. Indeed, the design of hard real-time systems differs from classical design processes in that the hardware is to be taken into consideration very early.

The validation step requires the knowledge of both hardware and software. In fact, it is particularly difficult to know the time parameters of tasks, including their worst case execution time. Indeed, computation methods of WCET are based on the knowledge of the hardware and on the software implementation. This second point is the most problematic since implementation and testing are expensive, and it may have to be re-done several times if the validation fails.

In this article, we propose techniques to limit this risk. We try to give an explicit representation of the system and its scheduling capacity usable even during the design step. Indeed, some time parameters of tasks can be known very early, such as for instance the period which often depends on the properties of external systems. The partitioning choice is also often made before the software implementation step.

Owing to this partial knowledge, we will determine processor utilization bounds which, if respected, will guarantee an execution without timing faults. This technique allows to conduct in parallel tasks software implementation and validation. The advantage is that the validation using this technique can detect some errors before the complete realization of the system, which can drastically cut down the design costs of hard real-time systems.

This article is structured as follows: the next section describes the system properties and presents some notations. Section 3 introduces four utilization bounds, and describes their properties and how to use them for validation. In section 4, we present methods, based on bounds, to allow the designer to find partitions parameters. Finally, we conclude our work in section 5.

2. BACKGROUND

The concept of partitioning induces that the processor allocation is not linear. This makes unusable the model of task commonly used [17]. That is why we will use *the generalized multiframe task* model [19–23].

Task notion

The concept of task uses in this article is relatively simple, but it makes possible to model and study many real-time systems [24, 16]. A task τ_i is defined as a couple (c_i, p_i), where c_i is the worst case execution time and p_i is the period of the task.
The study of partitioned systems highlights the difference between the concept of application and the concept of task. Indeed, these two concepts are often wrongly confused. In the case of partitioned systems this is not allowed because the concept of partition is used to separate the applications and not the tasks. Thus, the various tasks of a partition are considered as an application or a group of tasks ($\mathcal{G}$) to which a complete processor is assigned. In this article, we consider that this collection is partially ordered according to the task index set, thus the period of the first task is the shortest one ($\forall_{i=1...n}\ p_1 \leq p_i$).

Partitioning

We now introduce the concept of partitioning. Even if we will only study here the partitioning of the processor, we can notice that the following definition of partition can be extended to any kind of resource.

Definition 1 (Partition). *A partition Π is a tuple (Γ, P), where Γ is an array of N pairs $\{(S_1, E_1), ..., (S_N, E_N)\}$ that satisfies $(0 \leq S_1 < E_1 < S_2 < E_2 < ... < S_N < E_N \leq P)$ for some $N \geq 1$, and P is the partition period. The processor is available to a task group executing on this partition only during time intervals $[S_i + j \times P, E_i + j \times P], 1 \leq i \leq N, j \geq 0$.*

This representation of the partitioning has the advantage of being able to model any static behavior.

Definition 2 (Supply Function). *The supply function $S(t)$ of a partition Π is the total amount of time that is available for Π from time 0 to time t.*

Definition 3 (Demand Bound Function). *Let τ be a task, and t a positive number. The demand bound function $dbf(\tau, t)$ denotes the maximum cumulative execution requirement of the jobs of τ that have both arrival times and deadlines within any time interval of duration t.*

Theorem 1 ([21]). *A group $\mathcal{G}$ is infeasible on a partition Π if and only if $\sum_{\tau \in \mathcal{G}} dbf(\tau, t) > S(t_0 + t) - S(t_0)$ for some positive real numbers t_0 and t.*

The major interest of this theorem comes from that the complete knowledge of the task parameters is not needed. We will thereafter use this property to introduce new theorems based on a partial knowledge of the system.

Definition 4 (Least Supply Function). *The least supply function $S^*(t)$ of a partition Π is the minimum of $(S(t+d) - S(d))$ where t, $d \geq 0$.*

Definition 5 (Critical Partition). *A critical partition of a partition $\Pi = (\Gamma, P)$ is $\Pi^* = (\Gamma^*, P)$ where Γ^* has time pairs corresponding to the steps in $S^*(t)$ such that Π^*'s supply function equals $S^*(t)$ in $(0, P)$.*

The critical partition is an essential concept because it can express in a non-pessimistic way the worst situation, for the schedulability of a task group, relative to a partitioning (Π).
The following theorem was, up to this article, the best means to study effectively the schedulability of a partitioned real-time system (as far as we know).

Theorem 2 ([21]). *A task group $\mathcal{G}$ is infeasible on a partition Π if and only if:*
$\sum_{\tau \in \mathcal{G}} dbf(\tau, t) > S^*(t)$ *for some positive real number t.*

3.   SCHEDULABILITY AND UTILIZATION BOUNDS

The previously defined method allows to study the schedulability of a real-time partitioned system, without pessimism. However it has some disadvantages. Indeed, since it uses all the system characteristics (parameters of both, tasks and partition), a system modification, as negligible as it may be, implies to restart the process of validation from the beginning. For the same reason, it cannot be used in an interactive design of the system. Moreover, this method does not provide an intuitive idea of the capacity of the system to meet task time-constraints. Finally, towards the aim of adding the system some tasks dynamically, this method is too complex to be used as acceptance test for new tasks.
So there is a need of another kind of solutions. That is why we introduce four utilization bounds to study the schedulability of partitioned systems.

Demand bound function

In the particular situation where a task is defined only by its period and its worst case execution time, the demand bound function is defined as follow:
$\sum_{\tau \in \mathcal{G}} dbf(\tau, t) = \sum_{i=1}^{n} \lfloor \frac{t}{p_i} \rfloor \times c_i.$

Theorem 3. *A task group $\mathcal{G}$ is schedulable on a partition Π if and only if $\forall t \in \mathcal{D}$, $\sum_{\tau \in \mathcal{G}} dbf(\tau, t) \geq S^*(t)$ with $\mathcal{D}$ such as: $\mathcal{D} = \{k \times p_1, \ldots, k \times p_n\}$ $\forall_k$ such as $\forall_n k \times p_n \leq lcm(p_1, \ldots, p_n, P)$.*

The proof is commonplace because the demand bound function grows only at the instants t such that $t \in \mathcal{D}$.

Minimal partition

We introduce the concept of *minimal partition* which allows the designer to study the schedulability of a system in which some parameters are unknown.

Definition 6 (Minimal Partition). *The minimal partition is the partition such that its availability function $(S^{**}(t))$ is lower than or equal to all availability functions of every critical partition with same period (P) and period total availability $(A = \sum_{i=1}^{N}(E_i - S_i) = S(P))$.*

Thus we can easily deduce the formula of the minimal partition availability function, called *minimal function*:

$$S^{**}(t) = \left\lfloor \frac{t}{P} \right\rfloor \times A + \begin{cases} 0\,, if\ (t\ modulo\ P) \le P - A \\ (t\ mod\ P) - P + A\,, else \end{cases} \qquad (1)$$

As a consequence, the minimal critical partition is defined such as: $\Pi^{**} = (\{(P - S, P)\}, P)$.

The minimal partition is interesting because we can use it to validate partitioned systems with the following theorem.

Theorem 4. *If a task group $\mathcal{G}$ is schedulable in the minimal partition (Π^{**}), then $\mathcal{G}$ is schedulable in every partition (Π) with the same period (P) and same period total availability (A).*

Utilization bound

Using utilization bounds to study a real-time system is interesting, because it provides a means, to validate and design the system, less complex than the method based on the critical partition. But it also gives to the designer an intuitive idea of the availability of the system to schedule tasks without timing faults. To do so, we need to introduce a new hypothesis.

Hypothesis 1. *For any task group $\mathcal{G}$, the period of the first task must be greater than or equal to the period of the partition: $p_1 \ge P$.*

We can give these four following bounds:

$$\beta = \frac{\left\lfloor \frac{p_1}{P} \right\rfloor \times A}{\left\lfloor \frac{p_1}{P} \right\rfloor \times P + P - A} \qquad\qquad \beta' = \min\left(\frac{S^{**}(t)}{t}\right), \forall t \in \mathcal{D}$$

$$\beta'' = \min\left(\frac{S^*(t)}{t}\right), \forall t \in [p_1; \infty[\quad \beta''' = \min\left(\frac{S^*(t)}{t}\right), \forall t \in \mathcal{D}$$

with $\mathcal{D} = \{k \times p_1, \ldots, k \times p_n\}\ \forall_k$ such as $\forall_n\ k \times p_n \le lcm(p_1, \ldots, p_n, P)$.

Bounds properties

Pessimism.   One of the major advantages of the utilization bounds is their robustness. Indeed, the bounds being calculated only with parts of parameters of the system, their conclusions remain valid with some changes of the system. This property is interesting because it allows to use the utilization bounds during the design step. The partial knowledge needed to calculate the bounds, implies that they are pessimistic. In fact, the more parameters are needed to determine a bound, the less pessimistic it is. In order to quantify the precision of each bound we use a simulator varying the number of tasks and the parameters size [25]. The results show that the first bound (β), may be too pessimistic to use it to validate a system, contrary to the others. That's why we recommend to use it for the design.

Loss.   Pessimism makes it possible to characterize the behavior of a method based on a sufficient condition, compared to a perfect method based on a necessary and sufficient condition. The concept of loss makes it possible to measure, at the same time, the inaccuracy of the method of validation as well as the waste of processor time that comes from partitioning.

We can thus define the *loss* of an utilization bound B as follows:

Definition 7 (Loss). $\mathcal{P}_B(t) = \left(\frac{A}{P} - B \right) \times t$

The simulations show that the loss rate decreases quickly with the ratio p_1/P. We can also use the definition of the loss to prove the following theorem:

Theorem 5. *For any group $\mathcal{G}$ if $U_\mathcal{G} < \frac{A}{P}$, then whatever the characteristics of partitioning are, there is one period for the partition (P) short enough to schedule all the tasks of $\mathcal{G}$ without timing faults.*

Bound comparison

Until now we evaluated the precision of the various utilization bounds thanks to simulations. These results show that some bounds are less pessimistic than others. This observation intuitively seems logical; indeed it appears reasonable to think that a technique of validation based on a whole of knowledge is less pessimistic than another which requires less knowledge. In fact, we can prove the following partial order between the fourth utilization bounds: $\beta \leq \beta' \leq \beta'''$ and $\beta \leq \beta'' \leq \beta'''$.

Utilization of the bounds

We have four utilization bounds based on a partial knowledge of the system, we also know a partial order on their precision; it thus remains to recall in a clear way when to use each bound. Indeed, it is obvious to use the less pessimistic bound we can calculate. Thus, the designer must follow the instructions corresponding to its situation:

If only the total availability of the partition and the period of the partition or the smallest period of the tasks (or both), are known, then the utilization bound β should be used.

If the period of the partition and the total availability and the period of all the tasks are known then the bound β' should be used.

If the partition is completely known and the shortest period of the tasks is known to then the bound β'' should be used.

If the partition and the period of the tasks are known then the bound β''' should be used.

4.   BOUND-BASED DESIGN

In the previous section, we studied how to determine whether a real-time system with partition is schedulable. In this section, we will determine the values of the parameters of the partition so that the tasks are executed without timing faults.

Specific partitioning

We introduce here the concept of specific partition:

Definition 8 (Specific Partition). *The* specific partition *of tasks group $\mathcal{G}$ is a partition which allows to schedule all the tasks of $\mathcal{G}$ without timing faults, and for which the availability function is lower than or equal to all other scheduling of the tasks of $\mathcal{G}$.*

The specific partition of the task group $\mathcal{G}$ is denoted $\Pi_{\mathcal{G}}$ and $S_{\mathcal{G}}(t)$ its availability function. To determine the specific partition, we proceed in three steps: first find task constraints; second, keep the significant ones only, third calculate the steps of the specific partition.

The first stage consists in finding, for each task, when the demand bound function changes. The second stage consists in finding the instants when the constraints are the more restrictive (i.e. when the request of the resource is significant). To do that, we just have to find the pairs $(t, dbf(t))$ such that $t \in \mathcal{D}$ and to keep only those which bring an additional constraint. In fact, a pair $(t_i, \sum_{\tau \in \mathcal{G}} dbf(\tau, t_i))$ is not significant if $\exists t_j \geq t_i$ such that $S_{\mathcal{G}}(t_j) \geq \sum_{\tau \in \mathcal{G}} dbf(\tau, t_j) \Rightarrow S_{\mathcal{G}}(t_i) \geq \sum_{\tau \in \mathcal{G}} dbf(\tau, t_i)$. Once determined the significant pairs, we determine the various pairs (S_i, E_i). To do so, we associate with each t of a significant pair, one E_i; and to each corresponding instant where the request increases, a S_i.

Determining the total availability of the partition

It is possible to use the utilization bound β to find the total availability of a given partition A, from tasks parameters. To do that, one can use various methods according to the utilization bounds.

The first solution which can be used with all the bounds consists in proceeding in an iterative way by progressively increasing the availability per period way until the bound is verified.

However, there is another solution, more formal, based on the β bound use. This method makes it possible to calculate the smallest value of A which makes schedulable the tasks of the partition. The following equation makes it possible to calculate the smallest value of A:

$$A \geq U \times P \times \left(\frac{\lfloor \frac{p_1}{P} \rfloor + 1}{\lfloor \frac{p_1}{P} \rfloor + U} \right) \tag{2}$$

Determining the period of the partition

The utilization bounds also make it possible to determine the period of the partition. The use of the theorem given in the previous section makes it possible to state that the bounds enable to find a period of the partition, enough short, which schedules all the tasks of the partition, if the utilization ratio of the partition is lower than the availability of the partition.

There still are two solutions: one is iterative and consists in reducing the size of P gradually until the bound is verified, the other is based on the β bound. Indeed, we can demonstrate that if the following equation is checked, then the system is schedulable.

$$P \leq p_1 \times \left(\frac{\frac{A}{P} - U}{\frac{A}{P} - \frac{A}{P} \times U} \right) \tag{3}$$

5.   CONCLUSIONS

The main goal of this article is to provide guidelines for the designer to represent clearly the capacity of a system to schedule tasks without timing faults. For that, we propose four utilization bounds. These bounds provide an intuitive representation of a system whose designer has a partial knowledge, and this method thus makes it possible to provide a judgment on the schedulability of a system even if its design is not finished. A comparative study of these bounds enable to state in a clear way and specify some rules of their use, according to knowledge of the studied system.

The results obtained in this article are already concretely usable. However, taking into account other shared resources, whose access is controlled by protocols specific to real-time systems [24, 26], is mandatory to extend the field of application of the studied methods. This is why our future research will focus on the intra and inter partitions resource sharing using specific protocols. In this article, the speed of the processor was constant, but on the current processors it is common to be able to modify it. Thus, it would be interesting to vary the frequency of the processor on the different steps of partitioning.

REFERENCES

[1] A. Bondavalli, A. Fantechi, D. Latella, and L. Simoncini. Design validation of embedded dependable systems. *IEEE Micro*, 21:52–62, September/October 2001.

[2] Peter van der Stok and Paul T.A. Thijssen. Prevention of replication induced failures in the context of integrated modular avionics. In *Embedded System Applications*, pages 153–170. Kluwer Academic Publishers, 1997.

[3] P. Conmy and J. McDermid. High level failure analysis for integrated modular avionics. In *6th Australian Workshop on Safety Critical Systems and Software*, volume 3, 2001.

[4] Ben L. Di Vito. A model of cooperative noninterference for integrated modular avionics. In *Dependable Computing for Critical Applications (DCCA-7)*, 1999.

[5] M. Nicholson, P. Conmy, I. Bate, and J. McDermid. Generating and maintaining a safety argument for integrated modular systems. In *5th Australian Workshop on Industrial Experience with Safety Critical Systems and Software*, Melbourne, Australia, November 2000.

[6] J. Rushby. Partitioning in avionics architectures: Requirements, mechanisms, and assurance. Technical report, SRI International, Menlo Park USA, March 1999.

[7] B. L. Di Vito. A formal model of partitionning for integrated modular avionics. Technical report, NASA Langley Research Center, August 1998.

[8] B. Andersson and J. Jonsson. Fixed-priority preemptive multiprocessor scheduling: To partition or not to partition. In *Proceedings of the Int'l Conf. on Real-Time Computing and Applications*, pages 337–346, Cheju Island, Korea, December 2000. IEEE Computer Society Press.

[9] Airlines Electronic Engineering Committee. Arinc specification 653, January 1997.

[10] B. Ford and S. Susarla. Cpu inheritance scheduling. In *Usenix Association Second Symposium on Operating Systems Design and Implementation (OSDI)*, pages 91–105, 1996.

[11] P. Goyal, X.Guo, and H.M. Vin. A hierarchical CPU scheduler for multimedia operating systems. In *Usenix Association Second Symposium on Operating Systems Design and Implementation (OSDI)*, pages 107–121, 1996.

[12] John Regehr, Jack Stankovic, and Marty Humphrey. The case for hierarchical schedulers with performance guarantees. Technical Report CS-2000-07, Department of Computer Science, University of Virginia, march 2000.

[13] M. Nicholson and P. Hollow. Approaches to certification of reconfigurable ima systems, 2000.

[14] M.D. Bennett and N.C. Audsley. Developing a real-time micro kernel design process. In *22nd IEEE Real-Time Systems Symposium*, London , UK, December 2001. IEEE Computer Society Press.

[15] Michael Bennett and Neil Audsley. Developing an ima kernel based on l4 for avionic systems. Technical report, Dependable Computer Systems Centre, Dept. of Computer Science, University of York, UK, 2002.

[16] M. H. Klein, T. Ralya, B. Pollak, R. Obenza, and M. G. Harbour. *A Practitioner's Handbook for Real-Time Analysis: Guide to Rate Monotonic Analysis for Real-time Systems.* Software Engineering Institute, 1999.

[17] C.L. Liu and J.W. Layland. Scheduling algorithms for multiprogramming in hard real-time environment. *Association for Computing Machinery (ACM)*, 20:40–61, January 1973.

[18] J.P. Lehoczky, L. Sha, and Y. Ding. The rate monotonic scheduling algorithm: Exact characterization and average case behavior. In *IEEE Real-Time Systems Symposium*, pages 166–171, Los Alamitos, CA, 1989. IEEE Computer Society Press.

[19] A.K. Mok and D. Chen. A multiframe model for real-time tasks. In *17th IEEE Real-Time Systems Symposium (RTSS '96)*, page p.22. IEEE Computer Society, December 1997.

[20] S.K. Baruah, D. Chen, S. Gorinsky, and A. K. Mok. Generalized multiframe tasks. In *Real-Time Systems*, volume 17, pages 5–22, July 1999.

[21] A.K. Mok, A.X. Feng, and D. Chen. Resource partition for real-time systems. In *Seventh Real-Time Technology and Applications Symposium (RTAS '01)*, pages 75–84, Taipei, Taiwan, May-June 2001. IEEE Computer Society.

[22] A.K. Mok and A.X. Feng. Towards compositionality in real-time resource partitioning based on regularity bounds. In *22nd IEEE Real-Time Systems Symposium (RTSS'01)*, page 129, London, England, December 03-06 2001. IEEE Computer Society.

[23] A.X. Fen and A.K. Mok. A model of hierarchical real-time virtual resources. In *Real Time System Symposium*, pages 26–35, Austin, December 2002. IEEE Computer Society.

[24] L. Sha, R. Rajkumar, and J.P. Lehoczky. Priority inheritance protocols: An approach to real-time synchronization. *IEEE Transactions on Computers*, 39:1175–1185, September 1990.

[25] David Doose and Zoubir Mammeri. Analyse de bornes d'utilisation pour la validation de systèmes temps réel partitionnés. In *RTS 2004*, 2004.

[26] T. P. Baker. A stack-based resource allocation policy for realtime. In *Real-Time Systems Symposium*, pages 191–200. IEEE Computer Society Press, 1990.

FLEXIBLE RESOURCE MANAGEMENT

A Framework for Self-Optimizing Real-Time Systems

Carsten Boeke and Simon Oberthuer
Heinz Nixdorf Institut, Paderborn University
Fürstenallee 11, 33102 Paderborn, Germany
{boeke|oberthuer}@uni-paderborn.de

Abstract: The demand for highly flexible and reconfigurable applications for embedded systems under real-time constraints led to various demands for operating system capabilities. The resource manager of the operating system has to handle different service functions of the applications with different resource requirements and different qualities. Thereby, the grant of new resources has to be assured by an acceptance test. Whilst this issue is widely handled for the processor utilization and its schedulability analysis, it will be extended in the presented resource manager to a more general model. The profile model supports for an optimal resource utilization and also leads to a better system quality by enabling applications to use resources that are normally reserved for other applications. The resource manager also supports for a smooth integration of timing constraints and their acceptance tests for the resource allocation in a hard real-time environment.

1. INTRODUCTION

In the recent years real-time systems take over more versatile tasks and are more and more often used in dynamic scenarios. Systems of the future should be self-organizing, self-repairing, self-optimizing, self-adaptive, and self-reflective. To achieve this goal the system must be reconfigurable during runtime. Other challenging requirements for systems under this conditions are characterized by Schmidt, 2002: To adapt to the environment the systems must satisfy multiple QoS properties. Therefore, different *levels of services* are appropriate under different configurations and environmental conditions. The need for autonomous and time critical application behavior necessitates a flexible system substrate that adapts robustly to dynamic changes in mission requirements and environmental conditions.

Our basic approach to support reconfigurable applications follows the idea of service profiles. An application profile describes the configuration of the application, which in fact means what service function should be active. Additionally, the minimum and maximum resource usage boundaries are specified, which can be used to find an optimal profile for activation according to a feasible resource distribution. Besides the feasibility of the resource usage, the resource *utility* should be maximized. In order to support the process of finding an optimal set of all active application profiles, each profile is assigned a *quality* parameter. The quality parameter describes the benefit that the profile achieves when it would be active. This parameter is highly dynamic and can be changed from the application during runtime.

Important for these systems is that the flexibility does not harm the real-time constraints of the system. To describe the dynamic of applications for the operating system or other system components a model is required in which this dynamic can be represented.

The remainder of the article is organized as follows: Section 2 describes some previous experiences made with the configuration of real-time operating systems. Section 3 gives a short overview about reconfiguration approaches for embedded applications. Section 4 is the main part and describes our operating system driven resource manager that supports real-time reconfiguration and high resource utilization for embedded applications. Section 5 concludes this article with some general results.

2.   PREVIOUS WORK

Operating systems and run-time platforms for even heterogeneous processor architectures can be constructed from customizable components (*skeletons*) from the DREAMS's (**D**istributed **R**eal-time **E**xtensible **A**pplication **M**anagement **S**ystem) library [Ditze, 1995; Ditze, 1999; Ditze and Böke, 1998]. This process is done *a priori* during the design phase of a system. By creating a configuration description all desired objects of the system have to be interconnected and afterwards fine-grained customized. The primary goal of that process is to add only those components and properties that are really required by the application.

The creation of a final configuration description for DREAMS had been automated during the DFG project TEReCS (**T**ools for **E**mbedded **Re**al-Time **C**ommunication **S**ystems) [Böke, 1999; Böke, 2000; Böke, 2003]. During that project a methodology was developed in order to synthesize and configure the operating system for distributed embedded applications.

Another main issue of TEReCS is the integration of an off-line timing analysis into the design process for a configured distributed runtime platform. The design cycle of TEReCS specifies a loop. Within this loop a configuration is generated and its timeliness execution is checked as long as the check fails.

This implies that the configuration has impact on the analysis and the analysis has impact on the configuration.

During the exploration of this approach it had been revealed that configuration of software components increases dramatically their reuse. Contradictory goals, respectively trade-offs, for example, between performance and flexibility become highly adjustable. The operating system can be individually adapted to the concrete demands of the application. Hereby, the overall performance of the operating and communication system can be optimized.

3. RELATED WORK

The experiences about configuration of operating systems that have been gathered during the TEReCS project will be adapted to the application level. Therefore, applications must support for reconfiguration of their services. The approaches in the literature often introduce *service level* constructs. The application's state is divided into different *service levels*. In each of these service level states the application provides different functions with a different *resource usage, system benefit*, and *utility*.

Dertouzos and Mok, 1989 showed that for multi-processor systems no scheduling algorithm is optimal without a priori knowledge of the deadlines, computation times, and arrival times of the tasks. Popular algorithms like earliest deadline first and least laxity scheduling can be outperformed by other promising approaches that take resource requirements into account.

Lee et al., 1999 introduced *QoS dimensions* for a group of applications. In Q-RAM a utility function is used in order to dynamically optimize the resource requests of dynamic *application service levels*. The model requires *a priori* application profiles for each application.

Burns et al., 2000 presented a model that includes a set of different *service alternatives* for tasks. But their resource usage still is based on worst-case assumptions.

DQM [Brandt and Nutt, 2002] uses *QoS levels* to adapt multimedia applications to overload conditions. DQM uses worst-case execution time analysis to determine the resource usage. DQM does not reallocate tasks due to special situations.

In QuO [Loyall et al., 2002] applications adjust their own *service level* to improve performance. Applications react to the environment on their own accord.

ARM [Ecker et al., 2003] was especially developed to cope with unanticipated events, anomalies, or overload conditions. A system is seen as a dynamically allocated pool of resources. It is the job of a global scheduling policy to dispatch application tasks to all processors of the system. The software model incorporates knowledge of *application profiles*, network hardware, *utility*, and *service level* constructs for the applications. A service level s_a is represented by a value of R. An application can have assigned a set of service levels. Additionally, each application is assigned a workload w_a. For each application a and each host h with its defined workload and service level the response time $r_{a,h}(w_a, s_a)$ and the memory consumption $m_{a,h}(w_a, s_a)$ are determined. An *overall utility function* $U(s, w, r)$ can be defined, which must be monotonically non-decreasing in a combination of s, w, and r. An allocation of applications to hosts has to be found where the utility function is maximized.

The previously presented approaches define often a set of service alternatives per application that have different resource usages. This is named *service level* of the application. The benefit that the application achieves increases with higher service levels. Also the resource usage of an application is different according to its service level. It is the task of the resource manager to find a feasible resource distribution and to maximize the system's utility.

4.   FLEXIBLE RESOURCE MANAGER

In the scope of the Collaborative Research Center 614 is the challenge to make embedded applications self-optimizing. In this article an operating system driven approach is presented. For this approach applications must support several service alternatives, which claim for different resource usages. This means that applications are able to change their resource requirements. The maximal resource requirement of one service alternative is called *profile*. Due to the different resource usages per profile of an application task, the quality of the application can vary. It is the task of the resource manager of the operating system to support the tasks in finding their actual profile and to maximize the system's quality.

The following part defines the main features of our Flexible Resource Manager (FRM).

4.1   Profile definition

In our FRM per tasks τ_i the programmer can define a set of profiles P_i. In the following the actual number of tasks is assumed to be n, thus $1 \leq i \leq n$. The set must contain at least one profile. Profiles can be compared to different run or *service levels* of a task. At each time only one profile $\overline{\rho_i}$ of task τ_i is active. Each profile of a task implements another service level of the task. Inside of a profile the following information are stored:

Resource requirements.   Each profile describes a different level of recourse requirements of the task. A task can only allocate resources in the range that its active profile defines. The following data must be provided: The type of the resource (e.g. memory, CPU time, area on a FPGA, bandwidth on a communication medium, etc.), the quantity of the resource in ranges (e.g. 128-256kb, 20%-30%, 10-20 kbits/s, etc.), and the delay of the requests (e.g. $5\mu s$), which describes the *maximum* delay between the request and the assignment of the resource. When a task wants to allocate more resources than described in its active profile, it has to switch to a profile with appropriate resource requirements.

Switching conditions. The FRM is responsible for activating a profile. To support the FRM a task has to describe switching conditions in each profile. This conditions describe when and under which constraints a task can switch to another profile. Additionally, it is defined how long the switch will take, and which methods to execute. These methods are so-called enter and exit methods per profile, with their worst-case execution times (WCET) assigned.

Profile quality. The programmer or a quality manager application can order the profiles according their quality. The quality of a profile p is defined through the quality value $q_p \in [0, 1]$. The FRM uses this value to decide which profile to activate as described later in detail.

Service function. Each profile is assigned a main function that has to be executed when the profile is active. When switching between two profiles, the appropriate leave function of the old profile will immediately be activated, while the main function of the old profile is stopped. Hereafter, the enter function of the new profile will be executed. After this enter function terminates the main function of the new profile becomes immediately active. Thus, the active process of a profile is divided into an enter, main, and leave interval.

4.2   Profile configuration

We call a combination of profiles $c = (p_1, p_2, ..., p_n)$ with $p_1 \in P_1$, $p_2 \in P_2$, ..., $p_n \in P_n$ the configuration of the system. This means every configuration maps each task to one of its profiles. The configuration of all actual profiles $\overline{c} = (\overline{p_1}, \overline{p_2}, ..., \overline{p_n})$ is called active configuration.

4.3   Quality of the system

The FRM is responsible for switching between the profiles of the tasks under the switching conditions. To provide the FRM with information, which profile is the best for an application and which application to favor, the FRM considers the quality of the profile and the importance ($\iota_i \in [0, 1]$) of each task τ_i.

It represents the importance of this task inside of the whole system and the RTOS can consider it for optimizing the system. The value is set from the programmer, but can be changed dynamically online.

A quality function $Q(c)$ defines the quality of a configuration. The FRM uses this function to decide which configuration has to be activated, by maximizing the quality function. The programmer of the system has to define the quality function. For example, a simple quality function can be:

$$Q(c) = \sum_{\tau \in T} \iota_\tau \cdot q_{\rho_\tau}, \text{ with } \rho_\tau \in c$$

4.4 Configuration classification

In classical approaches for resource management, applications in real-time systems define worst-case requirements. The classical resource management has to assure that the upper limits from all applications do not exceed the system limits. When these upper limits are only reserved for worst-case resource requirements and do not represent the average case, then this leads often to an internal waste of resources. This means that the applications can only allocate resources in their a priori defined boundaries.

Guaranteed allocation. Per configuration, we define a resource to be in a guaranteed allocation state, when the normalized sum of all upper bounds of the resource requirements of the profiles of the configuration is lower than 100%. This means that the sum of all upper bounds of the resource requirements for the resource do not exceed the available amount of the resource. We define the configuration to be in a guaranteed allocation state, when all resources are in a guaranteed allocation state.

Over allocation. In a real-time environment applications want to have guaranteed resources. This leads to unused resources in the average case by reserving them for worst-case resource allocations.

We define per configuration a resource to be in an over allocation state, when not all upper bounds of the resource requirements of the configuration can be granted at the same time. This means that the sum of all upper bounds of the resource requirements for the resource exceeds the available amount of the resource in the system. We call a configuration to be in an over allocation state, when one or more resources are in an over allocation state.

When a conflict appears (more resources are required than available) this conflict must be solved, because in a real-time environment the applications need planning reliability. Denying of a resource requirement is normally not acceptable and can lead into catastrophic results. To deal with this fact our FRM allows transitions from a guaranteed allocation configuration to an over allocation configuration only under special circumstances. Transitions can only be granted if a guaranteed allocation configuration can be reached in time, when a conflict appears.

4.5   Profile reachability graph

We define a *profile reachability configuration graph*. This is a directed graph. Each configuration represents a node. From one node to another node a directed edge exists, if the system can switch from the first configuration to the second configuration. A weight is assigned to the edges, which indicates how long it takes to switch from the start configuration to the destination configuration. This weight is taken from the WCET of the enter and leave methods of the corresponding profiles. Each node is classified to be in a guaranteed allocation state or an over allocation state. This classification can also be done per resource.

4.6   Allowing over allocation

The basic idea is to allow the system to be in an over allocation state configuration, when the FRM can guarantee that a guaranteed allocation state configuration can be reached in time. Here, "in time" means that a new resource requirement that leads to a conflict must have a greater assignment delay than the switch time to a guaranteed allocation state configuration. In order to speed up the search time for a guaranteed allocation state configuration in the graph, the taken paths from the guaranteed to over allocation states will be recorded and cached.

Figure 1 shows a simple profile example with two tasks and the corresponding profile reachability graph. The first task τ_1 has two profiles $\rho_{\tau_1,1}$ and $\rho_{\tau_1,2}$, the second task τ_2 has only one profile $\rho_{\tau_2,1}$. From this follows that the corresponding profile reachability graph consists of two nodes: one for configuration $c_1 = (\rho_{\tau_1,1}, \rho_{\tau_2,1})$ and one for $c_2 = (\rho_{\tau_1,2}, \rho_{\tau_2,1})$. When we assume that our system has 1024kb memory for the application tasks, the configuration c_1 belongs to the set of guaranteed allocation states and the configuration c_2 to the set of over allocation states. We also assume that task τ_1 allows to activate the profile $\rho_{\tau_1,2}$ when it is in profile $\rho_{\tau_1,1}$ and vice versa. So, the two nodes of the profile reachability graph are connected with two directed edges, one from

T	ι	Profile					
		Profile name	q	Memory in kb	Delay	Enter	Leave
						WCET	
τ_1	1.0	$\rho_{\tau_1,1}$	0.6	128-256	$1\mu s$	$1\mu s$	$2\mu s$
	1.0	$\rho_{\tau_1,2}$	1.0	256-768	$1\mu s$	$3\mu s$	$4\mu s$
τ_2	0.6	$\rho_{\tau_2,1}$	1.0	256-512	$6\mu s$	$5\mu s$	$7\mu s$

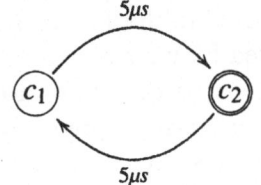

Figure 1.   A simple example for profiles and their reachability graph

c_1 to c_2 with the weight (switch time) 5 ($2\mu s + 3\mu s$) and one from c_2 to c_1 with weight 5 ($4\mu s + 1\mu s$).

Let us start with this scenario. We assume that our system is in the configuration c_1 and both tasks have each 256kb memory allocated. In this case, the tasks use only up to 512kb memory of the system memory. Our FRM checks whether task τ_1 can switch to profile $\rho_{\tau_1,2}$, which would bring the system in the over allocation state c_2. This can be granted, because when task τ_2 would allocate more memory, the assignments have to be fulfilled in $6\mu s$. Thus, the FRM has enough time to reconfigure the system in the guaranteed allocation state c_1, by forcing task τ_1 to go back from profile $\rho_{\tau_1,2}$ in profile $\rho_{\tau_1,1}$, which takes only $5\mu s$. The FRM grants the transition into the over allocation state c_2 and caches a way back to the guaranteed allocation state. This can help to optimize the system quality, while τ_2 uses less memory (in its average case only 256kb), task τ_1 is allowed to use up to 768kb memory by entering an over allocation configuration. When τ_2 wants to enter its worst-case scenario, then τ_1 has to switch back to its lower profile.

4.7   Resource allocation paradigm

This FRM assumes special requirements according the resource allocation by the applications:

1 The application specifies *a priori* the minimum and maximum limits per *resource usage*. The application cannot acquire less or more resources than specified. If the application wants to do so, then it has to specify a new profile with appropriate limits. The activation of the new profile underlies an *acceptance test* of the operating system.

2 The active profile of an application also registers the actual resource consumption (which must be in the specified limits).

3 All resource demands (also within the specified limits of the actual profile) require an announcement to the operating system. Between the announcement and the assignment a delay is assumed. The profile specifies a *maximal* delay per resource. Note, that this delay is a worst-case value.

Due to the fact that the maximal resource requirement per application is fixed for the active profile and that the assignment delays are greater than the activation delays for guaranteed allocation state profiles, the overall system quality can be improved. This can be achieved by allowing applications to have resource requirements that lead in the worst-case to an overload condition (refer to task τ_1 of the example). Such overload conflicts can be solved, because the FRM assures that a guaranteed allocation state profile can be activated before the resources for the worst-case scenario have to be assigned.

The existence of activation paths to guaranteed allocation state configurations implies that the applications assure to degrade their resource usages. For example, this means that the task τ_1 can improve its system quality by activating the over allocation state profile $\rho_{\tau_1,2}$, which means to be able to use more resources. This might have been possible, because task τ_2 did not use all of its maximal resources of its worst-case scenario. But when task τ_2 wants to enter the worst-case scenario by acquiring more resources, then task τ_1 will be forced to reactivate its lower profile $\rho_{\tau_1,1}$. The operating system supports the maximal assignment delay per resource request by a *resource demand* and a *resource acquire* programming interface. Thus, the application programmer should split resource requirements into a demand and acquire function. They have to recognize that between the call of both functions the operating system will assure an appropriate delay. For this reason, the resource request is split into these two functions in order to enable the application to make some other work before the resources are granted. This implies that resource requirements should be announced as early as possible in order to enable the operating system to handle them.

5. CONCLUSION

Our Flexible Resource Manager (FRM) is appropriate for application tasks that use moderate resource requirements in the average use case. Their resource requirements can increase during seldomly occurring worst-case conditions. Additionally, a well-known maximum delay can be specified during the recognition of the worst-case conditions (announcement for a higher resource demand) and the start of their handling (respectively, using more resources). Thus, the difference of the average resource usage and the worst-case resource usage can be used by other applications. Those applications must assure to degrade their resource usage in time, when the worst-case scenario will be announced by the other task. This will lead to a better resource utilization (wasting less resources due to worst-case reservations) and also to a better system quality (by allowing other applications to increase their resource usage in order to improve their service quality).

The shown FRM opens new potential of optimization in real-time applications. It helps to negotiate about resources between applications, even when the applications do not know each other. The programmers have to split their application into different service levels and have to use the FRM profile API. Also the FRM is flexible and supports dynamics, which is important for self-optimizing applications.

6. ACKNOWLEDGEMENTS

This work was developed in the course of the Collaborative Research Center 614 - Self-Optimizing Concepts and Structures in Mechanical Engineering - Paderborn University, and was published on its behalf and funded by the Deutsche Forschungsgemeinschaft.

REFERENCES

Böke, C. (1999). Software Synthesis of Real-Time Communication System Code for Distributed Embedded Applications. In *Proc. of the 6th Annual Australasian Conf. on Parallel and Real-Time Systems (PART)*, Melbourne, Australia. IFIP, IEEE.

Böke, C. (2000). Combining Two Customization Approaches: Extending the Customization Tool TEReCS for Software Synthesis of Real-Time Execution Platforms. In *Proc. of the Workshop on Architectures of Embedded Systems (AES)*, Karlsruhe, Germany.

Böke, C. (2003). *Automatic Configuration of Real-Time Operating Systems and Real-Time Communication Systems for Distributed Embedded Applications*. Phd thesis, Faculty of Computer Science, Electrical Engineering, and Mathematics, Paderborn University, Paderborn, Germany.

Brandt, S. and Nutt, G. J. (2002). Flexible soft real-time processing in middleware. *Real-Time Systems*, 22(1-2):77–118.

Burns, A., Prasad, D., Bondavalli, A., Giandomenico, F. D., Ramamritham, K., Stankovic, J., and Stringini, L. (2000). The meaning and role of value in scheduling flexible real-time systems. *Journal of Systems Architecture*, 46:305–325.

Dertouzos, M. L. and Mok, A. K. (1989). Multiprocessor on-line scheduling of hard-real-time tasks. In *IEEE Transactions on Software Engineering*, volume 15, pages 1497–1506.

Ditze, C. (1995). DREAMS – Concepts of a Distributed Real-Time Management System. In *Proc. of the 1995 IFIP/IFAC Workshop on Real-Time Programming (WRTP)*. (Another copy with quite identical contents appeared in journal *Control Engineering Practice*, Vol. 4 No. 10, 1996.).

Ditze, C. (1999). *Towards Operating System Synthesis*. Phd thesis, Department of Computer Science, Paderborn University, Paderborn, Germany.

Ditze, C. and Böke, C. (1998). Supporting Software Synthesis of Communication Infrastructures for Embedded Real-Time Applications. In *Proc. of the 15th IFAC Workshop on Distributed Computer Control Systems (DCCS)*, Como, Italy.

Ecker, K., Juedes, D., Welch, L., Chelberg, D., Bruggeman, C., Drews, F., Fleeman, D., and Parrott, D. (2003). An optimization framework for dynamic, distributed real-time systems. *International Parallel and Distributed Processing Symposium (IPDPS03)*, page 111b.

Lee, C., Lehoczky, J. P., Siewiorek, D. P., Rajkumar, R., and Hansen, J. P. (1999). A scalable solution to the multi-resource qos problem. In *IEEE Real-Time Systems Symposium*, pages 315–326.

Loyall, J. P., Rubel, P., Atighetchi, M., Schantz, R., and Zinky, J. (2002). Emerging patterns in adaptive, distributed real-time, embedded middleware. In *9th Conference on Pattern Language of Programs*.

Schmidt, D. C. (2002). Middleware for real time and embedded systems. *Communications of the ACM*, 45(6):43–48.

AUTOMATIC SYNTHESIS OF SYSTEMC-CODE FROM FORMAL SPECIFICATIONS*

Carsten Rust, Achim Rettberg
University of Paderborn, Germany
Carsten.Rust@c-lab.de, Achim.Rettberg@c-lab.de

Abstract: The paper presents an approach for realizing high-level Petri net models in SystemC. The approach contributes to an existing methodology for the Petri net based design of distributed embedded real-time systems. It is intended to be a vehicle for realizing Petri net components in hardware. The paper describes the use of standard SystemC language constructs to realize the execution of a high-level Petri net, which is assumed to be separated into partitions. Besides techniques for realizing the mechanisms of Petri net execution, the integration of the code generation into the overall design flow is discussed. To demonstrate the effectiveness of our approach we use the inverse discrete cosine transformation (IDCT) that is part of the MPEG-2 algorithm.

Keywords: Petri nets, SystemC, Embedded Systems, System Synthesis.

1.   INTRODUCTION

We describe a method for synthesizing SystemC-Code from high-level Petri nets. The synthesis method is part of a Petri net based methodology for the design of distributed embedded real-time systems [13]. The methodology leads through the complete design process from modelling on an abstract level using high-level Petri nets via analysis and partitioning of the model down to automatic synthesis of an implementation. Within the synthesis stage, we currently are able to automatically generate target code for different microcontrollers that are interconnected by a communication media, for instance a CAN bus. Such a software implementation is sufficient for many applications. In certain cases, however, it is necessary to realize components of an embedded system in hardware in order to meet real-time constraints.

For realizing a component in hardware, a specification in a Hardware Description Language (HDL) has to be generated. Appropriate languages are

*This work was supported by the German Science Foundation (DFG) project SFB-376

for instance Verilog and VHDL. In addition to these languages, C/C++ based languages for hardware design and hardware software codesign respectively emerged in recent years. Prominent examples are SystemC [14] and SpecC [3]. Especially SystemC has been developed towards a standardized modelling language, that is intended to enable system level design and IP exchange at multiple levels of abstraction for hardware and software components in embedded systems. Developed for today's System-on-Chip (SoC) design with increasing complexity, it offers executable specifications with high performance in early design phases. Hence, SystemC can be a particularly suited vehicle for realizing Petri net components in hardware. In order to accomplish that, techniques for realizing the basic operations of Petri net execution in SystemC are needed. A description of these techniques is the main topic of this paper.

In the remaining sections of the paper, we first give an overview of approaches related to our work (Section 2) and provide some background concerning SystemC (Section 3). Section 4 gives an overview of the entire synthesis process and its integration into our design methodology, while Section 5 presents several details of the realization of high-level Petri net execution in SystemC. Finally, in Section 6 an application example is described.

2.   RELATED WORK

Many applications of Petri nets to various aspects of hardware design can be found in literature (cf. for instance [16]). One reason for the usage of Petri nets in this area is their ability to express concurrency and parallelism. Furthermore, Petri nets are a well-investigated formal model offering a variety of analysis methods. They are used e.g. for behavioural modelling, analysis and verification, synthesis, and performance analysis. There are even complete Petri net based systems for hardware design, e.g. the CAMAD high-level synthesis system [9]. A canonical method for interfacing suchlike Petri net based methodologies to standard hardware design tools is to generate VHDL- or Verilog-code. For generating HDLs from Petri nets, again several approaches can be found in literature. In [10] behavioural VHDL code is generated from Petri nets. The generated code is not synthesizable, but it can be used for simulation of the model. Another approach is described in [11]. Here, structural – fully synthesizable – code is generated from so called Hardware Petri nets, an extension of Place/Transition nets.

In order to develop similar approaches for the relatively new C-based HDL SystemC, some basic techniques for realizing Petri nets in SystemC should be provided.

Concerning SystemC, currently no approach for coupling it with a formal graphical modelling language like Petri nets is known to us. Methodologies based on SystemC use either this language directly (as for instance [4]) or blockdiagrams for representing the entire system (e.g. [8]). Blockdiagrams however are rather a means for visualization than a formal model. Hence, our work is a contribution to interface a formal implementation independent high-level Petri net-model to the implementation oriented language SystemC.

3. BACKGROUND

In this section, we give a brief overview of our target language SystemC. We pass on a detailed description of our Petri net model used for specification. A small example net is depicted in Figure 2 on page 191. Basically, our formal model is a form of high-level Petri nets. An overview of several high-level Petri net-models is given in [5]. A general introduction into Petri nets can be found for instance in [7]. Beyond standard constructs of high-level Petri nets, our formal model includes a hierarchy concept in order to support easy modelling of complex systems. Furthermore, we support delay specifications.

As regards SystemC, introductions can be found in [14, 6]. Similar to other HDLs, users can construct structural descriptions of designs in SystemC using modules, ports and signals. To enable structural design hierarchies, modules (SC_MODULE) can be instantiated within other modules. Communication between different modules is enabled by ports (single directional or bi-directional) and signals. All ports and signals are declared by the user to have a specific data type. Typical data types include single bits, bit vectors, characters, integers, floating point numbers, vectors of integers, etc. Four-state logic signals (i.e. signals that model 0, 1, X, and Z) are also supported by SystemC. For the behavioural part of a hardware specification, concurrent behaviours can be modeled using processes. Such a process can be thought of as an independent thread of control which resumes execution when some set of events occur or some signals change, and suspends execution after performing some action. Generally SystemC process instances have their own independent execution stack. Code within processes is executed sequentially. Certain processes in SystemC that suspend at restricted points in their execution do actually not require an independent execution stack - these process types are termed SC_METHODs. Optimizing SystemC designs to take advantage of SC_METHODs leads to great improvements of simulation performance when the number of process instances in a design is large, see [14]. In SystemC a set of features for generalized modelling of communication and synchronization is available. These are channels, interfaces and events. They enable designers to model the wide range of communication and synchronization found in system designs. Examples include HW signals, queues (FIFO, LIFO, message queues, etc.), semaphores, memories and busses (both as RTL and transaction-based models), see [14].

4.   SYNTHESIS PROCESS

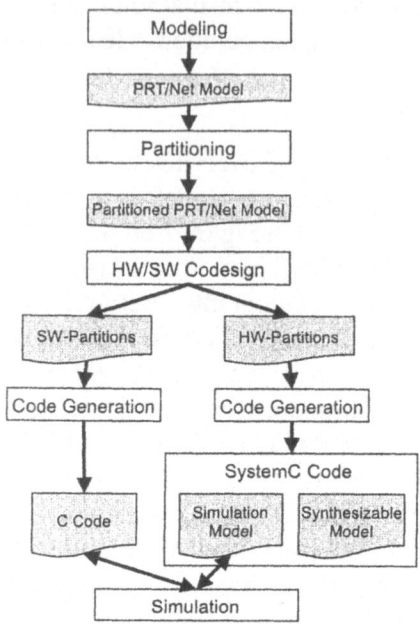

Figure 1.   Overview of entire synthesis process

The synthesis method presented in this paper is integrated into our methodology [13] as shown in Figure 1. We first give an overview of the first three steps, which are not in the scope of this paper. The step *modelling* leads to a hierarchical high-level Petri net of a system under construction. The next step is to flatten the net specification, which is straightforward, and to partition it. For *Partitioning*, we use a method introduced in [15]. The basic characteristics of this method are on the one hand that very small partitions are produced and on the other hand that the connections between different partitions have a simple structure. The latter is reached by encapsulating conflicts into single partitions. Due to the simple connection structure, communication between different partitions can be realized using a simple 'send and forget' mechanism. For more details concerning modelling and partitioning, we refer to [13].

After the step of partitioning, the system under consideration is given as a set of small Petri net-units with a simple connection structure. For each unit, it now has to be decided whether to realize it as hardware or as software. This non-trivial and usually iterative process is represented by the item *HW/SW Codesign*. Without going into the details of this process we can state that it leads to a separation of the Petri net-model into Hardware- and Software-partitions. The software parts are typically implemented in C or C++. To the hardware parts, the code generation presented in this paper is applied. In general, each Petri net can be mapped to an equivalent SystemC-specification, since SystemC is a superset of C. However, with the aim of realizing a Petri net component in hardware, the approach may be applied only to subnets that use a certain set of transition types. Petri nets that breach this condition, e.g. because a transition is annotated with a complex C function, have to be realized in software or to be modified by the engineer. With standard tools already available, the SystemC-code can be simulated together with the software parts, that were realized in C or C++. Tools for automatic synthesis of hardware from SystemC-Code are not available yet. However, these tools are under development. Guidelines for specifying synthesizable SystemC-models are given in [2].

5.   PETRI NET REALIZATION

We first describe the basic concepts for execution of high-level Petri nets in SystemC using the example depicted in Figure 2. Afterwards, the coupling of subnets will be described. The SystemC-Code for the net in Figure 2 is (partly) depicted in Figure 3. The entire net is realized as a SystemC-module. Hence, it can define several methods to be executed on activation of the module. In our SystemC-realization for high-level Petri nets, the constructor of the module (SC_CTOR, line 58) determines the method for Petri net execution (PO2_main, line 16) to be executed on activation. Therefore, this routine is executed – concurrently to the routines of other modules – each time the module is triggered. The routine itself is executed sequentially. The constructor also includes – besides the definition of the main method – the initialization of the module: For all inner places (in the example just one), the capacity and the initial marking is set (line 59) by means of methods that are not depicted in Figure 3. The mechanisms for triggering in line 64 are related to the interface specification, which has – as usual in hardware specification – to be defined for

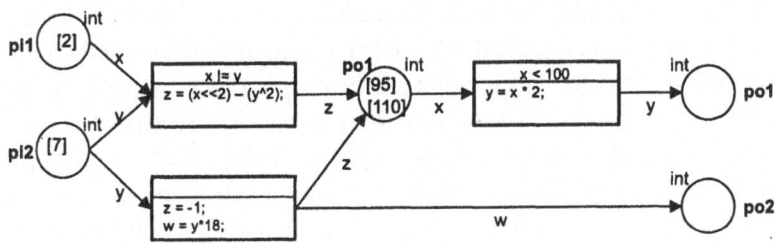

Figure 2.   High-Level Petri Net Example

```
 1: SC_MODULE(Partition_P02) {              35:                // check transition preset
 2:     // module not clocked                36:                for (i_p1=0; i_p1<p1->get_num();
 3:     // triggered by pi1, pi2, po1 and po2               i_p1++) {
 4:                                           37:                    x = p1->read( i_p1 );
 5:     // in-/output places                  38:
 6:     sc_port<place_int_in_if> pi1;         39:                    // check guard
 7:     sc_port<place_int_in_if> pi2;         40:                    if (x < 100) {
 8:     sc_port<place_int_out_if> po1;        41:                        enabled = true;
 9:     sc_port<place_int_out_if> po2;        42:                        break;
10:                                           43:                    }
11:     // internal places                    44:                } // END for()
12:     place_int p1;                         45:            } // END if
13:                                           46:
14:         ...                               47:            if (enabled) {
15:                                           48:                // transition can fire
16:     void P02_main() {                     49:                p1->demark( i_p1 );
17:         // variable declaration           50:                y = x * x;
18:         sc_bit enabled, fired;            51:                po1->mark( y );
19:         sc_int<32> i_p1, x, y;            52:                fired = true;
20:                                           53:            } // END if
21:         fired = true;                     54:
22:         while (fired) {                   55:        } // END while
23:             fired = false;                56:    } // END P02_main
24:                                           57:
25:             // process transition t1      58:    SC_CTOR(Partition_P02) {
26:                 ...                       59:        // set capacities of internal places
27:             // process transition t2      60:        set_place_capacities();
28:                 ...                       61:        set_initial_marking();
29:             // process transition t3      62:
30:             enabled = false;              63:        SC_METHOD(P02_main);
31:                                           64:        sensitive << pi1 << pi2 << po1 <<
32:             // check transition postset   po2;
33:             if (po1->get_capacity() > 0) {  65:    }
34:                                           66: };
```

Figure 3.   SystemC-Code for Example in Figure 2

each module in addition to the behavioural specification. The interface of the module for subnet P02 is specified in lines 5 to 9 of Figure 3. For each place of the net that is to be connected to other components, an instance of SC_PORT is defined. When instanciating the subnet, an object has to be provided for each port that implements the interface specified for the port (`place_int_in_if` and `place_int_out_if` respectively). The specification of the triggering mechanism in line 64 has the effect that the module is activated each time the value of one of the ports changes. Since the module is triggered only by changes on in- and outports, it is independent from the system clock.

The behavioural specification for executing the transitions of a net is like a standard software implementation using C or C++. In a loop (lines 22 to 55), which is executed until no more transition-firing can occur, each transition is evaluated. As an example, the evaluation code for transition t3 is included in lines 29 to 53. First, it is checked whether the transition is enabled (lines 30 to 45). The check starts with testing whether the output places provide enough capacity for the token produced by a transition firing. Afterwards it is examined whether the input places contain enough token. Finally, the transition guard is evaluated. If the transition has concession to fire, the corresponding changes in the place marking are realized (lines 48 to 51). This includes removal of token from incoming places, evaluation of the transition annotation and creation of token for outgoing places. As shown in the source code in Figure 3, places are realized by instanciating a place class generated therefor (line 12). The decla-

```
1: // Main Routine
2: int sc_main(int argc, char* argv[])
3: {
4:      // Partitions
5:      Partition_P01 Partition_P01("Partition_P01");
6:      Partition_P02 Partition_P02("Partition_P02");
7:
8:      // Testbench
9:      Stimulus Stim("Stimulus");
10:     Monitor Monitor("Monitor");
11:
12:     // Clock
13:     sc_clock Main_Clock("Main_Clock", 50, SC_NS);
14:
15:     // Channels
16:     place_int_fusion P02ToP01_1("P02ToP01_1");
17:     ...
18:
19:     // connect to clock
20:     Partition_P01.clock(Main_Clock);
21:     Stim.clock(Main_Clock);
22:     Monitor.clock(Main_Clock);
23:
24:     // connect partitions
25:     Partition_P02.po1(P02ToP01_1);
26:     Partition_P01.pi3(P02ToP01_1);
27:     ...
28:     ...
29: };
```

```
1: class place_int
2: {
3:   public:
4:       sc_int<32> read(sc_int<2>);       // read token
5:       void demark(sc_int<2>);  // delete token
6:       sc_int<2> get_num();      // current number of tokens
7:       sc_int<2> get_max();      // place capacity
8:       sc_int<2> get_capacity(); // free token space
9:       void reserve(sc_int<2>);  // reserve in token space
10:      bool mark(sc_int<32>);    // store token
11: };
```

```
1: class place_int_in_if: virtual public sc_interface
2: {
3:   public:
4:       virtual sc_int<32> read(sc_int<2>) = 0;// read token
5:       virtual void demark(sc_int<2>) = 0;    // delete token
6:       virtual sc_int<2> get_num() = 0;    // nu. of tokens
7:       virtual sc_int<2> get_max() = 0;    // capacity
8: };
9:
10: class place_int_out_if: virtual public sc_interface
11: {
12:   public:
13:      virtual sc_int<2> get_capacity() = 0;   // free space
14:      virtual void reserve(sc_int<2>) = 0;    // reserve
space
15:      virtual bool mark(sc_int<32>) = 0; // store token
16: };
```

Figure 4.   SystemC-Code for entire net and for a place / a channel

ration of the place class used for place p1 of the example net is depicted in the upper right part of Figure 4. For the example net, only the depicted place class `place_int` is needed. In general, one class is generated for each place type occuring in a net specification.

Beyond evaluation of single transitions, a Petri net-implementation has to provide mechanisms for resolving conflicts, for instance the conflict between transition t1 and transition t2, when both places pi1 and pi2 are marked with appropriate token. Conflict resolving is however realized implicitly when transitions are implemented in one module as indicated in Figure 3, since the code of one SystemC-module is executed sequentially. Furthermore, our partitioning method ensures that transitions realized in different modules are not conflicting (cf. Section 4).

Obviously, the simulation algorithm for a single subnet is pretty simple. The strategy of evaluating all transitions of a net in a loop would be very inefficient for large nets. We do however assume only small subnets to be realized in each partition (cf. Section 4), for which the simple strategy is sustainable. For the execution of the entire net, a less clumsy simulation strategy is realized, which avoids steady evaluation of all transitions. Instead, after each change of the net marking of one partition, only those other partitions are evaluated, whose transitions are affected from the change (since they are connected to a place with a modified marking). This is realized implicitly by using adequate primitives for communication between different partitions.

For coupling of subnets, our code generation approach assumes partitions that communicate with each other via shared places. For building partitions, we hence assume an algorithm that – like our partitioning algorithm mentioned in Section 4 – cuts a given net at places, leaving a copy of a cut place in both partitions built through cutting. The connections between partitions are realized by means of channels. In the SystemC-Code for the partitioned net, partly provided in Figure 4, the channels needed for communication between partitions are created in lines 15 to 17. For each connection, we create a channel, in our example net an instance of class place_int_fusion. The channel class implements the interfaces place_int_in_if and place_int_out_if, which are depicted in the lower right part of Figure 4. Naturally, these classes have the same methods as the class for inner places of the same type int. Since place_int_fusion implements these interfaces, an instance of the class is qualified to connect for instance the outport po1 of partition P02 (cf. Figure 2 and 3, line 8) with the inport pi3 of another – not further specified – partition P01. The – straightforward – implementation of the channel class is omitted. In general, channels are not synthesizable. Due to the simple communication structure between partitions, we suppose however, that the corresponding channels can be refined to synthesizable code using signals. In order to enable evaluation of the specified system by simulation, a testbench consisting of a stimulus (line 9) and a monitor (line 10) are created. A clock is needed for the testbench as well as for timed subnets as partition P01. For the realization of this timed component we refer to [12]. For the testbench, standard SystemC-classes are used.

6.   APPLICATION EXAMPLE

In order to evaluate our approach, we have implemented the inverse discrete cosine transformation (IDCT) according to the approach of Chen-Wang [1] as a Petri net. The IDCT consist of 13 additions, 13 subtractions, and 14 constant coefficient multiplications. The data-flow graph of the IDCT is depicted in figure 5. The boxes indicate a partitioning into so-called butterfly components. These components each consist of one addition and one subtraction with crossed inputs. In some cases, a butterfly component has constant coefficient multiplications for each input of the addition and subtraction. Other possibilities for partitioning are to include the entire IDCT into one partition or to include into each partition one operation only.

Based on a Petri net library containing all required elements, the depicted data-flow graph could easily be transformed into a high-level Petri net and - using the approach presented in this paper - into SystemC-Code. Hence, we were able to compare the generated code with an already existing hand-written implementation. A comparison concerning simulation time has shown no sig-

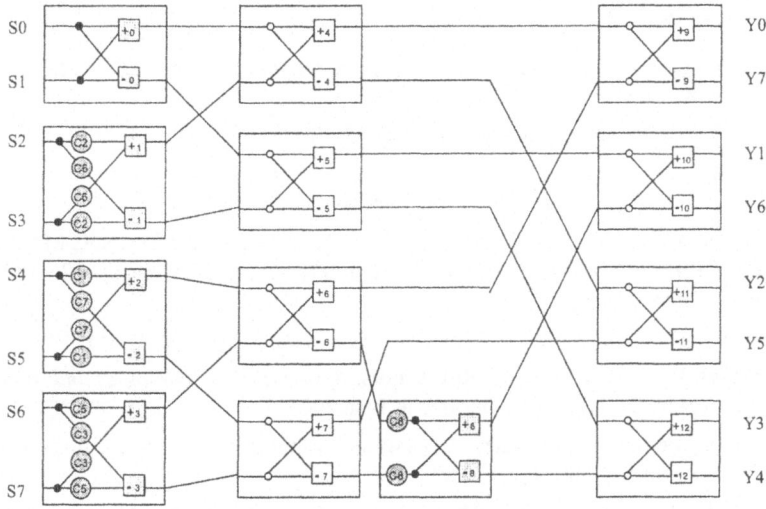

Figure 5.   Data-flow graph of the inverse discrete cosine transformation (IDCT)

nificant differences between the implementations. An advantage of the transformation into Petri nets is for instance that tests with different partitionings of the model can easily be achieved. The partitioning can be influenced by the user or by design parameters in the sense of design space exploration. Furthermore, we are able to annotate timing information from previously synthesized components into the Petri net model. Starting with single partitions, we then are able to gradually analyse the timing behaviour of the specified system. This leads to a hierarchical design approach based on our SystemC code generation from Petri nets.

7.   CONCLUSION

An approach for the realization of high-level Petri net-models in SystemC was introduced. The approach aims at providing a code generation component for realizing Petri net-models of embedded real-time systems in hardware. We presented SystemC-implementations for several aspects of high-level Petri net execution. Furthermore, we described how the SystemC-code generation is integrated into our existing methodology for the design of distributed embedded real-time systems. As an application example, we implemented the IDCT that is part of MPEG-2. We specified this example using Petri nets as well as using SystemC directly. The comparison between the manually and the generated SystemC code for simulation have shown no significant differences. With the presented approach, we are able to perform a design space exploration based on a partitioning of the system.

REFERENCES

[1] Chen-Wang, *Inverse two dimensional DCT, in Proceedings of the IEEE ASSP-32*, pp. 803-816, August 1984

[2] Doulos Ltd., *SystemC Golden Reference Guide*, 2002.

[3] D. D. Gajski, J. Zhu, R. Domer, A. Gerstlauer, and S. Zhao, *SpecC: Specification Language and Methodology*.   Kluwer Academic Publishers, January 2000.

[4] J. Gerlach and W. Rosenstiel, "System Level Design Using the SystemC Modeling Plat-form," in *Proc. of Workshop on System Design Automation (SDA'00)*, pp. 185-189, Rathen, Germany, March 2000.

[5] K. Jensen, G. Rozenberg, Eds., *High-Level Petri Nets*.   Springer Verlag, 1991.

[6] W. Müller, W. Rosenstiel, and J. Ruf, editors. *SystemC - Methodologies and Applications.* Kluwer Academic Publishers, Dordrecht, June 2003.

[7] T. Murata, "Petri Nets: Properties, Analysis and Applications," in *Proceedings of the IEEE*, Vol.77, No.4 pp.541-580, April, 1989.

[8] S. Pasricha, "Transaction Level Modeling of SoC using SystemC 2.0," in *Synopsys User Group Conference (SNUG 2002)*, Bangalore, May 2002.

[9] Z. Peng and K. Kuchcinski, "Automated Transformation of Algorithms into Register-Transfer Level Implementations," in *IEEE Transactions on Computer-Aided Design of Integrated Circuits and Systems*, 13(2):150-166., Feb. 1994.

[10] D. Prothero, "Modelling and Implementation of Petri Nets Using VHDL," in *Hardware Design and Petri Nets*, Yakovlev, A.; Gomes, L.; Lavagno, L., Eds., Boston: Kluwer Academic Publishers, 2000, pp. 223-236.

[11] P. Rokyta, W. Fengler, and T. Hummel, "Electronic System Design Automation using High Level Petri Nets,", in *Workshop for Hardware Design and Petri Nets*, Lisboa, June 22-26, 1998, pp. 129-138. 1998

[12] C. Rust and A. Rettberg. Generating systemc code for the execution of high-level petri nets.
     URL: http://wwwhni.uni-paderborn.de/eps/uni/publications/, May 2004.

[13] C. Rust, J. Tacken, and C. Böke, "Pr/T-Net Based Seamless Design of Embedded Real-Time Systems," in *LNCS 2075; International Conference in Application and Theory of Petri Nets (ICATPN)*, J.-M. Colom and M. Kounty, Eds., vol. 2075.   Newcastle upon Tyne, U.K.: Springer Verlag, 2001, pp. 343–362.

[14] S. Swan, "An Introduction to System Level Modeling in SystemC 2.0," published on technical paper section of Open SystemC Initiative (OSCI) website (www.systemc.org), 2001.

[15] J. Tacken, C. Rust und B. Kleinjohann. A method for prepartitioning of Petri net models for parallel embedded real-time systems, in *Proceedings of the 6th Annual Australian Conference on Parallel and Real-Time Systems, (PART'99)*, Melbourne, Australia, 1999.

[16] A. Yakovlev, L. Gomes, and L. Lavagno, Eds., *Hardware Design and Petri Nets*.   Kluwer Academic Publishers, March 2000.

HARDWARE SYNTHESIS OF A PARALLEL JPEG DECODER FROM ITS FUNCTIONAL SPECIFICATION

John Hawkins and Ali E. Abdallah
Centre for Applied Formal Methods,
London South Bank University,
103 Borough Road,
London SE1 0AA, U.K.
John.Hawkins@lsbu.ac.uk, A.Abdallah@lsbu.ac.uk

Abstract: Recent advances in manufacturing programmable logic devices, such as the FPGA, have made it possible to obtain reconfigurable circuits with upwards of one hundred million gates. Although we have such enormously powerful hardware at our fingertips, we are still somewhat lacking in techniques to properly exploit this technology to its full potential. In previous work, we have proposed a development methodology based on transformational programming and process refinement for producing provably correct solutions. Starting with a clear, intuitively correct specification of the problem, in a functional language such as Haskell, we apply a set of formal transformation laws to refine it into a behavioural definition in Handel-C, exposing the implicit parallelism along the way. This definition can then be compiled onto an FPGA. We apply this technique to a non-trivial, real world problem - a JPEG decompression algorithm, and achieve a truly scalable, parallel hardware implementation.

1.   INTRODUCTION

Greatly increased efficiency in solutions to real world problems can be achieved through parallelism and implementation in hardware. Unfortunately this comes at a cost; principally in terms of complexity. This complexity, coupled with the increased consequences of making mistakes, can make this a very costly process indeed.

A good example of a class of real world problems to illustrate these issues is that of image compression, particularly the JPEG standard [10, 11]. JPEG decoders and encoders are widely used, but not nearly as widely understood. Developers tend, quite naturally, to rely on tried and tested library code under normal circumstances. However, in some situations performance requirements force developers to leave behind the comfort of such libraries and look to new implementations.

At this point it is very important to have clear, unambiguous, and if possible, provably correct specifications to work from. We propose that functional programming languages [4], such as Haskell [5], facilitate exactly this. Indeed, we are not the first to consider the functional style a good foundation for a specification of JPEG decompression [7]. Not only do functional languages provide a good framework for specification, but also they give us scope for transformation and refinement not present in imperative languages. Such capabilities allow an efficient and correct implementation to be derived formally, and in part mechanically from the specification, by exploiting known efficient implementations for commonly used patterns of computation. This approach is often broadly referred to as patterns or skeletons [1, 2, 6].

Recent advances in FPGA chip manufacturing, coupled with the emergence of higher level compilation tools, such as Celloxia's Handel-C compiler [8], have together revolutionised hardware design from the exceedingly costly process it once was, to now being within the grasp of even the smallest company or academic institution. The Handel-C language has many desirable features including CSP [9] style communication, and an explicit means for denoting parallelism. However, it is an imperative language (being based on C), and as such, we argue, does not necessarily form a good basis for specifications, nor a good starting point for deriving a parallel algorithm. In this work, we use Handel-C as a target for implementation, deriving code in this language from specifications given in a functional style.

The rest of this work proceeds as follows. In Section 2, we give a brief overview of the notation used, and introduce the concept of refinement to explain how behavioural implementations can be derived from functional specifications. In Section 3 we discuss some issues relevant to the JPEG decompression process. In Section 4 we provide a functional specficiation of a JPEG decompressor. Then, in Section 5, we use this specification to derive a parallel implementation in Handel-C. This paper concludes in Section 6.

2.   NOTATION AND REFINEMENT CONCEPTS

Functional Notation.   As already noted, functional languages such as Haskell provide an extremely good environment for clear specification of algorithms. Details of functional notation in general can be found in

[4], with more specific information relating to Haskell in [5]. Also, certain aspects and properties of the particular notation we use in this work are explored in [1–3].

Handel-C.   Handel-C [8] is a C style language, and fundamentally imperative. Execution progresses by assignment. Communication is effectively a special form of assignment. As previously noted, communication in Handel-C follows the style of CSP. The same operators are used for sending and receiving messages on channels (! and ?), and communication is synchronous - there must be a process willling to send and a process willing to receive on a given channel at the same time for the communication to take place. Additionally, note that channels in Handel-C are typed - this is so the compiler knows how wide to make them. Parallelism in Handel-C can be declared with the **par** keyword. Handel-C has an equivalent of CSP's choice operator in the form of the **prialt** statement.

Refinement.   Having stated our specification environment (Haskell) and our target environment (Handel-C) it is now necessary to consider how we are to refine definitions in one to the other. These techniques are explained in more detail elsewhere [1–3], we shall provide only a very brief overview here.

Data Refinement.   Given that our implementation in Handel-C will rely on message passing, we need to consider how the types derived from our specification will be communicated. Most interesting to us are list types, and we will examine the alternative refinements for these here. Broadly we have two intuitive strategies for communication of a linear data structure (i.e. a list) - either sequentially or in parallel. We term these techniques streams and vectors respectively.

Streams facilitate a functional, or pipeline parallel scheme. To communicate a list as a stream, we send each value in order along a channel, and then signal the end of transmission (EOT). Although there are a number of possible options for how to signal the end of transmission, we have found the use of a second single bit channel the most widely applicable.

Vectors implement a data parallel scheme. To communicate a list as a vector each item is communicated independently, in parallel, on its own channel. There may be several variations to the vector, depending on the type of the items in the list.

These two structures may then be combined together to form refinements for lists of lists. One example of this is the vector of streams, which is a parallel composition of n streams, each communicating a sublist independently as a stream. Another example is the stream of vectors, in which at each stage an entire sublist is communicated in a single step, in parallel

Process Refinement.   Higher-order functions in our specifications can be refined into Handel-C implementations from a library of processes. We may have more than one implementation for any given higher order function depending on the setting in which we choose to use it (i.e. with streams or vectors). More detail on higher order process refinement can be found in [3].

As noted, the composition operator forms an important part of functional definitions. In terms of processes and parallelism, functional composition maps on to pipelining. Given a process P that outputs on a particular channel, and a process Q that takes input of the same type on a particular channel, we can pipe the result from one to the other simply by parameterising the name of their respective output and input channels and composing them together in parallel. This simple but powerful scheme can apply to both the stream and vector setting. We can pass in streams and vectors as parameters to processes in exactly the same way as we would simple channels.

3.   JPEG DECODING

We shall focus our efforts on a decoder for JPEG's baseline DCT method of compression. This is almost certainly the most commonly used method within the JPEG set of standards.

We shall require the use of restart markers in our compressed data. A JPEG decoder must maintain a set of predictors. The predictors will be modified each time a unit of data is decoded, and their values will affect the decoding of each unit. As such, for every single unit in the compressed file, we require that the previous unit has been at least partially decoded before it in turn can be decoded. This makes for a largely sequential decoding process. Thankfully, the JPEG standard recognises applications in which JPEG images might be communicated over unreliable media, and as such, data may have been lost part way through transmission. To this end, the standard includes the definition of restart markers. Whenever one of these markers is encountered, the predictors can be safely reset. This has the effect of defining a number of sections within the compressed data that can be decoded completely independently of each other.

It is important to clearly consider the hierarchy within a compressed JPEG file, when considering writing the specification for a decoder. To begin with we have a file. This can be split into two areas, the headers and the compressed scan data. The headers contain information about the compressed data (size, format and so on) as well as tables for dequantization and Huffman decoding.

Where restart markers are used, the scan can be decomposed into a number of independent sections which we shall call intervals. An interval can be further decomposed into one or more minimum coding units (MCUs). The number of MCUs per interval is defined in the headers. The MCU is a collection of units. Each unit, when fully decompressed, will form an 8×8 matrix of samples for a given component (usually one of Y, C_b or C_r for colour images). Generally, the chromincance components will be downsampled to achieve better compression. A typical scheme has an MCU representing a 16×16 block of pixels in the fully decoded output image. Within this, there will have been a unique Y (luminance) value for every pixel. However, each chrominance value will be shared by a 2×2 pixel block. As such, an MCU in this scheme will contain four units of Y samples, followed by one of C_b samples, and one of C_r samples.

4.　　FUNCTIONAL SPECIFICATION

We may find the following type definitions useful. A unit is an 8×8 matrix of coefficients (before transformation) or samples (after transformation). An MCU is a list of units. These types may therefore be defined as follows:

```
type UnitRow = [Int]
type Unit = [UnitRow]
type MCU = [Unit]
```

Now, to consider the functions that will comprise our decoder. At the highest level we require a function that will take in a list of compressed bytes representing the entire file, and will return an uncompressed image.

```
decodeJpeg :: [Byte] -> Image
decodeJpeg data = decodeScan hdrInfo scanData
  where (scanData,hdrInfo) = decodeHeaders data
```

An **Image** here can be considered as a simple two dimensional array of pixel values. This definition relies on two auxilary defintions. The first decodes the headers in the data, and returns both a **HeaderInfo** object and a list of the remaining data in the file, following the headers.

```
decodeHeaders :: [Byte] -> ([Byte],HeaderInfo)
```

The exact definition of `decodeHeaders` and the `HeaderInfo` type will not be shown in full here due to lack of space. Broadly, the header information should include all the numeric parameters and structures required for decoding. The second function, `decodeScan`, is where the bulk of the decoding effort takes place.

```
decodeScan :: HeaderInfo -> [Byte] -> Image
decodeScan hdrInfo = composeImage hdrInfo .
                  map (decodeInterval hdrInfo) .
                  readIntervals
```

This function is a composition of three stages. In the first, we use the function `readIntervals` to split the compressed scan data into a list of intervals which can be decoded independently of each other. Next, we map the function `decodeInterval` to each interval in the list of decoded sections within the image. Finally we apply `composeImage` to compose these sections together, a function which we shall keep deliberately vague.

The function `readIntervals` is simple, but crucial in terms of scope for parallelism, as we shall see later. It reads through the input list of bytes, and splits it into sublists based on the occurrence of restart markers. A restart marker will be a single byte with value ff in hex, followed by a value from d0 up to d7. The *encoder* will 'pad' any byte values of ff naturally occurring in the compressed data with a single zero byte to ensure they are never confused with a restart marker. This means that `readIntervals` can safely split up the compressed data without any greater level of detail than simply examining individual byte values. As such, this task should be very fast.

```
readIntervals :: [Byte] -> [[Byte]]
```

The next function, `decodeInterval`, will take a list of compressed bytes that form a single interval, and return a list of totally decompressed MCUs that, when reconstructed, will form the corresponding section of the output image. The definition is as follows:

```
decodeInterval :: HeaderInfo -> [Byte] -> [MCU]
decodeInterval hdrInfo
= map (transformMCU) . intervalToMCUs hdrInfo . bytesToBits
```

Here again we have a composition of three stages. Firstly, given that Huffman decoding works at the bit rather than byte level (due to the use of variable length codes), we employ `bytesToBits` to transform our input list of bytes into a list of bits. Next we apply `intervalToMCUs` which should supply us with a list of MCUs, each, at this stage, containing untransformed coefficients. Finally we map transformMCU, such that each MCU is transformed from a list of matrices of coefficients to a list of matrices of samples (Y, C_b, and C_r values). The type of intervalToMCUs is as follows:

intervalToMCUs :: HeaderInfo -> [Bit] -> [MCU]

We shall have to brush somewhat briefly over the goings on inside this function due to lack of space. Suffice to say we shall have a repeated application of a function which reads in an MCU, and maintains the state of the predictors between calls. Reading an MCU is in turn a repeated application of a function which reads in units.

Let us return now to the function transformMCU. This takes an MCU, containing units of untransformed coefficients, and returns an MCU containing units of fully decoded sample data. It maps the function transformUnit to each unit in the MCU.

transformMCU :: HeaderInfo -> MCU -> MCU
transformMCU hdrInfo = map (transformUnit)

The transformUnit function performs the familiar stages of transforming an 8×8 unit of coefficients into an 8×8 unit of output sample values. Firstly it performs zig-zag reordering, then dequantization (making use of the appropriate quantization table in the HeaderInfo structure), and finally applies the inverse discrete cosine transform.

transformUnit :: HeaderInfo -> Unit -> Unit
transformUnit hdrInfo = idct. dequantize hdrInfo . zigzag

5. IMPLEMENTATION

The majority of interesting functionality in the specification is concealed within the function decodeInterval, upon which we shall concentrate in this section. Given that an MCU is a list of units, and the number of units per MCU can be derived from the header information, it should be straightforward to flatten a list of MCUs into units and vice verse. This can be achieved with the functions unitsToMCUs and MCUsToUnits. Thus, with a little simple program transformation, we can arrive at the following definition:

```
decodeInterval' hdrInfo
 = unitsToMCUs hdrInfo .
   map idct . map (dequantize hdrInfo) . map zigzag .
```

```
MCUsToUnits . intervalToMCUs hdrInfo . bytesToBits
```

We may find the following 'shortcut' useful:

```
intervalToUnits hdrInfo
 = MCUsToUnits . intervalToMCUs hdrInfo . bytesToBits
```

This compositional form is now well suited to process refinement. An overview of the definition of DECODEINTERVAL could therefore proceed as follows. Communication between intermediate stages of the process (and indeed the final output of the process) will be in the form of a stream of vectors. At each stage a whole unit (sixty four values) is communicated in parallel. We have:

```
macro proc DECODEINTERVAL (streamin,vectorout)
{
    StreamOfVectors (64,Int) vsmida, vsmidb, vsmidc, vsmidd;
    par
    {
        INTERVALTOUNITS (smid,vsmida);
        SMAP (vsmida,vsmidb,ZIGZAG);
        SMAP (vsmidb,vsmidc,DEQUANTIZE);
        SMAP (vsmidc,vsmidd,IDCT);
        UNITSTOMCUS (vsmidd,vectorout);
    }
}
```

Now we have a definition for DECODEINTERVAL, we can construct our overall refinement of decodeScan. Let us consider the three stages of decodeScan in turn. Firstly we have readIntervals. A process refinement of this function, READINTERVALS, should take a stream of bytes as input - it needs to process these sequentially. The output, a list of lists of bytes, can be produced as a vector - each interval can be processed independently. At the next stage, we map decodeInterval to each interval produced by readIntervals. As the input to this stage will be a vector, we shall choose VMAP to refine the map in the original specification.

We shall leave the output type of the compose image stage (which forms the output of the decoder as a whole) deliberately vague - we may want it in any one of several forms depending on the process that receives the data. Regardless of the exact structure of the output, the overall outline for the DECODESCAN process can proceed as in Figure 1. The implementation is depicted in Figure 2.

```
macro proc DECODESCAN (streamin,vectorout)
{
    VectorOfStreams (n,Byte) vectormida;
    StreamOfVectors (n,Byte) vectormidb;
    par
    {
        READINTERVALS (n,streamin,vectormida);
        VMAP(n,vectormida,vectormidb,DECODEINTERVAL);
        VFOLDR (n,vectormidb,vectorout,ADDINTERVAL);
    }
}
```

Figure 1.   The DECODESCAN process.

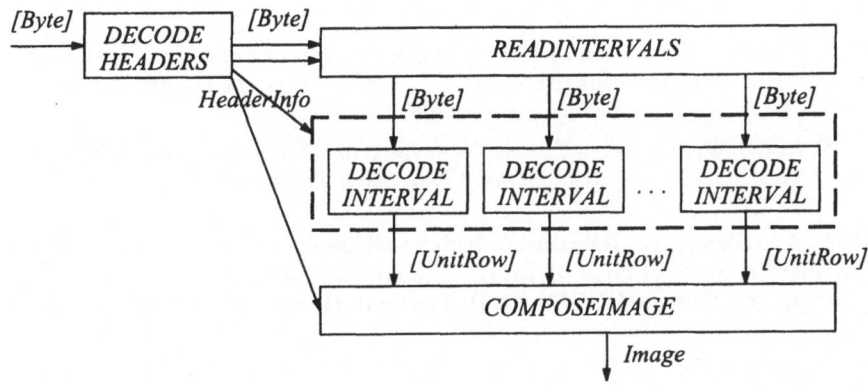

Figure 2.   The JPEG decoder process network

6.   CONCLUSION

We have presented a framework in which non-trivial algorithms can be specified in a clear, well structured environment, and then transformed formally, and in part mechanically, into an efficient behavioural implementation.

We have illustrated this with the development of a JPEG decoding algorithm, starting from a high level and intuitive specification in Haskell, and using this to derive a parallel Handel-C program that in turn can be compiled into a circuit design for an FPGA.

Given that the intervals (defined by the restart markers) in the compressed data are decoded independently of each other in parallel, our implementation is scalable, and as we are required to deal with larger problem sizes (effectively higher resolution images) we simply need to add more processing elements. Effectively this means we should use an FPGA with more gates, or combine more than one FPGA together, and the resulting execution time should not be greatly increased. This assumes, of course, that higher resolution images will contain more restart markers.

It is important to point out that restart markers are optional in the official JPEG specification, and the benefits of the implementation presented here on an image encoded without restart markers would be somewhat limited. It is worth noting however, that several newer compression standards derived from JPEG (including most notably MPEG-2, the worldwide standard for digital television), have adopted a version of restart markers which are mandatory.

REFERENCES

[1] A.E. Abdallah, Derivation of Parallel Algorithms from Functional Specifications to CSP Processes, in Bernhard Möller, ed., *Mathematics of Program Construction*, LNCS **947**, (Springer Verlag, 1995) 67-96

[2] A. E. Abdallah, Functional Process Modelling, in K Hammond and G. Michealson (eds), *Research Directions in Parallel Functional Programming*, (Springer Verlag, October 1999). pp339-360.

[3] A. E. Abdallah and J. Hawkins, Calculational Design of Special Purpose Parallel Algorithms, in *Proceedings of 7th IEEE International Conference on Electronics, Circuits and Systems* (ICECS 2000), Lebanon, (IEEE, December 2000). pp261-267.

[4] R. S. Bird and P. Wadler, *Introduction to Functional Programming*, (Prentice-Hall, 1988).

[5] R. S. Bird *Introduction to Functional Programming Using Haskell*, (Prentice-Hall, 1998).

[6] M. I. Cole, *Algorithmic Skeletons: Structured Management of Parallel Computation*, in Research Monographs in Parallel and Distributed Computing, (Pitman 1989).

[7] J. Fokker, Functional Specification of the JPEG algorithm, and an Implementation for Free, in R.C. Veltkamp and E.H.Blake, (eds), *Programming Paradigms in Graphics, Proceedings of the Eurographics workshop in Maastricht*, The Netherlands, September 1995. (Wien, Springer 1995). pp. 102-120.

[8] *Handel-C   Documentation*,   Available   from   Celoxica (http://www.celoxica.com/).

[9] C. A. R. Hoare, *Communicating Sequential Processes*. (Prentice-Hall, 1985).

[10] International Standards Organisation, *Digital Compression and Coding of Continuous Still Tone Images*. Draft International Standard DIS 10918-1.

[11] G. Wallace, The JPEG Still Picture Compression Standard, in *Communications of the ACM*, 43, 4, 1991. Draft International Standard DIS 10918-1.

A SELF-CONTROLLED AND DYNAMICALLY RECONFIGURABLE ARCHITECTURE*

Florian Dittmann, Achim Rettberg
University of Paderborn, Germany
roichen@upb.de, achim@c-lab.de

Abstract: Reconfigurable systems have the potential to combine the performance of ASICs with the flexibility of software. The architecture presented in this paper offers a new concept for reconfiguration by operating self-timed and self-controlling. Data is routed together with its control information in a so-called packet through the operator network to make local decisions concerning the behavior of the network. Therefore, we can realize different paths without a central control unit. In this paper, we describe the architecture from the aspect of reconfiguration. An example shows the architecture in practical operation.

Keywords: High-Level Synthesis, Reconfigurable Architectures, Embedded Systems.

1. INTRODUCTION

Nowadays processors work with clocks running in gigahertz and are programmable to execute all imaginable software programs. The flexibility is bought dearly by high power consumption and goes along with barely influenceable possibilities to use the available parallelism of algorithms. In contrast, ASICs provide high parallelism at low power consumption, yet only for fixed algorithms. Both concepts only partly fit in the requirements of data processing today. E. g. mobile devices demand for low power consumption and real-time data processing. Furthermore, all existing and in future arising standards should be supported. Such devices need the combination of the performance of ASICs with the flexibility of General Purpose Processors (GPP), more precisely their software.

Reconfigurable systems and their concepts address this problem area [2]. In such systems, existing modules are reused for other tasks and dynamically adjusted for current requirements. This procedure is supported by FPGAs. FPGAs are no longer only programmable at the beginning of appropriate applica-

*This work was partly funded by the *Deutsche Forschungsgemeinschaft (SPP 1148)*

tions; they can be partial reconfigured during operation. At the same time alternative architectures, like the PACT XPP (eXtreme Processing Platform) [7] or Quicksilver's ACM (Adaptive Computing Machine) [9] come on the market.

Thus, technical opportunities for dynamic reconfiguration are given, being constantly improved, and optimized. Besides the basic technical aspects, we need additional methods to realize simplified and flexible automated and concrete design cycles. By considering all the given arguments, it is not desirable to use centralized control processes, which represent a complex energy and area consuming control unit.

The MACT (Mauro, Achim, Christophe and Tom) architecture [11–13] developed at the University of Paderborn describes a concept to flexibly decentralize considerable tasks of reconfiguration by self-controlling. Necessary information for reconfiguration exists locally due to the combination of control information and data word. It is possible to adapt the processing of each data packet according to individual requirements. Required operators are requested and released. The clear identification of data allows direct and serial processing of different data.

In this paper, we firstly describe related work including the development of the MACT architecture and all necessary operators. Secondly, we give an overview of the requirement analysis for the data packet of the MACT architecture w. r. t. reconfiguration. Finally we present an example with an application that shows how MACT realizes the adaptation to exogenous effects.

2.   RELATED WORK

The PACT XPP, which addresses coarse grain reconfiguration, resembles the MACT architecture. A typical realization of the PACT XPP is similar to an array with processing nodes. The nodes are always alive, yet the functionality is dynamically changeable. The configuration respectively the reconfiguration is implemented by an appropriated flow. Therefore, it is essential to transform the instruction flow of a GPP into a configuration flow. This flow is mapped into a control flow graph representing the alternating configuration of the processing nodes over time. The control flow graph is executed sequentially.

The ACM approach by Quicksilver is based on run-time reconfigurable PLDs (Programmable Logic Device). Technical details concerning the implementation are hardly available. The main goal is to include algorithmic concepts in the architecture. Several ACMs are switched together according to requirements of the algorithms.

The MACT architecture is close to the concept of dataflow computation [14], as it is based on dataflow graphs. Further, concepts of dataflow computation often base on the inter-digitations of control- and dataflow. There, the processed data is combined with tokens to symbolize the status of affiliation.

The operators are triggered by the tokens evaluated from compare elements leading to demand-oriented execution similar to the MACT architecture. Synchronization at not unary operators does not have to be planned by a compiler in advanced, rather it is implicitly contained in the architecture.

A self reconfigurable platform based on FPGAs is described in [1]. In this example, the reconfiguration is executed by a microprocessor. The overhead of reconfiguration w. r. t. to power consumption is characterized in [10]. In this approach, the time of reconfiguration is reduced by pre-fetching. This leads to a more compact schedule.

3. MACT ARCHITECTURE

We describe the MACT architecture from two points of view. On one hand, the architecture is similar to the concept of the Internet on hardware level. On the other hand, it can be interpreted as a systematic approach for bit-serial calculation.

Within the Internet, data is transported without a central control element. All necessary information is transmitted in packets, with decisions done locally by routers or switches. Arriving packets activate nodes. These nodes decide how to proceed according to temporal circumstances. MACT uses a similar concept to transmit on dataflow level. This concept is especially suitable for processing of streaming-data. The architecture consists of an operator network derived from a dataflow graph. Data-words are assembled with suitable meta information and sent into the operator network. Each data-word activates self-controlled the next operator and ensures a minimal distance between the following packets. Valid data-words are alternated with minimal idle times. Thus, the processing of data within the MACT architecture is free of deadlocks and similar to operating in waves. Meta information of the packets is evaluated at specific points in the operator network to select the path.

Bit-serial processing is characterized by small operators, less area usage, low number of I/O pins, but higher latency in opposite to parallel calculation [3]. MACT is a systematic approach to process data bit-serial. Data of the addressed application classes, like control algorithms or signal processing, often is bit-serial. Therefore, conversion is not necessary. Further, we use advanced operators (e. g. [4]) and pipelining to considerably reduce the latency.

Data packets are transmitted synchronously into the operator network. The network can be interpreted as a clocked shift register. Due to the fixed length of data packets, scanners allow a precise evaluation and modification of the information at any time. Typical operators are addition, multiplication, etc. that are cascaded and assembled directly. Therefore, there exists no buffer storage. The local self-control cares for necessary synchronization of not unary operators, provoked by different path length.

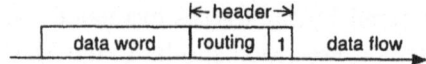

Figure 1.   Data packet

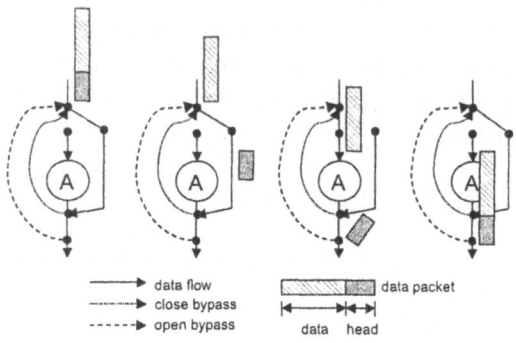

Figure 2.   Bypass

3.1   Realization

The functionality of the architecture is exemplary described by means of a data packet (see Fig. 1). Valid data packets consist of a leading flag ('1') in front of the data. The flag is needed to identify arriving packets at operators. Furthermore, we use the flag for local control. Additional information for routing in the operator network is stored between the leading bit and the data word. The bit length of the header information (flag and routing information) and the data word length are fixed at implementation. As mentioned before, such data packets are transported bit-serial on one wire.

When packets arrive at arithmetic operations, header information and data word have to be split, as the arithmetic operation should not process the head information. This is realized by so-called *Bypass* signals. The *Bypass* is implemented parallel to the operator (see Fig. 2). Initially the *Bypass* is active. When the flag of the header information reaches a specific point in the network the *Bypass* is deactivated and the following part of the data packet (data word) is directed to the operator. The *Bypass* is set to the active state when the data packet is outside the operator, again signaled by the leading flag of the header information. Details concerning the implementation of the *Bypass* can be found in [5].

It is necessary to synchronize the dataflow within the operator network at non-unary operators. We do this by *Stall* signals that are directed in opposite direction of the dataflow. These *Stall* signals can stop the dataflow. So-called *Synchronizers* in front of each non-unary operator implement this functionality. Yet, it is only necessary to delay a minimal amount of operators and not

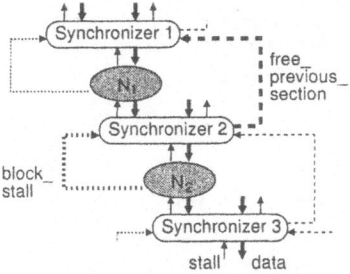

Figure 3. Synchronizer: A packet activates the *Block_Stall* signal at N_2, that is transmitted to Synchronizier 2. This one generates a *Free_Previous_Section* signal and transmitted it to Synchronizier 1. Consequently section N_1 is released.

the complete network. Only the block of operators actually processing the data packet is delayed. We implement the *Block_Stall* therefore. The signal is gripped from the shift register and directed to the corresponding *Synchronizers*.

Synchronizers having received a *Block_Stall* accept new data packets, but will not dispatch them. If necessary a *Stall* is produced. The reactivation of the block that is blocked by a *Block_Stall* is done by a *Free_Previous_Section* signal generated from a *Block_Stall* of the following operator block, see Fig. 3.

The interaction of the signals leads to local consistency of data and forces minimal distances to consecutive data packets. Therefore, the data processing is conflict free and operates in waves. The entire control is based only on local signals and not on long control wires from a central controller. This concept of locally based control elements realizes a deadlock free pipeline processing. The MACT architecture is the second approach implementing a deadlock free pipeline architecture (the interlocking problem) after that one from [6].

3.2 Router

We integrated routing nodes called *Routers* in order to be able to process similar to concepts of the Internet. The *Routers* evaluate the routing information in data packets and decide which paths are selected. We use such path decisions to assemble or to reload suitable operator networks. Further requirements for routers are compactness by high flexibility and minimal latency (decision delay). A first variant of router implementations are multiplexers. In this case, the routing information of data packets is used to set the parameters of operators. This leads to operators with integrated routing structures. If data packets achieve e. g. a constant multiplication with different hard implemented constants, it is possible to select the constant from the routing information grabbed by *Scanners*. This implementation style is useful for low numbers of constants in opposite to include constants within the data packets.

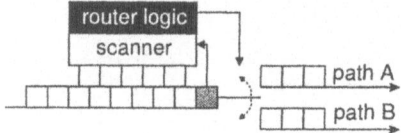

Figure 4.   Router example

We achieve more freedom concerning the path selection by implementing the routers as independent elements. Fig. 4 shows a router with two paths. A *Scanner* detects after the arrival of the flag (leading '1', see grey shaded register) the head information of the data packet. Thus, the logic of the routers interprets the head information. Depending on the result, the corresponding paths are triggered.

The router concept tends to result in two levels of reconfiguration. The first level selects between available paths of the operator network with the existing head information. A higher-level reconfiguration is based on this path selection mechanism. At this level e. g. the realization on an FPGA leads to reloading specific parts of a dataflow graph. At this point, the router has to be equipped with an intelligent replacement strategy similar to caching methods to minimize the reconfiguration of the FPGA. Both concepts have enough potential to operate locally and individually for each data packet. In this case, a central control element to generate signals and to track the data is not necessary. Therefore, it is practicable to process sequentially different applications with different requirements in the same operator network.

We integrate *Scanners* on the shift register before routers. These *Scanners* track the head information independently from the following elements (operators, synchronizers, or delay elements). The leading flag of each data packet is used to control the grabbing time. Routers represent an additional element in the shift register. This further delay is used for the decision of the router logic. Thus, we achieve a short latency of one clock cycle and a small area usage.

4.   RECONFIGURATION

In the previous section we described the routers and showed how a simple reconfiguration of the MACT architecture is achieved. In this section, we discuss the procedure in detail and examine the problem when using a surrounding system. Thereby, the MACT architecture offers a variety of possibilities for the implementation. Furthermore, we examine the possibilities towards practicability.

The goal to be reached for reconfigurable architectures is the realization of intelligent systems. Such systems have the capability to independently adjust the behavior and structure due to exogenous (environmental influences, user

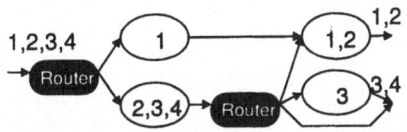

Figure 5.   Network with two routers and four paths

interaction) and endogenous effects (ageing, component failure, altered target parameters, etc.). Systems have to be adapted permanently and efficiently to changing requirements without additional control overhead. Comparing this adaptation with a GPP, it is a context switch, which should be as short as possible, because most reconfigurable systems are used under real-time constraints. Reconfigurable architectures allow a context switch on hardware respectively wiring level. The dataflow is manipulated from outside by a control system. Therefore, an external and complex control element is necessary to track the data and to provide appropriate networks and follow-on operations.

MACT offers the possibility to reduce the overhead of a context switch by local presence of the control and routing information. Not a control element, but the data itself controls the way to the operators. Therefore, data is assembled with explicit identification to distinguish between each other. Thus, it is possible to have data from different applications in the same operator network. This offers the freedom to use paths and operators without a central control element. Furthermore, we realize a dynamical extension of algorithms simply according to given facts. This is achieved by assembling data and suitable head information before entering the network. The peripheral preprocessed logic is only responsible for the attachment and generation of the data packet. Further control tasks are decentralized and operate independently in the local control elements (synchronizers, routers).

5.   IMPLEMENTATION OF THE SYSTEM

The implementation of the system should make profitable use of the characteristics of the MACT architecture. Thus, we distinguish between two tasks.

Firstly, we assume a hard implemented operator network with routers at suitable locations. These routers offer the possibility of multiple usages of areas of the graph (see Fig. 5). This kind of reconfiguration may be used for different coding standards like TDMA and GSM or refinements of compression algorithms. We code the path into the header of the data package. Concerning the example, we need 2 bits for the four possibilities. In general, the amount of n path possibilities can be realized with b_1 digits referring to $2^{b_1} = n$. The logarithmic dependency realizes many different paths to be coded by few bits.

Further, if data from different applications is intended to use the same path, the header must be extended with additional identification. The same formula

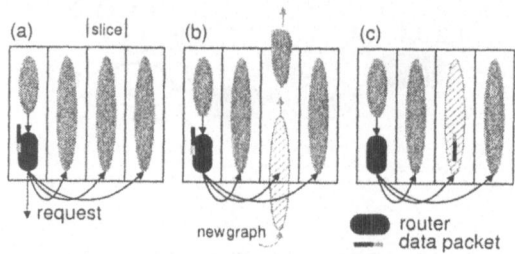

Figure 6.   Reconfiguration: In situation (a) a packet reaches a router on an existing path stored in a slice. The router sends a *Request*-signal so that the slice is configured with a new operator network (b). Then the packet is routed to the network (c).

leads to an amount of $m = 2^{b_2}$ possibilities for identification with b_2 bits. Here, we can combine both the path and identification information, as the first is needed inside the network, the latter after exiting the network. Each individual case demands for special care taken concerning possible double usage of bits. E. g. if there are less than 2^{b_1}, but more tan 2^{b_1-1} paths, one of those b_1 bits may be used for the additional identification of the different packets.

If path decisions are located early in the data flow network, we realize a further way of optimization. Parts of the header can be removed after the path decision is done, leading to shorter data packets for the ongoing processing.

We modify the above explained system in order to be able to adapt to new requirements. These new requirements are new versions of processing standard or complete new algorithms for data processing. In most cases, we will have to modify and add paths or exchange operator nodes. We can think of 3G and 4G mobile communication problems.

In order to be able to reconfigure hardware, there has to be the technical condition. We assume an FPGA, which contains the whole MACT architecture. We have multiple possibilities to reconfigure the network. Firstly, the FPGA may be programmed completely. All calculations have to be stopped for this task. The duration may take up to several milliseconds and the package generation part must be reconfigured. Now, we try to avoid these disadvantages.

FPGAs are dynamically partial programmable. It is possible to exchange parts of the circuit during operation. Still, this takes some time. We try to reduce the requirements for the reconfiguration, in order to speed up the reconfiguration phase. Therefore, we adapt the MACT architecture to these requirements. Basically, possible branches i. e. new paths can be found directly after routers. Thus, we extend routers with the possbility to request new paths. The header of the data packet is extended by one additional bit, which signals the need to establish a new path or not.

In order to be able to omit a central controller, the router itself will generate a data package that requests the new path. This data package consists

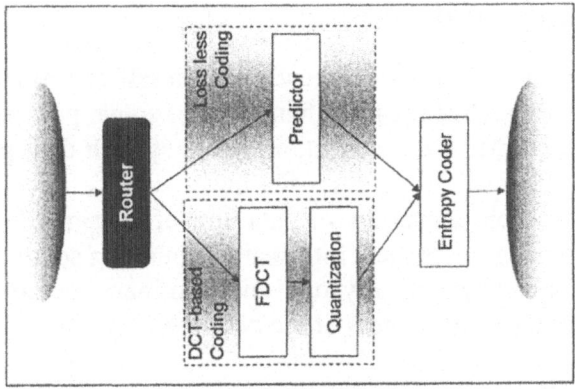

Figure 7. JPEG coding

of a location address (a number of slices of the FPGA) for the new operators. Thus, the reconfiguration data can be retrieved. The data packet generation unit buffered this reconfiguration information. To sum up, the process of reconfiguration is not controlled by a central controller, but organized locally and demand-oriented. Refer to Fig. 6 for a graphical example.

Using this order for the reconfiguration, we are able to reduce the control flow to a minimum. There is no need for a central controller, which would have to track the state of every data within the network. Again, different data packets of different applications can be calculated within one implementation of the MACT architecture. In order to reduce the busy waiting for new operators during the reconfiguration, we have planned to re-locate the scanners for the routers. Placing them earlier will mean additional time until the data will actually need the new path, thus hiding reconfiguration.

6.   EXAMPLE

As an example we present a part of the JPEG algorithm [8]. JPEG compresses images according to individual quality requirements. Fig. 7 shows a relevant part of the JPEG algorithm. Following a preprocessing, it is possible to either choose a lossy DCT (Discrete Cosine Transformation) or a lossless coding, before there is the entropy coding or compressing. We find different paths within the JPEG algorithm, initialized by a router. According to the meta information in the header, each data packet gets assigned the correct paths by the routers. Thus, data of different images with different requirements can be found in the same network.

The example JPEG consists of multiple possibilities to realize reconfiguration with the MACT architecture. This is especially true for an easy realization of dynamically adoptions of the data flow graph to new requirements.

7. CONCLUSION

In this paper we have shown how a new bit-serial self-controlled architecture can be used to easily realize the reconfiguration of signal processing systems. This architecture, the MACT architecture, operates with data packets which carry all relevant information and thus offer the possibility of local controlling. Especially path decisions changing the data flow of the signal processing can be realized by referring to the meta information. In doing so, the functionality of the circuit is adapted dynamically, or even reconfigured completely. Further work will consider the effectiveness of the described system.

REFERENCES

[1] B. Blodget, P. James-Roxby, E. Keller, S. McMillian, and P. Sundararajan. A Self-reconfiguring Platform. In *Proceedings of the International Conference on Field Programmable Logic*, Lisbon, Portugal, Sept. 2003.

[2] K. Compton and S. Hauck. Reconfigurable Computing: A Survey of Systems and Software. *ACM Computing Surveys*, 34(2):171–210, June 2002.

[3] P. Denyer and D. Renshaw. *VLSI Signal Processing: A Bit-Serial Approach*. Addison-Wesley Publishing Company, 1985.

[4] F. Dittmann, B. Kleinjohann, and A. Rettberg. Efficient Bit-Serial Constant Multiplication for FPGAs. In *Proceedings of the 11th NASA Symposium VLSI Design*, May 2003.

[5] F. Dittmann, A. Rettberg, T. Lehmann, and M. C. Zanella. Invariants for Distributed Local Control Elements of a New Synchronous Bit-Serial Architecture. In *Proceedings of the Delta*, Perth, Australia, 28 - 30 Jan. 2004.

[6] H. M. Jacobson, P. N. Kudva, P. Bose, P. W. Cook, S. E. Schuster, E. G. Mercer, and C. J. Myers. Synchronous Interlocked Pipelines. In *8th International Symposium on Asynchronous Circuits and Systems (ASYNC 02)*, Apr. 2002.

[7] PACT. The XPP White Paper. PACT Informationstechnologie GmbH, 2002.

[8] W. B. Pennebaker and J. L. Mitchell. *JPEG: Still Image Data Compression Standard*. van Nostrand Reinhold, New York, 1993.

[9] Quicksilver. Technology Backgrounder. QuickSilver Technology, 2000.

[10] J. Resano, D. Mozos, D. Verkest, S. Vernalde, and F. Catthoor. Run-Time Minimization of Reconfiguration Overhead in Dynamically Reconfigurable Systems. In *Proceedings of the International Conference on Field Programmable Logic*, Lisbon, Portugal, Sept. 2003.

[11] A. Rettberg, M. C. Zanella, C. Bobda, and T. Lehmann. A Fully Self-Timed Bit-Serial Pipeline Architecture for Embedded Systems. In *Proceedings of the Design Automation and Test Conference (DATE)*, Munich, Germany, Mar. 2003.

[12] A. Rettberg, M. C. Zanella, T. Lehmann, and C. Bobda. A New Approach of a Self-Timed Bit-Serial Synchronous Pipeline Architecture. In *Proceedings of the Rapid System Prototyping Workshop*, San Diego, CA, USA, June 2003.

[13] A. Rettberg, M. C. Zanella, T. Lehmann, U. Dierkes, and C. Rustemeier. Control Development for Mechatronic Systems with a Fully Reconfig. Pipeline Architecture. In *Proc. of the 16th Symposium on Integrated Circuits and System Design*, Sao Paulo, Brazil, 2003.

[14] T. Ungerer. *Datenflußrechner*. Teubner Verlag, Stuttgart, 1993.

PROFILING SPECIFICATION PEARL DESIGNS
"Try before build"

Roman Gumzej[1], Matjaž Colnarič[1] and Wolfgang A. Halang[2]
[1]University of Maribor, Faculty of Electrical Engineering and Computer Science, Smetanova 17, SI-2000 Maribor, Slovenia, Email: roman.gumzej@uni-mb.si;
[2]FernUniversität in Hagen, Faculty of Electrical and Computer Engineering, 58084 Hagen, Germany, Email: wolfgang.halang@fernuni-hagen.de

Abstract: An approach to holistic system modelling is presented, based on the Specification PEARL hardware/software co-design methodology, having its origin in the standard Multiprocessor PEARL specification language. Specification PEARL specifications and models represent prototypes of systems and programs, based on the PEARL program model. The system models built are checked for timely execution by co-simulation. The resulting information shall be used for fine-tuning the designs. Through the analysis of simulation traces a profiling process takes place. An integral CASE tool facilitating this holistic approach has also been devised.

After the profiling process has produced a feasible system model, the program prototypes may be enhanced to their full functionality. As long as their timing properties are not changed by this, utilising this methodology should minimise the possibility of implementing an infeasible system.

Key words: Real-time systems, co-design, co-simulation, verification, PEARL.

1. INTRODUCTION

With the ever increasing complexity of embedded control systems, the traditional development process of manual coding followed by extensive and lengthy testing is becoming inadequate. The main design concern, which first moved from low to high level program languages, recently moved to a higher abstraction level, which relies on automatic or semi-automatic code generators to produce code in traditional programming languages. Examples of these include the Unified Modelling Language (UML) [17], Model-Driven Architecture (MDA) [16] and Model-Integrated Computing (MIC) [14]. For real-time systems, timeliness and safety issues are just as important as functional correctness. Hence, to avoid exhaustive testing, they should be designed holistically, taking all their temporal and functional properties into consideration as early as possible, with their subsequent verification in mind.

To enable verification, often formal languages and/or mathematical notations are used, for which subsequently a proof can be worked out (e.g., formalisms supported by differential equations, which describe a system's operation in time and space [4], formal languages and timed automata [1], combinations of conventional CASE methods and state charts [15], graphical techniques with the expressive power of their formal language counterparts [3]). While enabling formal verification, most of these methods lack the versatility of basic constructs and user friendliness. Therefore, graphical formalisms with a greater set of basic constructs have been defined (e.g., CSR/CCSR [7], TTM/RTTL [9]), while keeping enough "strictness" to enable verification. Dedicated state transition automata like CRSM [9] are often used as basic internal computation model (e.g., POLIS [2]).

A wide variety of different verification methods has been combined with VHDL based design tools, ranging from formal methods to simulation with fault insertion and combinations thereof (e.g., [6]).

For pragmatic reasons, simulation is often used to check the correctness of a system designed or parts thereof. Hence, verifying systems with time limitations led to the introduction of real-time scheduling algorithms into their co-design and simulation (e.g., [8]). This approach is also used to check our designs for timeliness. The design and profiling processes are described in the forthcoming sections followed by a concluding summary.

2.   SPECIFICATION PEARL METHODOLOGY

Our co-design method [5] is based on the notation of the standardised Multiprocessor PEARL [12] specification language. It enables the construction of a conceptual system model, whereby its hardware and software architectures may be designed in parallel. The system model is built as a result of running the associated CAD tool. For each hardware and software component its timing information is specified for the later timeliness checking by co-simulation.

The main motives for using the mentioned method with the mentioned profile are:

1. the concepts of the modelling (specification) language and of the PEARL real-time programming language are syntactically and

conceptually closely related,

2. the ability to use software specifications as program prototypes as well as to extend them to fully functional programs in a straightforward manner,
3. the ability for early reasoning on system integration,
4. the ability to apply timing parameters to hardware and software constructs, and
5. the ability to simulate a modelled solution and to check its feasibility before implementation.

3. VERIFICATION METHOD

Our verification method is based on co-simulation with earliest-deadline-first (EDF) scheduling and time boundaries [5]. It is primarily meant to profile the timing properties of designs in order to make them feasible. A design is transformed into an internal representation for simulation, whose primary result is a successful execution or a failure, whereas the secondary result is an execution trace, from which additional profiling information is extracted. This is used to discover bottlenecks and unreachable states, as well as to fine-tune the resource parameters and to balance the load on the designed prototypes.

For successful verification, it is assumed that the designed system model is consistent. Intermediate checks on the following points may be performed during the design of the system architecture, and a final check has to be performed prior to verification to ensure this:

1. completeness check (all components are present and fully described),
2. range and compatibility check (parameter compatibility), and
3. software to hardware mapping check (complete coverage and consideration of resource limitations).

In the forthcoming sections the structure of system models is described, followed by the explanation of the co-simulation (verification) method.

3.1 System Model

The *hardware model* is represented by STATIONs, being the processing nodes of a system. Their properties are determined by their components (e.g., processors, memories, interfaces). There are four different types of processing nodes in a system architecture: BASIC (program and operating system), TASK (program), KERNEL (operating system) and COMPOSITE (multi-station node). A processing node may have one or more communication lines attached to it, each one connecting it to another node.

The components of the *software model* are COLLECTIONs of tasks, which are mapped to the stations of the *hardware model*. They are composed of sub-layers of nodes representing program tasks. The tasks themselves are represented by Timed State Transition Diagrams (TSTD), cp. [8]. For inter-task co-operation, collections communicate via PORTs, which represent references to "physical" communication lines between stations of the hardware model.

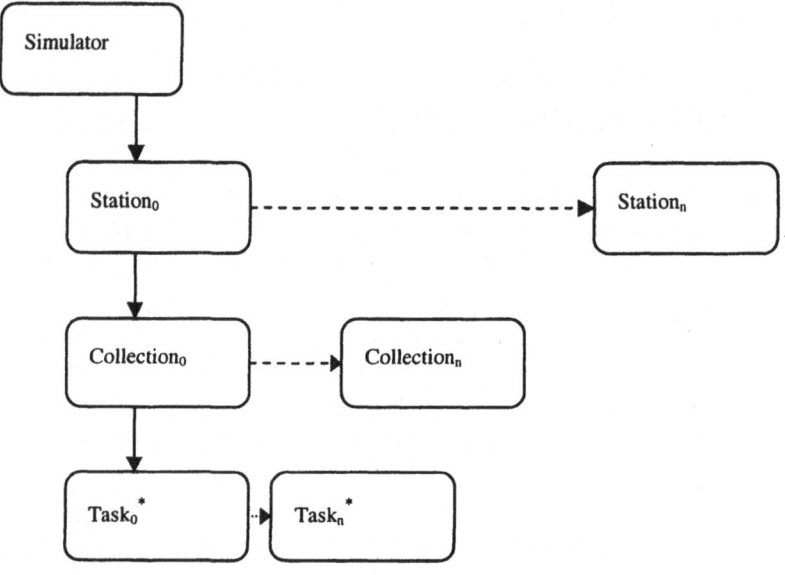

*task TSTD representation

Figure 1: Structure of simulation units

While being designed on separate layers, the mapping of collections to stations is made explicit for co-simulation. The structure of the simulation units is shown in Fig. 1.

The structure of a task is represented by the start/end and action states of the TSTDs (see Fig. 3):

- start states (representing task trigger conditions),
- working states (having continuation pre-conditions, timeout condition, on-timeout action, and actions to be performed within the current state),
- super-states (representing a working state's decomposition into a sub-diagram), and
- final states (representing finalisation actions).

Since the state transition conditions relate to the (operating) system's internal states, they are formed around system calls, changing these states. Naturally, they have to outline the task's structure together with its control structures and conditions.

For co-simulation, the execution times of individual states need to be estimated. A task's execution time is calculated based on the longest path in the corresponding TSTD.

The *hardware* and *software models* are glued together by a *Configuration Manager* (CM) including a real-time operating system (RTOS), which supports the tasking model and system services of the PEARL language [10, 11] chosen as most suitable for our tasks.

Functionally, the CM module has the same role in co-simulation (Fig. 3) as in execution on the target platform. The main difference lies in the global real-time clock, which is maintained by the simulation environment, and the context switches, which are performed virtually in the case of simulation (the context refers to task states - not processor registers). Pre-emption points remain the same in both cases - the atomic execution of task states is maintained in both cases.

The CM also represents the hardware abstraction layer for the executing application. The hardware abstraction layer, as configured by the hardware architecture model, is mainly used to define the properties and interfaces of stations. It is the only visible hardware simulation unit, and is also considered as a whole, with the properties specified in the target platform implementation. The resource access functions and interface device drivers of stations perform virtual functions in case of simulation, and concrete functions in case of target platform implementations.

Our RTOS supports earliest-deadline-first scheduling (later enhancements for other strategies are foreseen). Its resources are parameterised (e.g., number of tasks, synchronisers, signals, events, queued events) by setting the parameters of the KERNEL station or BASIC station, which are RTOS host nodes for any TASK station nodes.

Each RTOS processing node maintains a real-time clock. In a simulation environment, all these clocks need to be synchronised with the global simulation time.

3.2 Verification Presumptions and Criteria Function

Verification is based on the following presumptions:
1. there is only one global simulation clock in the system and all real-time clocks (timers) relate to it;
2. the time events relate to the corresponding station's real-time clock;
3. tasks are assigned deadlines for their execution (the only exception are short initialisation tasks);

4. task states (TSTDs) have a time frame for the activity being performed within the state (in real-time clock time units).

The time required to execute the operating system itself (schedule and dispatch cycle) is assumed constant. This time is considered to be a part of the system call service time and is, therefore, not modelled separately. The time needed to service a system call is considered to be included in the time frame of the calling task's state. Its sole function is to change the system state and to trigger task states, whose trigger conditions relate to the internal data structures of the (operating) system.

Every verification method requires the definition of a *criteria function*, which tells when a system fails, i.e., what the limits of the "normal" execution of the system being checked are.

The *concept of correctness* had been defined as follows: "The system fails if it holds true during co-simulation: the system reaches an undefined state, or its pre-defined time frame is violated and no timeout-action is defined."

By trying the shortest and taking the longest transition times through the task states (TSTD) of the system, it is assumed that enough of the time domain can be covered to be able to generalise the results to an arbitrary transition time (within these time limits) of every state and herewith also of the system as a whole.

3.3   Co-simulation with EDF Scheduling

The station clock rate is translated into the step size of the station in the simulation, and is used when the next event time is being calculated. For feasibility profiling, next critical event simulation and (EDF) scheduling are used. The time instant of the next critical moment is always determined by the simulation unit whose activation time is the closest. This time is forwarded to all its parent units and, finally, it becomes the next global critical moment.

On each step it is checked, whether timing or synchronisation errors have occurred. A "timeout-action" (performed upon violation of the state's timeout condition) represents a controlled program fault. Herewith, a transition is performed into a final state, from which there is no further transition. If, upon the same error, this action is not defined for the current state, the system fails and the error is logged. Otherwise, the transition into the next state is always tried in the minimum and performed in the maximum time variant, if the pre-conditions for the transition are fulfilled. The transitions through the task states executing at their stations are performed first for all nodes, which share the current critical moment, and the previous state is remembered on every transition. The execution protocol is logged instantly for all simulation nodes.

3.3.1   EDF Next Event Scheduling

Earliest-deadline-first next event scheduling is based on the following timing information (see Fig. 2):

A : task activation time,

R : accumulated task run time (updated with the next critical event),

E : task end time (the time when the normal task end is expected based on its maximum run time; upon a context switch the current time t1 needs to be remembered, because this parameter needs to be reset based on the current time t2 and the formula $E'=E+(t2-t1)$ when the task is re-run), and

D: task deadline (set, when A is known).

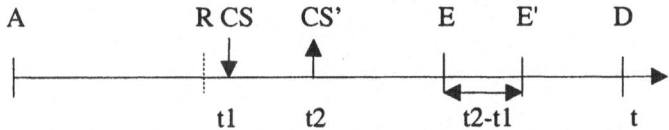

Figure 2: Task run with a single context switch

Re-scheduling takes place when a task is activated due to a scheduled event or on request. The task with the earliest deadline is chosen for execution, and its current state is assigned the current time t as its next critical moment.

While re-scheduling, the following criteria (failure conditions) need to be checked for all tasks:

$t < Z=D-(E-(A+R))$, where Z represents the latest time when the task needs to start/continue in order to meet its deadline; and

$t < E \leq D$ must be true for all active tasks, since they would have missed their deadlines, otherwise.

Tasks can be scheduled to be executed on events. For simulation purposes, they are assigned occurrence times regardless if they represent timers or external interrupts. They represent a special simulation unit, which takes its next critical moments' data from an occurrence table. When these events occur, they are fed into the stations' CM interfaces, and appropriate tasks are woken up through the RTOS.

3.4   Course of Simulation

During co-simulation (Fig. 3), the time of progression to the next state is calculated in two variants for each state:

1. RTC + minT (to check the pre-conditions), and
2. RTC + maxT (for transition to a new state).

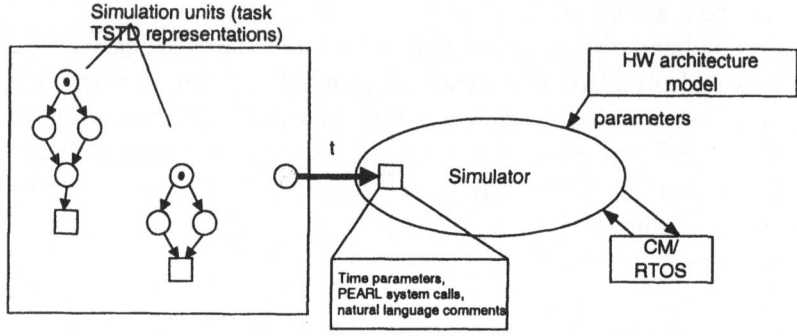

Figure 3: The course of simulation

If in critical moment (2) the pre-condition for the transition to any further state is not fulfilled, the on-timeout action is executed. If it is not defined, the system fails.

During simulation, the E and D parameters are set for each task when it is activated (the A parameter is set). When a critical moment is reached, it is checked if herewith the time frame given for the task has been violated, which results in the following consequences: (1) subtraction of the overhead from the task's slack time, or (2) the system fails as the task deadline is missed.

The simulation results are logged during the execution of every simulation unit, and each step is accounted for also within all its parent simulation units.

This means that every task state logs its actions into the task log, whereas a task logs its beginning and end into the module/collection log. The collection logs the time when it was first allocated at the station, possible subsequent re-loads, and the changes of states which triggered them into the station log. The stations also log the times when they were communicating among each other.

3.5   Interpretation of Results

The simulation logs are checked manually for irregularities, which could represent faults in the original design, or timing/synchronisation errors that might have occurred during the virtual "execution" of the system model.

Busy and idle times are considered for each station and, if necessary and possible, load balancing actions are taken.

The process of analysing and fine-tuning, also known as profiling process, cannot be unified due to the great diversity of possible designs. For this reason, it must be carried out manually and remains the responsibility of the designer.

4. CONCLUSION

Some "design for verification" methodologies and formalisms, used to design and verify real-time systems, have been mentioned. In particular, the part to verify temporal feasibility of the Specification PEARL co-design methodology for real-time systems has been presented. Our goal is to be able to determine a priori the feasibility of a program part on a specified hardware architecture without the need to implement it first.

A feasible design model, which is produced by the presented modelling and profiling process, retains its value if the foreseen execution time frames were chosen correctly (i.e., the circumstances on the time scale shall not change when the program part is extended to a fully functional program and run on the target platform).

ACKNOWLEDGEMENTS

This article presents results of the research project "Holistic Embedded Control Systems Design" (Z2-3493), financed by the Slovenian Ministry of Education, Science and Sport.

REFERENCES

1   G. Agha. The Structure and Semantics of Actor Languages. J.W. de Bakker, W.P. de Roever, and G. Rozenberg, editors, Foundations of Object-Oriented Languages, pp. 1-59, Springer-Verlag, 1991.

2   F. Balarin, M. Chiodo, P. Giusto, H. Hsieh, A. Jurecska, L. Lavagno, C. Passerone, A. Sangiovanni-Vincentelli, E. Sentovich, K. Suzuki and B. Tabarra. Hardware-Software Co-Design of Embedded Systems: The POLIS Approach. Kluwer Academic Publishers, 1997.

3   C. Dietz. Action Diagrams. Proc. 22nd IFAC/IFIP Workshop on Real-Time Programming, Lyon, 1997.

4   T. J. Eriksen, S. T. Heilmann, M. Holdgaard and A.P. Ravn. Hybrid Systems: A Real-Time Interface to Control Engineering. Proc. 8th Euromicro Workshop on Real-Time Systems, pp. 114-120, 1996.

5   R. Gumzej. Embedded System Architecture Co-Design and its Validation, Doctoral thesis, University of Maribor, Slovenia, 1999.

6   M. Khalil, Y. Le Traon and C. Robach. Control-flow System Diagnosis: An Evolutive Method. Proc. 24th Euromicro Conf., Västerås, 1998.

7   I. Lee, S. Davidson, and R. Gerber. Communicating Shared Resources: A Paradigm for Integrating Real-Time Specification and Implementation. Foundations of Real-Time Computing: Formal Specifications and Methods. Kluwer Academic Publishers, 1991.

8   V. J. Mooney III. Hardware/Software Co-Design of Run-Time Sytems. PhD thesis.

9   J. S. Ostroff. A Visual Toolset for the Design of Real-Time Discrete Event Systems. IEEE Trans. Control Systems Technology, May 1997.

10   Basic PEARL, DIN 66253, Part 1.

11   Full PEARL, DIN 66253, Part 2.

12   Multiprocessor PEARL, DIN 66253, Part 3.

13   A.C.Shaw. Communicating Real-Time State Machines. IEEE Trans. Software Engineering, Vol. 18, No. 9, pp. 805-816.

14   Janos Stipanovits and Gabor Karsai. Model-integrated computing. IEEE Computer 30(4):110-111, April 1997.

15   I. Traore and Abd-el-Kader Sahraoui. A Multiformalism Specification Framework with Statecharts and VDM. Proc. 22nd IFAC/IFIP Workshop on Real-Time Programming, Lyon, 1997.

16   OMG MDA website. www.omg.org/mda.

17   OMG UML website. www.omg.org/uml.

A MULTIOBJECTIVE TABU SEARCH ALGORITHM FOR THE DESIGN SPACE EXPLORATION OF EMBEDDED SYSTEMS

Frank Slomka[1], Karsten Albers[1], Richard Hofmann[2]

[1]*Department of Computer Science, University of Oldenburg, Ammerländer Heerstraße 114-118, 26111 Oldenburg, Germany, {slomka,albers}@informatik.uni-oldenburg.de;*
[2]*Department of Computer Science 7, University of Erlangen-Nürnberg, Martensstr. 3, 91058 Erlangen, Germany, richard.hofmann@informatik.uni-erlangen.de*

Abstract: An important step during the design of embedded systems is to allocate suitable architectural components and to optimally bind functions (tasks) to these components. This design step is called system synthesis. The automation of system synthesis is limited in recent research by developing models only for standard optimization algorithms. This paper describes the first approach to improve a standard optimization technique itself for the use in embedded system design. Our solution extends the heuristic optimization algorithm tabu search by multiobjective optimization. Using the multiobjective approach, domain specific heuristics could easily be included into the algorithm. By performing experiments with the new algorithm, a new effect was discovered: In contrast to known results from literature, the quality of optimization was depending on the size of the neighborhood if the moves in the neighborhood were sorted by domain specific estimation.

Key words: Tabu-Search, Multiobjective, Optimization, System Synthesis.

1.   INTRODUCTION

A number of approaches for system synthesis have been proposed in the relevant literature. The common goal of such approaches is to build an optimization model and to use heuristic optimization techniques to solve the synthesis problem. The optimization problem itself is tackled using simulated annealing [1], [6], genetic algorithms [1], [2], [5] and tabu search [1], [6], [10]. In some papers, self-made heuristics are used [4], [7], [11].

Most of the papers considering the analysis of real-time systems, which means different system tasks with different priorities running on one processor, must hold given deadlines. Only in [2] just the latency of the problem is considered.

Embedded system design is a multiobjective optimization challenge. The most important objectives are time, area and power. Many papers in system synthesis do not consider this aspect. The authors describe optimization as a cost or area optimization problem with time constraints. Only [2] and [5] describe multiobjective algorithms using a Pareto approach. Both papers deal with genetic algorithms, but [2] do not consider real-time systems. The algorithm described in [5] deals with real-time systems, but it disregards communication synthesis.

However, no paper deals with aspects for improving the quality of the optimization heuristic by information coming from the application domain, which in our case is embedded system design. The results of [1],[5], and [11] are based on an effective real-time analysis algorithm. In this paper, we present a technique that uses the multiobjective nature of the problem as a chance for improving the optimization technique itself. In contrast to recent literature on tabu search, which uses randomly generated neighborhoods [1], [6], we revealed that a sorted multiobjective neighborhood can improve the optimization algorithm.

2. EXPLORATION MODEL

Our approach to the system synthesis is based on two input models, (1) the problem graph to specify the application, and (2) the architecture graph to describe the maximal available hardware [2]. To synthesize a system architecture, the problem graph is mapped onto the architecture graph, along with the determination of additional parameters. A major difference of our modeling approach to related work is the use of different types of program nodes for modeling semantic aspects, e.g. to describe asynchronous communication between system-level tasks (processes) and other semantic peculiarities of languages based on the model of finite state machines.

2.1 Problem Graph

The problem model consists of two types of graphs: a control-flow graph (CFG) to model the behavior of the system (the control-flow of the specification, given in a formal description technique, e.g. SDL [12]) and a set of data-flow graphs (DFG). The two types of graphs are combined to a control data flow graph (CDFG), or *problem graph* for short. Each DFG refines a node of the CFG to model computational tasks.

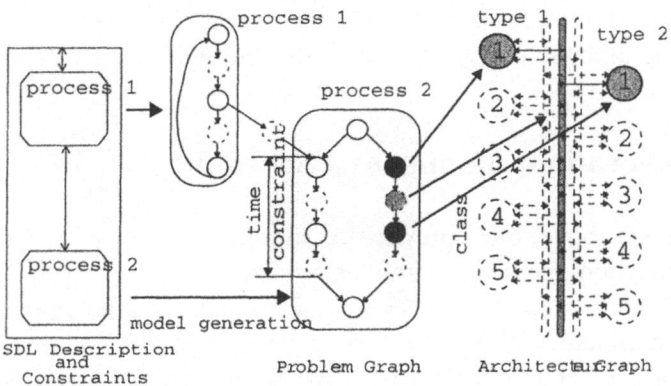

Figure 1. Optimization Modell

In order to derive the problem graph, the behavioral description of the system, as given by e.g. an SDL description, is transformed to the problem graph. The problem graph is a directed graph, where the nodes may represent computation or communication tasks. The edges of the problem graph specify the control flow. In addition to the nodes of the CDFG, we define super nodes that allow to model system-level tasks. A system-level task represents an instance of code with its own memory, i.e. a process running on an architecture component. In our model, a super node is defined as a set of nodes, where each node has the same process identifier and the same priority. The priorities of system-level tasks influence scheduling decisions where two or more super nodes are mapped onto the same architecture component, e.g. a processor.

In order to define time constraints, labels are assigned to the nodes. All nodes of the graph marked with the same label are associated to the same timing constraint.

2.2 Architecture Graph

The architecture graph defines the maximal available configuration of the hardware. It contains different types of nodes to model different types of components. The node types are used to model different scheduling strategies of processing elements: preemptive scheduling, nonpreemptive scheduling, no scheduling and communication. In this terminology, no scheduling means that a resource can only be used by one task exclusively.

All architecture nodes contain a class attribute that specifies different classes of components (e.g. different processor types and technologies). Fig. 1 outlines how the behavioral description — in our case an SDL description — is transformed to a problem graph, which in turn is mapped onto an architecture graph. In the problem graph, dotted nodes represent communication nodes. In the architecture graph, dotted nodes represent architecture nodes not yet allocated.

2.3   Allocation, Binding and Scheduling

As outlined above, our optimization algorithm for system synthesis defines the allocation, the binding and the schedule.

The **allocation** defines the selection of the architecture components from the available architecture components as defined by the architecture graph. The decisions are implicitly defined by the binding, i.e. each architecture node to which a program node is bound to is allocated.

Binding: Each node of the problem graph is bound to exactly one architecture node. The binding of the nodes of the problem graph to the architecture graph is achieved by edges between the two graphs.

Scheduling: We assume that the derived implementation employs runtime scheduling. Thus, decisions made by the system synthesis implicitly define the schedule. The factors influencing the schedule comprise 1) the scheduling strategies employed by the architecture nodes, 2) the binding of the program nodes on architecture nodes, 3) the priorities of the program nodes (super nodes).

3.   MULTIOBJECTIVE OPTIMIZATION WITH TABU-SEARCH

3.1   Multiobjective Optimization

Optimization of embedded systems is a multiobjective search problem. Different design parameters like time, area and power need consideration. Using a weighted cost function in a multiobjective optimization problem is questionable [5]. The weights are depending on the problem and finding the right set of weights could be as expensive as the optimization problem itself.

In multiobjective optimization, an effective method for ranking solutions is used: the Pareto approach. Consider a two dimensional objective space, e.g. area and power. For each solution, a value for each objective, power and area, can be calculated. This results in a point in the two dimensional objective space. A point in the objective space is *dominating* when it is in all objectives at least equal or better then the dominated point. Pareto points are points which are not dominated by other points. Thus, all system implementations represented by Pareto points are equal in terms of their design quality. To further discriminate them requires additional constraints. An optimization tool can find the Pareto points by using an algorithm called Pareto ranking [5]. Pareto ranking sorts all solutions according to the number of solutions that dominate them. The Pareto points are dominated by no other points, so they are on the top of the list.

3.2 Tabu Search

Tabu search is a heuristic optimization algorithm. In contrast to simulated annealing and genetic algorithms, tabu search represents a purely deterministic approach. Similar to simulated annealing, tabu search is based on a neighborhood search. Thus, any new solution is derived from the previous solution. In order to support this, the definition of the neighborhood of a solution and the definition of the moves to transform a previous solution to a new solution is of importance.

Different from greedy algorithms, e.g. as gradient search, tabu search also allows moves to solutions with higher cost. This is important for escaping from local minima. However, allowing non-improving steps may result in a cyclic search. To avoid cycles, tabu search employs a memory, typically called tabu list. The purpose is to prevent moves, which can lead to cycles. This list could have very different implementations. One possible way is to store a fixed number of previous moves, whose recurrence is inhibited.

3.3 Structure of Multiobjective Tabu Search

The idea of Pareto ranking can be used to construct a multiobjective tabu search algorithm. As tabu search defines moves for constructing new solutions and all moves are put to a list, called neighborhood, it is easy to construct a single neighborhood for each objective. The moves are evaluated only by the single objective of the neighborhood. Additionally, it is possible to use estimation techniques to find fast evaluation results. Such a fast estimation technique may be the use of Liu and Laylands real-time analysis instead of a computation expensive worst-case response time analysis or simulation. By using this technique, it is possible to explore a lot of possible system implementations or solutions. All neighborhoods will then be sorted separately. These lists are than merged with Pareto ranking.

However, constructing an optimal solution requires an extended analysis of complex objectives, which is in our approach carried out by selecting the

N best moves given by the Pareto ranking. For the chosen solutions, an extended and precise evaluation is performed.

3.4   Moves and Neighborhood

3.4.1   Definition of Moves

Priority Changing of Processes: To each process, a priority is attached. The priority defines the scheduling priority of a process. This means that all processes bound to the same component will be scheduled with respect to this priority. The actual priority of a process can be increased or decreased within a move.

Partitioning of Processes: Each process can be partitioned. A process partitioning is supported by the super node concept. Each process can be split into a number of super nodes. If a process is split into different super nodes, it is possible to bind the super nodes to different components of the component graph. This is used to support fine grain hardware/software partitioning in a hierarchical environment.

Binding of Super Nodes: This move changes the binding of the super nodes to hardware components. Only the binding of super nodes can be changed.

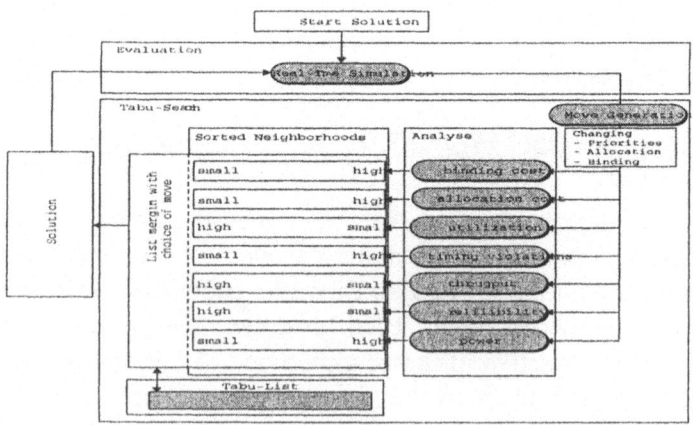

Figure 2. Multiobjective Tabu-Search

Allocation of Components: Moves to allocate and deallocate components are very important. If allocation were implicitly performed by binding moves, in many cases it would take a few moves to deallocate a component.

These intermediate steps are problematical because the not yet deallocated component still needs area, while its workload is moved to other components, which reduces their quality in other objectives like the performance. Deallocating moves prevent this overall stepwise degradation.

3.4.2 Neighborhood

The result of these moves is the neighborhood of a solution. In many cases, the resulting number of different moves is too high for a reasonable performance of the optimization process. Every move in a neighborhood is evaluated separately for each objective. Therefore, a separate list of moves is built for each objective.

Allocation Cost: The total system cost consist of the allocation cost, which represent the fixed cost of architecture components and the binding cost that is caused by binding the program nodes on architecture nodes. Each allocated node of the architecture graph results in a fixed cost. The fixed cost of an architecture component depends on its type and its class.

Binding Cost is caused by the need for memory (software) or cost for registers, ALUs, etc., on ASICs. Similar to allocation cost, binding cost depends on the type and class of the architecture component to which the program node is bound.

Timing Constraints: In order to evaluate meeting of time constraints, the actual execution schedule has to be derived. This schedule not only depends on the allocation and the binding of the processes but also on the distribution of the priorities. In this work, a simple event-driven simulation analyzes the temporal behavior of a given system (for more information see [10]). The problem to verify a given system and scheduling is NP-complete [5]. For that reason, it is problematic to verify a large neighborhood in an exact manner. As a rough estimation about the real-time behavior, the utilization formula in Liu und Layland [8] is used. The calculated utilization is then used as a metric to sort the solutions into the neighborhood.

3.4.3 The Tabu List

A new approach combines a problem independent sizing of the tabu list with a reduction of program memory size: It uses the multiobjective nature of the problem to implement an effective tabu list. The evaluation parameter of each neighborhood is stored separately. Although the used data structure is very compact, it describes a solution very exactly: Let us assume e.g., a system implementation needs 100 mm^2 allocation area, 50 mm^2 program memory (binding cost) at 70% processor utilization. In such a case, the set

{100, 50, 70} completely describes the system. As equivalent solutions have the same evaluation parameter, they can be mapped to the same description.

4. EXPERIMENTAL RESULTS

Using a multiobjective search for hierarchical problems in combination with neighborhood estimation reduces the run-time and the cost of the final system implementation. We verified this by experiments based on given examples from the literature [11]. Fig. 3 gives an idea about the quality improvement achieved by sorted neighborhoods. The figure shows the two objectives, number of real-time violations and total system cost. The total system cost is the sum of binding and allocation cost. The figure shows the effect of sorted neighborhoods for the examples *random1* and *random2*. Tab. 1 gives a detailed overview, how the algorithm's run-time depends on the size of the neighborhood.

The table shows three experiments with a small neighborhood and a large neighborhood to find an optimal value for the length of a sorted neighborhood. The first number in the neighborhood size row gives the number of estimated moves and the second number gives the number of total evaluated (using a detailed real-time simulation) moves. This number is equivalent to a neighborhood size in standard tabu-search. The given run-time is the complete run-time for 10,000 iterations fixed given by starting the program. The number in the brackets gives the number of iterations after which the best solution was found. As can be seen, a neighborhood of 6000 yields better results than a small neighborhood of 600 moves. In detailed experiments, we found that a size of 4000 is a break-even in run-time and quality. A neighborhood with a size larger than 8000 again increases the run-time of the algorithm, without improving quality. However, a neighborhood size between 4000 and 8000 is a good value for optimization with sorted neighborhoods.

The experiments reveal that the result from tabu search literature, which states that the quality of optimization is independent from the neighborhood size, only holds for unsorted or randomly generated neighborhoods. Our newly found result allows the design of fast system synthesis algorithms based on tabu search. Note that the experiments in [1] show that the quality of tabu search is as good as the quality of genetic algorithms. Sorting the neighborhood gives the possibility to include embedded system designers knowledge to the heuristic search algorithm and to improve the results given in [1], [2], and [5].

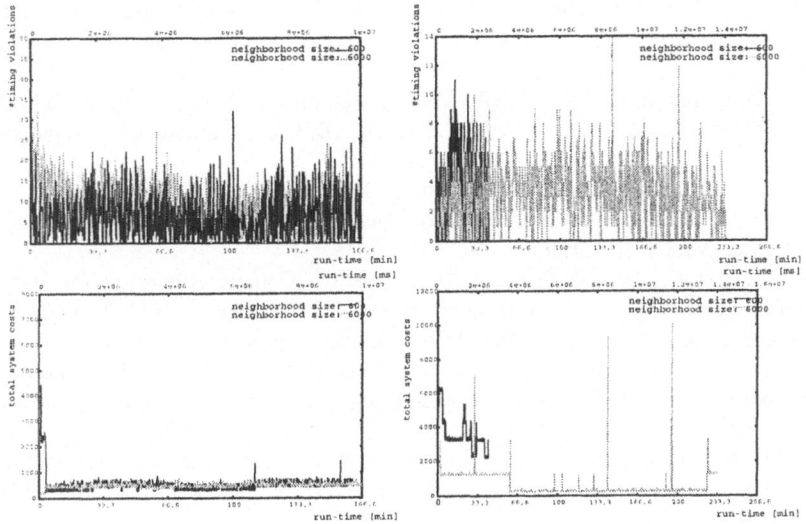

Figure 3. Results

Table 1. Results: Different Sizes of the Neighborhood

Experiment	Small Neighborhood			Large Neighborhood		
	Size	Cost	run-time[ms]	Size	Cost	Run-Time [ms]
Random-1.20	600/20	310	424212 (4652)	6000/20	195	133910 (36)
Random-2.20	600/40	2192	2421560 (3397)	6000/40	222	4671360 (789)
Random-3.100	600760	500	6194830 (631)	8000/20	417	73440 (11)

5.   CONCLUSION

In this paper, a new multiobjective tabu search heuristic is presented: Including domain-specific heuristics into a general optimization algorithm improves the quality of the optimization results and reduces the algorithm's run time. For that reason, the heuristic was extended to work with both estimation and evaluation algorithms for the different objectives. This enables the use of large neighborhoods without loosing quality of the optimization results. It also combines for the first time tabu-search with Pareto-ranking.

REFERENCES

1. J. Axelsson. Analysis and Synthesis of Heterogeneous Real-Time Systems. Dissertation, Linköping Studies in Science and Technology, 502. 1997.

2. T. Blickle, J. Teich, L. Thiele. System-Level Synthesis Using Evolutionary Algorithms. Design Automation For Embedded Systems, Kluwer Academic Publisher, Boston, 3(1), 1998.
3. Dave, B.P. und Jha, N.K. COHRA. Hardware-Software Cosynthesis on Hierarchical Heterogeneous Distributed Embedded Systems. IEEE Transactions on Computer-Aided Design of Integrated Circuits and Systems. 17(10). 1998.
4. B.P. Dave, G. Lakshminarayana, N.K. Jha. COSYN: Hardware-Software Co-Synthesis of Heterogeneous Distributed Embedded Systems. IEEE Transactions on Very Large Scale Integration (VLSI). 7(1), 1999.
5. R.P. Dick, N.K. Jha. MOGAC: A Multiobjective Genetic Algorithm for Hardware-Software Cosynthesis of Distributed Embedded Systems. IEEE Transactions on Computer-Aided Design of Integrated Circuits and Systems. 17(10). 1998.
6. P. Eles, Z. Peng, K. Kuchcinski, A. Doboli. System-Level Hardware/Software Partitioning based on Simulated Annealing and Tabu Search. Design Automation For Embedded Systems, Kluwer Academic Publisher, Boston, 2(1), 1997.
7. C. Lee, ,M. Potkonjak, W. Wolf. Synthesis of Hard Real-Time Application Specific Systems. Design Automation for Embedded Systems. Kluwer Academic Publisher, Boston, 4(4), 1999.
8. C. Liu, J. Layland Scheduling Algorithms for Multiprogramming in Hard Real-Time Environments, Journal of the ACM, 20(1), 46-61, 1973
9. F. Slomka, J. Zant, L. Lambert. Schedulability Analysis of Heterogeneous Systems for Performance Message Sequence Chart. 6th International Workshop on Hardware/Software Codesign. IEEE Computer Society Press. Seattle, 1998.
10. F. Slomka, S. Kocher, A. Mitschele-Thiel. A Three-Level Heuristic for System Synthesis Based on Tabu Search. Technical Report IMMD7 3/99. University of Erlangen-Nuremberg.
11. T. Yen, W. Wolf. Hardware-Software Co-Synthesis of Distributed Embedded Systems. Kluwer Academic Publisher, Boston. 1996.
12. ITU-T. Z.100, Appendix I. ITU, SDL Methodology Guidelines. ITU, 1993

DESIGN SPACE EXPLORATION WITH AUTOMATIC GENERATION OF IP-BASED EMBEDDED SOFTWARE

Júlio C. B. de Mattos[1], Lisane Brisolara[1], Renato Hentschke[1], Luigi Carro[1,2], Flávio R. Wagner[1]

[1] *Federal University of Rio Grande do Sul, Computer Science Institute, Av. Bento Gonçalves, 9500 - Campus do Vale - Porto Alegre, Brasil;*
[2] *Federal University of Rio Grande do Sul, Electrical Engineering*
Av. Oswaldo Aranha 103 - Porto Alegre, Brasil

Abstract: Automatic embedded software generation and IP-based design are good approaches to achieve a short design cycle due to stringent time-to-market requirements. But design automation must also consider application-specific requirements. This paper presents a mechanism for the automatic selection of software IP components for embedded applications, which is based on a software IP library and a design space exploration tool. The software IP library has different algorithmic implementations of several routines commonly found in different application domains. These routines have been characterized in terms of power, performance, and area, for a given architectural platform. The design exploration tool allows the automatic configuration of an optimized solution for a specific application, by selecting routines whose combination best match system requirements. Experimental results are presented and demonstrate that a very expressive design space can be explored with this approach.

Key words: Design Space Exploration; Embedded Software, IP Components.

1.   INTRODUCTION

The fast technological development in the last decades exposed a new reality: the widespread use of embedded systems. Nowadays, one can find these systems everywhere, in consumer electronics, entertainment, communication systems and so on. In embedded applications, requirements like performance, reduced power consumption and program size, among others, must be considered. Since different platforms and cores are available, precise technical metrics regarding these factors are essential for a correct comparison among alternative architectural solutions, when running a particular application.

To the above physically related metrics, one should add another dimension, which is software development cost. In platform-based design, design derivatives are mainly configured by software, and software development is where most of the design time is spent. But the quality of the software development also directly impacts the mentioned physical metrics.

Presently, the software designer writes the application code and relies on a compiler to optimize it. Compiler code optimizations for embedded systems have been traditionally oriented towards improving performance, reducing memory accesses or space [1,2,3], for instance targeting code to specialized architectures, reducing cache misses, or compressing code.

It is widely known that design decisions taken at higher abstraction levels can lead to substantially superior improvements. Software engineers involved with software configuration of embedded platforms, however, do not have enough experience to measure the impact of their algorithmic decisions on issues such as performance and power. Therefore, this paper proposes a more pragmatic approach, consisting in the use of a software library and a design space exploration tool to allow an automatic software IP selection. The software IP library contains alternative algorithmic implementations for routines commonly found in embedded applications, whose implementations are previously characterized regarding performance, power, and memory requirements on a given platform. A similar approach is followed in [6], but restricted to implementations of Simulink blocks.

By offering a range of algorithmic solutions for usual problems that may be critical in several applications, the designer may choose the solution that best matches particular application requirements. By exploring design alternatives at the algorithmic level, that offer a much wider range of power, performance, and memory size values, the designer is able to automatically find, through the exploration tool, corner cases that result in optimizations far better that those reported by later code optimizations. As a very important side effect, the choice of an algorithm that exactly fits the requirements of the application, without unnecessarily wasting resources, may allow a more efficient use of the underlying hardware, for instance reducing supply voltage, clock frequency, and area to a minimum.

This paper is organized as follows. Section 2 discusses related work in the field of embedded software optimization. Section 3 gives an overview of the target architecture. Section 4 presents our approach to design space exploration, introducing the library with its characterization and the exploration tool. Section 5 presents experimental results, and, finally, section 6 draws conclusions and introduces future work.

2. RELATED WORK

Power-aware software optimization has gained attention in recent years. It has been shown [8] that each instruction of a processor has a different power cost. By taking these costs in consideration, a 40% power improvement obtained by code optimizations is reported [8]. Reordering of instructions in the source code has been also proposed [9], considering that power consumption depends on the switching activity and thus also on the particular sequence of instructions, and improvements of up to 30% are reported. In [10], an energy profiler is used to identify critical arithmetic functions and replace them by using polynomial approximations and floating-point to fixed-point conversions.

Recent efforts are oriented towards automatic exploration tools that identify several points in the design space that correspond to different trade-offs between performance and power. In [4], Pareto-optimal configurations are found for a parameterized architecture running a given application. Among the solutions, the performance range varies by a factor of 10, while the power range varies by a factor of 7.5. In [5], the best performance/power figures are selected among various application-to-architecture mappings.

In [6], a library of alternative hardware and software parameterized implementations for Simulink blocks that present different performance, power, and area figures is characterized. Our approach is similar, but instead of aiming at a partitioning between software and hardware functions, it concentrates on algorithmic variations of software routines that are commonly found in a wide range of embedded applications. This way, it provides design space exploration for given platforms.

3. TARGET ARCHITECTURE

The software library characterization has been performed for a platform based on a Java microcontroller, called femtoJava [7], although the methodology is general and can be applied for other processor architectures as well. The Java microcontroller implements a hardware execution engine through a stack machine that is compatible with the Java Virtual Machine (JVM) specification. A CAD environment that automatically synthesizes the microcontroller for a target application [7] is available, using only a subset of instructions critical to the specific application. This way, the impact of algorithmic-level optimizations against compiler level optimizations can be measured.

4. THE PROPOSED APPROACH

Figure 1a shows a traditional design flow, where the designer receives the application specification and, after coding it in some language, compiles it for a chosen platform. In this approach, the designer must know the target platform, and all optimizations are trusted to the compiler.

In our approach, illustrated in Figure 1b, the design starts with an application specification at a high level of abstraction, and the application code is generated automatically by a tool. This tool allows design space exploration based on a software IP library, the application specification, and the designer knowledge. Note that, in this approach, the designer does not need to know the target platform, because this information is used only for the library characterization. This methodology allows the automatic selection of software IPs to better match a certain platform. Moreover, if the application constraints might change, for example with tighter energy demands or smaller memory footprint, a different set of SW IPs might be selected. The same reasoning applies when the underlying platform is changed.

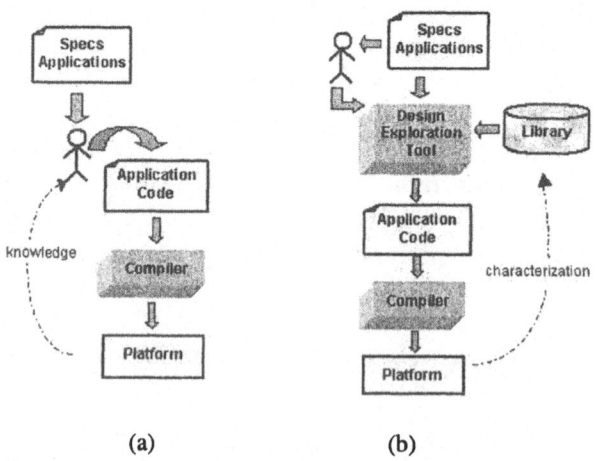

(a)   (b)
Figure 1. (a) Traditional approach   (b) Our approach.

In this work, a configurable power estimation simulator, called CACO-PS [11], was used to collect all measures during library characterization. Specifically, considering a certain platform and for each algorithmic implementation of the library functions, it measures the performance (in cycles), the memory usage (for data and instruction memories), and the power dissipation (in gate capacitances – GC – that switch during execution, considering CPU, RAM, and ROM). In the next sections, the software IP library and the design space exploration tool are presented in more detail.

4.1   Software IP library

As it has been already mentioned, the library contains different algorithmic versions of the same function, thus supporting design space exploration. Since embedded systems are found in many different application domains, this investigation has been started using classical functions: Sine – Two ways to compute the sine of an angle are provided. One is a simple table search, and the other one uses the CORDIC (Coordinate Rotation Digital Computer) algorithm [12]; IMDCT – The Inverse Modified Discrete Cosine Transform is a critical step in decompression algorithms like those found in MP3 players. Together with windowing, it takes roughly 70% of the processing time [13]. Others functions are implemented like Table Search, Square Root and Sort.

4.2   Library characterization

To illustrate the results of library characterization using different algorithmic versions of the same function, there are two routines selected: the sine and the Inverse Modified Discrete Cosine Transform. Table 1 shows the main results of the characterization of the four different implementations of the IMDCT function. The IMDCT4 implementation has the better results in terms of performance and power dissipation, but the size of program memory significantly increases. The opposite happens with the IMDCT1 implementation, which has far better results in terms of program memory, but consumes about 3 times more cycles and power.

Table 1. IMDCT characterization

Characteristic	IMDCT1	IMDCT2	IMDCT3	IMDCT4
Program size (bytes)	344	2,137	4,260	15,294
Data mem (bytes)	3546	3546	3546	3546
Performance (cycles)	140,300	97,354	92,882	51,345
Power (x 10^6 GCs)	1,149.43	940.83	1,021	905.89

Table 2 illustrates the characterization of the alternative implementations of the sine function. There are some entries in Table 2 that are pretty obvious. Since Cordic is a more complex algorithm, program memory size is larger than with Table Look-up, as well as the number of cycles required for computation. It is interesting to notice, however, that the data memory size seems to be almost the same. This, however, is caused by the fact that data in Table 2 was obtained for a sine resolution of 1 degree. As the resolution increases, the amount of data memory increases exponentially for the Table Look-up algorithm, but only sublinearly for the Cordic algorithm. The increase in memory reflects not only in the required amount of memory, but also in the power dissipation of a larger memory.

Table 2. Sine characterization

Characteristic		Cordic	Table
Program size (bytes)		206	88
Data mem (bytes)	1°	184	220
	0.5°	184	400
	0.1°	184	1840
Performance (cycles)		2,447	136
Power (GCs)	1°	6,274,770	350,237
	0.5°	6,274,770	391,197
	0.1°	6,274,770	637,117

4.3   Evaluating a complete application

In all examples presented above, the design space concerning performance, power, and memory footprint was large. However, the availability of different alternatives of the same routine is just a first step in the design space exploration of the application software. One must notice that embedded applications are seldom implemented with a single routine. There is another level of optimization, which concerns finding the best mix of routines among all possible combinations that may exist in an embedded application.

In order to better illustrate the concept, let us take as an example the IMDCT function. Taking into account program and data memory sizes, performance, and power, there are 16 possible combinations of the four versions of the IMDCT and cosine functions. Some of them are very interesting, depending on particular application requirements:

- If memory space has the highest priority, one can combine the IMDCT1 core with a table look-up cosine calculation with a resolution of 1 degree. This requires only 3,730 bytes of data memory and 432 bytes of program memory, although it presents the worst figures for performance and power;
- If an application must respond in at most 200,000 cycles and the cosine calculation requires a high resolution (0.1 degree), then the best is to combine the IMDCT2 core and the CORDIC-based cosine calculation. This is the combination that fulfils the above restrictions and requires less

memory space (3,730 bytes of program memory and 2,343 bytes of data memory);

- If performance and power have the highest priority, combining the IMDCT4 core with a table look-up cosine is the best alternative. It requires only 56,242 cycles and 906.25×10^6 gate capacitances of power consumption.

4.4 Design space exploration tool

The Dragon Lemon tool maps the routines of an embedded program to an implementation using instances of the software IP library, so as to fulfil given system requirements. The user program is modeled as a graph, where the nodes represent the routines, while the arcs determine the program sequence. The weight of the arcs represents the number of times a certain routine is instantiated. It is also possible to model parallel routine calls, in case the underlying hardware has parallel processing capabilities.

To generate the application graph representing the dynamic behavior of the application, an instrumentation tool was developed. It is based on BIT (*Bytecodes Instrumentation Tool*) [14] that allows the dynamic analysis of Java Class files, generating a list of invoked methods with its corresponding number of calls, which can be mapped to the application graph.

In the exploration tool, before the search begins, the user may determine weights for power, delay and memory optimization. It is also possible to set maximum values for each of these variables. The tool automatically explores the design space and finds the optimal or near optimal mapping for that configuration. The cost function of the search is based on a trade-off between power, timing, and area. Each library option is characterized by these three factors. The exploration tool normalizes these parameters by the maximum power, timing and area found in the library. The user can then select weights for the three variables. This way, the search can be directed according to the application requirements. If area cost, for example, must be prioritized because of small memory space, the user may increase the area weight. Although one characteristic might be prioritized, the others are still considered in the search mechanisms. As output, Dragon Lemon also provides 2D and 3D Paretto curves. For both curves, the user may select which variables (power, delay, or memory) will be used in each axis (x, y and z).

5.   RESULTS

Two sets of experiments have been executed. First, our methodology has been evaluated with small synthetic examples, but trying to address real applications, like an Address Book and a Game, running in parallel with a MP3 player. The second experiment shows that the design exploration tool is also able to explore much larger search spaces.

The application A_Book+MP3 is implemented as two parallel processes. The first one runs typical Address Book tasks, such as *table search, insert,* and *sort*. Calculator features, such as *square root* and *sine* calculation, have also been added. In parallel to this process, an MP3 player is executed. The design space exploration for the MP3 considers the different implementations of the IMDCT function, which is dominant in the MP3 decode routine. Two different architectural variations have been tried. In the first one, a single processor has been used. In the second option, one processor executes the MP3 algorithm, while the other processor deals with the other tasks of the Address Book. The results are shown in Table 4. For the option with equal weights for power, timing and area, the best solution is to use *hash* and *quick-sort* routines. However, this configuration is changed when the area weight increases. *Hash* is replaced with a *sequential search*, while the *quick-sort* is replaced with *insert-sort*. Table 4 also shows that increasing the number of processors does not significantly decreases the running time. This happens simply because the IMDCT calculation running time is much larger than the other tasks.

The Game application is implemented by three parallel processes. There is a rendering part, which allows the exploration of sine and square root routines. In parallel, there is the MP3 decoder part, with the IMDCT exploration. The third part comprises the game logic itself and AI computation, which will perform table searches, insertions, and sort functions. The difference from the previous application is that the parallel processes will have similar running times, while in the Address Book the IMDCT time determines the total running time. Results are also presented in Table 4. It is clear that this time we took advantage of additional processors in the architecture, because of the higher parallelism of tasks with equal complexity.

All results in Table 4 come from an exhaustive search, running in less than a second of execution time. Figure 3 shows the Paretto curve found for the first row of Table 4. The curve shows Running Time in the x-axis and Area in the y-axis. It is clear that by increasing the expected running time the designer is able to use smaller memory spaces.

Table 4. Results of design space exploration for Address Book + MP3 and Game*

Application	#	Weights			Power	Delay	Memory
	proc	P	T	A	(x 10^7)	(x 10^7)	Area
A_Book + MP3	1	1	1	1	36,23	20,54	20175
A_Book + MP3	2	1	1	1	36,23	20,52	20089
A_Book + MP3	1	1	1	10	36,23	20,54	20089
A_Book + MP3	2	1	1	10^4	37,63	38,93	6711
Game	1	1	1	1	40,10	43,69	20175
Game	3	1	1	1	40,10	20,48	20175

*Power in gate capacitances, delay in clock cycles, memory area in bytes.

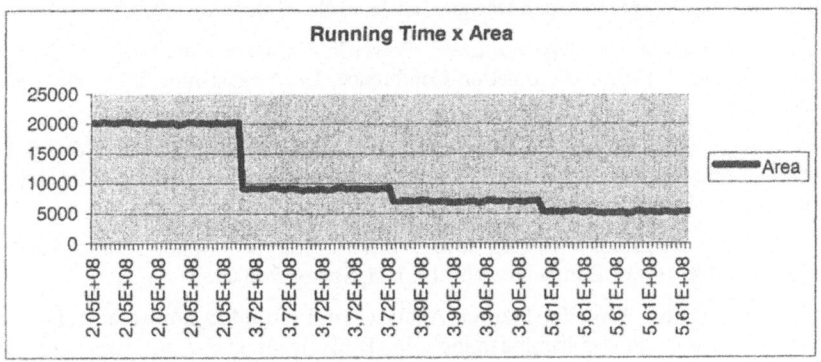

Figure 3. Paretto curve for first row of Table 4.

6.   CONCLUSIONS AND FUTURE WORK

This paper proposed a new methodology for software IP selection in a design space exploration context, considering performance, power, and memory area requirements. It is based on software IP library that is previously characterized for a given architectural platform and uses a genetic tool for automatic design space exploration and IP selection.

Experimental results have confirmed the hypothesis that there is a large space to explore based on algorithmic decisions taken at higher levels of abstraction, much before compiler intervention. Selecting the right algorithm might give orders of magnitude of gain in terms of physical characteristics like memory usage, performance, and power dissipation. As a future work, we plan to enlarge the library and to investigate the impact of different memories with different power-delay products, so that one can better tune the algorithms to the underlying platform.

REFERENCES

[1] N.Dutt, A.Nicolau, H.Tomiyama, A.Halambi. "New Directions in Compiler Technology for Embedded Systems." *Asia-Pacific Design Automation Conference*, Jan. 2001. Proceedings, IEEE Computer Society Press, 2001.

[2] V.Dalal, C.P.Ravikumar. "Software Power Optimizations in an Embedded System". VLSI Design Conference, Jan. 2001. Proceedings, IEEE Computer Science Press, 2001.

[3] M.Kandemir, V.Vijaykrishnan, M.J.Irwin, W.Ye. "Influence of Compiler Optimizations on System Power". In: IEEE Transactions on VLSI Systems, vol. 9, n. 6, Dec. 2001.

[4] T.Givargis, F.Vahid, J.Henkel. "System-Level Exploration for Pareto-optimal Configurations in Parameterized Systems-on-a-chip". ICCAD'01 - International Conference on Computer-Aided Design, San Jose, Nov. 2001.

[5] A.Nandi. R.Marculescu. "System-Level Power/Performance Analysis for Embedded Systems Design". Design Automation Conference, Las Vegas, June 2001. Proceedings, ACM, 2001.

[6] L.M.Reyneri, F.Cucinotta, A.Serra, L.Lavagno. "A Hardware/Software Co-design Flow and IP Library Based on Simulink". DAC'01 - Design Automation Conference, Las Vegas, June 2001. Proceedings, ACM, 2001.

[7] S.Ito, L.Carro, R.Jacobi. "Making Java Work for Microcontroller Applications". In: IEEE Design & Test of Computers. vol. 18, n. 5, Sept-Oct 2001.

[8] V.Tiwari, S.Malik, A.Wolfe. "Power Analysis of Embedded Software: a First Step Towards Software Power Minimization". In: IEEE Transactions on Very Large Scale Integration *(VLSI) Systems*, vol. 2, n. 4; Dec. 1994.

[9] K.Choi, A.Chatterjee. "Efficient Instruction-Level Optimization Methodology for Low-Power Embedded Systems". International Symposium on System Synthesis, Montréal, Oct. 2001. Proceedings, ACM, 2001.

[10] A.Peymandoust, T.Simunic, G. de Micheli. "Complex Library Mapping for Embedded Software Using Symbolic Algebra". DAC'02 - Design Automation Conference, New Orleans, June 2002. Proceedings, ACM, 2002.

[11] A.C.Beck Filho, F.R.Wagner, L.Carro. "CACO-PS: A General Purpose Cycle-Accurate Configurable Power Simulator". SBCCI'03 – 16th Symposium on Integrated Circuits and Systems Design. São Paulo, Brazil, Sept. 2003. Proceedings, IEEE Computer Society Press, 2003.

[12] A.Omondi. Computer Arithmetic Systems: Algorithms, Architecture and Implementation. Prentice Hall, 1994.

[13] K.Salomonsen, S.Søgaard, E.P.Larsen. Design and Implementation of an MPEG/Audio Layer III Bitstream Processor, Master Thesis, Aalborg University, 1997.

[14] H.B.Lee, B.G.Zorn. "BIT: A Tool for Instrumenting Java Bytecodes". USITS'97 - USENIX Symposium on Internet Technologies and Systems, Dec. 1997.

A MULTI-LEVEL DESIGN PATTERN FOR EMBEDDED SOFTWARE*

Ricardo J. Machado and João M. Fernandes
Dept. Sistemas de Informação & Dept. Informática, Universidade do Minho, Portugal

Abstract: It is a common practice amongst programmers to construct parts of software programs by imitating parts of programs constructed by more experienced professionals. This "learn by example" approach can be applied at the design level by using patterns as sets of rules and recommendations to solve well-defined tasks within the development of computer-based systems. This paper describes the multi-level ICIS pattern, to be used at various design levels of industrial control-based information systems, where embedded devices are networked to interact with the industrial processes and equipment. The proposed pattern is described using several UML diagrams.

1. INTRODUCTION

The research work of Edsger Dijkstra has demonstrated that it is advantageous to "waste time to think" in the organization, structure and internal partition of a system, instead of going directly to the implementation just after the requirements' modelling [1]. This methodological position, nowadays perfectly accepted by any professional system designer, has originated, at that time, several research lines that culminated in the emergence of a new sub-discipline called *systems architecture* [2], or *software architecture* in the particular situation of software intensive systems [3].

Architectural design involves the manipulation of general abstract models that can be applied to distinct systems, as long as these systems share a set of

---

* Research funded by FCT and FEDER under project *METHODES* (POSI/37334/CHS/2001).

common requirements. These general abstract models of systems' organization are called *design patterns* [4].

It is a common practice amongst programmers to construct parts of software programs by imitating parts of programs constructed by more experienced professionals. This current practice, at the implementation level, demands the search for a pattern within a third-party software code and the adaptation to the specific problem at hand. This "learn by example" approach can be applied at the design level by using patterns as sets of rules and recommendations to solve well-defined tasks within the development of computer-based systems [5].

2. DESIGN PATTERNS

One of the traditional problems of design patterns is the inexistence of a standard notation for its description, which allows different interpretations for each existing pattern [7]. A pattern can be characterized by using: (1) a pictorial diagram to describe the general context of the pattern; (2) a class/object diagram in a well-known notation (UML, for instance), to model the static relations amongst the pattern entities; (3) a sequence diagram to model the dynamic relations within the pattern; (4) any other semantic diagram, as long as the syntax is well-defined, to characterize a particular view of the pattern. Recently, Fontoura [8] has proposed the UML-F profile to describe framework architectures and to support framework modeling and annotation by using UML-compliant extensions.

Nowadays, design patterns have reached such a very mature state that they are organized in a catalogue fashion just like the old databooks of digital integrated circuits [9-13]. There are also some pattern catalogues for the analysis phase [14].

The idea of documenting the best practices in software development as patterns for building embedded and real-time systems is a recent research topic. The first important work on this topic was the "Recursive Control" pattern for real-time control systems [15]. Another major landmark is the collection of patterns proposed by Douglass to design object-oriented real-time systems [5]. Other work in defining patterns for embedded and real-time systems were also proposed in the last years [16-22].

3. THE MULTI-LEVEL ICIS PATTERN

A new design pattern, named *multi-level ICIS*, was defined as a result of the development of several industrial information systems [23, 28]. Within these developments, embedded systems, web-services, and control applications had to work together to accomplish the easy interconnection between the lower (0, 1 and 2) and the upper (3 and 4) CIM (computer integrated manufacturing) levels [24]. These ICIS (industrial control-based information system) solutions are complementary, within the industrial organizations, to the well-known management information systems (MISs) [25]. Industrial information systems (IIS), which result from the integration of a MIS with an ICIS, are the answer to accomplish the definition of an applicational platform, based on ERP (enterprise resource planning) approaches, in order to integrate and unify the management and control of all organizational information.

The proposed pattern, based on the MVC pattern [6], was defined to support both the levels 2 and 3 of co-design [26]: (1) at level 2, the embedded software engineer must decide which functionalities will run directly on the processor and which ones will be synthesized for the reconfigurable devices; (2) at level 3, the information systems engineer integrates the previously designed components with the existing MIS. With this pattern we avoid the designer to follow a strict class-driven approach, where class diagrams are built before the object diagram [27]. The defined pattern provides a set of recommendations to support the architectural design of ICIS solutions.

Fig. 1 depicts a pictorial diagram of the multi-level ICIS pattern. This pattern is composed of four architectural blocks: (1) the *access interface* block, is responsible for the interface implementation with the MIS subsystem; (2) the *supervision interface* block is responsible for the interface implementation with the industrial processes and equipments (shop-floor); (3) the *operator interface* block is responsible for the interface implementation with the human operators that interact directly with the ICIS subsystem; (4) the *production, quality and management (pre-)processing* block is responsible for the data processing (stubbing and transformation) to support the interconnection of the three previous interfaces. Each architectural block can be implemented by adopting a reuse approach, based on the specialization or refinement of previously existing classes. This is the reason why, in fig. 1, there are one inheritance relation between each block and one class library. Additionally, each block can be developed within a CBD (component-based design) approach by using aggregation and composition of sub-objects as instances of specialized or refined classes from libraries.

To thoroughly understand the proposed pattern it is important to analyse the typical network topologies of final IIS solutions. In fig. 2, two distinct "zones" can be identified: (1) the first one corresponds to the CAN network supporting the ICIS implementation by using several embedded devices

(CANit, CANio, CAN-FPGA, CAN-RF and CAN-Server execute embedded software to support CIM level 2) and one (or more) PC-VAP (gateway executing LabVIEW software); (2) the second one corresponds to the Ethernet network supporting the MIS implementation by typical ERP and POS (plant operations system) software.

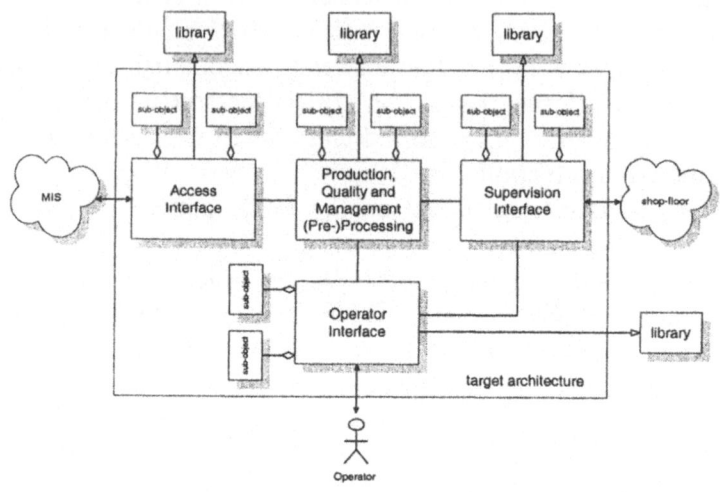

Figure 1. Pictorial diagram of the multi-level ICIS pattern.

UML deployment diagrams can be used to illustrate the three typical application scenarios for the multi-level ICIS pattern:

(1) *ICIS architecture.* The deployment diagram of the ICIS architecture is depicted in fig. 3, where the multi-level ICIS pattern is being used as follows: (i) the *PC-VAP* node supports the *access interface* component; (ii) the *CANio* node (embedded device topologically located near the industrial processes and equipments to acquire and send supervision information) supports the *supervision interface* component; (iii) the *CAN-RF* node (wireless embedded device used by human operators, along their walkthroughs the factory plant, to acquire and send supervision information) supports the *operator interface* component; (iv) the *CANit* node (embedded device that controls one or more groups of nodes, based on *CANio* and *CAN-RF* architectures, to coordinate the acquisition and sending of supervision information) supports the *(pre-)processing* component. Each *PC-VAP* node can concentrate, in a star topology, several sets of nodes based on *CANio* and *CAN-RF* architectures. Within this application context, the multi-level ICIS pattern is intended to clarify the kind of topology the information systems engineer should use to structure the existent computing nodes in a particular ICIS final solution.

(2) *Software architecture of the PC-VAP node.* The software architecture of the *PC-VAP* node is depicted in fig. 4. The *access interface* component of fig. 3 is being decomposed into a set of sub-components organized by the architecture defined by the multi-level ICIS pattern. The *access interface*, *supervision interface*, *operator interface* and *(pre-)processing* components appear again, but now within the *PC-VAP* software. For instance (and only just an example, since the graphical LabVIEW language has not been introduced here), it is possible to identify, within a portion of LabVIEW code depicted in fig. 5, the code blocks that correspond to those components.

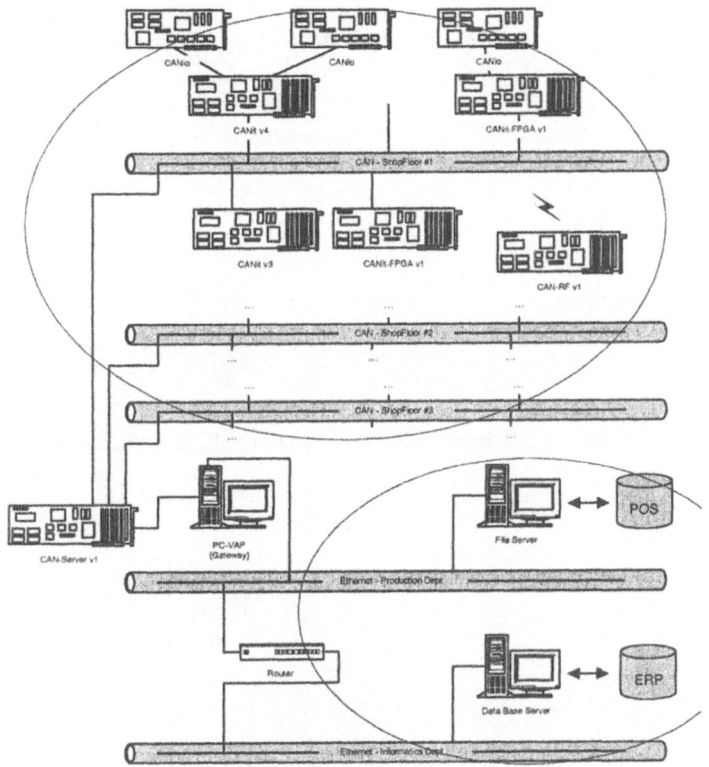

Figure 2. Network topology for typical IIS solutions.

(3) *Software architecture of the embedded components.* The *(pre-)processing* component of fig. 3 is decomposed into a set of sub-components organized by the architecture defined by the multi-level ICIS pattern. Again, *access interface*, *supervision interface*, *operator interface* and *(pre-)processing* components appear, but this time within the *CANit* embedded device, by using aggregates of objects in the Oblog language, just as referred in [29], following the methodology described in [30], with some well-known limitations [32].

A class diagram that describes, generically, the relations between the entities involved in the components suggested by the pattern is depicted in fig. 6. This diagram follows a class-driven approach (since it defines an instantiation template) and identifies six distinct classes: *Access, Supervision, Controller, Sub-Controller, DataRepository* and *Operator*.

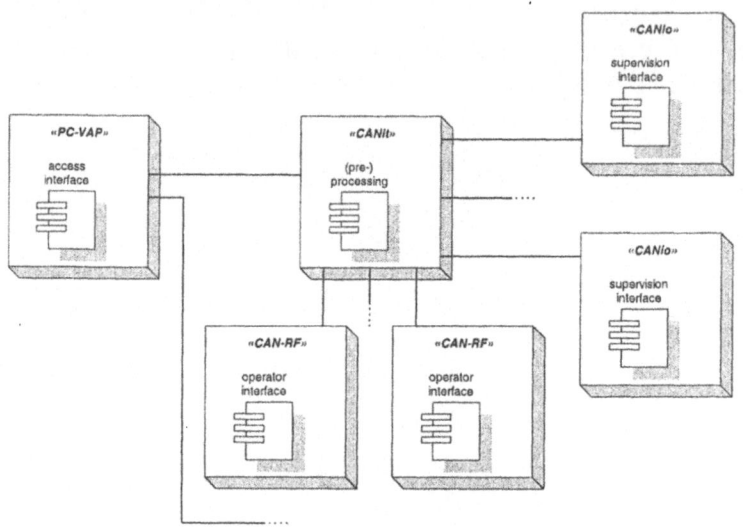

Figure 3. UML deployment diagram of the ICIS architecture.

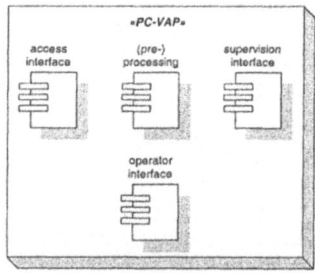

Figure 4. UML deployment diagram of the PC-VAP node.

Access, Supervision and *Operator* are *«interface»* classes (according to [32], an *«interface»* class models behaviour and information dependent on the system's interface) and allow *Controller* e *Sub-Controller* classes to be considerably independent from the particular mechanisms adopted to implement the relation with the outside world (the system's environment). Both the access (border between the embedded architecture and the upper MIS) and the supervision interfaces (border between the embedded architecture and the industrial process and equipment) deal with external entities topologically located very far from the embedded device, thus adopting an asynchronous flow mechanism in relation with the embedded device's main thread responsible for the system's general control.

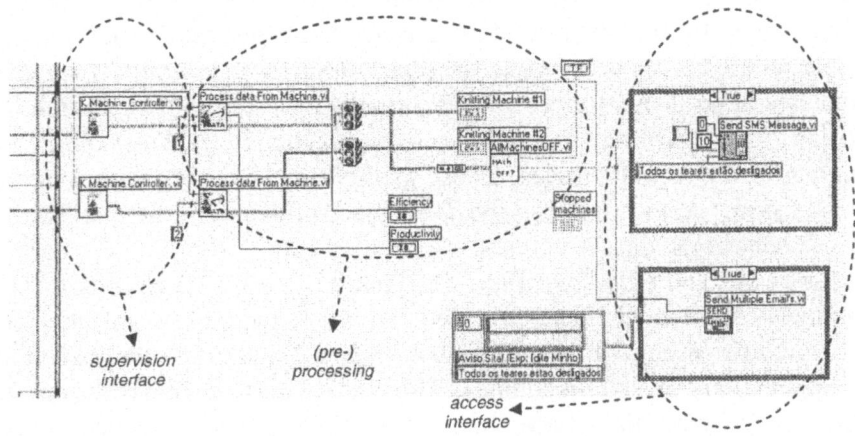

Figure 5. Multi-level ICIS pattern implemented in LabVIEW code.

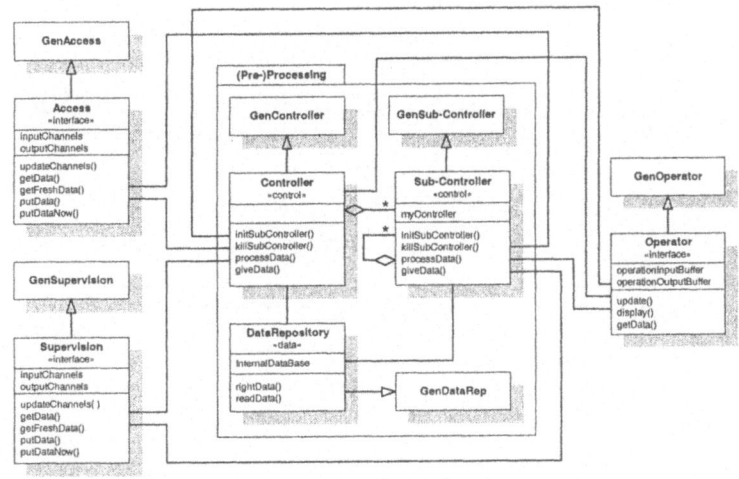

Figure 6. UML class diagram for the multi-level ICIS pattern.

The embedded device should have another tread that acknowledges the *access* and *supervision* objects (instances of *Access* and *Supervision* classes) about: (1) the arrival of information from the environment to be stored in the interface objects by using the *putData()* method; (2) the need to update all the values stored in the interface objects by using the *updateChannels()* method. Each *access* and *supervision* objects must implement, as attributes, two distinct data structures, one to store the interface input values (*inputChannels*) and another to store the interface output values (*outputChannels*), before they are disseminated throughout the other system components. In the main thread, the methods *getData()* and *putData()* should be used to have access to the *inputChannels* and *outputChannels* data structures in an asynchronous way. To assure a synchronous execution of the reading and writing operations the methods *getFreshData()* and *putDataNow()* should be used. These methods are blocking within the main thread, since *access* and *supervision* objects force an effective hardware refreshment of the data structures.

Controller and *Sub-Controller* are «*control*» classes (according to [32], a «*control*» class models behaviour that can not be naturally associated to any other kind of object, i.e., «*interface*» *or* «*data*») and allow the instantiation of aggregations of state-machines. These state-machine aggregations have access to a small data base, internal to the embedded device, to store temporarily information about the industrial processes and equipment. This set of objects constitutes the *(pre-)processing* architectural block to be executed within the main thread. Fig. 7 presents an UML sequence diagram for the multi-level ICIS pattern.

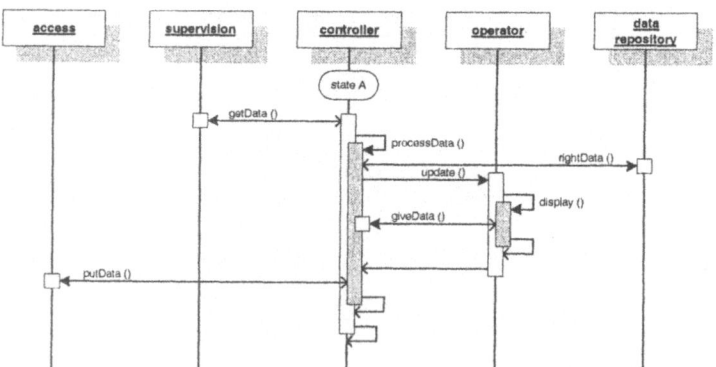

Figure 7. UML sequence diagram for the multi-level ICIS pattern.

4.   CONCLUSIONS

The implementation of a pattern with the characteristics of the one presented here must be carefully thought for real-time applications, since it is very easy to adopt technological solutions that will introduce an enormous temporal and space inefficiency. This additional implementation difficulty must be explicitly assumed as being the price to pay to benefit from the usage of patterns. The multi-level ICIS pattern should be faced as a semantic guideline for conducting the design of networked solutions for the supervision of industrial processes and equipment.

In practice, it is common to implement a simplified version of the architecture in which the three kinds of interfaces (*access*, *supervision* and *operator*) and the data repository are melted into a unique entity, named *interface controller*. This solution is more efficient than the one presented in fig. 7, since it is only necessary to maintain a unique set of data structures, which implies that the memory requirements can be significantly reduced and, consequently, the data processing operations can be speedup.

REFERENCES

1. E. Dijkstra, *The Structure of the 'T.H.E.' Multiprogramming System*, Communications of the ACM, vol. 18, no. 8, pp. 453-457, 1968.
2. E. Rechtin, M. Maier, *The Art of Systems Architecting*, Systems Engineering Series, CRC Press LLC, 1997.
3. P. C. Clements, *From Subroutines to Subsystems: Component-Based Software Development*, in A. W. Brown, *Component-Based Software Engineering*, Selected Papers from the Software Engineering Institute, IEEE CS Press, 1996.
4. W. Pree, *Design Patterns for Object-Oriented Software Development*, Addison-Wesley, ACM Press, 1995.
5. B. P. Douglass, *Doing Hard Time: Developing Real-Time Systems with UML, Objects, Frameworks, and Patterns*, Addison-Wesley, 1999.
6. G. E. Krasner, S. T. Pope, *A Cookbook for Using the Model-View-Controller User Interface Paradigm in Smalltalk-80*, Journal of Object-Oriented Programming, vol. 1, no. 3, pp. 27-49, ACM Press, 1988.
7. A. Lauder, S. Kent, *Precise Visual Specification of Design Patterns*, 12th European Conference on Object-Oriented Programming, LNCS 1445, pp. 114-134, Springer Verlag, 1998.
8. M. Fontoura, W. Pree, B. Rumpe, *The UML Profile for Framework Architectures*, Addison-Wesley, 2001.
9. E. Gamma, R. Helm, R. Johnson, J. Vlissides, *Design Patterns: Elements of Reusable Object-Oriented Software*, Addison-Wesley, 1995.
10. F. Buschmann, R. Meunier, H. Rohnert, P. Sommerlad, M. Stal, *Pattern-Oriented Software Architecture: A System of Patterns*, John Wiley & Sons, 1996.
11. J. Coplien, D. Schmidt, *Pattern Languages of Program Design*, Addison-Wesley, 1995
12. J. Vlissides, J. Coplien, N. Kerth, *Pattern Languages of Program Design 2*, Addison-Wesley, 1996.
13. R. Martin, D. Riehle, F. Buschmann, *Pattern Languages of Program Design 3*, Addison-Wesley, 1998.

14. M. Fowler, *Analysis Patterns: Reusable Object Models*, Addison-Wesley, 1997.
15. B. Selic, *An Architectural Pattern for Real-Time Control Software*, Third Annual Pattern Languages of Programming Conference, pp. 4-6, 1996.
16. M. Bottomley, *A Pattern Language for Simple Embedded Systems*, 6th Annual Pattern Languages of Programming Conference, pp. 15-18, 1999.
17. R. Mckegney, T. Shepard, *Design Patterns and Real-Time Object-Oriented Modeling*, Conference on Object-Oriented Programming, Systems, Languages, and Applications , pp. 55-56, 2000.
18. R. Mckegney, *Small Memory Software: Patterns for Systems with Limited Memory*, Addison-Wesley, 2000.
19. M. Pont, *Patterns for Time-Triggered Embedded Systems: Building Reliable Applications with the 8051 Family of Microcontrollers*, Addison-Wesley, 2001.
20. J. Zalewski, *Patterns Real-Time Software Design Patterns*, 9th Conf. on Real-Time Systems, 2002.
21. B. P. Douglas, *Real-Time Design Patterns: Robust Scalable Architecture for Real-Time Systems*, Addison-Wesley, 2002.
22. S. Sauer, G. Engels, *MVC-Based Modeling Support for Embedded Real-Time Systems: Position Statement*, Workshop on Object-Oriented Modeling of Embedded Realtime Systems, pp. 11-14, 1999.
23. J. M. Fernandes, R. J. Machado, H. D. Santos, *Modeling Industrial Embedded Systems with UML*, 8th Int. Workshop on Hardware/Software Codesign (CODES 2000), pp. 18-22, ACM Press, 2000.
24. P. G. Ranky, *Computer Networks for World Class CIM Systems*, CIMware Limited, 1990.
25. B. Scholz-Reiter, *CIM Interfaces: Concepts, Standards and Problems of Interfaces in Computer Integrated Manufacturing*, Chapman & Hall, 1992.
26. R. J. Machado, J. M. Fernandes, *Heterogeneous Information Systems Integration: Organizations and Methodologies,* Product Focused Software Process Improvement, pp. 629-643, M. Oivo e S. Komi-Sirviö (editors), Lecture Notes in Computer Science, LNCS vol. 2559, Springer-Verlag, 2002.
27. J. M. Fernandes, R. J. Machado, *From Use Cases to Objects: An Industrial Information Systems Case Study Analysis*, Object-Oriented Information Systems, pp. 319-328, Y. Wang, S. Patel e R. Johnston (editors), Springer-Verlag, 2001.
28. J. M. Fernandes, R. J. Machado, *System-Level Object-Orientation in the Specification and Validation of Embedded Systems*, 14th Symp. on Integrated Circuits and System Design (SBCCI'01), IEEE CS Press, 2001.
29. R. J. Machado, J. M. Fernandes, *A Petri Net Meta-Model to Develop Software Components for Embedded Systems*, 2nd Int. Conf. on Application of Concurrency to System Design (ACSD'01), pp. 113-22, IEEE CS Press, 2001.
30. R. J. Machado, J. M. Fernandes, H. D. Santos, *A Methodology for Complex Embedded Systems Design: Petri Nets within a UML Approach*, Architecture and Design of Distributed Embedded Systems, B. Kleinjohann (editor), chapter 1, pp. 1-10, Kluwer A.P., 2001.
31. J. M. Fernandes, R. J. Machado, *Can UML be a System-Level Language for Embedded Software?* Design and Analysis of Distributed Embedded Systems, B. Kleinjohann, K. Kim, L. Kleinjohann e A. Rettberg (editors), chapter. 1, pp. 1-10, Kluwer A.P.2002.
32. I. Jacobson, M. Christerson, P. Jonsson, G. Övergaard, *Object-Oriented Software Engineering: A Use Case Driven Approach*, Addison-Wesley, 1992.

A PETRI NET APPROACH FOR THE DESIGN OF DYNAMICALLY MODIFIABLE EMBEDDED SYSTEMS*

Carsten Rust, Franz Josef Rammig
University of Paderborn, Germany
car@c-lab.de, franz@upb.de

Abstract: A Petri net based approach for modeling dynamically modifiable embedded real-time systems is presented. The presented work contributes to the extension of a Petri net based design methodology for distributed embedded systems towards the handling of dynamically modifiable systems. Extensions to the underlying high-level Petri net model are introduced that allow for dynamic modifications of a net at run time.

1. INTRODUCTION AND RELATED WORK

To an increasing extent, embedded real-time systems these days are dynamically modifiable. As an example, consider an adaptive robot control, where components of the control software are changed at run time due to results of online learning algorithms. Another application scenario is a group of mobile robots that cooperatively solve a problem. Since robots may enter or leave the scenario or just change their location, the entire system is highly dynamic. Such systems gain increasing interest, e. g. when studying autonomic computing. Even in traditional application domains like automotive systems, dynamically modifying control systems are considered, for instance for the handling of so called fail-over situations, that is in error situations, where functionality has to be relocated. For the design of these systems, dynamically evolving subsystems – which imply a powerful basic model for specification – have to be considered together with basic controllers running under hard reliability constraints.

For the design of these systems, we propose to use a methodology based on high-level Petri nets as the underlying formal model [11]. We have chosen a

---

*This work was supported by the German Science Foundation (DFG) project SFB-376

high-level Petri net model for several reasons, for instance in order to benefit from the multitude of existing verification and analysis methods based on
Petri nets. While Petri nets are well-established for the design of static systems, they lack support for dynamically modifiable systems. We propose an
extension in such a way that an engineer is enabled to annotate transitions with
transformation rules. A transformation rule specifies a modification of the system that is performed when the annotated transition fires. The basic concepts
of our approach were first introduced in [10]. In [8] and [6], the extended
design methodology and a tool for the simulation of dynamically modifiable
systems were presented. In this paper, we concentrate on the formal Petri net
model. We will define a self-modifying Petri net model as the extension of a
hierarchical high-level Petri net model.

In the literature, dynamically modifiable Petri nets were often considered
in the context of object-oriented Petri nets. An example are Object Petri nets
introduced by Valk [13]. They support a two-stage modeling method: a main
net called system net contains several object nets, which are instanciated via
tokens of the system net. Transition firings in the system net, which lead to
changes of its net marking, obviously can change the overall net. However, the
dynamics is reflected in the marking of the net. No changes to the net structure
are made. An early approach to self-modifying Petri nets was presented by
Valk in the late seventies [12]. More recently, Badouel and Darondeau introduced Stratified Petri nets, a subset of Valks self-modifying nets. Both models
are based on standard Petri nets without annotations. Modifications of a net
are due to a simple mechanism switching edges on and off dependant on the
current net marking. An approach for high-level nets which is based on similar
ideas is presented in [1].

We propose a more generic approach, where modifications of the net structure at run time result from coupling a net model with graph transformation
rules (productions), as they are known from graph grammars and high-level
replacement systems respectively. Several other approaches for coupling Petri
nets and graph transformation techniques can be found in literature (see for instance [2] for an overview). One example is the concept of net transformation
systems [7]. Roughly speaking, a net transformation system is a graph grammar, where the generated graphs are Petri nets and the definition of productions
is based on Petri net morphisms. Basically, we use very similar concepts. The
characteristic feature of our approach is that the transformation system is integrated into the Petri net formalism by annotating transitions with productions.
In the aforementioned approaches, graph transformations are applied to Petri
nets at design time only. Our approach integrates them into the firing-rule.

In the following section, we will first give an informal brief overview of
the hierarchical high-level Petri net model, that forms the basis for introducing dynamic modification. The specification of Petri net transformation rules

and their integration into the high-level Petri net model will then be defined formally in Sections 3 and 4. Finally, a small application example will be considered in Section 5.

2.   BASIC PETRI NET MODEL

The basis for definining dynamically modifiable Petri nets in the following section is a high-level form of Petri nets. Petri nets are bipartite directed graphs augmented by a marking and firing rules. The Petri net graph consists of a finite set of places P, a finite set of transitions T, directed edges from places to transitions and from transitions to places. Places model conditions. For this purpose they may be marked by tokens. Driven by specific firing rules, a transition can fire based on the local marking of those places it is directly connected with. By firing, the marking of these places is modified.

With regard to the definition of Petri net morphisms, we adopt the so-called algebraic notation for the formal description of Petri nets. Hence, a Petri net graph is a tuple $F = (P, T, pre, post)$ where $pre : T \rightarrow \mu(P)$ assigns a multiset of places (the preset) to each transition, while $post : T \rightarrow \mu(P)$ specifies the postset of each transition. Figure 1 a) shows an example net. Its formal definition is $N_1 = (\ \{p_5, p_6, p_7\}, \{t_8\}, \{(t_8, 3p_5 + 2p_6)\}, \{(t_8, p_7)\}\ )$.

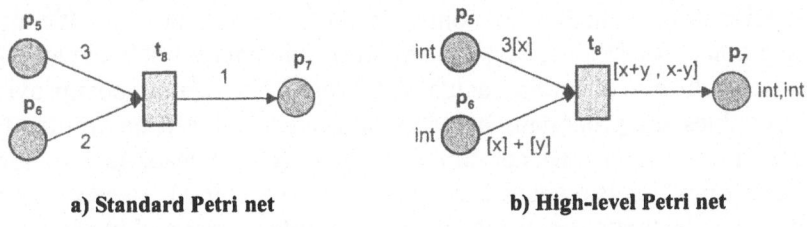

a) Standard Petri net   b) High-level Petri net

Figure 1.   Petri net examples

In the case of high-level nets the tokens are typed individuals. The other net components are annotated accordingly: places with data types, transition in-edges with variable expressions, transitions with a guard and transition out-edges with term expressions, i. e. sums of functional expressions. Now a transition can fire only if the formal edge expressions can be unified with actually available tokens and this unification passes the guard expression of the transition. By firing, the input tokens are consumed and calculations associated with the transition out-edges are executed. That way new tokens are produced that are routed to output places of the transition. A simple high-level net is depicted in Figure 1 b). Different from this example, we usually annotate transition out-edges with variable expressions and transitions with corresponding variable assignments, since to our experience this representation has some advantages

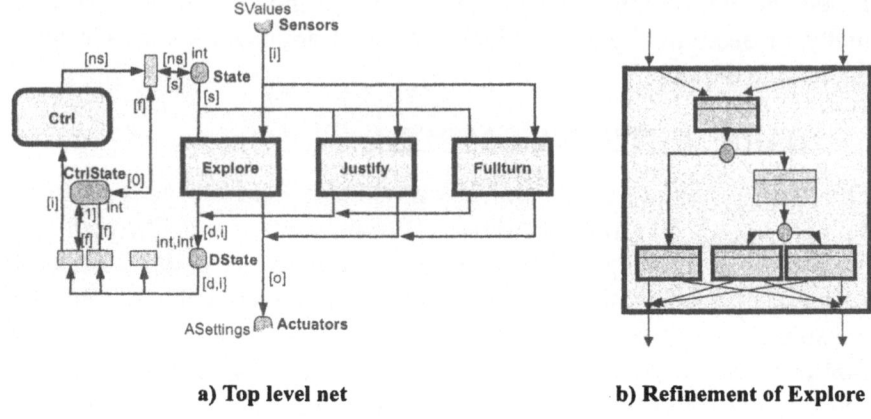

a) Top level net   b) Refinement of Explore

Figure 2.   Hierarchical high-level Petri net

in practical applications. Obviously, both alternatives for annotating the out-going edges of transitions are equivalent. The depicted notation was chosen, because the resulting formal definitions are more readable. In order to handle complex systems we added a hierarchy concept. As an example for a hierar-chical specification, a small robot control is depicted in Figure 2 a). It contains three hierarchical transitions, each instantiating a distinct robot behavior which maps sensor values to according actuator settings. The components providing the sensor values and processing actuator values respectively are omitted from the figure. Furthermore, the net contains a hierarchical place instantiating a discrete control which is responsible for properly switching between the possi-ble modes. The instantiation of the Explore-module is depicted in Figure 2 b).

Besides support for easy modeling, another reason for presuming a hierar-chical Petri net model as the basis of our dynamically reconfigurable model is that the structure induced by hierarchy may be used for defining scopes, to which transformation rules can be applied. In order to define a hierarchical structure, we assume a function s which assigns a parent node to each node of the net. A node acting as a parent node is called hierarchical node. The inverse function of s assigns to each hierarchical node the set of nodes which constitute the module instanciated by this node. In order to keep the definitions reasonably simple, we assume that each hierarchical Petri net can be realized by a flat net constituted by the basic, i. e. non-hierarchical, nodes of the net. This holds for many hierarchy concepts. In some cases however, extensions to the net model are necessary in order to facilitate this mapping. Since hierarchy is not in the focus of the presented work, we neglect these cases. Thus, in the following we consider flat Petri nets, which have a structure imposed by an original hierarchical definition.

3. RULES FOR DYNAMIC MODIFICATION

In the case of a static system, the entire system can be modeled in advance. To specify these systems, we propose to use the hierarchical high-level Petri net model outlined in the previous section. For dynamically modifiable systems however, only the generating system of a set of potentially resulting systems can be provided. A straightforward approach for describing the generating system is given by graph grammars, since a Petri net specification is strongly based on a graph, and graph grammars are a standard formalism for specifying graph manipulations. From the various existing approaches for defining graph grammars, we have chosen an algebraic approach, which was first introduced by Ehrig et. al. in the early seventies [4]. Algebraic approaches typically make use of constructs from category theory in order to describe graph transformation rules (productions) and their semantics, i. e. the precondition for applying a production to a given graph as well as the effect to the graph. In order to apply category theory, categories of graphs are considered, where relationships between graphs are modeled by graph morphisms.

Hence, in order to define productions for Petri nets, we first have to define Petri net morphisms. At this point, a - merely technical - problem arises: Productions and likewise Petri net morphisms shall be formulated over high-level Petri nets as well as be part of the annotation of high-level Petri nets. In order to solve this cyclic dependency, we define morphisms for a generic model of annotated nets complying with standard high-level nets, but also with the dynamically modifiable nets we are aiming at. An annotated net combines a Petri net graph $F = (P, T, pre, post)$, as it was introduced in the previous section, with a tuple of functions $A = (A_P : P \rightarrow L_P, A_T : T \rightarrow L_T, A_{F_i} : T \rightarrow L_{F_i} \times P, A_{F_o} : T \rightarrow L_{F_o} \times P)$, where L_P, L_T, L_{F_i}, and L_{F_o} are languages. Each function assigns annotations to Petri net elements. Given two annotated Petri nets, a Petri net morphism is a tuple of functions $f : N \rightarrow M = (f_P : P^N \rightarrow P^M, f_T : T^N \rightarrow T^M, f_A : A^N \rightarrow A^M)$ which maps the places, transitions, and annotations of one net N to those of another net M. For f being a morphism, it is required that for all net components (i. e. places, transitions, and edges), the corresponding morphism component commutes with the annotation function. For the complete formal definition we refer to [9].

Having introduced Petri net morphisms, we are able to define productions for Petri net transformations in the usual way. Thereby we follow the double pushout approach which was introduced in [4]. A comprehensive tutorial can for instance be found in [3]. In the double pushout approach applied to Petri nets, each production p consists of two Petri net morphisms $l : K \rightarrow L$ and $r : K \rightarrow R$. Basically, p correlates an annotated Petri net L (the left side of the production) with an annotated Petri net R (the right side). Furthermore,

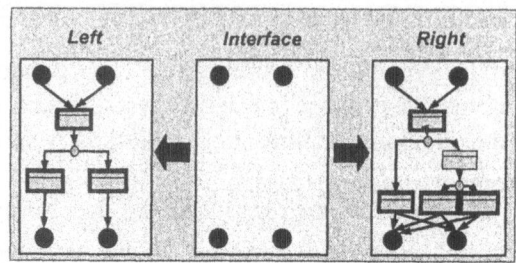

Figure 3.   Rule for Dynamic Transformation of Petri nets

the production explicitly specifies the interface object K, typically a common subnet of L and R. An example for a production is depicted in Figure 3. The rule can be applied to a net N, if N contains the net on the left hand side of the rule (*Left*). When the rule is applied, the left hand side is replaced with the net on the right hand side (*Right*). The common interface object (*Interface*) must be part of the net N for application of a rule, but it remains unchanged during replacement. Hence, it specifies the interface of the modified net to the surrounding net.

In general, the application of a production to a graph leading to another graph (in our case the application to a Petri net leading to another Petri net) is called a direct derivation. In algebraic approaches to graph grammars, direct derivations are defined by gluing constructions of graphs, that are formally characterized as pushouts, a standard construct from category theory. As the name suggests, a direct derivation step in the double pushout approach is modeled by two pushout diagrams. They are depicted in Figure 4. The first diagram (1) describes the deletion of all elements of N which have a pre-image in L, but none in K. The diagram contains the graphs K, L, N, and C, the latter being the graph resulting from the first step. In addition to the morphisms l and n, the diagram contains $k : K \rightarrow C$, which embeds K into C, and $l' : C \rightarrow K$. In terms of category theory, N is called the pushout object of l and k, while C is the pushout complement object of l and m. The second pushout diagram (2) describes the second step, where all elements of R are inserted that do not

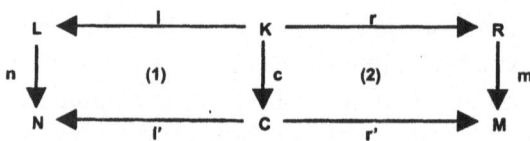

Figure 4.   Diagram of a direct derivation

have a pre-image in K. In this diagram, the resulting graph M is the pushout object of r and k. Summarized in terms of category theory, given a production $p = (l : K \to L, r : K \to R)$, a Petri net N and a match $m : L \to N$, p is applied to N by first building the pushout complement object C of l and m and then building the pushout object of r and $k : K \to C$. We pass on a formal definition of pushouts and direct derivations and conclude this section by characterizing three objects from Figure 4 that are substantial for the application of a production $p = (l : K \to L, r : K \to R)$ to a given annotated Petri net N. These are the Petri net morphisms n (which embeds the left side of the rule into N), l'^{-1} (which removes the left side from N), and r' (which adds the right side). In the following we denote these objects by the tuple $D = (D_m, D_r, D_a)$.

4.   INTEGRATION OF DYNAMIC MODIFICATION

With a formalism for describing net transformations, we now are able to define dynamically modifiable high-level Petri nets. They consist of a Petri net graph $F = (P, T, pre, post)$ as described in section 2 and a tuple of annotation functions $A_N = (A_P : P \to S, A_I : T \to \mathcal{L}_d \times P, A_G : T \to \mathcal{L}_{Op}(bool)$, $A_O : T \to \mathcal{L}_m \times P, A_T : T \to \mathcal{R}, A_M : P \to \mathcal{L}_{Const})$. A_P annotates places with sorts, i.e. with datatypes, A_I annotates transition in-edges with variable expressions. Transitions are annotated with a guard (by A_G) and with a transformation rule (by A_T). A_O annotates transition out-edges with sums of terms. Finally, the initial marking is specified by A_M. The definition of a signature including a set of sorts S as well as of the languages $\mathcal{L}_d$, $\mathcal{L}_{Op}(bool)$, $\mathcal{L}_m$, and $\mathcal{L}_{Const}$ is straightforward. $\mathcal{R}$ is the set of rules. Each element of $\mathcal{R}$ is a tuple $r = (p, v)$, where p is a production as described in the previous section, and v is a (hierarchical) Petri net node, the scope of r.

Annotating a transition t_{mod} of a Petri net N with a rule $r = (p, v)$ specifies that, during firing of t_{mod}, the production p is applied to the subnet instantiated by v. If several matches of the production are feasible, one of them is chosen non-deterministically. For defining the semantics of a dynamically modifiable net formally, the definition of net markings as well as the transition firing rule have to be extended. As usual, markings assign tokens to the places of a net, whereby the sort of each token must fit to that of the place. For dynamically modifiable nets, the notion of a Petri net marking is extended towards a Petri net configuration consisting of a marking and a Petri net. Petri net configurations are modified by firing of transitions. For enabling a transition firing, a match of the transition's transformation rule has to be found in the current net as well as a consistent substitution of the transition's variables by values of the current marking. Hence, a transition t, a tuple $D = (D_m, D_r, D_a)$ characterizing a direct derivation, and a variable binding B are combined to form a transition step $S = (t, D, B)$. B must be a consistent substitution of the transition's variables, for which the transition guard is true. If a transformation rule is specified for the transition, the transition guard as well as the out-edge annotations may include references to the rule components, for instance in order to specify additional conditions. Therefor, the set of transition variables includes the places and transitions of the rule's left side. Accordingly, a consistent substitution B being part of a transition step $S = (t, D, B)$ must assign values to these variables, which comply with D.

The semantics of a transition step S is defined in terms of its incremental effects describing the effect of the demarking process of a transition and of the marking process respectively. For dynamically modifiable nets, the incremental effects of a transition step are twofold. We have to define the effects of S on the current net $E_N^-(S)$ and $E_N^+(S)$ as well as the effects on the current marking $E_M^-(S)$ and $E_M^+(S)$. Given a transition step $S = (t, D, B)$, where $D = (D_m, D_r, D_a)$, and a configuration $C = (N, M)$, the effects on the current net N are given directly by the two functions D_r and D_a applied to N. From these functions, the two nodesets $E_V^-(S)$ and $E_V^+(S)$ can be derived. $E_V^-(S)$ contains all nodes of N that are removed by D_r, while $E_V^+(S)$ contains all nodes added by D_a. As in static nets, the negative effect of a transition step results from evaluating the in-edge annotations of t with the substitution B. Similarly, the out-edge annotations are evaluated for generating the positive incremental effect $E_M^+(S)$. In addition, modifications to the net must be taken into account. The positive effect $E_M^+(S)$ has to be restricted to the marking of those places, that remain in the net after modification, i. e. the elements of $E_V^-(S)$ are not marked. Places contained in $E_V^+(S)$, i. e. places created by the transition step, are assigned their initial marking.

Based on these definitions, the firing rule of dynamically modifiable high-level Petri nets can be defined expectedly. Let t be a transition with the transformation rule $A_T(t) = (p, v)$, where $p = (l : K \rightarrow L, r : K \rightarrow R)$. Let $D = (D_m, D_r, D_a)$ be a direct derivation, $S = (t, D, B)$ a transition step, and $C_1 = (N_1, M_1)$ a configuration. S is enabled, i. e. t can fire, in C_1, if the following conditions hold. (1) The transition t is an element of N_1. (2) The scope of the transformation rule v is a hierarchical node of N_1. (3) v instantiates $D_m(L)$. (4) The negative incremental effect $E_M^-(S)$ is included in the current marking M_1. If S is enabled in C_1, it may fire leading to a configuration $C_2 = (N_2, M_2)$ where N_2 results from applying D_r and D_a to N_1 and M_2 results from subtracting $E_M^-(S)$ from M_1 and adding $E_M^+(S)$.

5.   APPLICATION

Using the Petri net transformation features introduced in the previous sections, a more concise specification of the robot control presented in Figure 2 is

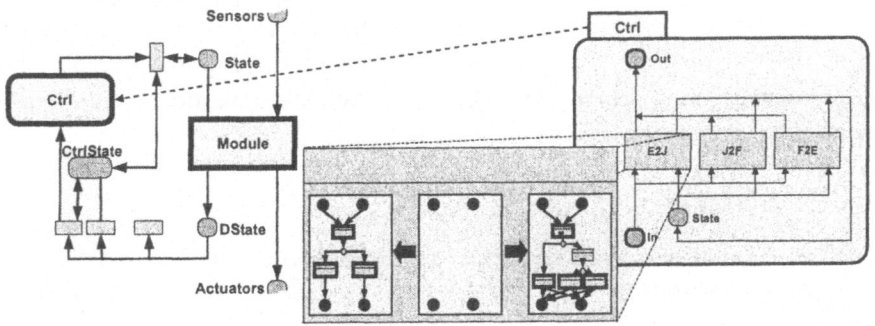

Figure 5.   Petri Net with dynamic modification

feasible. An excerpt of the revised specification is depicted in Figure 5. The hierarchical transitions *Explore*, *Justify*, and *Fullturn* specifying the behaviour in each possible mode of the robot have been folded into one transition *Module*. The mode switching transitions of the discrete control *Ctrl* are annotated with transformation rules changing the refinement of *Module* as exemplarily shown for one transition in Figure 5. This specification is more compact than the original one. Beyond that, it is more flexible, since transformation rules determining the refinement can depend on run time data.

The presented application example is comparatively small. An application of our approach to a larger robot scenario, a small robot contest called 'Capture the Flag', is described in [5]. In both cases the extended high-level Petri net model has proven useful for the specification of dynamically modifiable systems. For an evaluation of the system behavior, we provide an execution platform [6], which allows to simulate the execution of a dynamically modifiable high-level Petri net on the simplified model of the target hardware. The execution platform will also serve as a basis for the automated implementation of dynamically modifiable Petri nets. For the realization of the above described applications, it was necessary to transform the dynamic Petri net models into equivalent static nets, since a direct implementation of truly dynamic behavior on the available small microcontrollers was not feasible. However, with regard to more powerful backends, we made first experiments with a direct implementation of the dynamic nets in Java, whose results were very promising. Compared to the implementation of an equivalent static net, the time for executing a modifiable net increased by a factor of 1,5 only.

6.   CONCLUSION

We have presented an extension of our high-level Petri net model in order to capture dynamically modifiable embedded systems, for instance adaptive robot controls. In order to achieve a formal definition of dynamically modifiable Petri nets, the existing high-level Petri net model was coupled with transformation rules as they are known from graph grammars. In our approach, these productions annotate transitions. The firing rule for transitions was modified accordingly.

REFERENCES

[1] E. Badouel and J. Oliver. Reconfigurable Nets, a Class of High Level Petri Nets Supporting Dynamic Changes. In *Proc. of a workshop within the 19th Int'l Conf. on Applications and Theory of Petri Nets*, 1998.

[2] B. Braatz, K. Ehrig, K. Hoffmann, J. Padberg, and M. Urbasek. Application of Graph Transformation Techniques to the Area of Petri Nets. In *Proc. of APPLIGRAPH Workshop on Applied Graph Transformation (AGT 2002)*, pages 35–44, Grenoble, France, 2002.

[3] H. Ehrig, M. Korff, and M. Löwe. Tutorial introduction to the algebraic approach of graph grammars based on double and single pushouts. In H. Ehrig, H.-J. Kreowski, and G. Rozenberg, editors, *Proceedings of 4th International Workshop on Graph-Grammars and Their Application to Computer Science*, volume 532 of *Lecture Notes in Computer Science*, Bremen, Germany, Mar. 1990. Springer.

[4] H. Ehrig, M. Pfender, and H. J. Schneider. Graph-grammars: An algebraic approach. In *14th Annual Symposium on Switching and Automata Theory*, pages 167–180. IEEE, Oct. 1973.

[5] M. Koch and C. Rust. Design of intelligent mechatronical systems with high-level petri nets. *submitted to:* IEEE/ASME Transactions on Mechatronics, Sept. 2004.

[6] W. Y. Liu, C. Rust, and F. Stappert. A simulation platform for petri net models of dynamically modifiable embedded systems. In *The European Simulation and Modeling Conference (ESMC 2003)*, Naples, Italy, Oct. 2003.

[7] J. Padberg, H. Ehrig, and L. Ribiero. Algebraic high-level net transformation systems. *Mathematical Structures in Computer Science*, 5:217–256, 1995.

[8] F. J. Rammig and C. Rust. Modeling of dynamically modifiable embedded real-time systems. In *9th IEEE International Workshop on Object-oriented Real-time Dependable Systems (WORDS 2003F)*, Capri, Italy, Oct. 2003.

[9] C. Rust. A High-Level Petri Net Model for the Design of Dynamically Modifiable Systems. *Internal Report*, URL: http://wwwhni.uni-paderborn.de/eps/uni/publications/, May 2004.

[10] C. Rust, F. Stappert, and R. Bernhardi-Grisson. Petri Net Based Design of Reconfigurable Embedded Real-Time Systems. In *Distributed And Parallel Embedded Systems*. Kluwer Academic Publishers, 2002.

[11] C. Rust, J. Tacken, and C. Böke. Pr/T–Net based Seamless Design of Embedded Real-Time Systems. In *Applications and Theory of Petri Nets 2001*, LNCS 2075, pages 343–362. Springer Verlag, 2001.

[12] R. Valk. Self-modifying nets, a natural extension of petri nets. *Lecture Notes in Computer Science: Automata, Languages and Programming*, 62:464–476, 1978.

[13] R. Valk. Petri nets as token objects, an introduction to elementary object nets. In J. D. und M. Silva, editor, *Applications and Theory of Petri Nets 1998*, LNCS 1420, pages 1–25. Springer Verlag, 1998.

INTERNET PREMIUM SERVICES FOR FLEXIBLE FORMAT DISTRIBUTED DEVICES

Brigitte Oesterdiekhoff
University of Paderborn
& Siemens Business Services, C-LAB
Fuerstenallee 11
33102 Paderborn
Germany
brigitte@c-lab.de

Abstract: This paper presents the provision of an internet premium service on different format output devices, which are embedded devices. In particular, we developed a tool for automatic generation of different profile depending target formats, which are used to present the service information on distributed mobile embedded devices like mobile phones, personal digital assistants (PDAs) or smart phones. In this approach XML-[Extensible Markup Language]-based user interface descriptions will be transcoded into other target formats. Used examples are cHTML [compact Hypertext Markup language] for web-enabled mobile devices and WML [Wireless Markup language] for WAP [Wireless Application Protocol]-enabled mobile devices.

Keywords: Transcoding, User Interface.

1. INTRODUCTION

The huge amount of information possibly much unstructured that is received by users every day for example by internet, email or newsletter make it difficult to select important and individual user information out of it. Users like to get special very personal information. Additionally users work more and more with mobile devices like PDAs, mobile phones and smart phones and wish to have their information on these embedded devices. Dealing with this problem a service called MEMPHIS[1] [1] is

---

[1] MEMPHIS [Multilingual Content for flexible format Internet Premium Service] supported by the European Commission: IST 5th Framework Programme

developed and implemented. This service system collects premium service information according to user profile depending topics, transforms these information in various ways like extraction, summarization and translation and transcodes these information to special target output formats. Information will be provided in form of push or pull services. For the pull service on distributed mobile devices the transcoding tool performs the automatic generation of different target formats. In fact, as an example a XML-based description will be transcoded into cHTML and WML format descriptions.

The increasing use and the growing variety of different mobile devices induce the introduction of special purpose content presentation languages, like WAP [Wireless Application Protocol] / WML [2] and W3C [World Wide Web Consortium] / cHTML [3] as well as techniques for automatic conversion of traditional HTML [Hypertext Markup language] format to these formats by using XSLT [Extensible Stylesheet Language Transformation] methods [4]. Further developments are transcoding tools for automatic conversion of arbitrary different formats [5], which are based on generic rules in the description language RDL/TT [Rule description language for tree transformation] that operates on the DOM [Document Object Model] tree representations of HTML or XML-based documents [6]. Additional work is spent for comparing different methods [7]. A classification of transcoding functions with respect to user and hardware profiles can be realized by a Fuzzy-RDL/TT [8].

This contribution is organized as follows: Section 1 describes briefly the architecture of the internet premium service. The transcoding mechanism is discussed in section 2. The portals on the different mobile devices are described in section 3. The next section 4 gives examples of the internet premium service. The final section 5 comprises a summary and an outlook.

2.   INTERNET PREMIUM SERVICE ARCHITECTURE

The internet premium service collects premium service information according to user profile depending topics, transforms these information and distributes individual information to users. The rough architecture of the Internet Premium Service (Figure 1) contains three main parts, namely acquisition, transformation and distribution. Participating to premium service information needs a registration of user data to the system. The user can select different service profiles and he has choices of a variety of device profile definitions. The premium service information

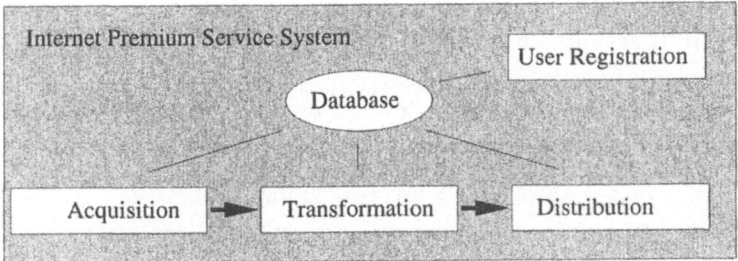

Figure 1. Internet Premium Service Architecture

and the user information will be managed by a user and information document database.

The acquisition part works with mobile agents that collect high premium information according to user profile depending topics from special databases or news providers like nationwide newspapers.

The transformation part (Figure 2) transforms the information in var-

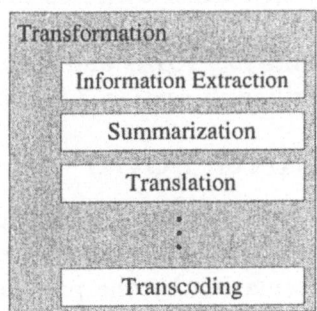

Figure 2. Components of Transformation

ious ways like information extraction, summarization of information, combining of several information that belongs together, translation in different human languages and transcoding to special target output formats depending on users device profiles. In our approach of internet premium service the human languages English, German and Italian are supported. Output formats that are supported in our demonstrator are WML and cHTML, i.e. we focus on limited mobile embedded devices. In section 2 the transcoding mechanism that produces the different output formats on mobile devices is described in detail.

The distribution part delivers the formatted service information to the users. The user has the option to get information by a push service and also by a pull service (Figure 3). Concerning the push service the user

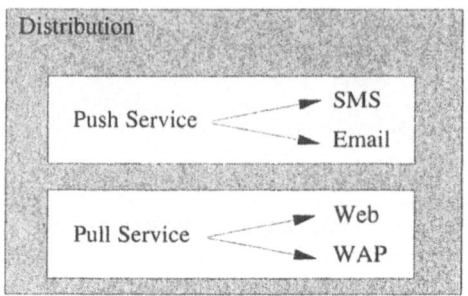

Figure 3.   Distribution

gets his information by SMS on his mobile phone or by email. The pull service uses the formats that are produced by the transcoding tool. The output information that are produced in special content presentation language formats can be pulled either by a web-browser or WAP-browser so that the user can browse in his personal information for example on PC or on small mobile clients like PDAs and mobile phones. The Portal for the pull service is described in section 3 in detail.

3.   TRANSCODING TOOL

The Transcoding Tool component of the transformation layer formats the output information for different small limited devices. The users can get the formatted information by the pull functionality of the service (see section 3). Because of a great variety of mobile devices a generic transcoding tool is used. This tool generates automatically output formats depending on the output device parameters. The transcoding tool is a rule based system to transform automatically between different markup languages like HTML, XML, cHTML or WML by passing the DOM tree presentation of XML-based user interface descriptions with the deapth-first-search method and modifying for example tags, attributes or content. Therefore the transcoding system needs some parameters like device profiles, rule description files and tool settings (see Figure 4).

In our use case of internet premium service, special structured XML-files are transcoded to cHTML-files and also to WML-files by passing the DOM-tree of the XML-file and modifying the tree according to the

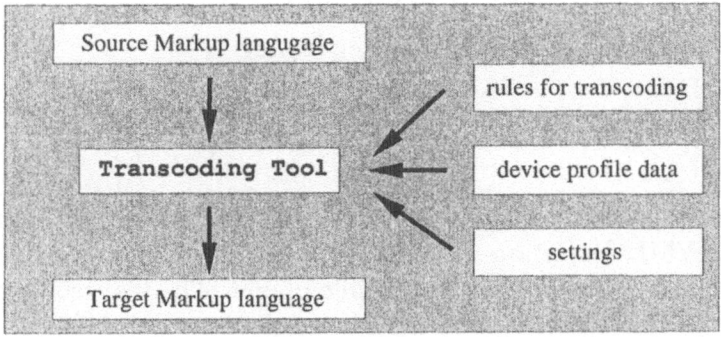

Figure 4.   Conceptual overview of the transcoding tool

rules in rule-description-language-file. The following example shows an XML-based description for books.

```
<BOOK doc-lang="en">
  <TITLE>The Official Price Guide to The Beatles Records
  and Memorabilia</TITLE>
  <SUBTITLE>2nd Edition</SUBTITLE>
  <AUTHOR>Perry Cox</AUTHOR>
  <ISBN>0-676-60181-2</ISBN>
  <PUBLISHER>House of Collectibles</PUBLISHER>
  <RESELLER>Random House</RESELLER>
  <YEAR>1999</YEAR>
  <SUMMARY_ANALYSIS>
    <tu id="7" weight="12.5" rank="1">The Official Price
    Guide to The Beatles:  Records and Memorabilia has
    everything to please, please you--including CD and
    record listings (artist compilations, singles, EPs,
    and LPs from Meet The Beatles!  to Abbey Road)
    </tu>
    <tu id="8" weight="8.744023868654244" rank="3">-
    COMPLETE DISCOGRAPHIES for The Beatles, Apple label
    artists--plus the individual albums of John, Paul,
    George, and Ringo.
    </tu>
    <tu id="10" weight="11.454508341506713" rank="2">
    Valuable information on pricing and grading records
```

```
          and memorabilia, what to expect when selling your
          records to a dealer, and a handy chapter on
          authenticating Beatles autographs.
          </tu>
       </SUMMARY_ANALYSIS>
     </BOOK>
```

This example will be transformed by special rules for example to the following WML-desription. WML-files are divided in special cards and each card will be one site on the mobile phone. The transcoding will be done by rules that are implemented in a rule-description-file.

```
<wml>
<card id="first" title="MEMPHIS">
<p>-- NEW BOOK --<br>
<b>The Official Price Guide to The Beatles Records and
Memorabilia</b>
<br>2nd Edition
<br>BY Perry Cox<br>
<a href="#second">BOOK-INFORMATIONS</a><br>
<a href="#third">SUMMARY</a>
</p></card>
<card id="second" title="Book-Informations">
<p>BOOK-INFORMATIONS<br>
<b>ISBN</b>0-676-60181-2<br>
<b>PUBLISHER</b>House of Collectibles<br>
<b>RESELLER</b>Random House<br>
<b>YEAR</b>1999<br>
</p></card>
<card id="third" title="Summary">
<p>
<b>SUMMARY:</b><br>
The Official Price Guide to The Beatles: Records and
Memorabilia has everything to please, please
you--including CD and record listings (artist
compilations, singles, EPs, and LPs from Meet The
Beatles!  to Abbey Road)  
Valuable information on pricing and grading records and
memorabilia, what to expect when selling your records
to a dealer, and a handy chapter on authenticating
```

```
Beatles autographs. 
- COMPLETE DISCOGRAPHIES for The Beatles, Apple label
artists--plus the individual albums of John, Paul, George,
and Ringo. 
</p></card>
</wml>
```

The produced WML or cHTML formats will be used for the representation of information for the individual users. The representation will be described in the next section.

4. PORTALS ON LIMITED DEVICES

In this section we describe the pull service of the distribution part by explaining the portals on small mobile devices like mobile phones and PDAs. The users can login to the service and can browse in his personal information. PDAs have own browsers, often http-browser for example a special Internet Explorer on Pocket PCs. Mobile phones use WAP-browsers.

4.1 Pull Service on PDAs

The internet premium service offers a pull service on PDAs by the Web. This functionality offers the possibility to get service information by a Web-browser on the PDAs.

Users often work with PDAs when they are on the way and when they have no online connection to their office or private PC. In order to support this use case, PDAs use conduit-browsers. That means users synchronize their PDA and PC at some points of time and afterwards they use their PDA offline. In our case of internet premium service system it is possible to configure the conduit-browser in such a way that the user can synchronize the PDA and PC and afterwards he can read his personal service information offline.

Usual online browsing on the PDA just like browsing on a PC will also be supported.

By calling the Internet Premium Service portal page on the PDA, a start page for the input of login and password will be presented. Additionally a function for password forgotten is implemented. The user can ask for his password and gets an email with his password. Otherwise the user can enter the portal and gets the home page of the system by username and password.

Once the user has logged in the system he gets some web pages, in which he can navigate. In these web sites the functionalities L (logout),

H (home), A (archive), S (Search) and U (user data) are implemented. We work on small display clients, so that we use only one letter to describe a function. Additional there is a button, where the user can choose the language for representation of the websites and of service information content. The language which the user has selected during the registration to the internet premium service is used optionally. The available languages will be English and German. The default language will be English.

In detail, the functions on the web sites work in the following way. After clicking L for logout the user will leave the pull service portal.

If the user goes to home by clicking H, he get a site containing a list of service information items which have been selected by the system according to the users service profiles since the last users login. Each list item contains an icon that hints to the topic of information and a links to a new page with a more detailed description of the information.

New information will not be deleted at once, they will at first be written to an archive. These information will appear in the archive functionality during the next login of the user. This functionality by clicking to the letter A will present all the items of the information list, which have been read once by the user and which are not older than 30 days. The archive function will be designed in a similar way as the list on the main page. That means there are also icons that hint to the topics and links to the information description.

The function U for user data allows the user to get to the internet premium service registration portal and allows to modify his user data and his service and device profile data. This functionality is only available in the online mode and not for the offline application, because there is no back writing during the next synchronization.

An additional function in the Portal is S for searching. By this function the user can search for a special term in the database of the internet premium service system.

The user can configure a notification email alerting service for his pull service in the registration portal, which will remind him that there are new information arrived. The default value for this alerting service is every 7 days, but the user can change this value or he can stop this service by the registration portal.

4.2   Pull Service on Mobile Phones

The second part of the pull service is a WAP-service on mobile phones. The portal for this service is designed in a similar way as for the Web-service on PDAs, unless one has to design several cards instead of sites.

When the user browses in his information per WAP he is always connected online to the Internet Premium Service System, so that all the functionalities in the portal could work.

The user can configure a notification by sms, which will send him an SMS to remind him that new information are arrived. The notification sms connects automatically to the right site in the WAP-Portal and the user can read immediately his personal information.

5.   EXAMPLE

As an example we implemented an internet premium service for new book publications and financial news on small clients like PDAs and mobile phones. For each of these two cases the user can select personal individual topics.

6.   CONCLUSION AND OUTLOOK

This paper presents an internet premium service for flexible format limited output devices. In particular we implement a rule based system to transcode XML-based user interface descriptions to cHTML and WML in order to present premium service information by Web and WAP on embedded devices like mobile phones, PDAs and Smartphones. It is possible to enhanced the system by speech generation and to support graphics.

However, the idea and the tool of a rule based system for automatic transcoding is universal and can be used in other applications that work also with a variety of different devices and consequently with a variety of different output formats.

ACKNOWLEDGEMENT

The work in this paper has been done in the Project MEMPHIS and was supported by the European Commission within the IST 5th Framework programme.

I would like to thank Wolfgang Müller and Robbie Schäfer for fruitful discussions concerning user interface description formats and the use of transcoding.

REFERENCES

[1] MEMPHIS [Multilingual Content for flexible format Internet Premium Service], supported by the European Commission, IST 5th Framework programme. http://www.ist-memphis.org/

[2] WAP Forum. Wireless Markup Language Specification Version 2.0, June 2001. http://www.wapforum.org/tech/documents/WAP-238-WML-20010626-p.pdf

[3] Tomihisa Kamada. Compact HTML for Small Information Appliances, W3CNote. World Wide Web Consortium, February 1998. http://www.w3.org/TR/1998/NOTE-compactHTML-19980209/

[4] Korva, Jari, Johann Plomp, Petri Määttä and Maija Metso, On-line service adaptation for mobile and fixed terminal devices, Proc. of the 2nd Int. Conf. on Mobile Data Management (MDM 2001), Hong Kong, 2001

[5] R. Schaefer, Rule Based System to Transcode XML-based UI Descriptions. http://www.c-lab.de/vhelab/rdl.html

[6] R. Schaefer, A. Dangberg, W. Müller. RDL/TT A Description Language for Profile-Dependent Transcoding of XML Documents, Proceedings of ITEA VHE Workshop, Paderborn, Germany, February 2002

[7] J. Plomp, R. Schaefer, W. Müller. Comparing Transcoding Tools for Use With a Generic User Interface Format, Extreme Markup Languages, Montreal, Canada, August 2002

[8] R. Schaefer, A. Dangberg, W. Müller. Fuzzy Rules for the Transcoding of HTML Files, Hawai'ian International Conference on System Sciences (HICSS-35), Hawaii, USA, January 2002

EVALUATING HIGH-LEVEL MODELS FOR REAL-TIME EMBEDDED SYSTEMS DESIGN

Lisane Brisolara[1], Leandro B. Becker[1, 3], Luigi Carro[1, 2], Flávio R. Wagner[1], and Carlos Eduardo Pereira[1, 2]

[1] *Computer Science Institute, Federal University of Rio Grande do Sul (UFRGS), Brazil*
[2] *Electrical Engineering Depart., Federal University of Rio Grande do Sul (UFRGS), Brazil*
[3] *Faculty of Informatics, Pontific Catholic University of Rio Grande do Sul (PUCRS), Brazil*

Abstract: This paper compares different high-level modeling approaches for real-time embedded systems design: an object-oriented approach using UML diagrams against the block diagram approach provided by Simulink. This investigates the facilities provided by both approaches for expressing system requirements and functional specification. A Crane Control System is used as a case study for conducting the proposed comparison.

Key words: High-Level Modeling, Real-Time Embedded System Design, UML, Simulink.

1.   INTRODUCTION

Traditionally, the function block (FB) modeling approach has been used by the signal processing and control engineering communities for the development of real-time embedded systems. These models are widely accepted in industrial design, driven by an extensive set of design tools, as for instance Matlab/Simulink from MathWorks. On the other hand, as a result from a standardization process among different object-oriented (OO) design methodologies, the OMG promoted the creation of the Unified Modeling Language (UML) [1], which is considered the de facto modeling notation for any OO system. UML has gained in popularity also for real-time embedded systems specification and design [2, 3]. Efforts that describe the use of UML in different phases of an embedded system design process are shown in [4]. A relevant question is whether the use of UML presents real advantages over traditional approaches for real-time embedded systems design. Therefore, an analysis is necessary in order to argue about the facilities provided by the approaches. Such analysis should reflect aspects like model readability, model validation, and model implementability.

This paper presents a study comparing the use of the UML and FB modeling approaches. In order to reach a fair comparison, a collection of criteria based on the work conducted by Ardis et al [5] is established. A case study is developed using the proposed evaluation methodology, consisting in the modeling of a Crane Control System, as proposed in [6]. The remaining of the paper is organized as follows. Section 2 gives an overview of high-level modeling applied to real-time embedded systems. In Section 3, the comparison criteria are defined. Section 4 presents the case study and shows the description of the UML and Simulink models. Section 5 discusses and summarizes the obtained results. Section 6 gives an overview of related work. In the last section, conclusions are drawn.

2.   EMBEDDED SYSTEMS DESIGN OVERVIEW

The design of an embedded system consists of several steps, as follows. The first step is the development of a high-level system model, containing both requirements and a functional specification. The requirements specification relies on defining three main elements: desired behavior or functionality; quality-of-service (QoS) requirements (performance, timing, power); and problem domain structure. Once these elements are specified, designers can proceed with the development of the formal solution, that results in the system functional specification. The high-level model should reflect the nature of the application domain. It is important to use the most appropriate Model of Computation (MoC) [7], so that the model applicability is enhanced. Up to this point, no platform information has been added to the model. The concerned aspects relate only to user needs and their detailed description, which is expressed by means of specific diagrams.

The following step consists of translating the high-level model into an executable description. This process should be automatic, but depending on the modeling notation it may need different degrees of designer interaction. Such executable description is generally obtained by means of a program code, written in the programming language that best fits the adopted modeling approach and MoC. Further steps must take the executable description as input for the architectural exploration, where alternative hardware and software solutions that fulfill system requirements should be taken into account, and for the final system generation.

The high-level modeling language should be able to express both the application requirements and the functional specification. Also, it should provide facilities to allow model validation, as well as features that can be used to guide implementation.

3. EVALUATION CRITERIA

To develop a comparison between the modeling approaches, several evaluation criteria have been established. These criteria are based on the work conducted by Ardis et al [5], which performs a qualitative comparison among several design languages for reactive systems. This work is extended here in the direction of searching for aspects that could be used to perform a quantitative evaluation of the designed models. For those criteria where a quantitative evaluation is not possible, a qualitative one is established. Moreover, additional evaluation criteria are added together with a new organization for the set of criteria. They are organized in groups that reflect the design steps introduced in the previous section as listed bellow.

a) Requirements Specification: evaluates the capacity to express and document user needs and system requirements;

b) Functional Specification: evaluates the model abstraction level and expressiveness, i.e. if it describes the problem domain and the system behavior/functionalities in a natural and straightforward manner;

c) Validation/simulation: evaluates if the specification can be validated before its implementation;

d) Implementability: evaluates if the specification can be easily refined or translated into an implementation compatible with the rest of the system;

e) Design Space Exploration Facilities: criteria evaluate whether the model incorporates facilities that can be used for design space exploration.

The comparison is based on criteria subgroups, as detailed below:

a.1) Functional requirements: capability of expressing and documenting the problem domain elements that provide interaction with the system to be designed and its desired functionalities; expressed by the number of modeling diagrams that can be used to implement the desired feature.

a.2) QoS requirements: capability of expressing the application QoS requirements and/or restrictions. This is expressed by the number of QoS requirements that can be specified.

b.1) Applicability: capability of representing system behavior or functionality by using different MoCs, according to systems nature; This criteria is expressed by the number of supported MoCs.

b.2) Modularity/Hierarchy: capability of dividing a large specification into independent modules, which could be decomposed into smaller parts;

b.3) Expressiveness: capability of the modeling language primitives to describe the specification; This is expressed by three main aspects: (1) Number of modeling primitives, (2) Number of different modeling primitives in use, (3) Number of lines of code programmed by the designer;

c.1) Simulation (qualitative): capability of verifying if the specification can be used to validate the implementation.

c.2) Verifiability (qualitative): capability of demonstrating formally that the specification or generated program fulfils the requirements.

d.1) Code generation (qualitative): capability of generating an executable application from the model.

e.1) Synthesis (qualitative): capability of synthesizing the model (into hardware) or generating a program.

e.2) System tuning (qualitative): capability of adjusting the generated model by correct tuning of parameters like performance and power.

4.   CASE STUDY

The crane system, proposed as a benchmark for system-level modeling [6], was developed for the comparison using UML and block diagrams.

4.1   UML Model Description

The UML model development has followed the design steps proposed by Gomaa [3]. According to this approach, the first development concerns the Use Case model to represent the system functionality that must be fulfilled and its interaction with the real-world. Each proposed Use Case has been further detailed as UML Collaboration Diagrams. After detailing all Use Cases, the Class Diagram has been derived, containing the whole static structure of the system (see Fig. 1).

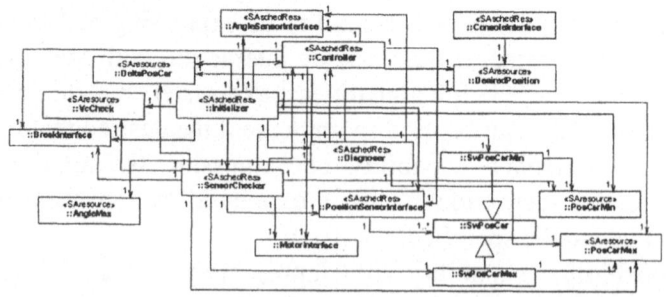

Fig. 1: UML Class Diagram of the Crane System

An important consideration regards the fact that UML models have been decorated with the stereotypes and tags suggested by RT-UML [8].

Therefore, it has been possible to state the timing information about the system. As an example, in Fig. 2 one can see the collaboration diagram for the control algorithm, which represents a periodic activity that is triggered every 10 ms, starting after the user selects a new position for the crane.

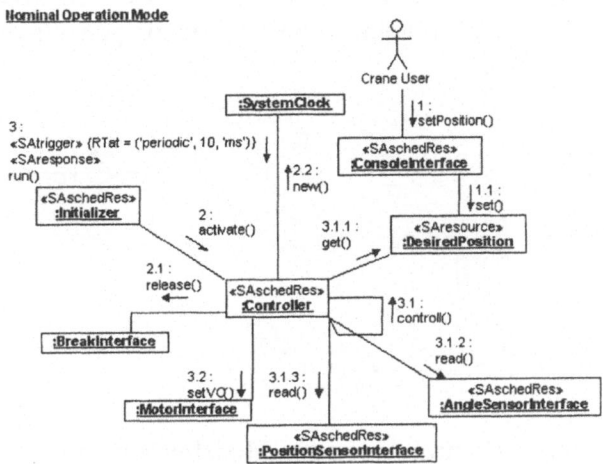

Fig. 2: UML Collaboration Diagram of the Control Algorithm

4.2   FB Model Description

The crane model developed using FBs starts with the definition of the elements that interact during the system execution. The model is composed by four modules: PlantActuators, Sensors, ControlAlgorithm, and JobControl, as presented in Fig. 3. Each module is further detailed to represent its intrinsic behavior, by creating different hierarchical levels.

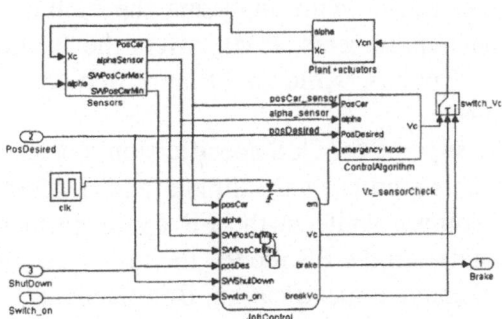

Fig. 3: Crane Model using Simulink

The crane system is composed by both data-driven and event-driven parts, as can be observed in Fig. 3. The JobControl module is represented by a finite state machine (event-based), while the other modules are data-driven.

Fig. 4 illustrates details of the ControlAlgorithm module, which is responsible for computing the control of the crane-motor. As it can be observed in the figure, this functional block contains two implicit MoCs, which are characterized as continuous-time and discrete-time. For example, it contains a discrete-space state component used for differential equations resolution (top-left), which is combined with those components that work in the time-continuous domain.

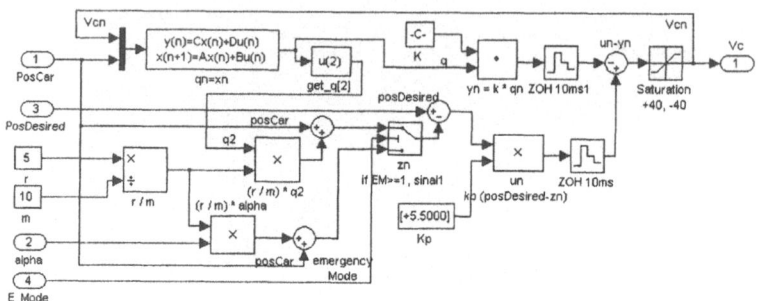

Fig. 4: Control Algorithm Model in Simulink

5.   COMPARISON OF THE MODELS

This section presents an analysis and comparison of the developed models according to the criteria discussed in Section 3. The obtained results are summarized in Table 1. For evaluating the qualitative aspects, we have used the symbol + to indicate a particular strength of the approach, - to indicate a clear weakness of the model, and * to indicate that the model meets the criterion in a way that is adequate, but less than ideal.

This evaluation begins with analyzing the facilities for expressing the system functional requirements. UML offers the facilities provided by the use case diagram (1 point), while the FB approach does not support this kind of facility (0 points).

Regarding the support for QoS specification, one can see that the profile for the RT-UML supports both timing and performance requirements specification (2 points), while in the FB approach there is no support for such issues (0 points). In the FB model, the timing requirements are implicit in the functional/behavior specification. Both languages do not give support to the specification of power consumption and cost requirements.

Analyzing the model applicability by means of the number of supported MoCs, it is possible to observe the advantages provided by the FB approach, as it supports three different MoCs (3 points): time-continuous (analog), time-discrete (digital), and event-based. Regarding UML, it supports only the event-based model (1 point). Nevertheless, there are efforts in the literature that already address the lack of dataflow in UML (see [9, 13]).

Table 1: Comparison between UML and block-diagram models

Evaluation Criteria	UML	FB
a) Requirements Specification		
a.1) Functional requirements	1	0
a.2) QoS requirements	2	0
b) Functional Specification		
b.1) Applicability	1	3
b.2) Modularity/Hierarchy	*	+
b.3.1) Number of used modeling primitives	55	42
b:3.2) Number of different modeling primitives in use	4	4
b.3.3) Number of line codes programmed by the designer	>>	<
c) Validation/Simulation		
c.1) Simulation	*	+
c.2) Verifiability	-	-
d) Implementability		
d.1) Code generation	*	0

Considering modularity/hierarchy aspects, it is possible to observe that the FB model leads to a better decomposition. This can be observed by comparing the Simulink high-level model against the UML class diagram. The first contains fewer elements, making the interpretation of the physical behavior easier. The UML class diagram maintains the whole system elements within the same abstraction level, which is somewhat not suitable, considering the desired hierarchical features. Nevertheless, one should mention that this is not a problem of the OO paradigm itself, but rather stems from the decomposition nature allowed by UML diagrams.

The next criteria relate to model expressiveness. The first two aspects relate to the number of used modeling primitives and to the number of different modeling primitives in use. This reflects an interesting observation point. As expected, the UML model is depicted by means of classes, objects, their associations, and states. Therefore, it is natural to observe an equivalent number of different modeling primitives if compared to the FB model, which includes blocks, ports, connections, and states. Nevertheless, using a design tool like Simulink, the designer can make use of different pre-defined components available in a component library. Such aspect has a direct influence in the total number of modeling primitives in use, and the comparison shows a smaller number of elements in the FB model if compared to the UML one. Another point of interest relates to the number of lines of code programmed by designer in both models. It can be observed that in the UML model the designer has to manually code much more lines. On the other hand, by using the FB model and associated library, the designer is not required to code the program by hand.

Regarding model validation/simulation, it is possible to observe that in order to provide such features, suitable modeling/design tools are required. Regarding the crane case study, only the FB model could be simulated, thanks to the Simulink tool. The available version of the Real-time Studio tool, used for the construction of the UML model, does not support model simulation. Nevertheless, considering the authors' experience with other UML-like simulation tools, these provide support only for the event-based MoC. Also, one can state that for this task the FB model is more adequate, because the simulation environment supports all the three intrinsic MoCs.

Considering the model implementability, one can see that from both models an implementation can be derived. Nevertheless, there are two directly related aspects that lead to differentiations: amount of code provided by designer and number of pre-defined components. Regarding UML, most tools are able to generate code skeletons from the model static structure (classes, objects, and associations) and from the dynamic one (the state machines). Nevertheless, the need for designer intervention is higher. In the FB models, the whole code can be generated almost automatically, since it relies on the use of pre-defined libraries. Although Simulink provides facilities for simulation, the generation of the embedded software implies several modifications/optimizations of the initial code used for simulation, since it must be adapted/optimized to the target platform.

Regarding the design space exploration facilities, one can observe that both UML and FB lack features to tackle this issue. An up-to-date topic is the enhancing of their functionality to provide the desired capabilities.

6.   RELATED WORK

As of today, the authors are not aware of other similar work that directly compares the OO modeling approach from UML against the FB modeling approach provided by Simulink. Nevertheless, there are several proposals for combining both modeling paradigms. In [10], a profile for integrating FBs into UML is proposed. For this, the General Function Block Model is presented, working as a kind of adapter between classes and FBs. Another work [9] addresses the lack of a dataflow model in UML, and so presents an integration proposal for both mechanisms.

Additionally, other works concentrate on observing that UML is not suitable for representing other MoCs besides the event-based one. Therefore, other extensions are proposed. Axelsson [11] proposed an UML extension to represent continuous-time relationships, such as continuous variables, equations, time and derivatives.

The HASOC methodology [12] extends UML-RT to include annotations with mapping information. In this work, the authors propose the association of capsules with additional MoCs, such as Synchronous Dataflow and Codesign Finite State Machines. Another research group proposed an UML profile for embedded system platforms [13], which allows the modeling of platforms, quantifying QoS performance and budgeting constraints and revealing platform services. Nevertheless, the adopted modeling strategy is difficult to understand, once it is hard to see a direct correspondence between the UML model and its describing equation from the physical domain. Moreover, the model is overly verbose, since it uses several modules to describe a simple equation with two multiplications. Additionally, the model abstraction level is very low, going to the micro-operation level, and is not adequate for complex embedded system modeling.

7.   CONCLUSIONS

While several authors already proposed the unification between UML and the FB modeling approaches, this work focused on comparing both approaches. Our goal was to define the largest amount of quantitative evaluation criteria as possible, thus allowing a more consistent comparison.

Considering the obtained results, it seems that UML looks better for requirements specification. Nevertheless, none of the models properly deals with the specification of embedded systems requirements, since power, for example, is not included. An advantage of UML is that it can be extended to incorporate such feature. Comparing the developed functional specifications, a similar score is observed in Table 1 for both approaches. This leads to the conclusion that models are somehow equivalent, although each has pros and cons in this aspect. An observed weak aspect from UML is the lack of a suitable decomposition mechanism, which could be easily overcome by the modeling tools by adopting a hierarchical aggregation as in the SIMOO-RT framework [14]. Also, this aspect should be tackled in UML 2.0.

Moving to the facilities for validation/simulation, the FB model is advantageous especially because of the used modeling tool, coupled with its intrinsic simulation engine. Regarding the model implementability, one can see that from both approaches an implementation can be derived, although each approach has its own peculiarities. Considering the last comparison dimension, namely design space exploration facilities, one can observe that both UML and FB lack features to tackle such issue. Nevertheless, there are already proposed approaches focusing on providing the desired capabilities.

As a final remark, it must be observed that both models show clear advantages and disadvantages. One interesting research target is to combine both approaches with the care to keep the application of each one within the most adequate design phase and abstraction level, according to their original capabilities. This contrasts with other existing proposals, which extend the current models to allow their use at design levels for which the language abstraction does not provide real advantages. Future investigations should focus on enhancing the existing proposals for extending UML to support a higher degree of integration with the FB paradigm and to allow the design of models using different MoCs in a natural manner.

ACKNOWLEDGMENTS

This work has been supported by CNPq and CAPES grants for some of the authors. Thanks are also due to Artisan Sw for allowing the use of the Real-Time Studio modeling tool.

REFERENCES

1. G. Booch, I. Jacobson, and J. Rumbaugh. The Unified Modeling Language User Guide. Addison-Wesley, 1999.
2. B. Douglass. Real-Time UML: Developing Efficient Objects for Embedded Systems. Addison-Wesley, 1998.
3. H. Gomaa. Designing Concurrent, Distributed, and Real-Time Applications with UML. Addison-Wesley, 2000.
4. L. Lavagno, G. Martin, and B. Selic. UML for Real: Design of Embedded Real-Time Systems. Kluwer Academic Publishers, 2003.
5. M. Ardis et al. A Framework for Evaluating Specification Methods for Reactive Systems: Experience Report. IEEE Trans. on Sw Eng. v.22, n.6, 1996. pp. 378-389.
6. E. Moser and W. Nebel. Case Study: System Model of Crane and Embedded Control. In: Proc. of DATE'1999, Munich, Germany, March 1999.
7. S. Edwards, L. Lavagno, E. A. Lee, and A. Sangiovanni-Vincentelli, Design of Embedded Systems: Formal Models, Validation, and Synthesis. Proc. of IEEE, Mar. 1997, pp. 366-390.
8. Object Management Group (OMG). UML Profile for Schedulability, Performance, and Time, 2002. OMG document n. ptc/02-03-02.
9. L. Bichler, A. Radermacher, and A. Schürr. Integrating Data Flow Equations with UML/Realtime. Real-Time Systems, n. 26, 2004, pp. 107-125.
10. Th. Heverhagen, R. Tracht, and R. Hirschfeld. A Profile for Integrating Function Blocks into the Unified Modeling Language. In Proc. of Works. on Specification and Validation of UML models for RT and Embedded Systems, San Francisco, USA, Oct. 2003.
11. J. Axelsson. Real-World Modeling in UML. In Proc. 13th International Conference on Software and Systems Engineering and their Applications, Paris, December 2000.
12. P. N. Green and M. D Edwards. The Modeling of Embedded Systems Using HASoC. In Proc. of DATE'2002, Paris, France, Mar. 2002.
13. R. Chen, M. Sgroi, G. Martin, L. Lavagno, A. Sangiovanni-Vicentelli, and J. Rabaey. Embedded System Design Using UML and Platforms. In Proc. of FDL'2000 – Forum on Specification and Design Languages, Sep., 2002.
14. L. B. Becker and C. Pereira. SIMOO-RT - An Object-oriented Framework for the Development of Real-time Industrial Automation Systems. IEEE Transactions on Robots and Automation, v.18, no.4, 2002, pp. 421-430.

A DATAFLOW LANGUAGE (AVON) AS AN ARCHITECTURE DESCRIPTION LANGUAGE (ADL)

Ashoke Deb

Department of Computer Science, Memorial University, Canada

ashoke@cs.mun.ca

Abstract: Avon is a dataflow graph language which insists single-assignment side-effect free paradigm. While it is an asynchronous system, the synchronicity is achieved by explicit events, thus allowing a sub-system to have local sychronization, while being globally asynchronous. A powerful facility in Avon is line filters where a predicate can be associated with input as well as output ports. These filters can screen values from the streams either at the source or at the sink.

We demonstrate that a small subset of Avon allows us to describe a computer architecture of substantial complexity in a natural and intuitive setting.

Keywords: dataflow, single-assignment, stream, filter, strictness, asynchronous, nondeterminism, pipelining, speculative execution, flushing.

1.   DATAFLOW LANGUAGES [1, 2]

Tools shape our thoughts. The concept of dataflow is fundamentally different from that of control flow [3]. The discipline of thinking in terms of values about a solution of a problem may be a new experiences for a newcomer to this area.

As in other areas of computer science, designers of dataflow languages have different viewpoints – in terms of syntax, semantics and pragmatics of the language. These differences mostly originate from the philosophies or other considerations. For example, LUCID [4, 5] was originally designed as a declarative language which makes proving programs easy; Id [6] was designed to run on a fine-grain dataflow machine, called Tagged-token machine; Sisal [7] was designed as an applicative language to run on different multiprocessors systems; and Avon [8] was designed as a minimalist dataflow graph language.

1.1   Introduction to Avon [8]

Avon is a dataflow language with a small number of powerful constructs. Dataflow programs written using Avon are actually dataflow graphs [9]. We will introduce some of its main language constructs via simple examples.

In Avon, a line (or, a variable) associates with a stream of arbitrary length. Each output is singularly defined, and hence no side-effect is allowed.

Filters in Avon:

In Avon, a filter is a predicate which can be associated with a line – either an input line or an output line. The purpose of a filter is to 'remove' the current value from the line if the associated filter is not satisfied for the current values. A filter on an input line is a conditional expression which can involve the names of input lines, but not the names of output lines. A filter can also be attached to an output line, in which case the output line filter can involve the input line names and also the output line names. Absence of a filter with a line is the same as having a filter *TRUE*, which will allow values unfiltered.

Example 1: *To find the largest numbers so far from a stream of integers.*

An Avon program graph which computes the sequence of largest numbers found so far is shown at the top of Figure 1(a). An example of execution of the program is shown in four stages. The initial value in the line L is 0; and, say, the values appearing in line A are 5, 4, 3, 9, 7, 2 ... and so on. There is a *filter*, $(A > L)$, attached to the line A. The purpose of this filter is to 'remove' the values in line A which do not 'pass through the filter' ie. do not satisfy the condition. In other words, if the 'current' value in A is less than or equal to the current value in L, then that value is removed from the line A, and the subsequent values in A will 'move forward'. For instance, the value 4 in line A gets removed, because $4 \not> 5$.

In *textual form* the Avon dataflow graph in Figure 1(a) will be written as:

```
LARGEST-SO-FAR:
        {IN A,L; OUT C; INIT L [0];
        INCOND A (A > L);
        A → C ;
        L ← C;}
```

Elements of Avon:

In Avon, **semicolon** (;) is used to imply relaxed ordering or *unordering*. This means that any two syntactic entities separated by a semicolon

(;) can be permuted without any effect on the program correctness. The *input* and *output* lines have distinct names. For example, A and L are used for two input lines; and C is the output line. **IN,OUT,INIT** and **INCOND** are keywords. Input line names are given after the keyword **IN**. Output line names appear after **OUT**. An input line may have an *initial stream* of values, and these values are given between **square brackets** ([and]) following the keyword **INIT**. An *input predicate, or filter*, for an input line, appears after the keyword **INCOND**. Absence of a predicate (or, empty predicate) implies constant $TRUE$.

The *body* of the node contains one or more definitions, defining output(s) in terms of input(s). The symbol for definition is **right arrow** ($\rightarrow$). An output name cannot have more than one definition.

A program may have a set of *line connectors* as well – where, a line connector connects an output line to an input line. The symbol used for connection is **left arrow** ($\leftarrow$).

Types as filters and polymorphism:

In *Example 1(a)*, the input line A may carry any type of values, which is of course not what is specified. In Avon, types are treated as filters. There is a generalised predicative function **IS**, which can be used *to define type of a line as a filter*. In Figure 1(b) , the input line A has an additional filter *IS(A, INTEGER)* – the keyword **INTEGER** represents the set of all the integer values. This filter will accept only the integer values appearing on the line A.

One advantage of using types as line filters in dataflow is that we can associate types of a fairly complex nature, including *negative type*, to a name. For example, a filter *IS (A, COMPLEX OR REAL AND NOT INTEGER)* will allow all the reals and complex, but not the integers.

Using types as filters in this manner gives us a means of allowing values of different types to appear for an input or output line name (called *restricted polymorphism*). Of course, not having any type filter allows all types of values –ie. *unrestricted polymorphism*.

In *Example 1* the output from the line C will be a stream of values. One may wish to see only the ultimate largest number, but not largest numbers so far. In Figure 1(b), we do just that. **EOD** stands for end-of-data value. The output filter (A = EOD) will then absorb all the results appearing on the line G until the input line gets to the end-of-data value.

A note on the difference between Input Filters and Output Filters:

Although, at first glance, it may seem that with the availability of input filters the output filters are redundant; but they are not. The presence of a filter on an input line removes values from that line only if the associated filter is not satisfied, and before the node fires, thus keeping the values on the other input lines. Whereas, an output filter is

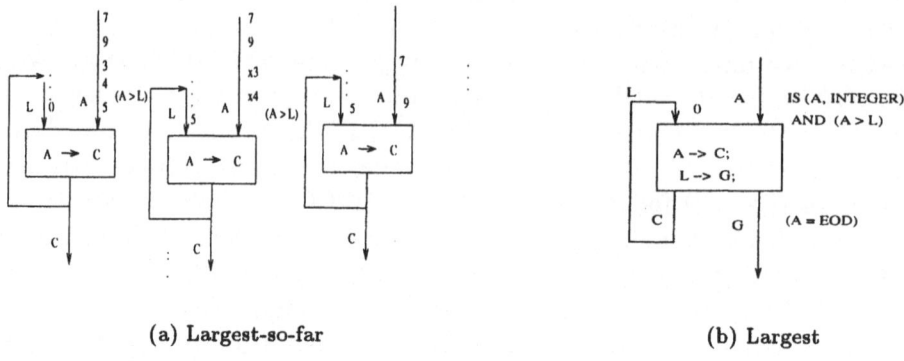

(a) Largest-so-far	(b) Largest

Figure 1. An example of Avon Program

"active" only after the node fires by which time the current values from all the input lines have been "consumed" (and essentially are removed from the input lines).

2. DESCRIBING MACHINE ARCHITECTURE

2.1 von Neumann machine and IPC

Since the introduction of APL (Iverson, 1962), there were about 200 different languages proposed, although only some of them are best known. For example, ISP (Bell and Newell, 1970), ISPL (Barbacci, 1976), ISPS (1977, Barbacci), SA* (Dasgupta, 1981), AADL (Damn, 1984), MIMOLA (Marwedei, 1984), VHDL (DOD, Intermetrics, IBM, TI, 1985) [10].

Most of these languages, with the exception of APL which is a functional and side-effect free language, are very much control flow oriented and imperative in their behaviour. Some of them succeed in classifying computers in terms of their processors, memory and switches. But most are specification languages to be used to automatically convert the specification into hardware, or to study performance. Some attempt to express the "dataflow" nature of a computer using control flow paradigm; some would express "parallelism" using cumbersome syntax, or introduce the concept of "stream" as an artifact. There are other systems proposed which deviate from traditional control flow style. For example, Johnson [11] suggested using recursive equations to describe digital design; Cardelli [12] suggested an algebraic approach to hardware description; and more recently Arvind and Shen [13] suggested using term rewriting system for description of processors.

Dataflow concepts have been applied in some languages, such as Kahn Network of Processes (KNP) [14], Synchronous Data Flow (SDF) [15] and SIGNAL [16]. These languages are useful in modelling signal processors. SDF do not allow asynchronicity, although KNP does. Also, unlike KNP, SDF insists on finite size streams. But, they do not restrict themselves to "pure" dataflow paradigm – eg. side-effects are allowed, and single-assignment is not necessary. SIGNAL differs from KNP in the sense that it allows "no value" ($\perp$) in the trace so that handling process deadlock (or, non-firing) can be accommodated in an unified manner. In SIGNAL, an elementary process produces an output value (at time t) by acting on all input values (at time t).

Avon, on the other hand, insists on single-assignment, absence of side-effect; it is asynchronous, and its streams are of arbitrary lengths. It does not insist on the output port to be empty in order for a node to fire. It allows independent "filters' on any of the input or output ports, which provides a powerful tool for modelling – eg, streams can be screened both by the destination (receiver) node as well as the source (sender) node. Synchronicity is achieved by explicit events, and thus different subsystems can synchronize locally, still maintaining global asynchronicity.

In this paper, we exploit only a subset of facilities available in Avon, and demonstrate that dataflow graph language provides a natural and transparent way of describing machines.

Traditionally, a von Neumann machine, executing one instruction per cycle, is described by a control-flow algorithm, known as Instruction Processing Cycle (IPC). For example, consider a machine with three instructions – *ADD, LW* and *BRZ*. Instructions are single address, with Accumulator (ACC) as the implied operand.

```
Repeat
        (* Sequential address generator stage *)
                PC = PC + 1;
        (* New Instruction generator stage *)
                IR = M[PC]
        (* Ins   truction Preparation and Issuing stage *)
                OP = DC (IR)
                OPR = IA (IR)
        (* Execution Stage *)
                Case OP of
                        ADD: ACC = ACC + M[OPR]
                        LW: ACC = M[OPR]
                        BRZ: If (ACC = 0) Then PC = OPR
                Endcase
Forever.
```

In the example above, PC stands for the traditional program counter, M stands for Memory where both instructions as well as data reside, and for the time being can be viewed as an one-dimensional array; IR stands for the instruction register; DC and IA stand, respectively, for a functional unit which extracts the opcode (OP) and operand (OPR) from IR;

The IPC given above can be hierarchically expanded to introduce, for example, multilevel memory, complex instruction formats, addressing schemes and larger instruction repertoir.

It can also be used for simulation purposes, and datapath and control section designs.

But, the control-flow oriented description of IPC, and the related imperative semantics, make it very difficult to augment the IPC in a natural way to describe advanced concepts of overlapped instruction execution (instruction pipelining), data pipelining, multifunctional machines with multiple instruction issuing, pipeline bubbles, branch hazards and "flushing" pipeline stages, conditional issuing of instructions etc.

2.2   Using Avon as Architecture Description Language

In this paper, we demonstrate, as an example, how Avon can be used to describe a pipelined machine with speculative execution. We will start with a machine which is *not pipelined*, has only ADD and LW type instructions, and does not have branch instructions. Then we will show that this description can easily be augmented to turn that machine into a pipelined machine. Following that we will include a branch type instruction, BRZ, to the pipelined machine, and show how branch hazards are represented.

Non-pipelined Sequential machine, with no branch type instructions.   Figure 2(a) describes a strictly sequential von Neumann machine.

Note that this description is very similar to the imperative style IPC given earlier, although with several significant differences.

Avon, being single assignment language, cannot have more than one function assigning values to the same output line, nor can it have the same line name both as input as well as output. Therefore, the imperative construct like PC = PC + 1 will be illegal. Similarly, both of ACC = M[OPR] + ACC and ACC = M[OPR] are not allowed.

Two lines are shown joined, explicitly, by a non-deterministic OR, or, sometimes implicitly, by simple fan-in.

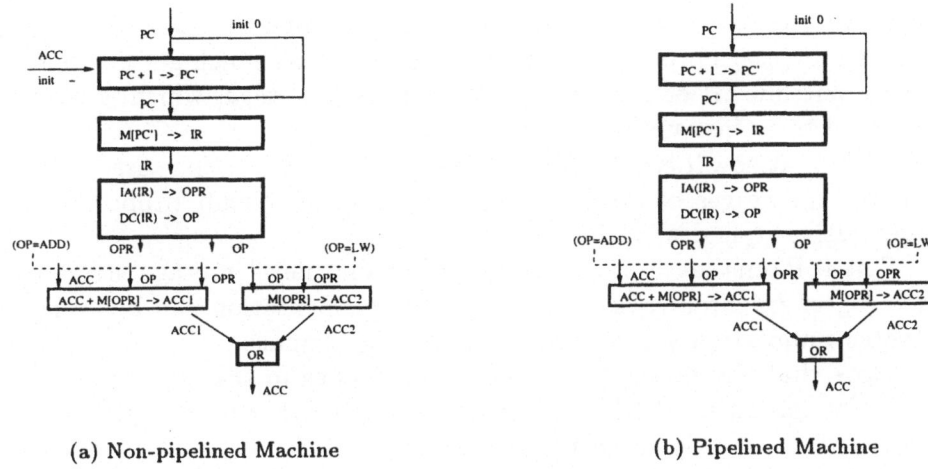

(a) Non-pipelined Machine   (b) Pipelined Machine

Figure 2. Non-pipelined and Pipelined Machine - no branch instructions

To further save us from redundant drawings, when two lines are labeled with the same name, it means that they represent the same physical line.

The input condition attached to all the input lines, OP, OPR and ACC of the node which computes ADD, is (OP = ADD), meaning that if the current value of OP is ADD, then this node will "fire" and thus will produce a value via ACC1; if the condition is false, then the current values from these lines of this node will be "absorbed" or discarded. Similarly, for the node which computes LW.

In order to "sync" the address generation station so that it generates a new value only when the previous instruction is complete, we have an "extra" input line ACC to the node PC + 1 → PC', which although has no effect on the value generated, has the effect on the node's firing intervals. Note that the "sync" line did not have to be fed from ACC, it was just convenient in this example.– it simply mimics the behaviour of "repeat forever" construction of the imperative style IPC shown earlier.

Pipelined machine with no branch type instructions. A simple modification of the first diagram (describing a sequential machine) gives the description of a pipelined machine – we had to remove the "sync" input line ACC from the address generation stage!! (See Figure 2b).

With this modification, the address generation stage produces a stream of addresses which get buffered in the input line to next stage

- the instruction generation stage. So, the input line PC' refers to the address cache. Using these addresses from the line PC', the instruction generation stage produces a stream of instructions which get buffered in the input line IR of the instruction preparation stage, which is usually referred to as instruction cache. And so on.

Note that now it is not difficult to see how the instructions are "moving along" the stages of the pipeline, which was a difficult proposition in imperative style description.

These interstage buffers can be either multilevel storage structures (to reflect its infiniteness), or its finite implementation can be done by proper annotation and demand/acknowledge signals.

Note that the presence of two distinct nodes in the execution stage (one for computing ADD instructions and the other for computing LW instructions) clearly reveals the possibilities of issuing multiple instructions to a multifunctional machine, Of course, in that case the data dependencies among instructions will have to be taken into consideration.

If we are to restrict ourselves to pipelined but single issue machines, then that can be easily described by introducing a "sync" line ACC to the instruction issue stage.

Pipelined machine with branch type instructions . In addition to the system described in the last section, let us introduce a branch type instruction BRZ (defined earlier). To keep the matter simple, we will make a fair and realistic assumption that each stage takes equal amount of time, and hence each stage may have at most one value.

In a pipelined machine, if a branch instruction is successfully executed, a number of things will have to considered – the target address will be the address of the next instruction to be executed; and as a result of which, all previously generated addresses and the instructions which are already in the pipeline have to be discarded. (Please refer to Figure 3.)

Modifying the execution stage: With the introduction of this new instruction, we modify the execution stage by introducing two nodes (see parts 1 and 2.)

The first node computes if the branch condition is true. And then, if the branch is true (indicated by a T token on the *branch* line, the following node computes OPR $\rightarrow$ PC" In fact, if the branch is evaluated to be true, a four value stream (T, F, F, F) will be generated. Reader can ignore this for the time being without loss of continuity, and it will be explained shortly.

Updating the next PC value to be the value of PC": Now, PC' and PC" are OR-ed (multiplexed) using the value of the line *branch*.

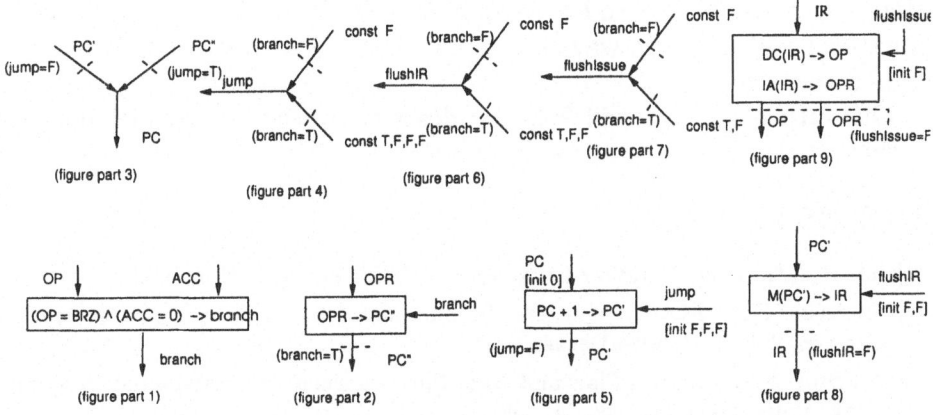

Figure 3.   Segments of the Avon description of a speculative pipelined machine with branch instruction

Initially, the value on the line *branch* would of course be F (false), and as long as the current instruction executed is a non-branch type, then a stream of F values will be on *branch* line, allowing sequential addresses to be generated. If the value of *branch* becomes T, then the value on PC" comes to PC. (See parts 3, 4 and 5.)

Flushing all intermediate stages of the pipeline:

In order to "flush" all the intermediate stages, ie "discard" all the values from the internal lines PC' (gateway to instruction generator), IR (gateway to instruction issuing stage) and the lines OP and OPR (gateway to the execution stage) we associate a new line condition (*branch = F*). Thus, if and when *branch* value becomes true, the values from PC', IR, OP and OPR will be discarded. (See parts 6 and 7.)

As a consequence though, this will create "bubbles" in the three stages, and so no further values for *branch* will be generated. To make these bubbles progress through the stages, we need extra F values following a T value on the *branch* line.

Similarly, to initially "fill" the pipe, the *init* values of *branch* are to be set accordingly for each stage of the pipeline, and are shown on the diagram.

Finally, putting together the entire description is simply a matter of connecting the appropriate lines. (Please note that the ADD and the LW units were left out from the diagram for space.)

3.   CONCLUSION

In this paper, we have attempted to show that Avon, a dataflow graph language, is not only a powerful language for general purpose computation, but it also proved to be useful in describing machine architecture in a natural and intuitive way that is not possible with control flow based imperative languages.

Our future research will focus on describing other aspects of machine architecture and constructs of communicating sequential processes.

REFERENCES

[1] W. B. Ackerman, Dataflow Languages, *IEEE Computer*, Feb, 1982.

[2] A. Deb, Data Flow Languages, In *Encyclopedia of Library and Information Science*, Vol. 66, Marcel Dekker, 2000.

[3] M. Broy, Ed., Control Flow and Data Flow - concepts of Distributed Programming, Springer-Verlag, vol. 14, 1985.

[4] E. A. Ashcroft et. al., Lucid - A formal system for writing and proving programs, *SIAM J. Comp.*, 5, pp. 519 - 526.

[5] E.A. Ashcroft and W. W. Wadge, Lucid, the Dataflow Programming Language, Academic Press, 1985.

[6] R. S. Nikhil, The Parallel Programming Language Id and its Compilation for Parallel Machines, In *Proc. of the Workshop on Massive Parallelism: Hardware, Programming and Applications*, Academic Press, 1990.

[7] J. R. McGraw, et. al., SISAL: Streams and Iteration in a Single Assignment Language, Reference Manual 1.2, M-146, Lawrence Livermore National Laboratory, Livermore, CA, March 1985.

[8] A. Deb, Avon: A Dataflow Language, In *Second International Conference on Supercomputing*, Florida, USA, pp. 9 -19, International Supercomputing Institute, 1987.

[9] A. L. Davis and R. M. Keller, Data Flow Program Graphs, *IEEE Computer*, pp. 26 - 41, Feb. 1982.

[10] Lipsch R. et al, VHDL: Hardware Description & Design, Kluwer, 1989.

[11] S. Johnson, Synthesis of Digital Design from Recursive Equations, MIT Press, 1983.

[12] L. Cardelli, An Algebraic Approach to Hardware Description and Verification, Ph.D dissertation, Univ. of Edinburgh, 1982.

[13] Arvind end Shen, Using Term Rewriting Systems to Design and Verify Processors, *IEEE Micro*, pp. 36-46, June 1999.

[14] Kahn, G. The semantics of a simple language for parallel programming, In *Information Processing 74*, pp. 471-475, North-Holland, 1974.

[15] Lee, E. A. et all, Synchronous Data Flow, In *Proc. of IEEE*, pp. 55-64, Sept 1987.

[16] Gautier, T. et al, SIGNAL: A declarative language for synchronous programming of real-time systems, In *Conference on Functional Programming Languages and Computer Architecture*, pp.257-277, LNCS, 274, Springer-Verlag, 1987.

ENGINEERING CONCURRENT AND REACTIVE SYSTEMS WITH DISTRIBUTED REAL-TIME ABSTRACT STATE MACHINES
Bridging the gap between formal and empirical approaches

Uwe Glässer and Mona Vajihollahi
School of Computing Science, Simon Fraser University, Burnaby, BC, Canada V5A 1S6
{glaesser/mvajihol@cs.sfu.ca}

Abstract: This paper revisits the distributed real-time abstract state machine (ASM) paradigm as a feasible, yet robust, approach to high-level specification and design of distributed embedded systems. The flexibility in modeling reactive system behavior, the well defined underlying concurrency framework, and the ability to gradually sharpen requirements into specifications, inspires viewing the ASM paradigm as an *agile* formalization method that directly supports fundamental practical needs in modeling such systems.

Key words: distributed embedded systems, requirements specification, agile formalization.

1. INTRODUCTION

Distributed embedded systems implicate decentralized control structures and asynchronous communication protocols. As such, they are characterized by their concurrent and reactive behavior, making it particularly difficult to predict dynamic system properties with a sufficient degree of detail and precision under all circumstances. Typical examples are embedded control systems and distributed protocol architectures used in automotive control, industrial automation, e-business applications and wireless communication. The inherent complexity and intricate nature of such systems clearly demand for reliable and predictable design approaches in order to establish the key system attributes in early design phases prior to coding. Unfortunately, it is common practice, even when dealing with complex concurrent and reactive behavior, to deeply rely on informal requirements—regardless of the lessons that should have been learned from previous experiences:

> *"There is a strong tendency on the part of people in general, and engineers in particular, to pass quickly and casually through the problem-definition phase of system design and focus almost immediately on solutions. A satisfactory solution to the right problem is often better than an excellent solution to the wrong problem."*[6]

Classical engineering disciplines, in contrast, widely use well established formalisms (such as the circuit diagrams and blueprints in electrical and mechanical engineering) for gaining the mathematical precision needed to sharpen informal requirements into reliable specifications. Inevitably, the evolution of systems design will eventually lead to a shift in the design culture towards mathematically well founded approaches. Not yet clear is *how* formalization can effectively be used as a design instrument that serves the fundamental practical needs.

The goal of this paper is to critically review the abstract state machine (ASM) paradigm [14], [4] regarding its potential for high level specification and validation of concurrent and reactive systems. Specifically, we discuss fundamental issues related to suitability, practicability and robustness of the approach. How can on gradually sharpen requirements into specifications? How to draw the boundary between formal and informal specifications, and how can they complement each other?

ASM models have been used extensively for specification and reverse engineering of hardware and software architectures (e.g. [11],[7],[12],[1]), semantic foundations of system modeling languages (including SDL [9], SystemC [16] and VHDL [5]) and programming languages (like Java [17]), and a variety of protocols (including real-time aspects [15]). A computation model that is frequently used for concurrent and reactive systems is the *distributed ASM* (DASM) model, a generalization of all other ASM models. Practical applications dealing with distributed embedded systems often use a restricted form obtained by imposing additional real-time constraints [9], [12],[1]. In this paper, we concentrate on the DASM model and its variant, the real-time DASM model.

Section 2 discusses the idea of agile formalization. Section 3 illustrates the semantics of concurrency, reactivity and time. Section 4 exemplifies the embedding of an ASM into its environment. Section 5 concludes the paper.

2.   AGILE FORMALIZATION

This section briefly illuminates some fundamental aspects of combining a formal semantics framework with informally described requirements.

Informal descriptions are useful and necessary for dealing with abstract requirements in early design phases. However, they are usually ambiguous, incomplete, and often even inconsistent. Furthermore, informal descriptions are not *executable* and thus provide very limited support for experimental validation of the correctness and completeness of requirements. To eliminate such deficiencies, one would like to gradually sharpen informal requirements into precise specifications (effectively turning "English" into mathematics) with a degree of detail and precision as needed.

Formal methods indeed seem to work best at the requirements level [2]. However, formalization may not help us to identify missing requirements, and *"difficulties caused by lack of understanding of the real world situation are not eliminated by use of FMs; instead the misunderstanding gets formalized into the specifications, and may even be harder to recognize simply because formal definitions are harder to read by the clients"* [2]. Still, formalization prior to coding results in a much better understanding of the requirements in early design phases, where it is most meaningful, and thus can indeed improve the quality of the resulting software dramatically.

Viewing the ASM paradigm in the light of *agile* software development [8], the very nature of this formalism clearly is that of a "light-weight" formal method (in the spirit of agile methods). Oriented towards practical system design needs, the ASM formalism emphasizes feasibility, flexibility and robustness instead of heavy mathematical machinery. As such, it offers a good compromise between mathematical elegance and practical relevance. This is accomplished by combining a universal abstraction for representing system states with a minimal state transition language. Since there is no a priori fixed language for defining the initial states of an ASM, one may use whatever language is appropriate (e.g., first-order logic, algebraic languages, etc.). Conceptually, this even allows for combining formal and informal notations in the form of literate specifications where this is appropriate.

The idea of 'agile formalization' materializes in the notion of *ASM ground model* as discussed in [3],[4]. Particularly interesting for dealing with concurrent and reactive behavior are the underlying abstraction mechanisms for modeling the continuous interaction between a system and the *operational environment* into which the system is embedded—especially as one usually starts from a fuzzy understanding of how actions and events in this environment actually affect the system behavior.

3.   CONCURRENCY, REACTIVITY, TIME

Abstract state machines (originally called *evolving algebras*) have been introduced by Yuri Gurevich in [14]. We assume here some familiarity with the basic ASM concepts and will recall only definitions that we explicitly address in this paper. For further details on theoretical foundations, see [13].

3.1   Concurrent Computations

A DASM A is defined over a given vocabulary V by a program Π_A and a non-empty set I_A of initial states. An initial state of A specifies a valid interpretation of V over some potentially infinite base set X. A consists of a collection of autonomously operating *agents* from some finite domain *AGENT*. Intuitively, the agents of A model the concurrent control threads in distributed computations of A. Agents interact with each other by reading and writing shared locations of global machine states. The underlying semantic model regulates such interactions so that potential conflicts are resolved according to the definition of *partially ordered runs*.

A (partially ordered) *run* ρ of a distributed ASM A is given by a triple (M, λ, σ) satisfying all of the following four conditions [14]:

1. M is a partially ordered set of moves where each move has only finitely many predecessors.
2. λ is a function on M associating agents with moves such that the moves of any single agent of A are linearly ordered.
3. σ assigns a state of A to each initial segment Y of M, where $\sigma(Y)$ is the result of performing all moves in Y; $\sigma(Y)$ is an initial state if Y is empty.
4. The *coherence condition*: If x is a maximal element in a finite initial segment X of M and $Y = X - \{x\}$ then $\lambda(x)$ is an agent in $\sigma(Y)$ and $\sigma(X)$ is obtained from $\sigma(Y)$ by firing $\lambda(x)$ at $\sigma(Y)$.

While the above definition is elegant and concise, it may not be obvious how one can imagine DASM runs in concrete applications, and, particularly, what does the coherent constraint mean?

Intuitively, a run specifies a class of possible executions of A. In general, there is more than one partial order required to specify all the possible executions of A. For a given partial order ρ, there may be more than one (even infinitely many) actual executions of the underlying DASM model that can be derived from ρ. Of particular interest among these are the *linearly* ordered runs, each of which is the result of a linear transformation applied on ρ (effectively ordering all those moves that are incomparable under ρ in an arbitrary way). In that respect, there are two interesting observations [14]:

- All *linearizations* of the same finite initial segment of ρ have the same final state.
- A property holds in every reachable state of a run ρ if and only if it holds in every reachable state of every linearization of ρ.

To further illustrate the meaning of the coherence condition in the above definition, Section 3.2 considers two simple but meaningful examples.

3.2   Sample DASM models

We illustrate here fundamental semantic aspects of partially ordered runs by means of two sample DASMs, where the first one is derived from [10].

Example 1. Suppose that we have three propositional variables (dynamic nullary relation symbols) *door, window* and *light*. Intuitively *door = true* means that "the door is open", *window = true* means that "the window is open" and *light = true* means that "the light is on". Now, consider a DASM consisting of three agents: a *door manager* (agent *d*), a *window manager* (agent *w*) and a *light manager* (agent *l*). The door manager opens the door only when the window is closed (move *x*), the window manager opens the window only when the door is closed (move *y*), and the light manager turns on the light when either the door or the window is closed (move *z*).

```
WindowManagerProgram ≡ if ¬door then window := true
DoorManagerProgram ≡ if ¬window then door := true
LightManagerProgram ≡ if ¬door or ¬window then light := true
```

Figure 1 shows all the possible DASM runs assuming that in the initial state S_0 the door and the window are closed and the light is turned off. There are six possible runs (M_1-M_6), yielding to two different final states (S_4, S_5).

$$M_1 = (\{x, z\}, \langle \rangle), \quad M_2 = (\{x, z\}, \langle x < z \rangle), \quad M_3 = (\{x, z\}, \langle z < x \rangle),$$
$$M_4 = (\{y, z\}, \langle \rangle), \quad M_5 = (\{y, z\}, \langle y < z \rangle), \quad M_6 = (\{y, z\}, \langle z < y \rangle).$$

We cannot have $x < y$ because *w* is disabled in the state S_1 obtained from S_0 by performing *x*. Similarly we cannot have $y < x$ because *d* is disabled in the state S_3 obtained from S_0 by performing *y*. Finally, we also cannot have a run where *x* and *y* are incomparable, that is neither $x < y$ nor $y < x$. This follows from the fact that all the linearization of such a run must result in the same state (thus it is impossible to go from S_0 to S_6 or S_7, or from S_2 to S_7).

Example 2. Suppose a single *producer* agent placing items, one by one, into a queue. Two *consumer* agents concurrently attempt to remove these items by popping the head of the queue. This example shows the effect of the coherence condition in the presence of a race condition (between the two consumers simultaneously trying to remove the same item of the queue).

We abstract from the details of adding items to the queue and removing items from it. In each step of the producer, it adds a single new item to the queue (move *p*). In each step of a consumer, it removes the head item if the queue is nonempty (moves *c1, c2*). The programs of the producer agent and the consumer agents can be written as follows.

```
ProducerProgram ≡ ADD_ITEM(queue, newItem)
ConsumerProgram ≡ if queue ≠ empty then item := headItem(queue)
```

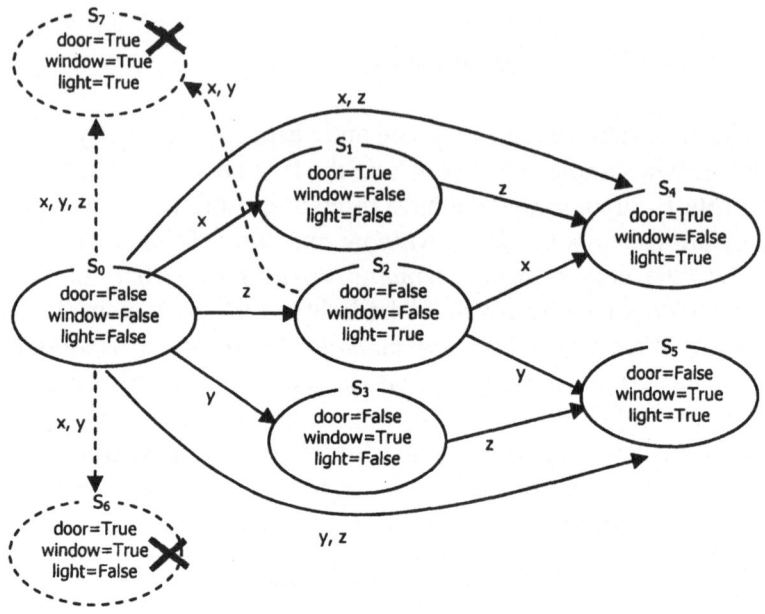

Figure 1. All possible runs of Example 1

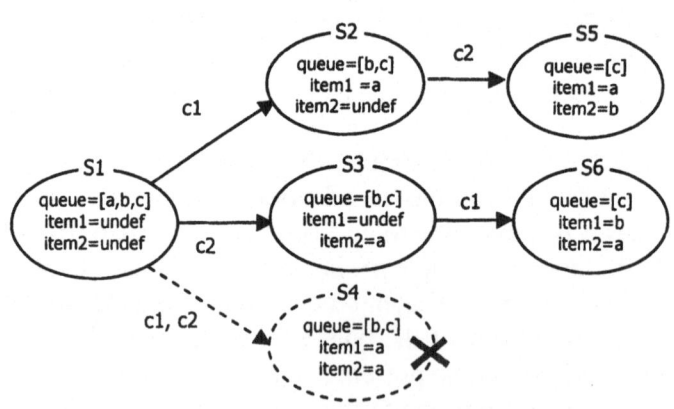

Figure 2. Some segment of possible runs of Example 2

In the initial state the queue is empty. The most important property of this DASM is that there is no run where $c1$ and $c2$ are incomparable. Note that if both consumers would make an attempt to remove the same head item at the same time (incomparable $c1$ and $c2$), this would not cause conflicting update operations on the queue; rather it would produce a logical conflict (notably, a duplication of this item). The coherence condition prohibits this behavior as any linear execution of such a run, for instance $c1 < c2$, can not produce the same result. *Figure 2* shows some segment of possible runs of this DASM and helps clarifying this argument. Clearly, it is not possible to go from states S_2 and S_3 to S_4; hence $c1$ and $c2$ are not incomparable.

3.3 Reactivity and Time

Externally controlled actions and events that may affect the system behavior in any way are encapsulated in abstract interface functions, called *monitored functions*. Such functions change their values dynamically under control of the system environment and, by definition, are read-only within the model. A typical example is a real time extension of the DASM model[1] based on a notion of *global system time* as implied by a globally accessible system clock. One can model such a clock by a nullary function *now* taking values in a linearly ordered domain *TIME*. As an integrity constraint on *now*, we assume that the values of *now* change monotonically over DASM runs.

 monitored *now: TIME*

Conceptually, monitored functions formalize abstract interfaces making the boundary between the system and its environment explicit and visible. Also, they have a crucial role in shaping abstraction levels by allowing us to move irrelevant details to the "background". In practice, however, it is often not obvious how to delineate the system from the environment and the background as this problem is tightly linked to the question of how to find the "right" level of abstraction. We try to give some answers below.

4. AN ABSTRACT CASH MACHINE CONTROL

In this section, we abstractly model an automated transaction machine, or ATM, to illustrate the role of ground models in defining the embedding of a system into a given operational environment.

4.1 Informal requirements for ATM transactions

Assume an asynchronous interaction model between three autonomously operating entities involved in ATM transactions, namely: an *ATM manager*, an *authentication manager*, and an *account manager*. For simplicity, we restrict here on withdrawal transactions. A withdrawal transaction requires

---

[1] Real time behavior actually imposes additional constraints on DASM runs, for instance, to ensure that the agents react instantaneously (see [15] for details).

the following logical steps: *(1) input the bank card and PIN code; (2) check the validity of both the bank card and PIN code; (3) input the amount to be withdrawn; (4) check the account balance against the credit line; (5) on approval update the account balance; (6) output cash or denial notification.*

Assuming an unreliable communication medium, timeout mechanisms may cause the cancellation of a transaction spontaneously at any time.

4.2   ATM abstract machine model

Basically, the ATM control forms a distributed embedded system which should be modeled in terms of a DASM consisting of three separate agents (each of which represents one of the interacting entities). Nonetheless, one may start by modeling only the ATM manager assuming the roles of both the authentication manager and the account manager to be marginal. That is, the latter two entities are considered to be part of the global environment of the ATM manager. This view allows us to focus on the key behavioral aspects first. In subsequent refinement steps, this model then can easily be extended to a DASM by making the behavior of the two other agents explicit.

Intuitively, an ATM *activation event* occurs whenever a user requests the service. The user then enters the card number, PIN code and the desired amount. Beyond reading this data from the global environment, the machine can also perform more complex interactions with the global environment to get other, non-trivial information like authentication approval/rejection and transaction approval/denial. The abstraction mechanisms allow us not only to define (and decide about) the environment, but also enable us to freely choose the level of detail and precision. Here, we abstract from all the inter-actions between the ATM and its global environment (including the user and the two other services) by assuming that they take place in the background (called the *local* environment). The ATM agent communicates with its local environment through various monitored functions. Henceforth, we refer to the local environment as environment. In this initial ATM control model, neither the behavior of the authentication manager nor that of the account manager will be formally defined; still, we have of course some idea of the operations they perform and the constraints that do apply.

The machine is idle in the initial state. ActivationEvent is a monitored Boolean-valued function. Two other monitored functions getCardData and getPinCode serve to obtain the input data as specified by the user.

| ATMIdle ≡ **if** ActivationEvent **then** |
| data := getCardData, code := getPinCode, mode := checking |

This way, a series of interactions between the ASM and the environment takes place, and in each step some required information, ranging from the requested withdrawal amount to the user authentication, is obtained from the environment and is used to perform the operation. Authenticated is another important monitored function that abstractly provides the authentication service to the ATM abstract machine. Once the information is authenticated, the ATM obtains the requested amount.

```
ATMChecking ≡ if mode = checking ∧ Authenticated(date, code) then
                amnt := getWithdrawAmount, mode := Processing
```

While in the processing mode, the abstract machine checks whether or not the requested amount gets approved by the account management service (as indicated by a monitored predicate ValidTransaction).

```
ATMProcessing ≡ if mode = processing ∧ ValidTransaction(data, amnt) then
                  ReleaseCash(amnt), UpdateBalance(data, amnt), mode := idle
```

On the other hand, if the card information is invalid or the requested amount exceeds the approved credit line, the transaction is cancelled and an error notification is generated.

```
ATMError ≡ if ¬Authenticated(date, code) ∨ ¬ValidTransaction(data, amnt) then
             OutputErrorNotification, mode := idle
```

This example also makes use of another convenient feature. ReleaseCash, UpdateBalance and OutputErrorNotification are parts of the model that are meant to perform the final operations. However, as we do not want to deal with the details of such operations at this level of abstraction, we left the definition of these rule abstract. The complete definition of these rules thereby is left to the next refinement step.

Furthermore, a transaction in progress may be canceled anytime due to an externally caused timeout event. CancellationEvent is a monitored Boolean-valued function indicating the occurrence of a timeout. Hence, the complete behavior of the ATM control is described as follows.

```
ATMProgram ≡
    if mode = idle then ATMIdle
    else if CancellatonEvent then OutputCancellationNotification, mode := idle
          else ATMChecking, ATMProcessing, ATMError
```

5.   CONCLUSIONS

Based on experience from extensive applications of the DASM paradigm to modeling distributed embedded systems and communications software, we review here its potential for agile formalization and literate specification. Specifically, we consider the problem of defining the boundary between a system and its environment in semantic modeling of concurrency, reactivity and time. This research contributes to the effective use of formal methods as practical system design tools rather than toys for academic pleasure.

REFERENCES

[1]   Ch. Beierle, E. Börger, I. Đurdanovic, U. Glässer and E. Riccobene. Refining Abstract
      Machine Specifications of the Steam Boiler Control to Well Documented Executable
      Code. In J.-R. Abrial, E. Börger and H. Langmaack, editors, *Formal Methods for
      Industrial Applications: Specifying and Programming the Steam Boiler Control*,
      volume 1165 of LNCS, State-of-the-Art Survey, 52-78, Springer-Verlag, 1996

[2]   D. Berry. Formal Methods: The Very Idea – Some thoughts about why they work when
      they work. *Science of Computer Programming* 42(1): 11-27 (2002)

[3]   E. Börger. High Level System Design and Analysis using Abstract State Machines. In
      D. Hutter et al., eds., *Current Trends in Applied Formal Methods* (FM-Trends 98).
      Springer LNCS 1641, pp. 1-43, 1999

[4]   E. Börger and R. Stärk. *Abstract State Machines: A Method for High-Level System
      Design and Analysis.* Springer, 2003

[5]   E. Börger, U. Glässer and W. Müller. Formal Definition of an Abstract VHDL'93
      Simulator by EA-Machines. In C. Delgado Kloos and Peter T. Breuer, editors, *Formal
      Semantics for VHDL*, Kluwer Academic Publishers, 1995, 107-139

[6]   N. Dorny. Systems Engineering. University of Pennsylvania, Philadelphia, PA, URL:
      www.seas.upenn.edu/~dorny/se.htm#si

[7]   R. Farahbod, U. Glässer and M. Vajihollahi. Specification and Validation of the
      Business Process Execution Language for Web Services. In *Proc. of the 11th
      International Workshop on Abstract State Machines* (ASM'2004), volume 3065 of
      LNCS, pages 69-86, Springer-Verlag, 2004

[8]   M. Fowler. The New Methodology, April 2003, online reference at URL:
      www.martinfowler.com/articles/newMethodology.html

[9]   U. Glässer, R. Gotzhein and A. Prinz. Formal Semantics of SDL-2000: Status and
      Perspectives. *Computer Networks* 42(3): 343-358, Elsevier, 2003

[10] U. Glässer, Y.Gurevich and M.Veanes. An Abstract Communication Model. Microsoft
      Research, Technical Report, MSR-TR-2002-55, May 2002

[11] U. Glässer, Y.Gurevich and M.Veanes. Abstract Communication Model for Distributed
      Systems. To appear in *IEEE Transactions on Software Engineering*.

[12] U. Glässer and M. Veanes. Universal Plug and Play Machine Models. In B.
      Kleinjohann et al. (Eds.): *Design and Analysis of Distributed Embedded Systems*, IFIP
      Conference Proceedings 219, Kluwer Academic Publishers, 2002

[13] Y. Gurevich. Sequential Abstract State Machines Capture Sequential Algorithms, *ACM
      Transactions on Computational Logic*, 1(1): 77-111, July 2000

[14] Y. Gurevich. Evolving Algebras 1993: Lipari Guide. In E. Börger, editor, *Specification
      and Validation Methods*, Oxford University Press, 1995, pages 9-36

[15] Gurevich and J. Huggins: The Railroad Crossing Problem: An Experiment with
      Instantaneous Actions and Immediate Reactions. In H. Kleine Büning, editor, *Computer
      Science Logic*, volume 1092 of LNCS, pages 266-290, Springer, 1996

[16] W. Müller, J. Ruf and W. Rosenstiel. An ASM Based SystemC Simulation Semantics.
      In W. Müller, W. Rosenstiel and J. Ruf. *SystemC – Methodologies and Applications*,
      Kluwer Academic Publishers, 2003

[17] R. Stärk, J. Schmid, and E. Börger, *Java and the Java Virtual Machine: Definition,
      Verification, Validation.* Springer-Verlag, 2001

THE IMPLICATIONS OF REAL-TIME BEHAVIOR IN NETWORKS-ON-CHIP ARCHITECTURES

Edgard de Faria Corrêa[1,2], Eduardo Wisnieski Basso[1], Gustavo Reis Wilke[1], Flávio Rech Wagner[1], Luigi Carro[1]

[1] *Instituto de Informática-Universidade Federal do Rio Grande do Sul – Porto Alegre-Brasil;*
[2] *Superintendência Informática-Universidade Federal do Rio Grande do Norte – Natal-Brasil*

Abstract: This work discusses the adaptation of NoCs to real-time requirements, in particular with respect to the fulfillment of task deadlines. It is shown that, for soft real-time systems, the number of missed deadlines can be substantially reduced by the utilization of a routing mechanism based on message priorities. A core placement strategy based on message bandwidth requirements and also on message priorities can also reduce the number of missed deadlines. The paper also discusses the impact of these strategies on the energy consumption of the system and shows that an interesting design space can be explored.

Key words: Systems-on-Chip, SoC, Networks-on-Chip, NoC, Real-Time.

1.   INTRODUCTION

Technology scaling improvements will allow SoCs with dozens of IP blocks and large amounts of embedded memory until the end of this decade[1]. IPs can be for instance CPU or DSP cores and video stream processors, allowing new applications in the fields of telecommunication, entertainment, and consumer electronics. Communication architectures providing from dozens to hundreds of Gbit/s (or Tbit/s)[2] will be required. Furthermore, these architectures must follow reusable templates, in order to amortize design costs among several designs and to meet time-to-market pressures[3].

The typical reusable communication template in current SoCs is based on the bus approach. But, this approach has strong constraints that will inhibit its use in future SoCs. First, a bus does not scale with the system size, and its bandwidth is shared by all the cores attached to it. Second, its operating frequency degrades with the increase in the number of cores, because of the growing capacitive loading in the wires. Finally, the power consumption increases with the wire length, which increases with the circuit size.

Recent works[1,2,4] have proposed the use of interconnection networks[5] as an alternative approach to interconnect cores in SoCs. The overall idea is that such NoCs will meet the major requirements for future SoCs: reusability, scalability, and parallelism, while coping with power constraints and clock distribution. Furthermore, the application requirements, such as time restrictions and performance, can be met with the correct customization of NoC features, like routing policy, speed of the router, and buffer size.

This work discusses the application of NoCs to real-time (RT) systems, in particular regarding task deadlines. Since predictability of execution and communication times is mandatory for these systems, NoCs add another level of complexity. For soft RT systems, the number of missed deadlines can be substantially reduced by a routing mechanism where messages with tighter deadlines have higher priority. A core placement strategy based on message priorities and bandwidth requirements can also reduce the number of missed deadlines. The paper also discusses the impact of these strategies on energy consumption. We show that an interesting design space exists, where a right combination of strategies may result in an adequate trade-off between soft RT requirements and energy consumption.

We discusse related work in Section 2. Section 3 presents concepts about NoCs. Requirements of RT applications and their impact on NoC design are considered in Section 4. Section 5 introduces the approach proposed in this paper. The placement methodology is detailed in Section 6. Experiments and results are shown in Section 7. Section 8 gives concluding remarks and discusses future work.

2.   RELATED WORK

High performance is obtained thanks to the available parallelism in the network, and scalability is achieved thanks to the network characteristic of regularity. Most of the works focus on the concept of using the regular NoC tile-based architecture, but they do not address the mapping problem.

Hu and Marculescu[6] present an algorithm to solve the mapping problem, by considering the communication energy consumption. This algorithm minimizes the energy consumption under specified performance constraints, but does not consider RT restrictions.

Bolotin[7] proposes a QoS NoC, where inter-module communication traffic is classified into four classes of service. Once communication requirements of the target SoC have been identified, the network is customized. First, the modules are placed so as to minimize spatial traffic density. After, unnecessary mesh links and switching nodes are removed, and bandwidth is allocated to the remaining links and switches according to their relative load, so that link utilization is balanced.

In our work, we embed the QoS aspect into the mapping problem, in order to achieve QoS while looking at smaller power consumption.

3. NETWORKS-ON-CHIP

Several NoCs are described in the literature[2,3,4,8]. A NoC is composed by a set of routers and point-to-point links interconnecting routers in a structured way. Each router has a set of ports that are used to connect routers with their neighbor's routers and with the processing cores of the system.

NoCs are based on the message passing communication model. Cores in the network communicate by sending and receiving messages with a header, a payload, and a trailer. A NoC is described by its topology and by strategies for routing, flow control, switching, arbitration, and buffering. The topology is the arrangement of nodes and channels in a graph. Routing determines how a message chooses a path in this graph, while flow control deals with the allocation of channels and buffers to a message as it traverses this path. Switching is the mechanism that removes data from an input and places it on an output channel, while arbitration is responsible for scheduling the use of channels and buffers by the messages. Buffering defines the approach used to store messages when the router arbitration circuits cannot schedule them.

3.1 THE SoCIN NoC MODEL

SoCIN[9] is a scalable network based on a parametric router architecture to be used in the synthesis of customized low-cost NoCs. It uses wormhole packet switching and a deterministic XY-routing in order to ensure deadlock freedom at a low cost. The communication model uses message passing, and cores communicate by sending and receiving requests and responses. SoCIN uses wormhole packet switching[10]. A distributed approach for arbitration is used, and there is a round-robin arbiter at each output channel of a router. Flow control is based on a handshake strategy. Buffering is performed at the input channels, and there exists a p-words FIFO buffer at each input channel, where **p** depends on the application costs and performance requirements.

4.   NOCS AND REAL-TIME REQUIREMENTS

Predictability represents the most important requirement for embedded applications with real-time restrictions. But other aspects of QoS, like performance, can be important too. Moreover, for embedded systems, application requirements (memory footprint, power) are more restrictive.

Embedded systems using NoCs may achieve reusability, scalability, and parallelism, while coping with power constraints. Furthermore, application requirements, such as timing restrictions and performance, can be met with the correct customization of NoC features. But the use of NoCs in RT systems adds complexity to the design, since the predictability of execution and communication time is mandatory. For predictability, it is necessary to know the time latency in the routers, since the communication time between two cores in the NoC must be smaller than the end-to-end deadline of the messages exchanged by them (i.e. from source to destination core).

In soft RT systems, a small number of deadlines may be missed, thus smoothly and temporarily degrading system performance. As shown in this paper, the number of missed deadlines in a NoC can be substantially reduced by the utilization of a routing mechanism based on message priorities, where higher priorities are given to messages with tighter deadlines. For hard RT systems, where deadlines cannot be missed, this mechanism must be eventually combined with a larger channel bandwidth. But it is important to notice that the required increase in bandwidth would be substantially larger in a hard RT system if there was no priority-based routing mechanism. Another important design aspect is the average time of the communications, which is directly related to the total energy consumption (of course the energy consumed in the core computations must also be considered). This average time may be reduced by a core placement strategy that maintains close to each other those cores that require a high communication bandwidth between them. Sometimes, however, these two requirements – reducing both missed deadlines and energy consumption – are conflicting, and an adequate trade-off may be found according to application requirements.

5.   THE PROPOSED APPROACH

The proposed approach considers two relevant aspects: the core placement in the NoC and the flow control of messages by the arbiters of the routers. The main idea is to improve QoS of soft RT systems by reducing the number of missed deadlines, while simultaneously trying to reduce the average transmission time of messages and thus the energy consumption.

For the placement, we compare a random strategy with two other ones where communication requirements are considered. In the first one, a straightforward approach assumes that the cost of a core in a given position is related only to the communication requirements with other cores. Cores communicating with a high rate should be placed nearby. In the second strategy, both the bandwidth and the priority (deadline-based) of the messages are considered. These strategies tend to decrease the average message transmission time, and thus the overall energy consumption.

Considering flow control, two policies are proposed besides the original round-robin arbitration mechanism of the SoCIN architecture. The first one is a priority-based arbiter, which is also based on message deadlines. The other alternative, besides priority-based flow control, uses multiple buffers at the output channels of the routers, allowing preemption of lower-priority messages by higher-priority ones. These priority-based mechanisms decrease the number of missed deadlines and thus increase QoS for soft RT systems. However, they also tend to increase the average message transmission time, since messages with lower priority may be blocked for larger time intervals.

Together, the arbitration mechanisms and the placement strategies build a design space that can be explored during the design of a NoC. For each application, with particular requirements considering task deadlines and energy consumption, an ideal combination of mechanisms may be found.

6.   PLACEMENT ALGORITHM

Given a distributed application, it is necessary to determine the best placement of the processing cores over the network in order to match the application RT constraints, while reducing the total energy consumption.

To model the placement problem, we define an Application Communication Characterization (ACC) graph as the way the task communications occur. It can be described by the relationships among the application tasks, by the parallelism among message exchanges, and by the bandwidth and priority required by each message. This behavior can be modeled as an oriented graph, where vertices represent the application tasks, that send and receive message, and arcs express the relationship among tasks. The oriented arcs thus implement the paths for the messages and express the communication pattern of the application. The arcs are weighted in two alternatives. In the first one, the weight corresponds only to the bandwidth required by the message modeled by the arc. In the second one, the weight is given by the product between message priority and bandwidth.

Definition 6.1. ACC $G=(V,A)$ is a directed graph, where each vertex $v_i \in V$ ($i=1,2,...,m$) represents an application task which sends and/or receives messages, and an arc $a_j \in A$ ($j=1,2,...,n$) is the directed path between the sender and receiver vertices of a message. For each directed arc $a_j=(u,v)$, a weight defines either the bandwidth $b(a_j)$ the application requires for the message represented by a_j, or the product bandwidth*priority. A position $p(v_i)$ is assigned to each i vertex.

The communication architectures can also be modeled as a graph, whose vertices represent the routers in the NoC and the set of oriented arcs express all the communication channels given by the topology. This data structure is defined as the Architecture Communication Graph (ACG).

Definition 6.2. ACG is a directed graph, $G'=(V',A')$, where each vertex $v_q' \in V'$ (q=1,2,...,m) represents a router in a NoC and each arc $a_r' \in A'$ (r=1,2,...,l) is a channel between two routers that are directly connected. Furthermore, each router has a single local port, where a processing core is attached to. For each directed arc $a_r'=(u',v')$, a weight expresses the available bandwidth $b'(a_r')$ of the communication channel it represents. This parameter is taken from the network physical features such as channel width and frequency. The way the arcs are connected represents the topology.

In order to find a placement, one must map each application task (vertex of ACC) to a local port associated to a router (vertex of ACG).

Definition 6.3. Given an ACC and an ACG, for each vertex $v_i \in G$ in ACC there exists a corresponding vertex $v_q' \in G'$ in ACG, and vice-versa, i.e. there is a bijective mapping function $F:V \rightarrow V'$ s.t. $\forall v_i \in V$, $\exists v_q' \in V'$ ($v_q'=F(v_i)$ $\wedge v_i=F^{-1}(v_q') \wedge p(v_i)=p(v_q')$).

Finally, for each application message, it is necessary to find in the ACG a path between its sender and receiver vertices, in order to determine if the bandwidth offered by this path matches the one required by the application.

Definition 6.4. A path $C = (v_1',a_1',v_2',a_2',...,v_{m-1}',a_{m-1}',v_m')$ in ACG is an alternating sequence of vertices and arcs from the sender to the receiver of a message. A path is formed according to the routing strategy implemented in the network routers the ACG represent.

Using the above graph representations, the problem of matching the application real-time constraints, while reducing the total energy consumption under performance constraints, can be formulated as the problem of covering the rows of a m-row, n column, zero-one matrix $M = (a_{ij})$ by a subset j; j=1,...,n; of the columns $M_j=(a_{ij})$; i =1,...,m; at minimal cost. If we define $x_j=1$, if column j (with cost $c_j>0$) is in the solution, and $x_j=0$ otherwise, then the problem can be formulated as:

$$\text{Minimize} \quad Z = \sum_{j=1}^{n} c_j x_j \quad \text{subject to} \quad \sum a_{ij} x_j = 1 \quad i = 1,...,m \tag{1}$$

$$x_j \in \{0,1\} \quad j = 1,...,n \tag{2}$$

Equation (1) ensures that each row is covered by one column, and statement (2) is the integratility constraint. We can now formulate our placement problem as a set covering problem: M is the set of vertices in the

ACG used for each application message, $G'=(V',A')$; $M \subseteq V'$. This is so because all n messages of an application cover the set M of routers in a NoC, when they are sent over a network through their paths C.

Definition 6.5. A set $M_j=(a_{ij}=1 \mid i \in M)$ is a path C_j for one of the n messages in an application: $M_j = (C_j \mid v_q' \in C_j, a_{ij}=1 \wedge i=p(v_q'))$.

In our problem, c_j expresses the bandwidth (or the product between bandwidth and priority) the message M_j can reach. The semantic we adopted for c_j in the objective function says that if $c_j=0$, its associated bandwidth is equal to or greater than the bandwidth required by the application; otherwise, if $c_j=1$, the required bandwidth was not reached by the current placement.

Definition 6.6. Let $b'(a_r')$ be the bandwidth for a given arc a_r' in a path C_j, and B the required bandwidth for the message j:

$$c_j = 0, \; if \; \underset{w=1}{\overset{m-1}{MIN}} b'(a_w') \le B \; ; \qquad c_j = 1, \text{ otherwise}$$

As a consequence, minimizing the objective function means setting its value as closer to zero as possible. When Z is zero, all bandwidths were reached. This mapping problem has been proven to be NP-complete[11], and a number of heuristic solution algorithms have been presented in the literature. We adopted for this purpose the Simulated Annealing (SA) algorithm[12].

SA is a generalization of a Monte Carlo method for examining the equations of state and frozen states of n-body systems. The concept is based on the way liquids freeze or metals recrystalize in the process of annealing. In this process, a melt, initially at high temperature (T) and disordered, is slowly cooled so that the system at any time is approximately in thermodynamic equilibrium. As cooling proceeds, the system becomes more ordered and approaches a "frozen" ground state (T=0). SA has been used in various combinatorial optimization problems and has been particularly successful in circuit design problems[13].

7. EXPERIMENTS AND RESULTS

Fig. 1 shows our experimental setting. The application cores are placed in the NoC based on the traffic density of the communication (bandwidth) and on the time priorities of the application (deadlines). Synthetic task graphs are generated using TGFF[14] and used as input to the placement tool[15]. The placed NoC is then evaluated by a NoC simulation tool (NoCSim) in the timing aspects. NoCSim simulates the exchange of messages according to a previously defined communication bandwidth between two tasks. NoCSim returns performance parameters as the maximum and average times required to send each type of message. The deadline, as well as the bandwidth, is also defined for each communication, therefore NoCSim also provides the number of messages that arrived after the deadline. NoCSim is specific to SoCIN, with the addition of multiple buffers in the routers to allow message preemption by priority, and has been developed in C++.

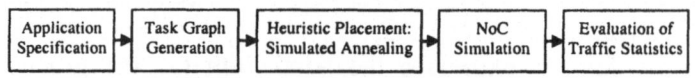

Figure 1. Experimental setting

To test impact of the placement and flow control strategies on the communication traffic, we carried out two experiments, using two sets of task graphs. The first set has tighter time restrictions than the second one, so that its deadlines are harder to respect. The design space is shown in Table 1.

Table 1. Strategies for placement and flow control

Placement:	**0** – without using SA (simulated annealing)
	I – with SA using only bandwidth as a weight
	II – with SA using bandwidth times priority as a weight
Flow control:	**R** – with round-robin arbiter
	P – with priority-based arbiter
	PP – with preemption (multiple buffers)

Results of the experiments, in terms of average message transmission time (which is directly related to overall energy consumption, measured in cycles) and percentage of missed deadlines, are shown in Table 2.

Table 2. Experimental results

		0-R	0-P	0-PP	I-R	I-P	I-PP	II-P	II-PP
	AvgTime	31.12	21.08	26.9	14.79	25.36	28.26	28.49	27.73
Experim.1	% deadline	35	23	25	33	18	15	17	17
Experim.2	% deadline	19	12	11	2	0.9	0.8	0.6	0.6

Following observations can be extracted from Table 2:

- If the bandwidth-based placement combined with round-robin is used (I-R), there is an average time reduction of 52.5% (from 31.12 down to 14.79) as compared to the original SoCIN network with arbitrary core placement (0-R). However, a reduction is not observed when a bandwidth-based placement is applied to NoCs using other arbiters.
- In the case of placement strategies applied with a priority-based arbiter (0-P, I-P, and II-P), there is a progressive reduction in the percentage of missed deadlines – from 23 to 18 and 17 in experiment 1, and from 12 to 0.6 in experiment 2. However, the average message transmission time increases (21.08, 25.36, and 28.49, respectively). The same behavior is noticed with a priority-based preemptive arbiter (0-PP, I-PP and II-PP).

As for the flow control, the use of a priority-based arbiter reduces the number of missed deadlines in comparison to the round-robin arbiter, both for random and bandwidth-based placements:

- From 0-R to 0-P there is a reduction from 35 to 23% of missed deadlines in experiment 1 and from 19 to 12% of missed deadlines in experiment 2;
- From I-R to I-P there is a reduction from 33 to 18% of missed deadlines in experiment 1 and from 2 to 0.9% of missed deadlines in experiment 2.
- However, the average transmission time increases from I-R to I-P by 71.5% (from 14.79 to 25.36).

When preemption is used in a priority-based arbiter, the number of missed deadlines decreases even more, but the average time increases again. For example, in the bandwidth-based placement the reduction (from I-P to I-PP) in the percentage of missed deadlines was aproximately 16% (18 to 15) and 11% (0.9 to 0.8) for the first and second experiments, respectively, but the average transmission time increased by 11,4% (25.36 to 28.26). By comparing II-P to II-PP, we see that a more complex arbiter with premption does not reduce the number of missed deadlines, since the priority-based placement already reduced this value to an apparent lower bound.

It can be concluded that the flow control with priority reduces the number of missed deadlines, but in general increases the energy consumption. The application of priority with preemption reduces even more the missed deadlines, but with an even higher energy consumption. In order to obtain a smaller increase in energy consumption in these cases, a new placement algorithm is required, considering the NoC dynamic behavior. The average transmission time increases because of messages that are blocked by other higher-priority ones: the placement algorithm should avoid communication bottlenecks in channels that are used frequently by high-priority messages.

It can also be observed that a prority-based placement has the same effect of reducing the percentage of missed deadlines as a priority-based arbiter, so that a more complex arbiter with premption is not useful in this case.

8.   FINAL REMARKS

In this paper we discussed two possible alternatives to adapt NoCs for RT applications, where the correct predictability of execution and communication time is required. The first was the impact of the placement of the cores in the network in the behaviour of messages with priority. The other alternative considered the way how the flow control is made by the arbiter from the routers. We discussed a priority mechanism where the router would dispatch first the message with highest priority, or still if there could be preemption, when the router would have multiple queues of priorities.

We proposed a core placement strategy based on message bandwidth requirements and also on message priorities, in order to reduce the number of missed deadlines. The paper also had discussed the impact of these strategies on the energy consumption of the system. We had shown that an interesting design space can be explored, where the right combination of strategies might result in an adequate trade-off between soft RT requirements and energy consumption.

As future work we plan to use an adaptive routing to reduce the average message transmission time and therefore the energy consumption, while sustaining RT behavior. Another approach is adapting the placement mechanism for reducing the average time of message transmission when the priority-based arbiters are used.

REFERENCES

1. L. Benini, and G. De Micheli. Networks on Chips: a New SOC Paradigm. IEEE Computer, Jan. 2002, pp. 70-78.
2. P. Guerrier and A. Greiner. A Generic Architecture for on-Chip Packet-Switched Interconnections. DATE'2000, IEEE Press, 2000. pp. 250-256.
3. S. Kumar et al. A Network on Chip Architecture and Design Methodology. IEEE Computer Society Annual Symposium on VLSI, April 2002. pp. 105-112.
4. W. J. Dally and B. Towles. Route Packets, Not Wires: On-Chip Interconnection Networks. DAC'2001, ACM Press, 2001. pp. 684-689.
5. J. Duato et al. Interconnection Networks: an Engineering Approach. IEEE CS Press, 1997.
6. J. Hu and R. Marculescu. Energy-Aware Mapping for Tile-based NoC Architectures Under Performance Constraints. VLSI-SoC'2003, IEEE Press, 2003.
7. E. Bolotin et al. QNoC: QoS architecture and design process for Network on Chip. Special issue on Networks on Chip, The Journal of Systems Architecture, Dec. 2003.
8. A. N. F. Karim et al. An Interconnect Architecture for Networking Systems on Chips. IEEE Micro, Sep.-Oct. 2002, pp.36-45.
9. C. A. ZEFERINO and A. A. SUSIN, "SoCIN: a Parametric and Scalable Network-on-Chip". In: Proceedings of the 16th Symposium on Integrated Circuits and Systems (SBCCI'2003), São Paulo, Brazil, Sept. 2003, IEEE CS Press, pp.169-174.
10. W. J. Dally and C. L. Seitz. The Torus Routing Chip. Journal of Distributed Computing, Oct. 1986. pp. 187-196.
11. M.R. Garey and D.S. Johnson, Computers and Intractability: A Guide to the Theory of NP-Completeness, W.H. Freeman and Co., San Francisco, 1979.
12. N. Metropolis et al. Equation of State Calculations by Fast Computing Machines. J. Chem. Phys., 21, 6, 1953, pp. 1087-1092.
13. S. Kirkpatrick et al. Optimization by Simulated Annealing. Science, 220, 4598, 1983, pp. 671-680.
14. R. P. Dick, D. L. Rhodes and W. Wolf. TGFF: task graphs for free. Proc. Intl. Workshop on Hardware/Software Codesign, March 1998.
15. Blue Macaw, http://www.inf.ufrgs.br/~renato/bluemacaw, Apr 2004.

ME64 – A PARALLEL HARDWARE ARCHITECTURE FOR MOTION ESTIMATION IMPLEMENTED IN FPGA

Diogo Zandonai [1,2], Sergio Bampi [1] and Marcel Bergerman [2]

[1] UFRGS – Federal University of Rio Grande do Sul, Porto Alegre, Brazil;
[2] GIT – Genius Institute of Technology, Manaus, Brazil l

Abstract: Digital video compression is a computationally intensive task, in which motion estimation accounts for a significant portion of the arithmetic operations. This paper presents ME64, a dedicated scalable hardware architecture for fast computation of motion vectors. ME64 is a highly parallel architecture, based on a matrix of 64 processing elements at its core, an I/O interface, and comparison and control units. The proposed architecture was implemented in an FPGA to treat reference and search blocks of 8x8 and 15x15 pixels, respectively. ME64 is scalable to be able to cover larger search blocks if needed. It implements the full search algorithm using the SAD criteria. ME64 was fully described in VHDL and prototyped in the Xilinx XC2S150 FPGA device, with a maximum frequency of 33 MHz. Using this FPGA device, ME64 reaches 2.1 GOps (billions of 8-bit operations per second) and 107.32 frames (640x480 pixels) per second. The results herein presented validate the ME64 against a software implementation, using an external I/O data driver.

Key words: Hardware Architecture for Motion Estimation, Motion Estimation, Video Compression.

1.   INTRODUCTION

1.1   Motivation

Digital video has a growing number of applications, such as in DVDs, digital television, videophone, and PC multimedia. All these applications require a large communication bandwidth and/or storage space. Compression makes these applications feasible by reducing the amount of data necessary to represent the video information.

Figure 1 shows a block diagram of a generic video compression system. The pre-processing block performs color conversion and sub-sampling, when necessary. Compression occurs inside the blocks: static image compression and motion estimation, which are responsible for removing spatial and temporal redundancy, respectively. Once compression is performed, the resulting data is packed in a bitstream according to some standard, MPEG-2, for example.

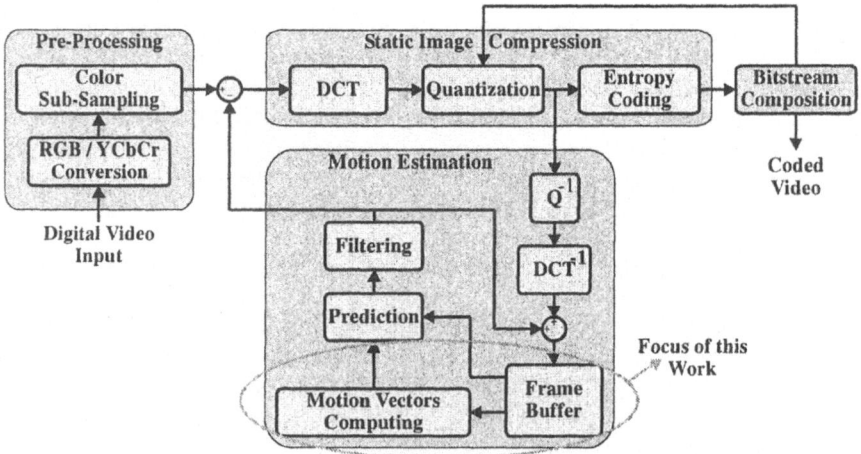

Figure 1. Generic video compression block diagram

Table 1 shows the computational effort to implement the main video compression tasks in MOp (millions of 8-bit operations) per frame. This table shows that the computational effort for motion estimation is more than three times the effort for image compression.

Table 1. Computational effort to run the main video compression tasks in MOp/frame

Video Format	Resolution (@ 30 fps)	Motion Estimation	Image Compression
CIF	352x288	6.49	2.13
VGA	640x480	19.66	6.45
SVGA	800x600	30.72	10.08
SVGA	1024x768	50.33	16.52
SXVGA	2048x1536	201.32	66.06

Since motion estimation is the most computationally intensive video compression task, its implementation in a dedicated hardware device saves hundreds of millions of operations and speeds up the task when compared to software solutions.

1.2 Motion vectors

Motion vectors are used to represent the reference frame based on the search frame, as shown in Figure 2. The reference blocks are represented by a portion of the search block that has the same size of the reference block. The motion vector points to the portion of the search block with the lowest distortion when compared to the reference block. Each possible portion is called a motion vector hypothesis.

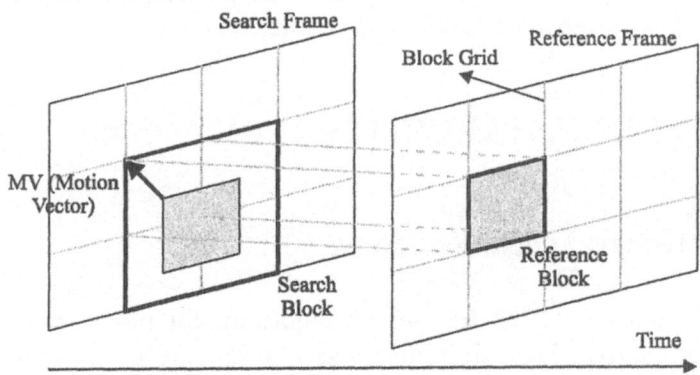

Figure 2. Motion vectors, search block and reference block

To find the best motion vector hypothesis, an algorithm that defines the search procedure and which hypotheses to consider is utilized in association with some criterion for distortion computing. In practice, the most common criterion is the SAD (sum of absolute differences) [5] [8]. Table 2 presents relevant algorithms for motion estimation and their operations requirement in MOp per frame.

Table 2. Algorithms for motion estimation and their operations requirement (MOp/frame)

Algorithm	Ref.	Operations Req.
Full Search	[1]	530
Circular Search	[8]	20
Logarithmic Search	[7]	37
Edge Matching Search	[2]	245
Hierarchical Search	[3]	20
Block Clustering	[4]	72

1.3   Previous works

Some relevant architectures for motion estimation have been developed, as in [5] [4] [6] [9]. Their common features are that they are comprised of linear or two-dimensional arrays of processing elements and all of them utilize the SAD as the distortion calculation criterion. Their main differences are the search block size, the I/O interface to input video data, the level of hardware parallelism and the clock frequency.

The remainder of article is organized as follows: Section 2 presents the proposed architecture, Section 3 presents the prototype used for validation and Section 4 presents the results and conclusions.

2.   THE ME64 ARCHITECTURE

2.1   General considerations

ME64 implements the full search algorithm for block matching-based motion estimation. This algorithm was chosen due to its regularity and precision. Full search is the most precise search algorithm, since it returns the optimal motion vector hypothesis for a given search block. The analysis is performed in a very regular way, which allows ME64 to save CPU time by speeding up memory access through an efficient I/O interface and high level of parallelism.

In ME64, the criterion for distortion computation is the SAD. This is a common criterion in motion estimation hardware implementations [4] [6] [9] because it does not involve multiplications or divisions.

ME64 was designed to treat reference and search blocks of 8x8 and 15x15 pixels, respectively; therefore, 64 hypotheses are considered. One motion vector is computed every 64 clock cycles. Motion estimation is performed based on luminance data [1].

2.2 Architectural description

Figure 3 presents the ME64 high-level block diagram. The input reference (Y) and search (S0 and S1) data are organized by the I/O interface in a way suitable for input to the Processing Matrix. The Processing Matrix computes the distortion for all motion vector hypotheses and presents one valid distortion value to the Comparison Unit at each clock cycle. The Comparison Unit analyses these hypotheses and indicates to the Control Unit through a NEW_MV signal pulse that a better hypothesis occurred. The Control Unit, upon receiving this pulse, generates the MV signal based on its own internal state.

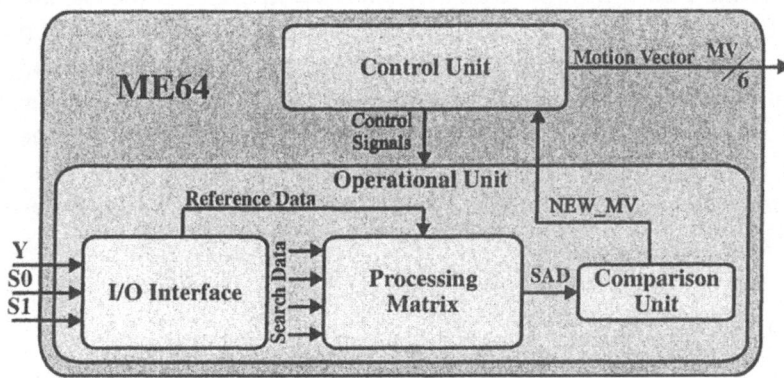

Figure 3. ME64 high-level block diagram

The Processing Matrix is composed of 64 processing elements (PE), each one responsible for the calculation of the distortion for one motion vector hypothesis. The PE architecture is presented in Figure 4. The reference data input Ri is stored in a register and presented in the output Ro, allowing for a pipeline organization of the PEs. The difference between the B and Ri signals is computed by ADR0. This difference may be inverted, depending on its signal, by a controlled inverter logic gate, implemented through XOR gates. The difference is then accumulated by ADR1 in the ACC register, which is 6 bits larger than the input signal to avoid overflow. After 64 clock cycles ACC stores the distortion in such a way that the SADij signal is valid.

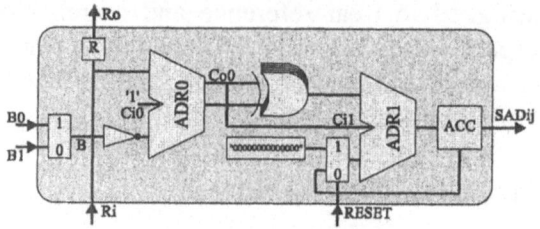

Figure 4. Processing element architecture

The Processing Matrix is presented in Figure 5. Each PE is named `PEij`, in which `i` stands for the line index and `j` stands for the column index of the element's position in the Processing Matrix. The `R` input signal feeds all PEs through a pipeline created by connecting a PE's `Ro` signal to the next PE's `Ri` signal. The four global buses feed local buses. The data from the `GB1` and `GB3` buses pass through a delay line with addressing function. Two local buses feed one line of PEs. The local buses named `LBi0` feed the `B0` input to the PEs while the local buses named `LBi1` feed the `B1` input to the PEs. Each `PEij` is responsible for the calculation of the distortion of the block whose first pixel is the one located at the coordinates (i,j) in the search block. Each PE starts computing one clock cycle that is delayed with respect to the previous PE in the pipeline. For this reason, only one `SADij` value is valid at each clock cycle. The `SADij` outputs from PEs feed the `M64` multiplexer which selects the unique valid `SADij` signal to feed the `SAD` signal.

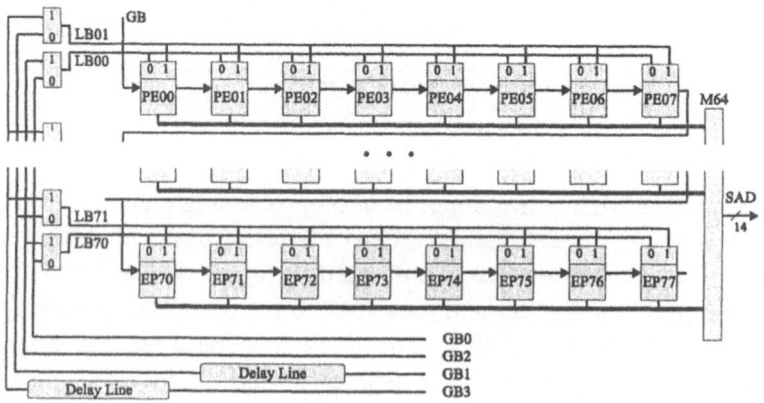

Figure 5. Processing Matrix architecture

The `SAD` signal is the input to the Comparison Unit. This unit, at each clock cycle, analyses one distortion value and, if it represents a minimum, it is stored in the `MIN` register and a `NEW_MV` pulse is generated.

The Control Unit is a finite state machine implemented using an 8-bit counter. The control signals are generated by applying a combinatorial logic to some bits of the 8-bit counter. The Control Unit is also responsible for generating the motion vector by sampling the addressing signal END at the time a pulse is received from the NEW_MV signal.

2.3   Scalability

The proposed architecture may be instantiated to support larger search blocks. For k^2 instances, the search block size is $(k*8+7)x(k*8+7)$. Figure 6 presents an example of four ME64 instances to support a search block of 23x23 pixels.

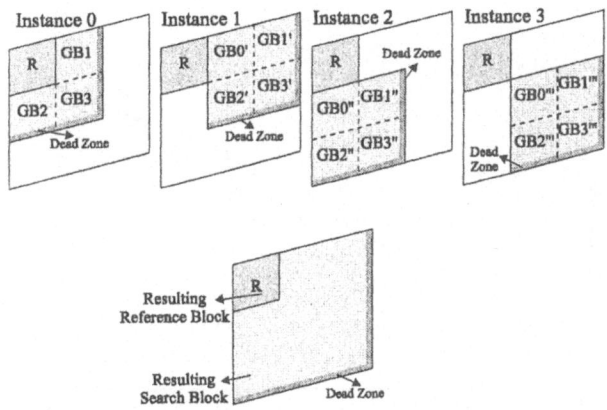

Figure 6. Scalability property of the ME64 architecture

The R bus of each region receives the same data while their global buses receive different partial search blocks. Note that the dead zones from inner instances are covered by adjacent instances.

3.   SYNTHESIS RESULTS

The proposed architecture was validated in simulation with the *ModelSim 5.5* tool and by a software tool (running on the PC platform) that feeds data to the actual ME64 hardware implementation and reads back the values of the motion vectors. In addition, to verify the quality of the ME64 hardware computation, the motion vectors were also computed by software in the PC, and compared to the ME64 results for the same frames. The main development tools used were:

• Hardware development tool *WebPack 4.2*, from Xilinx. This tool is integrated with the simulation tool *ModelSim 5.5*, from Mentor Graphics.

• Xilinx Spartan II Evaluation Kit, with the target FPGA prototyping device XC2S150.

• Pentium III 733 MHz microcomputer connected to a video source, running MSWindows.

The ME64 full description was written in VHDL language. In this description, the bit-width of the input signals Y, S0, and S1 were defined based on a generic parameter named n.

During the development, simulation was exhaustively used for validation. It also showed that the description with $n=8$ (as video is usually distributed) occupies 1,918 logic blocks, which is more than the 1,728 available in the XC2S150 device. Figure 7 presents the number of logic blocks taken up by ME64 for various values of n.

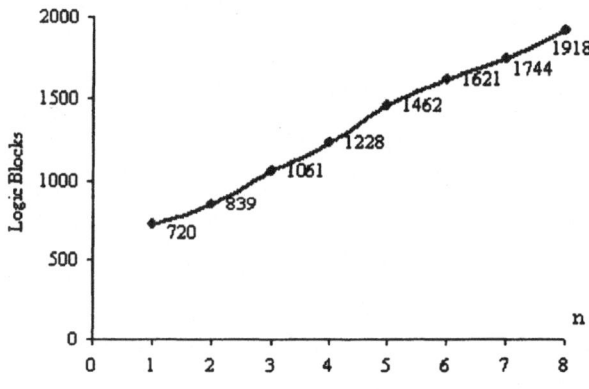

Figure 7. Number of logic blocks versus n

The XC2S150 device offers 12 configurable 4096-bit memory slices. The ME64 architecture requires simultaneous access to its ten 256-bit memory blocks. So unfortunately, each of ME64's memory blocks had to be mapped to different memory slice of the XC2S150, thus using up most of the available memory.

The software developed interfaces to the prototype via the PC parallel port. Due to the restrictions in the number of pins for communication using the parallel port and the low availability of logic blocks in the XC2S150 device, the prototype was initially tested with $n=4$.

The prototype was tested at a slow speed (9.76 KHz) to accommodate the slow communication channel provided by the PC parallel port. The hardware results for the motion vectors of a full frame were compared to the software calculation done in the PC for n=8. This way, the ME64 hardware calculations were validated.

4. CONCLUSION

With the FPGA running at 33 MHz, its maximum operating speed, the proposed architecture can estimate motion for video at a resolution of 640x480 pixels at the rate of 107.32 fps (frames per second) or 41.96 fps for a resolution of 1024x768 pixels.

Comparing the prototype against the PC software implementation, the FPGA hardware prototype is 19.67 times faster and performs 437 times more operations per second than a Pentium III 733 MHz running the compiled version of the motion estimation software.

The ME64 latency is 192 clock cycles. The prototype uses 16 I/O pins (for n=4), and the n=8 version would use 31 I/O pins. The prototype uses 71.1% of the logic blocks and 83.3% of the memory blocks available in the XC2S150 FPGA device.

Considering the high ME64 computing power there is no reason to use an algorithm other than the most precise, the full search. Moreover, in the implementation of another algorithm, the expected decrease in the operations rate requirement would not be directly converted to an increase in the speed, due to the limitations imposed by the I/O rate that the FPGA can sustain.

Table 3 presents a comparison of the proposed architecture against other solutions. The frame rate normalization was done considering frame size, reference block size and search block size.

Table 3. Comparison between ME64 and others

Architecture	Ref.	Max. Freq. (MHz)	Operations Rate (GOps)	Absolute Values		Normalized Values	
				fps	ms	fps	ms
STi3220	[5]	18.25	2.65	44.01	22.72	237.65	4.21
Architecture Based on Block Clustering	[3]	15	0.12	18.49	54.08	6.10	163.89
EST256	[6]	20	11	48.22	20.74	260.39	3.84
Linear array of 8 Processing Elements	[7]	8.32	0.06	3.38	295.86	3.38	295.86
ME64	-	33	2.11	107.32	9.32	107.32	9.32

The ME64 is among the fastest in Table 3. It is scalable, i.e. the frame rate may be increased further and the search block size parameterized. The

ME64 has a low I/O pin count and has a good ratio of operations to frame rate. Given the ME64 efficient I/O interface and its pipeline architecture, the hardware usage is 100% after initial pipeline fill latency.

Future developments include the design of different architectures of processing elements. The proposed architecture can be used to implement different algorithms such as hierarchical search or block clustering search. The prototype can be integrated with external memory and an image sensor aiming at a prototype running at the maximum simulated clock frequency. Another tool to be developed is an automatic generator of VHDL descriptions of motion estimation architectures based on the scalability property of ME64. These descriptions would have the same throughput as ME64 and a configurable search block size.

REFERENCES

[1] BHASKARAN, Vasudev; KONSTANTINIDES, Konstantinides. **Image and video compression standards:** algorithms and architectures. 2. ed. Massachusetts: Kluwer Academic Publisher, 1999. 454p.

[2] CHAN, Yui-Lam; SIU, Wan-Chi. Block motion vector estimation using edge matching: an approach with better frame quality as compared to full search algorithm. In: INT. SYMP. ON CIRCUITS AND SYSTEMS, Hong Kong, 1997. **Proceedings**, [S.l.]: IEEE Press, 1997, p. 1145-1148.

[3] CHU, Chung-Tao; ANASTASSIOU, Dimitris; CHANG, Shih-Fu. Hierarchical global motion estimation/compensation in low bitrate video coding. In: INT. SYMP. ON CIRCUITS AND SYSTEMS, Hong Kong, 1997. **Proceedings**, [S.l.]: IEEE Press, 1997, p. 1149-1152.

[4] FUJITA, Gen; ONOYE, Takao; SHIRAKAWA, Isao. A new motion estimation core dedicated to H.263 video coding. In: INT. SYMP. ON CIRCUITS AND SYSTEMS, Hong Kong, 1997. **Proceedings**, [S.l.]: IEEE Press, 1997, p. 1161-1164.

[5] QUEROL, Marc. **STI3220:** motion estimation processor codec. [S.l.]: SGS-Thomson Microelectronics, 2001. Available at: <http://www.st.com/stonline/books/pdf/docs/1648.pdf>. Access in: July, 18, 2002.

[6] SANZ, César; GARRIDO, Matías J.; MENESES, Juan M. VLSI architecture for motion estimation using the block-matching algorithm. In: AUTOMATION AND TEST EUROPE CONF., Paris, *1998*. **Proceedings**, [S.l.: s.n.], 1998, p. 45-49.

[7] SHI, Yun Q.; SUN, H. **Image and video compression for multimedia engineering:** fundamentals, algorithms and standards. United State: CRC Press, 2000. 480p.

[8] TOURAPIS Alexis M.; AU, Oscar C.; LIOU, M. L. Predictive motion vector field adaptive search technique (PMVFAST) enhancing block based motion estimation. In: VISUAL COMMUNICATIONS AND IMAGE PROCESSING, San Jose, 2001. **Proceedings**, [S.l.: s.n.], 2001.

[9] ZANDONAI, Diogo; BAMPI, S.; CARRO, L. An architecture for MPEG motion estimation. In: WORKSHOP IBERCHIP, 7., Montevideo, Uruguay, 2001. **Proceedings**, Montevideo, Uruguay: Universidad de la Republica, 2001, '1' CD.

Erratum to: Design Methods and Applications for Distributed Embedded Systems

Bernd Kleinjohann, Guang R. Gao, Hermann Kopetz, Lisa Kleinjohann and Achim Rettberg (eds.)

This book was originally published with a copyright holder in the name of the publisher in error, whereas IFIP International Federation for Information Processing holds the copyright.

The updated original online version for this book can be found at
DOI 10.1007/978-1-4020-8149-1

B. Kleinjohann, et al. (eds.), *Design Methods and Applications for Distributed Embedded Systems,*
DOI 10.1007/978-1-4020-8149-1_33, © IFIP International Federation for Information Processing, 2017   E1